THE BOMBING OF DUBLIN'S NORTH STRAND, 1941

The Untold Story

The Author

Kevin C. Kearns, Ph.D., is a social historian and Professor Emeritus at the University of Northern Colorado. He has made 34 research trips to Ireland, a number of which were funded by the National Geographic Society. Of his nine books on Dublin, four have been bestsellers, most notably *Dublin Tenement Life* which was number one on the *Irish Times* bestseller list for many weeks. He now resides in the coastal village of Camden, Maine.

THE BOMBING OF DUBLIN'S NORTH STRAND, 1941

The Untold Story

KEVIN C. KEARNS

Gill & Macmillan

Gill & Macmillan Ltd
Hume Avenue, Park West, Dublin 12
with associated companies throughout the world
www.gillmacmillan.ie

© Kevin C. Kearns 2009, 2010
First published in hard cover 2009
First published in paperback 2010
978 07171 4644 4

Index compiled by Kate Murphy
Typography design by Make Communication
Print origination by O'K Graphic Design, Dublin
Printed by J F Print Ltd, Somerset

The paper used in this book comes from the wood pulp
of managed forests. For every tree felled, at least one
tree is planted, thereby renewing natural resources.

A CIP catalogue record for this book is available from
the British Library.

5 4 3 2 1

To my grandsons, Owen and Leo, who have brought new meaning to my life.

By the same author

What the future will hold for us no man can tell. In time of war, the unpredictable, the unforeseeable event is the only certainty.

(SEÁN LEMASS, *Sunday Independent*, 25 January 1941)

May 1941

When Peace at last puts on her crown of crowns
And comes from that last cave where she is hid,
I'd like to take young airmen round the towns
And show them what they did.

Some day when rancour and when hate are done
And eyes are clear and hearts again are light,
And men no longer listen for the drone
Of engines in the night.

I would not trouble them with rubble heaps
That were old buildings generations loved
And history's most dear, remembered keeps
Where great and humble through the ages moved.

I would not say: This blackened dump was where
A poet penned his first, shy secret rhyme
Or, with a sonnet's opening, climbed a stair
To outlast Time.

But I would say: This terrace here was hit
On one May night. The worst raid of the year.
The warden said a land-mine fell on it.
A girl died here.

A girl who, sleeping in the room above,
Dreamed of the morning all that night of May,
The morning that would be the morning of
Her wedding day.

I'd say: I knew the family that lived there.
The crater's where their garden used to be.

I'd like to think that *these* would be the men,
The men who drove bright planes beneath the stars,
To see that this thing shall not be again
In what may be of wars.

(ANONYMOUS *Thirty Years of "Dublin Opinion,"* 1952)

CONTENTS

ACKNOWLEDGEMENTS

This book, based upon archival research and the exhaustive gathering of oral history testimonies, presented daunting challenges from the outset. The search for survivors, rescuers, other participants and eye-witnesses from 1941 demanded resourceful detective work and considerable patience. Reconstructing in detail the events of the German bombing of Dublin two-thirds of a century ago was dependent upon the kindness and co-operation of innumerable individuals. Most vital were those persons who shared their personal, first-hand accounts of the tragedy, with vivid recollection and often much emotion. Their oral testimony provided the heart of this book.

Many other individuals contributed in important ways to the writing of this long-untold historical tale. Their suggestions, guidance and personal assistance were of immeasurable value in the construction of the final manuscript. Particular gratitude is extended to the following for their generosity and contributions: Comdt P. B. Brennan, Irish Military Archives; Dr Máire Kennedy, Divisional Librarian, Special Collections, Dublin City Libraries; Dr Mary Clark, City Archivist, and the staff at the Dublin City Library; Paddy Farrell, *Irish Independent* photographic archivist; Ciara Farrell, Senior Librarian, Cabra Public Library; Noelle Dowling, Allen Library, Dublin; Bernie Pierce, Director, Lourdes Day Care Centre for Seniors; Pat O'Connor, Librarian, Charleville Mall Library, Dublin; Tony Gray; Bernard Share; Cathal O'Shannon; and Thomas P. Geraghty.

Special heartfelt appreciation is extended to my partner, Cathe A. Brown, for her unfailing support and patience during the four years of intensive research and writing. Her critical reading of sections of the manuscript helped to keep me on a tight track, and her companionship provided much-needed balance and joy in my life during this period.

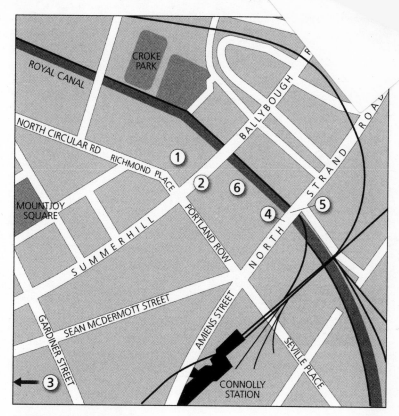

Bomb area reference map

1 First bomb site
2 Second bomb site
3 Third bomb site in Phoenix Park
4 Fourth and largest bomb site
5 Newcomen Bridge
6 Charleville Mall Library

PROLOGUE

These four bombs formed an incident which had all the features of a major air-raid ... search-lights, anti-aircraft fire, bomb explosions and fires, with the rise in terror as the tempo of the attack increased.

(DEPARTMENT OF DEFENCE)

Fear seized an entire city.

(LT-COL PADRAIC O'FARRELL)

Those of us who lived through that night of horror are not likely ever to forget it.

(MARY TWOMEY, 81)

Friday 30 May 1941

Dubliners were in a merry mood. The Whit holiday weekend was looming and the weather expected to be glorious. After the bleak winter of wet turf and wartime deprivations, people were desperate to burst out of the gloom into spring sunshine and outdoor activities.

Everyone had plans of some sort for the long-awaited break: a visit to the seaside, a cycling tour, an excursion by railway to resorts in the west, or simply a picnic in the Phoenix Park, a trip to the zoo, or visiting family and friends. The city's many dance halls and cinemas were expected to be packed, adding to the excitement. By Friday afternoon the celebratory spirit was in the air.

Friday evening was balmy, the starlit sky above Dublin as clear as a crystal goblet. The mild temperature and the fragrance of early spring flowers enticed some to do a bit of after-supper gardening. It seemed that everyone was outdoors. People stood outside their front doors or by railings, chatting amiably with neighbours and passing strangers. Drinking men, in top form, took their pints and banter out onto lamplit pathways. Children frolicked in the streets, shouting gleefully, and ice-cream vendors could hardly keep up with the flurry of outstretched arms. From toddlers to grannies, everyone seemed in buoyant spirit on this Whitsuntide Eve.

No-one wanted to go to bed early and see such a lovely evening end, and the streets were filled with cheerful talking and laughter. Patrons pouring out of the cinemas and dance halls were especially animated, still howling over the hilarious Laurel and Hardy film they had just seen or singing their favourite show tune. Fellas, seeking to impress their girls, attempted to duplicate a few snappy Fred Astaire dance steps, adding to the laughter in the streets. Men, flush-faced and boisterous, shuffled out of their local pubs. Late-night crowds were mobbing the city's fish-and-chip shops. It was one of those rare Friday nights in spring—Dublin at its most exuberant.

City-dwellers were accustomed to staying up late at weekends. Many people were still standing about in the North Strand area, some on Newcomen Bridge, their elbows on the old stone wall, puffing their Woodbines and looking down into the moonlit waters of the Royal Canal. A glance over at the big clock outside Corcoran's shop told them that midnight was approaching. Local people relied on the village clock to keep their lives on schedule.

Adults might dally till dawn if they wished, but children had to be put to bed. That afternoon thousands of them had received their inoculation against diphtheria. Doctors warned their mammies that they might be fussy, and restless in their sleep that night because of a sore arm.

As midnight neared, some adults felt fretful. "Something didn't *feel* right," they would later say. Father Jackie Masterson sensed it, as did Alec King. Both men possessed prescient powers that had been proved before. Their instincts told them of impending trouble, though they were not able to predict its nature. On this night there was no doubt in their minds that something was awry, or *about* to go awry.

Father Masterson resided at his presbytery at 595 North Circular Road. A gregarious priest with boundless energy—and quite handsome, women noted—he was immensely popular. He was preparing to retire about eleven o'clock when the ominous feeling came over him, and the nagging feeling kept him awake. A few miles away, Alec King was experiencing almost identical sensations, that "something was up," as he would later put it. He was the Chief Rescue and Demolitions Officer for his district. Intelligent and resolute, he was highly respected by the eighty men under his command. After surviving an excruciating brain operation at the age of twenty-one he felt he had acquired what he calls a sixth sense, some inexplicable instinct that forewarned him when anything in his universe was about to spin out of its natural alignment. This didn't happen often, but when it did his sixth sense was always correct.

After some evening gardening, he too climbed into bed about eleven o'clock but could not relax enough to doze off. His wife asked why he was so restless, fidgety in bed. She had never seen him so agitated over a warning from his sixth sense. Unable to sleep, he decided to get out of bed, put on his dressing-gown and slippers and go downstairs to read for a while. "I just had this awful sense that *something* terrible was about to happen."

At midnight that Whit weekend many Dubliners were still awake. At 12:02 the familiar drone of German bomber engines was heard overhead. For months, squadrons of Luftwaffe planes had been flying over the city at night on their northerly route towards targets in London, Manchester and elsewhere. But this night they sounded louder, perhaps because the air was so clear. Or was it that some of the planes were flying lower than usual?

At 12:04 a.m. huge anti-aircraft searchlights were switched on, making lazy sweeps back and forth across the starry canopy above the city. Shortly thereafter, warning flares were shot aloft; this was to alert pilots that they were over neutral territory and should depart immediately. Normally they did so— but not this night. Inexplicably, they seemed to be lingering in a strange, meandering manner. After about thirty minutes Air Defence Command, following precise procedure, ordered anti-aircraft gunners at several batteries to fire into the sky. This was meant as a final warning to intruding pilots.

For Dubliners it provided a dazzling show of lights and fireworks in a spectacle worth getting out of bed to watch at windows or from the streets. On this particularly lucid night it even drew "ooohs" and "aaahs". After all, it *was* Whit weekend. It seemed almost as if the military brass had planned the flashy aerial show as entertainment to welcome the arrival of the Whit weekend.

Neither Father Masterson nor Alec King regarded it as entertaining. Both were wondering if it could have anything to do with their unusually strong forewarnings of trouble. As the minutes passed their suspicions grew. Some odd things were indisputably occurring in the sky above Dublin. Normally, when Luftwaffe pilots were greeted with searchlights and gunfire they politely continued on their northerly path, out of Irish air space. This time they were lingering. More mystifying, and troubling, was the fact that the pilots seemed to be flying in disarray. Highly disciplined Luftwaffe crews ordinarily flew in precise, tight squadron formation. Owing to the clarity of the starry, moonlit sky and powerfully penetrating searchlights, the planes could be periodically spotted. King, trained to identify German aircraft, judged their numbers to be considerable—possibly thirty or more. "Why weren't they *leaving*?" he wondered.

When the activity began just after midnight Father Masterson arose from bed and got fully dressed. He began pacing the floor, continually looking out the window at the light display in the sky. When the anti-aircraft fire commenced, he decided to place his holy oils in his coat pocket, just to be prepared. Simultaneously, King was hurriedly dressing in his rescue and demolition gear. He then mounted his bicycle and headed for the depot where his men trained and kept all their rescue equipment. Both men were now feeling heightened warnings of an impending disaster. Of some sort.

By contrast, after an hour or so of watching the spectacle, most Dubliners grew weary and went to bed. Whit Saturday was going to be a busy, exciting day and they wanted to be rested. But as sleep was coming over them, many found themselves thinking that it was odd that the bombers would be sticking around for so long, especially as volleys of shells were now being fired.

At 1:28 a.m. the first bomb whistled earthward, then exploded. Dubliners leapt up. It fell near the intersection of the North Circular Road and North Richmond Street. One minute later a second one detonated, just around the corner at Summerhill. The two bombs toppled several houses and shops, trapping victims in the debris. Dublin Fire Brigade, members of the Local Defence Force (LDF) and other rescue groups raced to the scene.

At 1:31 a third explosion was heard. This bomb struck in the Phoenix Park; it gouged a large crater in the soft earth and blew apart the little house in which Joseph McNally lived with his eleven-year-old daughter, Winifred. He worked at the nearby Dog Pond pumping station. It also shattered windows and damaged the American Legation and Áras an Uachtaráin. In the zoo, frenzied animals, some of them dangerous, thrust themselves madly against their barriers, trying to escape. A large bison succeeded in thrashing its way out, as did Sara, a gentle elephant, who lumbered quickly down to the pond reeds in search of safety.

Three bomb blasts within four minutes. By now most of the city was awake, and worried. Was Dublin under attack? As Belfast had been six weeks before? But the city was *neutral!* And *no* air-raid sirens had been sounded. Confused and frightened, citizens watched the sky and waited.

After the third explosion, minutes passed and no more bombs fell. Some of the planes drifted off, but others remained overhead, one conspicuously so. This rogue aviator began engaging in daring aerobatics over the city, swooping low, veering sharply, then darting off to a safer altitude. His bizarre manoeuvres over the next half an hour would first spellbind, then terrify, all those who witnessed it.

At first, Air Defence Command officers observing this behaviour were perplexed. After fifteen minutes they were worried. They began to try to drive the plane away, as searchlights ceased making rhythmic sweeps across the sky and sought to pinpoint and illuminate a real target. Anti-aircraft fire became more intense, using larger shells. The pilot showed no fear. As recorded in the military log (kept in closed archives and marked "Secret" for the next sixty-five years), shortly before 2 a.m. military observers determined that the plane was "hovering" purposefully above, the pilot seemingly "awaiting instructions" of some sort.[1] This was an alarming realisation.

Dubliners watching the "show" were at first more entertained than worried. To them it had become the "mystery" plane. It was exciting, suspenseful. "What was the German pilot fella up to, anyway?" And were Irish gunners now really trying to bring down a German plane? Scores of citizens were fixated on the spectacle as they watched from streets, gardens and windows. The *Sunday Independent* the following day would lambaste these "thousands of fool-hardy" Dubliners who pressed their noses to glass windows as the bomber swooped not far above their heads.[2]

By 2 a.m. Air Defence Command was convinced that the pilot was now searching for something as he focused his low runs around the area of Amiens Street railway station. "But what could a Luftwaffe pilot be *searching* for in the heart of neutral Dublin?" Northsiders in his path were now becoming frightened, and his low sweeps over rooftops felt menacing. Nonetheless, they remained mesmerised. No matter *what* the pilot was up to, nobody wanted to *miss* it.

There were still no air-raid sirens heard anywhere in the city to alert citizens of imminent danger.

At 2:05 a.m. the clock outside Corcoran's shop on the North Strand was stilled for ever. A thunderous, deafening explosion—the most skull-piercing noise anyone had ever heard—struck with awful suddenness. The sky turned a fiery crimson and the earth shook violently from the ferocious force. Houses blew wildly apart; some just disintegrated. Steel lamp-posts and tram tracks bent like liquorice sticks. Windows shattered by the thousands as bricks and slates were fired like mortar shells great distances. Gas mains broke and blazes erupted. Decrepit, brittle old tenement houses throughout the city shuddered and cracked. Tremors from the mighty blast radiated outwards from the impact point, reaching to Mullingar, Enniskerry and beyond.

In a split second, masses of people were killed, injured, savagely mutilated. People out on the streets and in wrecked houses were tossed like rag dolls. Some bodies were catapulted onto rooftops. Shell-shocked victims floated eerily about in their night attire. Survivors were terrified, hysterical. Everywhere around the North Strand there was panic and pandemonium. Some truly thought that doomsday had come.

In type big enough to be read half a street away, the *Evening Herald* proclaimed it the "NIGHT OF HORROR".[3] To northsiders, the destruction was unfathomable. The *Evening Mail* told readers that the entire area from the Five Lamps to Newcomen Bridge had been "almost completely wiped out."[4] Surrounding streets suffered severe damage as well. In attempting to describe their experience, survivors could only compare it to nature's wrath, telling reporters that it had been like a colossal earthquake, hurricane or tornado, smashing their world to smithereens within seconds.

No ordinary bomb had done the deed. It was one of the most powerful weapons in the German arsenal at that time, a 500-lb high-explosive bomb created specifically for use against strategic targets constructed of the strongest steel and concrete, designed to detonate on impact with the surface for maximum destruction, unlike most bombs, which have some of their power blunted by penetration. Throughout the war the Luftwaffe used this large, specialised weapon purposefully and sparingly—not randomly against people in their homes.

As fate would have it, the one that fell on the little North Strand village proved to be the "perfect bomb" in its performance. It struck the hardest and densest surface possible in Dublin: steel tram tracks and thick cobblestones, instantly unleashing the full fury of its pulverising power in a circumferential pattern. As documented by the Department of Defence, it "exploded with the resulting cone of the blast very flat, and therefore had maximum effect."[5] Had it fallen on any other type of surface, its destructive power would have been at least partially smothered. As it turned out, all the bomb's other critical variables were also optimised. Dublin, a city of old brick, timber and slate, proved a pathetically vulnerable target. Of the millions of bombs dropped by the German air force during the Second World War, none could have performed more flawlessly.

The massive destruction was testimony to its effectiveness. Military and government authorities were astonished when the final assessments were completed. A total of 2,250 buildings had suffered some type of bomb damage.[6] Many were completely demolished or severely smashed. Shops and houses half a mile away suffered severe damage. So many thousands of windows were shattered all over the city that glass supplies ran out within days. More than forty people were killed, more than a hundred seriously injured and countless others wounded. Hospitals and morgues were filled to capacity within hours, and the city's blood supplies were running low. After only one day the Red Cross had to make a public appeal for help because their resources were being depleted. Nearly two thousand people would be rendered homeless.

When the first light of dawn crept over the city, illuminating the full magnitude of destruction, Dubliners were shocked and incredulous that their neutral capital had really been bombed. As the *Irish Press* affirmed:

Ireland has maintained its neutrality with a correctitude evident to all belligerents ... yet had to suffer the horrors of this awful tragedy ... this great calamity.[7]

The *Irish Independent* disclosed that not only had the "Irish people been horrified by the terrible tragedy ... [but] the outside world was shocked by the news" as well.[8] No-one seemed more stunned than the Taoiseach, Éamon de Valera. When he arrived at the scene at about nine o'clock on Saturday morning with a coterie of officials by his side, he stood at the edge of the bomb crater and was described by one reporter as appearing "dumbfounded."[9]

Yet everyone had been warned. Dublin had previously been bombed on several consecutive nights in January. Bombings had occurred also in five other counties. In mid-April, when Belfast was blitzed, de Valera despatched fire brigades from Dundalk, Dublin and Dún Laoghaire to assist with battling the conflagrations and rescuing victims. He subsequently took in three thousand refugees from the North, providing asylum, shelter, food and medical assistance.

These acts constituted clear breaches of neutrality. There had been other violations of the neutrality agreement, which surely did not please Hitler. Nonetheless, the majority of Irish people, and many in the Government and the military, remained complacent, convinced that the war "over there" would never come "within an ass's roar" of their shores.

On 26 January, only three weeks after the first Dublin bombings, Seán Lemass, the Minister for Supplies, scolded those citizens who acted as if the "war was being fought on another planet ... immune from the effects of it," while all around Ireland "cataclysmic things are happening."[10]

In February the *Irish Press* issued a similar warning, calling Ireland "a suburb of a city on fire" and stating that it would be naïve to believe that the Irish people would remain untouched by the blazes of war.[11] Even the Irish-American fascist William Joyce—known as "Lord Haw-Haw" because of his contrived English aristocratic accent—in his radio broadcasts foretold German retribution for Ireland's breaches of neutrality.

Despite such admonitions, the great majority of citizens remained unfazed, oblivious of real danger at their doorstep. Between the authorities and the public there were plenty of blunders and follies to go around.

For its part, the Government failed miserably to prepare Dublin for a real bomb attack. The air-raid defence system relied on flimsy above-ground concrete shelters, ridiculed from the outset as "hat boxes" and "hen houses", useless First World War gas masks and earthen trenches dug in the city's parks and squares. The tragic irony proved to be that the air-raid sirens, the only modern air-raid precaution device, remained silent during all Dublin's bombings—not because of mechanical failure but through human neglect. Perhaps it was no wonder that the populace failed to take war risks seriously.

On Whit Saturday morning, about seven hours after the "unthinkable" had happened, as de Valera, members of his Government and the Dáil trudged sorrowfully through the ruins, they could do little but shake their heads. Carnage on such a scale had not been witnessed since the first weeks of the Civil War in 1922. What did it mean for Ireland's policy of neutrality? Dubliners felt a loss of both their innocence and their security. By early morning the city's churches were packed with people in the throes of repentance, desperate to get into confession before another nightfall.

On the morning of Sunday 1 June, barely thirty-two hours after the violent bomb explosion, a related tragedy struck. In Old Bride Street in the Liberties three decrepit tenement houses that had been further destabilised by the bomb's rumbling quake gave way and collapsed. A young mother, her baby and an older man were killed; many more were injured. News of the collapse sent a chill through the city's vast tenement population and sent alarmed housing authorities into emergency session.

Over the next week Dubliners would experience more fear as well as profound grief when the funerals took place. It was a city truly bent in mourning. As the *Evening Mail* stated, "Never had the capital felt or expressed such sorrow."12

———

The little city village of North Strand had been a Dublin treasure. One of the most traditional and picturesque in the city, it was an uncommonly provincial, "old-fashioned" community where residents traced their roots back many generations. Its tranquil, bucolic character made it unique. The simple, countrified way of life endeared it to both residents and visitors. People from other parts of Dublin liked to ramble over and enjoy its charms.

The German bomb not only largely destroyed the village and killed and injured inhabitants but expunged forever a cherished way of life. Survivors who were made homeless were transplanted to the barren "wilds" of Cabra and Crumlin, lonely and soulless environments that left them not only homesick but heartsick. Profoundly dispirited, many were never the same again.

Regrettably, from the outset the Government failed to comprehend the significance of the loss of a community. Instead, it essentially perceived the bombing as a political and military incident:

In real terms in the eyes of de Valera, and perhaps the government at large, the bombing was a political and defence issue, as opposed to the destruction of a community.[13]

In the immediate aftermath the Government had to contend with a barrage of criticism from the public and the press for the failures in the city's defence system, as well as worrying about future relations with Germany. In the following weeks and months the Government concentrated its attention on the political and diplomatic ramifications, while the military authorities concentrated on defence matters. The devastated North Strand and its survivors were gradually neglected, then forgotten.

———

In historical perspective—taking into account the magnitude of physical destruction, death, injuries, homelessness, and housing resettlement—the German bombing was a catastrophe. In her book *Mud Island*, a general history of the North Strand area and Ballybough, Noelle Dowling asserts: "Within the history of Dublin it was a major tragedy."[14] Tom Geraghty, in *A History of the Dublin Fire Brigade*, calls it the most "grave crime against humanity" ever suffered by the city,[15] while the former Taoiseach Bertie Ahern considered it one of the "seismic events in our capital."[16] Tony Gray, in 1941 a young reporter for the *Irish Times*, hopped on his bike and arrived at the bomb scene within minutes. Some fifty years later he reflected:

In these days of on-the-spot television reportage of wars, earthquakes and other disasters, we are all inured to the sight of the injured, the dead and dying, but in those times ... I found the whole experience utterly shattering.[17]

Mary Cooke, one of a family of seventeen children, lived in a tenement house in Lower Gardiner Street, only a few streets from the explosion. At the age of seventy-four she draws an analogy:

I'm telling you, the disaster, it was equal to what happened at 9/11 in America. It was on a scale like that for us! Really and truly!

The German bombing of neutral Dublin for no apparent reason has long been historically fascinating because of the mystery and the speculation surrounding it for two-thirds of a century. Indeed Robert Fisk, author of the excellent work *In Time of War*, refers to the bombing as "the great mystery of Irish neutrality during World War II."[18] Was it simply a mistake, as many believed—an error on the part of the pilot? Or was it Hitler's retribution against de Valera for multiple breaches of neutrality, most notably despatching firefighters to assist Belfast during the blitz? Some alleged that it was due to the anger of German pilots being so intensely fired upon that night by Irish gunners. Others even suggested that Britain's new scientific technology had been used to distort or "bend" German aircraft navigational guidance beams, throwing aviators off course. Or was it a clever British plot carried out by Churchill and the Royal Air Force to draw Ireland into the war on their side? All these hypotheses have a certain credibility.

But surely one of the greatest mysteries about the bombing is why, after more than sixty years, not a single book had been written about such a seismic event in Dublin's history. Which raises the question, if the bomb had fallen in one of the more salubrious areas of Blackrock, Rathmines or Ballsbridge, killing and injuring scores, virtually wiping out the community, would the tragedy not have warranted a book or two? City-dwellers have long pondered, and openly expressed, this question. There is abundant evidence that Irish historians and other writers as well have traditionally not regarded the working class and their communities as worthy of serious research and documentation. Tom Geraghty contends that this prevailing mentality dissuaded chroniclers from undertaking a major work on the North Strand calamity:

> I think the reason why there has never been a book written about it is that people didn't realise about *social* history, particularly about the working class. The bomb survivors, *ordinary* people, are worth writing about—and there are *really stories* there![19]

Another contributing factor may have been that many important documents relating to the incident were in closed archives in the Dublin City Libraries and the Military Archives. Whatever the reason, the absence of a comprehensive work on the German bombing indisputably constitutes a glaring gap in the historical literature of Dublin.

Towards the close of the twentieth century several surprising developments conspired to renew interest in the event, stimulating some fresh analysis and speculation about the still-perplexing "mystery". In 1997 and 1998 two men claimed to possess new evidence pertaining to the reasons behind the bombing. Some newspapers treated this like an old police "cold case" being resurrected in the light of new DNA evidence, spurring public interest once again.

Coincidentally, and more importantly, in the late 1990s the Military Archives at Cathal Brugha Barracks, Dublin, declassified its documents on the bombing, including information from the Air Defence Command log for the night of the air raid, stamped "SECRET". Similarly in 2001, on the sixtieth anniversary of the bombing, Dublin City Library in Pearse Street finally opened its complete archive on the subject, including an extensive collection of rare photographs taken in the hours and days following the bombing. There has also long existed a wealth of documents in the possession of all the Dublin newspapers, inexplicably little tapped over the years.

However, archival documents and newspaper accounts are hardly sufficient for writing an authentic, comprehensive book on so human a tragedy. Also vital are oral history testimonies from survivors who lived through the experience. Only they can provide eye-witness accounts in great detail. Una Shaw, now seventy-five, a survivor, still lives in Rutland Street, in the same house in which she was born. It was severely bomb-damaged in 1941. She is among those who have long wondered why no book on the subject ever appeared, lamenting that "it's part of the *history* of Dublin, a *major* part—and the story hasn't come out!" It is her conviction that the "real story" must rely heavily on the words of the survivors themselves:

> With oral history you're *hearing* it, from the people who were *there*. Who *knew* what happened! You get the *real* facts ... as it *should* be in a book.

After two-thirds of a century, the search for survivors was challenging. While some remained around the North Strand, others were scattered in Cabra, Crumlin, Ballyfermot and beyond. Through historical detective work, and patience, a surprising number were tracked down. Most are today between seventy-five and ninety-five years of age. But their powers of recollection on the cataclysmic bombing are astonishing. It was, after all, they say, the "most memorable experience of my life." Details of what many still refer to as "that night of horror" are vividly etched in their minds.

Apart from survivors who were local residents there were other participants who experienced the bombing at first hand—firemen, policemen, nurses and orderlies, members of the Local Defence Force, as well as journalists who covered the scene, and even undertakers who buried the dead. They too were hunted down for their oral-history testimonies. Without their participatory, often gripping personal narratives the story would not be complete.

What emerges is a narrative social history of immense human drama that unfolds over a period of two years. Much of what preceded and followed the bombing was highly relevant, interesting, and dramatic in its own right. Thus it is not one story but many, intertwined to form the whole picture: stories of Government bungling and citizens' complacency, of terror, courage, heroism and survival; of mystery; of human loss—and the remarkable resilience of the human spirit; even humour amidst the panic and pandemonium.

The untold tale of great historical tragedy that has long needed telling.

———

On 5 April 2004

Una Shaw is happy to tell her story. As she's boiling water for the tea she points out to me where the bomb damage was done to her home in Rutland Street. How windows shattered and walls and ceilings cracked and crumbled as the earth quaked; where a great tree in the back garden was nearly plucked out of the ground as if in the teeth of an angry hurricane. She was one of the lucky survivors, being a few streets away from the point of impact.

The tea made, she is ready to reflect upon it all. The tape-recorder whirs softly. She needs "plenty of time," she explains—hours and hours—for it's a long story:

At the time of the bombing I was living right here, in *this* house. I can remember it *so well. Vividly!* It was Whit weekend ...

Chapter 1 ∾

"NOT WITHIN AN ASS'S ROAR"

Even to have attempted a policy of neutrality ... looks like a vast confidence trick. That it worked is still largely a matter for wonder and thanksgiving.

(BERNARD SHARE, *The Emergency*)

We felt very far away from the war, very remote. We weren't part of it ... we were neutral! Comfort, yeah.

(NICK HARRIS, 91)

Air-raid shelters—they were a joke!

(MARGARET LADRIGAN, 81)

"STOP PRESS—WAR DECLARED!" The news was blared through her tenement window in Lower Gardiner Street by "lorries going around with loudspeakers." Seven-year-old Mary Cooke scrambled down the stairs and plunged outside to see what the commotion was all about. People were filling the streets, talking excitedly. The Brits and the Jerries were "going at it," she was told. "Oh, I remember that day the war started!"

Everyone remembers. The news was being spread wildly across the city by legions of newsboys with their piercing cries of "Herald or Mail! Read all about it!" Around the Liberties, recalls Máirín Johnston, "even people who couldn't read what was on them" were buying papers, relying on others to interpret for them. After absorbing the news about the outbreak of war everyone wanted to know what it meant for Ireland. Children became worried on seeing adults turn so serious after putting their newspaper down. Twelve-year-old Phil O'Keeffe felt anxious and decided to ask her father if she should be frightened. His reassuring words put her young mind at ease:

The war is far away. It will never touch us ... the war'll not get within an ass's roar of us.[1]

Dev would see to that. Everyone was counting on him.

The Taoiseach, Éamon de Valera, had seen war clouds gathering on the horizon years earlier. Germany's enormous military build-up and Hitler's threatening rhetoric were alarming to surrounding countries. In an address to the League of Nations in 1936 de Valera reasoned that small countries were essentially defenceless against the military might of the great powers. If war erupted, the best they could do was to declare their neutrality, hope that it would be respected, then struggle against any pressures to be drawn into the conflict by the belligerents. In reality, the security of neutral countries depended on the will of the powerful warring states.

In September 1939, when war reared its ugly head, a state of national emergency was declared, and de Valera announced that the Irish state would be neutral. The policy of neutrality meant that Ireland would not align itself with any of the belligerents. With an expanding war raging around Ireland—on land and sea and in the skies—it was astonishingly bold to believe that a mere declaration of neutrality would keep the country secure and at peace. It would require great political and diplomatic skill. That it would last successfully for more than five years, against vast odds, was part political mastery, part pure miracle.

If the policy of neutrality was complex and delicate for the Government to uphold, the concept was simple enough for ordinary citizens. To most Irish people it meant "take no sides," "stay out of it," "play it *safe*"—the most common phrases heard in the streets. Let the Germans, the British and other European countries settle their disputes.

For de Valera, "staying out of it" was not quite so easy. Both Britain and Germany had interests in Ireland and saw real benefits in having the country join their side. From the outset of the war, Churchill was irked at de Valera's refusal to participate in the struggle for freedom throughout Europe. From a purely practical viewpoint he wanted to reclaim the use of the three strategic "treaty ports" of Cóbh, Castletown Bearhaven and Lough Swilly. These would be valuable for refuelling British naval vessels, for re-supplying, and for refuge from German submarines. De Valera stubbornly refused. Hitler too wanted to acquire Irish ports for his navy; he also saw strategic value in being able to install air bases on Irish soil from which his pilots could easily strike Britain at close range.

Both belligerents coaxed and pressured de Valera to align with them. Churchill promised a united Ireland if he would take up with the British. De Valera rejected the offer, believing that the British would be in no position to make good their offer, that the Ulster Unionists would surely block the way. Similarly, Hitler tried to tempt de Valera into supporting Germany by offering to play a role in settling the problem of partition once the British had been defeated. He even promised to give Ireland weapons with which to help fend off any invasion by Britain, which was a genuine worry at the time. Again, de Valera declined.

All the while, behind the cordial offers of assistance to de Valera was the veiled threat by both countries that they might ultimately decide to invade and take control of Ireland. This reality made it all the more difficult for the Taoiseach to carry out his skilful tight-rope act as the war progressed. But people had faith in his extraordinary ability to keep them wrapped safely in his neutrality blanket.

De Valera, however, understood quite well the fragility of his neutrality policy. As early as 1937 the German Minister in Ireland, Dr Eduard Hempel, personally told him of Hitler's expressed interests in Ireland. When the war began, however, Hempel gave de Valera a strong assurance that the German Foreign Minister, Joachim von Ribbentrop, had vowed that he would respect Ireland's neutrality—as long as de Valera *faithfully adhered* to the terms of absolute non-intervention, meaning no acts of interference or support of any sort. De Valera assured Hempel that he understood perfectly.

In May 1940, when France fell to the Germans and the two small neutral countries of Belgium and the Netherlands were invaded, it was a sobering blow to de Valera and his Government, confirming his prediction of 1936 about the vulnerability of neutral countries. What did it mean for Ireland? In fact there had been more worry about a British invasion than a German one. Churchill, it was thought, might decide that he had better act before Hitler in taking over Irish territory. As Bernard Share asserts, there was now genuine fear of a real invasion, at least among many in the Government and the military:

> The fall of France in May 1940 altered the picture. The invasion of territorial waters, or of Irish territory, by one or other of the belligerents no longer seemed a matter for humorous speculation.[3]

Among ordinary citizens there had indeed been plenty of humour, even derision, directed at Ireland's neutrality, at the "Emergency", and the paltry Defence Forces. Clara Gill, now seventy-nine, remembers well how men at her father's public house on the North Circular Road got great amusement out of making jokes about Ireland's status, how British or German troops might march into the country at mere whim. Open ridicule was heard in pubs all over the city. The risk of invasion was not taken seriously by the majority of citizens, rather it was fodder for joking and banter.

There was a prevalent feeling of remoteness, smug security. "We never bothered about the war then," said Agnes Daly, now eighty-one, of North

Clarence Street. "You didn't think the war would ever come here." Even when France fell and the neutral Low Countries were invaded, most Irish people were not a bit rattled. Indeed, as "Britain was blacked-out and blitzed, life in Ireland went on in an almost defiantly normal way."[4]

To de Valera and other members of the Government this complacency created a dangerously false sense of security. On 1 July 1940, following the fall of France, Seán MacEntee, Minister for Industry and Commerce, openly criticised the "illusion of security" so pervasive throughout Ireland. His message was one of reality:

> Destroy the illusion that while all the world rocked about them they might feel themselves secure and live unmolested.[5]

MacEntee's concerns were hardly unfounded. Ireland had no real air force, no tank corps, little infantry or heavy artillery with which to defend itself. The army still had many First World War rifles, with which it would have to repel any German Panzer divisions sweeping ashore. As Tony Gray speculated, "whether the Irish armed forces could have held an invading army at bay for more than a few hours at best is debatable."[6] Despite MacEntee's admonition, many people tended to see such warnings as unnecessarily alarmist.

———

At least Ireland could expand its defensive capability. The Air-Raid Precautions Act (1939) provided for the organising of citizens to participate in duties of guarding against aerial attack. Designated ARP wardens had the responsibility to "ensure that warning of expected air attacks be given to all citizens in their area. The means of achieving this was the use of the air-raid siren system."[7] They were to periodically carry out siren tests to make certain people knew the sound of the alert and what it meant. Wardens also had the duty of directing citizens into air-raid shelters and enforcing compliance with black-outs, if they were imposed. ARP wardens were issued with a helmet and an armband, which they wore proudly. Although the ARP service "attracted a hard core of enthusiastic volunteers, the populace at large remained apathetic."[8]

This apathy troubled de Valera, especially after German troops had stormed into France and the Low Countries. On 1 June 1940 he decided to address the people candidly in a national radio broadcast about his dual concerns of public apathy and weak defence. People from Co. Donegal to Co. Kerry gathered around their radio sets to listen to his words. "Our greatest danger here is complacency," he told them, "a complacency begotten by the fact that in the past we had not to defend ourselves directly."[9] Though the British had occupied Ireland for centuries, they had also prevented any other invaders from conquering the country. With independence, however, "the fact slowly began to sink in that, for the first time in seven hundred years, Ireland was on her own."[10] For the Irish to be oblivious of this reality while a brutal war was being waged all around them was both naïve and dangerous.

In his address de Valera announced the formation of the Local Security Force (LSF) as a reserve force for the Garda Síochána. He explained the need for citizens' service and appealed for recruits. His forceful, persuasive speech stirred patriotic zeal. Recruiting forms were sent to Garda stations, and within days 44,870 volunteers had signed up. Recruitment was going so well that on 22 June the new force was divided into an "A" section, to act as auxiliary to the army, and a "B" section to supplement the Garda in policing duties. Several months later the "A" group was placed under army control and renamed the Local Defence Force (LDF). By August more than 148,000 enthusiastic patriots had answered their nation's call to duty. By the time Christmas arrived, however, this number had declined sharply to about 84,000. Some 60,000 or so eager recruits quickly lost their enthusiasm when they learnt that membership in the force was not exactly what they had anticipated. They had expected to be properly outfitted with a uniform, boots, and real weapons. When they found out that they had to wear their civilian clothes, to drill in their own shoes, wearing only an armband and a cap (if they got even that), they had a hard time taking it seriously.

For those volunteers who stuck it out, marching in front of amused onlookers could be embarrassing. The father of the novelist Roddy Doyle, Rory Doyle, recalls joining the LDF in 1940 only to find that "we had no arms or equipment ... we drilled with pick-axe handles and shovels."[11] Observers often made jokes about them. It was dispiriting. The poet Paddy Kavanagh's caustic quip that Ireland's volunteer defence forces "would be hard put to defend a field of potatoes against an invasion of crows" did not endear him to many.[12]

One LDF volunteer, Frank Matthews, tells of his disappointment. "We were woefully equipped, we performed with wooden rifles."[13] Then one day they got their hands on real weapons. One of the platoon leaders somehow showed up with "a gift of sixty Brown Bess flintlock muskets and two brass flintlock blunderbusses, with a supply of powder and ball."[14] The muskets had originally been issued to the Louth Militia, about 1798. Recruitment declined, and members faded away as "the initial enthusiasm had been tempered by the equipment shortage, organisational muddles ... and morale was suffering."[15]

Clearly any invasion, real or imagined, had to be handled by the regular army. During 1940 rumours of a British or a German attack were commonly heard, a number of which were taken seriously by the army and police. One persistent rumour in Dublin had the belligerent naval vessels steaming straight up the River Liffey into the heart of the city, placing invaders within only paces of the best pubs. In the Garda barracks in Kevin Street, Senan Finucane, now seventy-seven, and his mate, the notorious James "Lugs" Brannigan, constantly heard such rumours. Several times he was even ordered down to the river to look for invaders:

> It was rumoured all the time that the Germans might invade here. Like an invasion up the Liffey. So I had to go down on the quays and keep an eye out for any boats coming up. They might as well give us a revolver and a candle—for what good it would be to anybody if they came upon a German boat! But I was never afraid.

Similar stories swirled around the army barracks. In 1922 Thomas Barry, concealing his real age of fifteen, joined the raw recruits of the new Irish army, "proud as a peacock" to wear his green uniform. Shortly after the fall of France he and his fellow-soldiers were told to be ready for action:

> In 1940 we were expecting an invasion of the Germans. We were getting toughened up. Training. One night we were taking up defence where the Germans were to be invading. I remember well the priest giving us his blessings. We were worried, all right.

Most citizens, however, remained unruffled by events in the faraway war. In fact at this time "the putative invader was the British army, since Churchill greatly wanted the Treaty Ports."[16] To Irish people it seemed more likely that the British would temporarily return to occupy Ireland's soil than that the Germans would invade. It was easier to imagine.

For the sake of debate, especially in pubs, Dubliners liked to take sides with the Brits or the Jerries. At the outset of the war, Clara Gill heard among the men in her father's pub "very little anti-German feeling." In fact many patrons "were IRA veterans and there was sympathy with Germany ... because the Black and Tan atrocities were familiar in living memory." Paddy Walsh, a fireman, born in 1916, agrees, noting that among many older men "there was a very pro-German feeling here, Hitlerites who blamed Britain for everything!" As Rory Doyle expressed it, at first "the Brits were getting a flaking from the Germans and we thought that was great. They deserved to be taken down a peg."[17] Taking a "good licking" might teach the British a much-needed lesson, many Irish people reasoned. However, as the war progressed and Hitler's madness became more apparent, they didn't seriously want to see Britain defeated. "We didn't really hate the British, just the Establishment," confesses Doyle. "We were hoping the Germans wouldn't be *too* successful."[18] Ultimately, the Irish wanted to see Britain defeat Hitler, for everyone's sake.

Though Ireland might not be able to repel invaders, it could at least provide some protection for citizens. Dublin, the capital and most populous city, was especially vulnerable. It required a system of both active and passive defences. The first comprised searchlights, flares, anti-aircraft guns and air-raid sirens. Passive protection depended upon bomb shelters, trenches, water tanks and gas masks, as well as the services of the Fire Brigade, the Gardaí, ARP, LDF, LSF, Red Cross and St John Ambulance Brigade, among others.

The active system of searchlights, flares and sirens was to spot belligerent aircraft, warn pilots they were over neutral territory, and alert citizens to danger. Anti-aircraft fire could be used to encourage intruding planes to depart. Gun emplacements were sited at Clontarf, Ringsend, Dalkey, Collinstown and elsewhere. Owing to limited stocks of ammunition, gunners got precious little practice. Air-raid sirens were regarded as a vital and reliable protection for citizens. They told people of impending danger and gave them time to seek safety. Similar to those used in Britain, they were affixed on buildings around Dublin in the autumn of 1940. Tested regularly, they worked flawlessly. Their high-pitched wail caused people to clasp their hands over their ears, and dogs to howl in harmony. The sirens were mechanically dependable; only human failure could cause them not to work.

Unfortunately, the city's passive protections were not regarded as dependable. From their first appearance they were riddled with problems and met with controversy and criticism—fodder for innumerable jokes in pubs and on theatre stages. The notion of an army invading Ireland or dropping bombs on Dublin was seen as so preposterous that such humour was regarded as harmless enough.

British bomb shelters in such cities as London and Manchester were engineering marvels of fortified steel and concrete, excavated deep below ground. They were costly, but saved lives. Ireland considered various types of bomb shelter, but economics won the day. It was determined that it was not financially justified for a neutral country to spend large sums on costly underground shelters that were highly unlikely ever to be needed. Instead, Dublin's shelters were blocks of concrete resting on the surface of streets. They looked like plain grey Jacob's biscuit boxes and afforded about as much protection, it was said. They were not designed to withstand a bomb strike, rather to prevent or minimise injury from flying debris or shrapnel. A few shallow tomb-like shelters were dug out in the soft earth of several parks and squares, which would have offered scant protection.

James Martin, a Dubliner, now eighty-seven, was living in Manchester during the early part of the war. Several times during heavy German bombing raids his life had been saved by clambering down into nearby deep shelters. When he returned home to Dublin at Christmas 1940 and saw the concrete shelters sitting atop the streets he could only shake his head. "I'd say if a bomb had fallen they'd have *blown over*, and anybody in them would have suffered, severely." A joke going around was that a person would be safer if they could find a fairy ring in which to stand than entering a shelter.

There were two types of shelter: open-door and locked-door. For the latter, Dublin Corporation (as Dublin City Council was then called) sought local men to be entrusted with the key in the unlikely event of their ever needing to be opened. Few men wanted the responsibility, saying it was too much of a bother. Noel Hughes, now seventy-eight, lived in Coleraine Street, just off North King Street, then a dense tenement district. His father was offered the key to a shelter directly across from their house. He declined. So did his neighbours. Once a man agreed to be the keyholder there was the question about him misplacing it in time of crisis. And what if the man himself could not be found? No-one seemed to worry about it.

The boxy, open-door shelters, says Margaret Ladrigan, now eighty-one, "were a *joke!*" Most Dubliners agreed. Before the concrete was even dry, people began using them for every imaginable purpose other than that for which they were created: playhouses for children, club houses for boys and men, trysts for passionate couples, and haunts for dossers, prostitutes, social miscreants of every kind. Noel Hughes kept a close eye on the shelter just across from his house. At first a Corporation man came around, swept it out, even washed it occasionally. It quickly became a popular hideaway for courting couples, who vied for coveted corners that afforded the most privacy for serious courting. Hughes claims that "more girls lost their virginity" in bomb shelters than anywhere else, adding that some of the unwanted "war babies", as he calls them, were then dumped in the shelters to be found by local women who turned them over to the authorities or adopted them.

From the outset, shelters were commonly used as public latrines. Before long the Corporation men ceased trying to clean them. It was hopeless. The ones around Mountjoy Square, recalls Winnie Brennan, now seventy-three, "became like cesspools. Somebody actually wrote 'Ladies' on one door and 'Gents' on the other. Oh, it was *dreadful!*" Reeking with a foul stench that flowed out the doors onto the street, nearly gagging passers-by, they drew flies, insects and rats. On hot summer days the squalid shelters putrefied the surrounding area. Even dogs ceased using them. Says Mary Cooke, "All along the middle of Gardiner Street there were air-raid shelters; they made public toilets out of them—*no way* anyone would *even dream* of going near them!"

There were also several dozen designated "basement shelters", as they were called, sited in the heart of the city beneath large buildings. They were essentially reserved for the elite members of government and business. They provided reasonable safety from a bomb blast. Throughout the rest of the city, ordinary Dubliners had access to basements below their old Georgian and Victorian buildings, many of which were decrepit tenements. They could seek safety there if they were willing to risk having the whole structure collapse and bury them. Conversely, a number of affluent people had private shelters erected in their back gardens. Most were the British Anderson type, which were dug about five to eight feet deep and covered with a corrugated metal roof.

The greatest folly was the Government's expenditure on digging primitive trenches in the city's parks and squares. To those knowledgeable about contemporary warfare in 1940, this archaic scheme was plain idiotic—scooping out soil so that citizens could huddle in open ditches. Tony Gray asked: "For what purpose? How could trenches dug in the Dublin parks protect anybody from anything? But trenches had become a part of the post-First World War mentality."[19] During 1940 nine large trench "shelters" were excavated, sizeable enough to hold more than six thousand trembling people. If heavy rain had fallen when they were nestled in, they would have been lucky not to have drowned.

Gas masks, or respirators, were another relic of the First World War. But Dublin Corporation was determined to distribute more than 400,000 of the weird contraptions to people—whether they wanted them or not. They were ugly, ill-fitting and smelly. To adults they looked silly, while children were frightened by the big snout and huge eyes. When Winnie Brennan's father took her by the hand and walked her down to Gardiner Street School to get theirs she took one look at the scary, insect-head mask. "I can remember trying it on me ... I was *shaking* from head to toe." Una Shaw's mask had the "most *awful smell*, I nearly *suffocated*. My father said, 'They're of no use, they wouldn't keep us alive if gas came here.'" That being the consensus, most were promptly stuffed under beds or behind cabinets. Claimed Mary Cooke in 2004, "There are still some in attics here in Dublin."

More useful, it first seemed, were concrete water tanks erected in streets around the city centre. If incendiary bombs ever fell they would ignite fires that could spread quickly, and instant access to water could help people douse smaller blazes in their homes. The tanks would also provide an auxiliary water supply for firemen. The plan seemed practical enough except for one flaw, according to Una Shaw:

These cement water tanks *never* had any water in them! Not an ounce of water—in the whole course of the war. Unless rain fell into it. These things really were supposedly put up just to calm us down.

There was never any public outcry to have them filled. Who thought they would ever be needed?

By the end of 1940 there were 64 above-ground concrete shelters dispersed around the city, compared with 9 trench shelters, 47 designated basement shelters and a few shallow underground chambers dug out in parks and squares.[20] People joked that if they ever heard a bomb whistling earthwards they would prefer to crouch beneath stairs or dive under a table. And that's exactly what they did.

——

Citizens may have been complacent about the war but they were hardly indifferent to the shortages it brought. It diminished the quality of their daily life and, for many, imposed real hardship. With safe shipping lanes gone, imported commodities declined or disappeared altogether. The scarcity of essential items created shortages and led eventually to rationing. Lacking domestic coal and oil, as well as other critical resources, isolated Ireland could not keep many factories going. Work at the docks dried up. Widespread unemployment sent droves of people across the water to work in British factories or to join their armed forces.

At home no-one starved, but many genuinely suffered, especially lower-income city-dwellers. The level of deprivation was a matter of class status:

> The restrictions in supplies in basic foodstuffs, though causing some discomfort among the middle classes, hit the poor hard, reducing them to a level of subsistence. Shortages and rationing certainly accentuated the very wide gap between rich and poor.[21]

To Pauline Bracken of affluent Blackrock, "war naturally affected supply and demand … yet it seemed quite irrelevant to our lives."[22] Residents of the inner city, however, felt it deeply. According to Una Shaw, "we were badly off, through [limited] supplies, through poverty and deprivation. We *suffered!* We were living from hand to mouth." Those with money could still get hold of almost anything they wanted through a thriving black market.

At first few thought it would last very long. Shortages could be temporarily endured. As months, then years, dragged on, people really felt the pinch. Scarcity of the most basic products imposed the greatest hardship: fuel, flour, sugar, clothing, soap, candles, tea and cigarettes. While milk, eggs and meat were in ample supply, people could no longer get imported flour for making good bread. Dark-brown or "black" bread had to be made from inferior domestic flour. It tasted awful and grew stale quickly. Nonetheless, though people grumbled they ate the detested bread. Around the Liberties, says Senan Finucane, women were "using a silk stocking, and they'd sieve the brown flour to get the dusty white flour off it, to get a few ounces to make a few nice scones." Resourcefulness helped people to cope.

Fuel shortages conspicuously crippled the functioning of the entire city. Owing to diminished petrol supplies, private cars all but vanished from the streets, except those for emergency purposes. This gave rise to a sea of bicycles. A limited number of buses were kept running, so packed with humanity that their tyres nearly burst. Thanks to the Shannon hydro-electric scheme, most trams continued to operate. The most visible and dramatic change in public transport and haulage was the massive revival of horse vehicles, as the *Evening Herald* explained: "We are obliged again to fall back on our dumb friends to help us in an emergency."[23]

With the return of thousands of horses, farriers enjoyed a resurrection. "Our craft was almost dead," James Colman, one of Dublin's veteran blacksmiths, told the *Irish Press*. "Now all the firms are going back to horses and our trouble will be to get apprentices."[24] Farriers were swamped with business, their forges open nearly eighteen hours a day. Soon the city was suffused once again with the sound of the smithy's hammer upon anvil.

A fascinating variety of horse-drawn vehicles appeared on the streets: side cars, drays, brakes, hansom cabs, broughams, three-horse minibuses, even some ancient coaches not seen for more than a century. With the marvellous profusion of horse vehicles, jarveys shouting and cursing and swarms of zigzagging cyclists, Dublin's streets had never been more lively and exciting. Or dangerous.

Within homes, fuel shortages struck a personal blow in kitchen and hearth. The absence of coal and the rationing of gas turned people's world topsy-turvy. Curtailed gas supplies meant that it was limited to a few precious hours each day. Gas remaining in the pipes gave off a glimmer in burners, but it was strictly forbidden to use this; yet many a decent woman, craving a cup of tea, Bovril or shell cocoa, dared to secretly squeeze a bit off the glimmer to boil water. Knowing she could be nabbed by the now-legendary "glimmer man", the Gas Company inspector sent around on his bicycle to catch violators. Sly mammies such as Una Shaw's would post their children on the street as sentries to watch for the glimmer man as they illicitly used an extra bit of gas. Shaw recalls how she and her pals would scream to high heaven when they spotted the glimmer man on their street; "We'd scramble—'it's the *glimmer man*, it's the *glimmer man!*'" If caught, most women were let off with a scolding and firm warning, but repeat violators could have their gas cut off.

Coal for heating and cooking seemed to disappear overnight. "We never *saw* coal during the war," Una Shaw says. Turf became the substitute for coal, often wet, smouldering and smoking but giving off little heat. The Government brought in mountains of turf to the Phoenix Park. People had to wheel a cart or pram over to get a load, which was back-breaking work. The turf was sodden, heavy, and infested with fleas. Una Shaw dreaded having to go and collect it for her mother, "bringing it home in an old pram, *wringing* wet, you wouldn't be able to light it—and you'd be *eaten alive* by fleas! You were freezing all winter." It was no wonder that poor tenement-dwellers ripped wooden doors off some bomb shelters for fuel in the depths of winter.

Hospitals were allotted a limited supply of coal, so valuable that it had to be guarded by policemen, including Senan Finucane. He made regular rounds to make certain that no coal was being stolen. There was a trick to protecting it, he explains: "Hospitals would whitewash the coal with lime so they would know if anybody was stealing it. See, the white part would be gone and the hole would be in the black. Oh yes." When alerted to theft, he would stake out and watch for the culprit.

One night he might be despatched to catch a coal thief, the next night down to the Liffey quays to watch for a German invasion. Such were the war years.

No shortages were more agonisingly suffered than those of tea and cigarettes. Tea was first rationed at two ounces per person per week. As supplies shrank, it was reduced to one ounce, then to half an ounce. To women especially it caused great anxiety and stress: tea was calming, it was their life's elixir; men always had their pints. John Ryan contends that to get their hands on a few precious ounces of tea women would "swap almost their soul." They tried to concoct substitutes from a mixture of ash and hawthorn leaves, or dried dandelion roots. Most people simply dried out used tea leaves and used them over and over again till they were anaemic and the tea nearly transparent.

Cigarettes were just as desperately sought. Almost every man smoked back in the 1940s and had cigarettes on his mind every waking hour. In his memoir, *Remembering How We Stood*, John Ryan recalls that in pubs such as the Palace, the Pearl and McDaid's, where the literary set convened, talk of strategies for finding cigarettes was taken as seriously as a discourse on Yeats or Joyce. "One had to get them by assiduous supplication, guile, blackmail, bribery, or plain begging."[25] One of the most persistent moochers was Brendan Behan. Woodbines and Player's were the old standards, but foreign sailors brought in cigarettes with all sorts of peculiar names, such as Tento, Drumhead, Lucky Strike, Yanks, State Express, 333 and 555. No-one could ever be sure what was actually in them. Cigarettes were then sold by twos, threes and even singly. Regardless of content or bitterness, they were smoked to the very nub.

Many a Dubliner wanted the war to end for no greater reason than to normalise their daily tea and cigarette habit.

Despite their deprivations, Dubliners knew they were very fortunate compared with the great hardships and suffering of those in war-torn countries. They were truly blessed, for every night they could go to bed in peace and security.

————

During the summer of 1940 Dubliners saw an increasing number of wartime newsreels in cinemas showing destruction by bombs, deaths of soldiers, suffering of civilians. They felt ever more fortunate to be so far away from the war "over there."

In August an Irish merchant vessel, the *Kerry*, was fired on by passing German aircraft. It barely received notice in the press. A few days later, on 26 August, Jim Hawkins of Duncormick, Co. Wexford, heard a "bang" close to his home. A bomb had fallen nearby, doing slight damage to his roof. Shortly thereafter, about five miles away, another bomb descended on a creamery at Campile, Co. Wexford. Three young women working in the creamery, two of them sisters, were killed. This incident, widely covered in the newspapers, elicited great sympathy but was readily perceived as an unfortunate accident, as the *Irish Independent* commented:

> The public accepted the explanation that this tragic occurrence was due to an error on the part of German airmen.[26]

A terrible mishap, hardly likely to happen again.

On 25 October a few more bombs fell in the open countryside about two miles from Rathdrum, Co. Wicklow. No damage or casualties. Wicklow folk wandered over to see the imprint in the earth. Dubliners didn't bat an eye. Then, in early December, when Dubliners were anticipating Christmas, the mail boat *Cambria* was machine-gunned by German pilots only forty minutes after leaving Dún Laoghaire. Two weeks later there was a snippet in the newspapers about German planes dropping a few bombs "in open country throughout Northern Ireland." There were no injuries or damage. Both incidents went largely unnoticed.

As Christmas week of 1940 approached, the city's streets were jammed with people in jubilant spirits. Inner-city residents, with little money to spare, were happy with a simple Christmas. Mammies had saved their shillings for the Christmas pudding. They bought a few inexpensive items for their children at Woolworth's or from the dealers along Henry Street. More affluent Dubliners shopped at Clery's, Brown Thomas, or Switzer's. Grafton Street was bedecked with garlands of red, green, silver and gold, while shop windows were a kaleidoscope of colour and activity, with animated Santas, reindeer and elves busy in their little workshops. Adults and children alike wriggled their way forward to get a close-up view.

Henry Street was bustling with traders and customers. The city was at its liveliest. Newspapers noted that people seemed even merrier than usual, as if they wanted to compensate for wartime hardships and shortages by celebrating Christmas more exuberantly this year. Carol-singers were on nearly every corner and Girl Guides out on streets collecting toys for poor children. During Christmas week the annual entertainment presented by the Children's Party Committee of the St Vincent de Paul Society was a smashing success, with more than 1,500 children attending.

The city's Christmas mood was made all the more joyful by the return for the holidays of Dubliners who had been working in Britain, relieved to get back home in a safe environment. James Martin remembers returning "just the day before Christmas" to stay until the new year with his family in Grosvenor Square, Rathmines. He had recently experienced heavy German bombings in Manchester, where he worked, surviving by plunging down into deep air-raid shelters. His parents were delighted to have their 26-year-old son home for the holidays, assuring him that his visit would be restful and peaceful, that he had heard his last bombs for a while.

On 20 December, shortly before 7 p.m., as residents of Dún Laoghaire were engaged in their own Christmas preparations, several bombs fell near Sandycove railway station. Three people were slightly injured and there was some minor damage to roofs and windows. People milled about the site, speculating about what had happened. When it was mentioned in the newspapers next day, busy Dubliners paid little attention to another minor "mishap". However, an astute follower of these bombing incidents might have pinpointed them and found an interesting pattern of occurrence along the line of Co. Wexford, Co. Wicklow and Dún Laoghaire—the regular northerly route followed by German pilots as they flew towards their targets in Britain.

An incident on 22 December reported in the newspapers doubtless caught the attention of many Dubliners. Another neutral country had been bombed: Switzerland, long renowned and respected for its neutrality. A cluster of bombs fell in the heart of Zürich, injuring eleven people. And Germany wasn't the culprit: it was the British. The Swiss legation in London issued a strong "protest to the British Government against grave violations of Swiss neutrality in flights over Switzerland."[27] The British apologised, ruling it an unfortunate accident of war. Some Dubliners reading about it surely must have wondered, "what if a belligerent's bombs fell on *our* capital city?" If it happened in neutral Switzerland it could happen anywhere.

On 24 December the *Irish Independent* wrote at length about another "war drama" in the heart of Dublin, affecting scores of citizens. Affluent customers had been worrying whether or not the shops would have a good variety of luxurious merchandise for Christmas, because of the perils facing ships in getting safely through dangerous shipping lanes. Without quality imported items, they said, their Christmas could be spoiled. In an article headed "It Was a Happy Ending Despite the War," the newspaper described the drama:

> The tens of thousands doing their Christmas shopping in Dublin stores were at the happy last acts of a war-drama that has spread over twelve months. That drama has been the struggle of Dublin shop-owners to provide normal Christmas shopping facilities in the face of war blockades, submarine campaigns, and bombing of docks and transport facilities.[28]

Happily, the shop managers reported, "Irish-made fabrics, toys and fancy wares are obtainable in greater variety than ever."[29] But top-class shops wanted their shelves to be filled with "fine French silk scarves and leather handbags from America." Some managers personally told customers "stories full of the drama of war," how some shipments had barely made it through treacherous waters, with lurking German submarines, right to their shelves.[30] However, when they heard other "stories of shipments gone astray or blown up," some customers seemed positively heartbroken:

> In one shop a department manageress seemed a little disconsolate thinking of what *should* have been the finest show in her department—a £500 order of the very best American hand-bags ... either at the bottom of the sea or among the debris of some burnt-out warehouse in an English dock.[31]

As much of the highest-quality merchandise had dodged German torpedoes in the Atlantic or the Irish Sea, concluded the newspaper, "thus it was that Dublin has been provided with its usual Christmas shopping carnival."[32]

As always, Christmas Eve was joyful and magical, a time of family and friendship and of religious celebration. Every Dublin newspaper published its Christmas greetings, typified by that in the *Irish Independent*:

Last year when we were celebrating our Christmas with the greater part of the world at war, we all hoped that when the holy season would come around again the clouds would have passed and men would once more be enjoying the peace on earth for which Christmas stands. But, instead of that, the war has grown more bitter. And very many more widows and orphans, refugees and homeless are experiencing its grim results.

We here have been happily spared the ravages of war.[33]

Dubliners had rarely savoured so much their Christmas pudding in peace and security.

————

Following Christmas, Dubliners looked forward to the New Year holiday. But those who would be saying goodbye to relatives and friends returning to jobs in Britain were worried. Hitler's ominous message to his forces, published in Irish newspapers, did not help:

Herr Hitler, in his New Year Order of the Day to the German forces, thanked them for defeating their enemies on land, at sea, in the air ... "We are ready—the year 1941 will bring the completion of the greatest victory in our history."[34]

While other countries were praying for peace, Germany was promising expanded war, destruction and death.

Despite Hitler's disquieting predictions of conquest, countries around the world tried to hold their traditional New Year celebrations. It was more important than ever to do so. Russians celebrated with their customary hotel parties and vodka drinking, while in Athens a Greek minister told his people to "be ready to fight to their last breath until the enemy was exterminated."[35] In Ottawa the Prime Minister, Mackenzie King, soberly prophesied that "before the end of 1941, events will have happened which will change for all time the world as we know it to-day."[36]

Londoners, who had much to fear from the coming year, held their traditional celebrations with a Churchillian show of confidence and resolve. Nature had helped by providing inclement weather over their part of Europe for several days, grounding German planes. New Year's Eve was London's second consecutive raid-free night. With a steely courage and high cheer, Londoners showed the outside world, and themselves, that the German blitzing had not broken their spirit. Amidst toppled buildings and mounds of rubble, crowds massed in the streets outside St Paul's Cathedral, celebrating unity and determination. They cheered and sang heartily, leading the *Evening Herald* to describe New Year's Eve in London as having "almost an air of normalcy in the streets."[37]

New Yorkers exhibited unusual exuberance in their parties and public demonstrations. Hundreds of thousands of revellers packed Broadway at midnight, singing and roaring out their wishes for a happy new year, "in defiance of an illuminated news projector which relentlessly flashed bulletins of a world at war."[38] Perhaps their gaiety reflected the feeling of a "last fling"—a sensing that the next New Year's Eve might not be so happy and carefree.

Dubliners on New Year's Eve were feeling grateful to their saviours, God and Dev, for having kept them safe through the first year of the war. In their New Year's Eve editions, newspapers wrote that through God's benevolence and de Valera's brilliant diplomacy they continued to live in peace while around them war raged. As Father P. J. Gannon wrote in a newspaper article, "we in Ireland have, through the mercy of God, escaped its horrors ... and we owe gratitude to God and to our leaders for this."[39] The *Irish Independent* expressed similar sentiments:

> We have to thank Providence for the inestimable blessings of having spared us from this terrible conflict which ravages so close to our very shores.
>
> 1940 goes out to-day. Having given us many heart-breaking tidings of war in other lands, it leaves us still at peace. A continuation of this favoured state is what we pray for in 1941.[40]

De Valera, MacEntee and Lemass may have thanked God as well, but talk of Ireland being a "favoured" nation in God's eyes worried them. The belief that Ireland was somehow protected by divine forces contributed to the feeling of complacency among the population. De Valera knew that this instilled a feeling of false security, one that could be shattered in the coming year.

New Year's Eve celebrations in Dublin were traditionally clamorous. Normally the more rackety and rowdy the better to welcome in the new year. By midnight, revellers had a good few sups on them and were primed for singing, cheering, shouting, clashing pots and pans, using any musical instrument they could get their hands on. Ships in the docks blew their whistles. The din of it all could be heard throughout the city.

This year, however, the *Evening Herald* reported an "almost silent welcome in Dublin."[41] This was the result of the Control of Sounds Order (1940), issued under the Emergency Powers Act, which prohibited the "use of sirens, hooters, rattles and other like instruments, except for giving air raid warnings." The restrictions silenced the ships and deprived citizens of loud noise-makers. They could still sing and shout at the top of their lungs, and certain moderate musical instruments were allowed.

Not to be denied their ancient tradition, by eleven o'clock excited revellers were gathering outside Christ Church Cathedral. Members of the Cathedral's Bell Ringer's Society, founded in 1670, had been up in the belfry for hours preparing for their biggest night of the year and setting out their large table with food and wine to be enjoyed after their duties had been carried out. As the final minutes of 1940 ticked away, the crowd swelled, people standing shoulder to shoulder, heads cocked upwards towards the great bells. But, as the *Irish Independent* reported, something was not quite the same as in past years:

> At 11.45 the bells began to peal, and at midnight came the first of twelve strokes to denote the passing of the old year and the advent of the new. There was cheering and shouting, and a number of accordion and mouth-organ players led the chorus of "Auld Lang Syne."
>
> But, somehow, one fancies that the cheering was less vigorous and the singing not so lusty as in former years ... it was as if most people felt that 1941 should be welcomed with a slight bit of reserve.[42]

Chapter 2 ～

A LUFTWAFFE NEW YEAR'S GREETING

Dublin City had its first experience of bombing yesterday morning.

(*Irish Times*, 3 January 1941)

We came out of Rathmines station and the plane came right over us. *And you could hear them releasing the bomb.*

(GARDA MAURICE WALSH, 88)

New Year's Day, 1941

The morning of New Year's Day was as tranquil as Dublin ever gets. Few were stirring in the streets. Inside, people were still drowsy, or hung over, from the night before.

The apocalyptic headline in the *Irish Times* opened droopy eyes and jarred some groggy brains, as it cast the new year in grave terms:

1941 YEAR OF DESTINY—WORLD'S FUTURE TO BE DECIDED

What did this mean for Ireland?

The rest of the New Year's Day news was not so grim. It was reported that, as was the custom on the first day of each new year, the German and Spanish Ministers, among others, would be calling to Áras an Uachtaráin to convey New Year's greetings to the President. For Dublin's cinema devotees who enjoyed following the exploits of American film stars, the news from Hollywood was that Bette Davis had just married Mr Arthur Farnsworth. At home Jack Doyle, the Irish heavyweight boxer, "stage variety artiste" and husband of Movita, the Mexican film star, declared bankruptcy. And, of course, Guiney's advertised their huge annual sale on a full page, billing it as the "Winter Sale All Ireland Is Waiting For." Despite wartime shortages they offered good selections at bargain prices for those who could afford them: men's overcoats for 19/11, women's evening frocks at 7/11, cardigans only 4/11, and Twilfit corsets for 2/11.

On a more serious note, the *Irish Times* revealed that the British air force had taken the offensive with some daring "raids over western Germany [that] claimed some direct hits."[1]

Most Dubliners traditionally spent New Year's Day in leisure at home or visiting family or friends. Cinemas always offered good films for those who liked to get out. A particularly big draw was the Baldoyle Races, both as a sporting event and fashion spectacle. The races attracted large crowds and a mixture of social classes. Newspapers sent their fashion reporters to cover the women, who often had no interest in horses but went solely to flaunt their new finery. It was fun for the "smart" set to show off before such an admiring crowd. According to the *Irish Independent*, the chilly day brought out ladies fashionably attired in furs, with muffs being the "in" thing:

> The air was filled with New Year's greetings and the attendance was good. It was a comfortably dressed meeting and in furs, boots, muffs and voluminous gloves, many women suggested a picture depicting Iceland rather than Ireland.[2]

Throughout the day, Dubliners were in good cheer, exchanging New Year greetings, determined to keep their new resolutions. Many expressed their hope that the awful war would be ended by next year at this time. With the holiday over, most people liked to go to bed at a reasonable hour and get a good night's sleep for the work week ahead.

At 9:43 that evening Mrs Thomas O'Rourke, a resident of Julianstown, near Drogheda, was wheeling her bicycle over a bridge on her way home when the "district was shaken and lit up" by several explosions. The bicycle was "wrenched from her grasp and flung against the wall" of the bridge.[3] In a house nearby, Agnes Johnston was so startled by the blast that she later told reporters, "For a moment I thought I was dead."[4] The next day the military and police would determine that five bombs had fallen at Duleek and three at Julianstown. All were relatively small, making shallow indentations in the fields. The roofs and ceilings of two small houses were slightly damaged. No-one was hurt.

As Dubliners turned off their lights to go to bed on New Year's night, most knew nothing of the eight bombs that had been dropped. The holiday now a memory, the next morning would bring a return to work and the usual humdrum of daily life. As they settled beneath their blankets a light snow began falling over most of Ireland.

———

1–2 January 1941, Knockroe, Co. Carlow

> When the eight members of the Shannon family knelt down and said the rosary in the cheery glow of the turf fire in their comfortable house at Knockroe they were, mercifully, unaware that death would snatch three of them from their sleep in the morning.[5]

Evening Rosary was the most comforting ritual for the Shannon family of isolated, ruggedly beautiful Knockroe. At Christmas and New Year's Day they always counted their blessings, particularly having one another.

Their farmstead comprised a two-storey stone and slated house with several outbuildings for cattle, farm implements and storage. Here lived John Shannon, a widower aged forty-five, his brothers Patrick (forty-eight), James (forty-three) and Michael (thirty-seven), also his sisters Mary Ellen (forty-four), and Bridget (thirty-seven), as well as his son Raymond, aged seventeen, and his sixteen-year-old daughter Kathleen, known to all as "young Katty". A close-knit family, they were all well known and "very popular" in their part of Co. Carlow. The menfolk tended to the farming and cattle on their 44-acre farm while the two unmarried sisters managed the house. The past year had been bountiful, with good crops and new calves born, and just before Christmas Mary Ellen had sold her pigs and poultry for the considerable sum of thirty pounds, now safely stashed away in a box in the kitchen. The new year looked equally promising.

The Shannon homestead lay in an undisturbed mountain valley about eight miles from Borris, almost on the Co. Wexford border. The setting was renowned for its natural beauty, but very isolated. "The family house lies in a lonely valley between the Blackstairs Mountain and Mount Leinster," the *Irish Independent* reported, "and there are scarcely half-a-dozen houses dotted over the square mile of desolate countryside."[6] Knockroe folk knew little of Hitler and the war. They had their hands full on the farm from morning till night.

New Year's night was biting cold and wintry, with a fresh snow blanketing the mountainsides and valley. The last acts were to bring their collie dog inside and tend to the turf fire. At 11:15 they gathered to say their nightly Rosary together, then exchanged goodnights.

By early morning the cover of snow had brought a hush over the land. Then, shortly before six o'clock, some neighbours heard the faint drone of plane engines breaking the perfect silence of the valley. The Shannons remained fast asleep, unaware. Then one plane, passing over the peak of Mount Leinster towards the Blackstairs, dropped flares over the snow-covered mountains and valley below. Suddenly "an aeroplane, streaking out of the frosty sky, rained bombs on the mountain district of Knockroe, and brought death and destruction to a peaceful farming homestead."[7] Eight bombs were dropped in rapid succession, in a straight line, with only a few miles between the first and the last, exploding as neatly as firecrackers on a string.

The first two bombs dug into the open earth, tossing out soil and stones. At 5:50 the third bomb sliced cleanly through the crisp air directly towards the Shannons' home and "must have struck their house plumb in the centre."[8] It crashed through the slate roof and exploded in the kitchen, next to the room in which Mary Ellen, Bridget and Kathleen were sleeping. All were killed instantly. Mary Ellen died from a stone striking her head; Bridget was flung clear through the roof, and bed parts were blown out into adjacent fields. Young Katty was discovered under debris, her school books by her side. Michael and James were seriously injured. Outbuildings were also destroyed and some cattle killed. The family collie survived.

Neighbours had heard the explosions and felt the impact. All rushed along the road leading to the Shannons'. Peter Breen, who lived three hundred yards away, ran faster than ever before in his life and was the first to arrive. As others showed up he was digging frantically with his hands through the rubble to free those trapped. Once extricated, the bodies of the three women were laid out in the barn, side by side. All through the long winter day relatives, friends and strangers showed up, viewed the lifeless bodies of Mary Ellen, Bridget and young Katty and wept. That evening, "as dark was falling, the military carried the three bodies on a kreel down the stony mountain lane" to the main road, where they were placed on army lorries and taken for inquest.[9]

The next day, army investigators determined that the bombs had been "of small calibre." Yet it only took a direct hit from one small bomb to cause such awful destruction and death. The *Irish Independent* emphasised the improbability of a single bomb hitting the Shannons' house:

> The most extraordinary feature of the Knockroe bombing tragedy is that the house which was struck stands almost alone in a mountainous district which is one of the loneliest in the country.[10]

It illustrated how a bomb, once released, was unpredictable in its path and its impact point. In the following days people all over Ireland would engage in conjecture, trying to calculate the odds of what had happened. Eight bombs dropped over a span of several miles, in a straight line. The Shannons' little farm had to be precisely on their line, at exactly the right distance between the second and fourth bombs, for the third one to have struck directly in the kitchen.

There was no doubt about it—a plummeting bomb might strike *anywhere*, against *any* odds.

2 January 1941, Dublin

A few minutes past six o'clock in the morning, as Peter Breen and other neighbours were digging through the debris at Knockroe, aircraft engines were heard over Dublin. A familiar sound by now, few people paid any attention. On this morning they were particularly reluctant to leave their warm beds to look out the window. The heavy frost on the glass told them of the frigid conditions outside. However, those who were already up, or who decided to rise and peer outside, saw Dublin at one of its loveliest moments. The freshly fallen snow made the city appear as white as a wedding dress. Snowy parks and squares looked like Christmas cards. But most Dubliners at six in the morning chose to ignore the drone of engines and pretty wintry scenes to remain comfortably in their beds.

At 6:10 many decided differently. For the first time, Dubliners heard the sound of bomb blasts in *their* city.

Four bombs fell in the Terenure area. Two dropped in Lavarna Grove on vacant land; a third struck near the end of Rathdown Park and a fourth near the centre of the park. Almost everyone within hearing distance popped out of bed and went to their windows. Not James Martin. He remained bundled in his bed in Grosvenor Square, unfazed by the four "thumps". "I was in bed and heard the bombs. But the week before I'd had a hell of a lot more in Manchester. So I was not the slightest disturbed."

Others were very disturbed. Over at Rathmines Garda station the guard on night duty immediately identified the drones as German bombers that were flying unusually low over the city. He alerted the other men, who scrambled outside. Maurice "Mossie" Walsh had come from Co. Kerry only a year before at the age of twenty-one to join the force. He had never expected to have to deal with bombs in Dublin, but when he pushed his way through the door beside a comrade the plane swooped "right over us." His more experienced colleague shouted at him to "hit the ground!" and to stuff his handkerchief into his mouth to cushion his teeth and jaw in case a bomb exploded near them. With fumbling hands he did so. When the bombs detonated over in Terenure he and the other guard were ordered to rush over to help with rescue work and crowd control.

Most Dubliners were more curious than frightened. At first, many had no idea they were bomb blasts. A number of men were already out on the streets or at work, such as milkmen, carters, lamplighters and those working in the fruit and vegetable markets. Farriers were in their forges, putting frost nails on horses so they wouldn't slip on the icy streets. Many of them saw the "blue flash, like a blue flame that comes from the tramway wires when there was something wrong."[11] Peter Wilson, a dairyman from Swords, was making his rounds and got a close look. Just as he approached Rathdown Park he saw "a plane flying very low overhead." Seconds later he felt the force of the blast and, "in a half-dazed condition, rushed into the nearest house for shelter."[12]

At 6:22 a.m. John McColl of 19 Rathdown Park excitedly phoned Tara Street fire station for help. Meanwhile local police and members of the ARP and LDF were rushing towards the scene. Paddy Walsh, at twenty-five one of the younger firemen at Tara Street fire station, was on duty that night. When the station bell rang out at 6:23 he and his colleagues leapt out of bed and into their uniforms and boots, mounted their vehicles and were ready to roar out of the station. Then they saw the glistening streets, covered with a layer of slick ice and frost. Only the most skilled drivers could take the wheel under such conditions. Paddy Walsh was one of those chosen. Now aged ninety, he recalls:

> The fire bell rung, but we didn't know it was a bomb till we went out. I thought it was an ordinary fire. The officer in charge, Richard Gorman, came and said I was to be the driver. It was very very frosty. One engine had already gone out.
>
> I was driving up Rathfarnham Road on this white frost—and no traffic on the road at this time. And I just tipped the brakes and the vehicle swung around and did a complete turn. But I readied it, and we headed on.

By 6:26 two fire engines and two ambulances were on the scene, under the direction of the superintendent of Dublin Fire Brigade, Major J. J. Comerford. Assisted by the LDF, firemen concentrated their efforts on numbers 25 and 27 Rathdown Park, owned by Mr and Mrs Plant and Louis Isaacson and his family. Here the "bomb apparently fell in the garden by the rear walls of the two houses ... almost demolishing them."[13] Eleven-year-old Jacqueline Isaacson recalled, "I was choked with the dust and there was glass flying and I screamed."[14] Unable to extricate his daughter, Louis Isaacson ran out into the snowy street, hysterically crying, "Save my daughter, save my daughter!" An ARP warden and several of his men responded immediately, removing bricks and mortar and freeing the girl unharmed.

Next door at number 29, Mr Benson, a Grafton Street jeweller, and his wife were abruptly awakened by the blast. Mrs Benson looked up and "I saw a hole in the roof of the room where my child Leonara (aged two) was asleep in her cot."[15] She took the child in her arms and gently rocked her back and forth. When the child was fully awake she looked up at her mother and, with Christmas fresh in her mind, asked, "Mammy, has Santa Claus come down the chimney?"[16]

By this time Paddy Walsh and his Fire Brigade colleagues were engaged in rescue work at a nearby house where the blast had ripped off the roof and left the structure in an unstable condition. From inside they had heard a woman's call for help:

This bomb hit the end of a terrace of houses, at the back garden. Made a crater in the garden and the house fell in, but not much fire. They were up-market houses, a place where there was a Jewish settlement. A woman was trapped there, in her bed. The roof had collapsed down and the joists were all criss-crossing on the bed.

Now I was just five foot nine but another lad with me was a hardy fella, Harry O'Keeffe. So we got in and everything was in a heap, the front of the house was still intact but the whole back was down. There was one joist holding most of the roof still on. So he got down on his hunker, if you like, and held it. Then he says to me, "I'll hold that and give you time to get in."

So we got in there, we made contact with her and talked to her. She was an old lady, a great character. Ah, she was *delighted* to see us! And we had a great chat. Then we had to drag her down. Somebody else looked after her then ... and that was the last I saw of her.

Only a few houses away, LDF rescuers were trying to free another trapped woman. They asked a bystander if he would assist them by knocking at doors along the street in hopes of fetching a saw they needed. He hurried off and within minutes had good luck. The door was opened by "a charming old lady", who told him, "I have a saw, certainly, but it may take me a few minutes to find it. Would you like a glass of champagne while you wait?"[17] Not wishing to be rude, he accepted. At 6:35 a.m. he was sitting there alone, sipping champagne and wondering if it was all a dream. When the woman came back with a saw in hand he thanked her and then apologised for having to leave so suddenly. He ran back and turned the saw over to the rescuers, quickly telling them his story and summing up, "I have never had a glass of champagne in such circumstances, or with such speed."[18]

By now people from other parts of the city were making their way by foot or bicycle to the Rathdown Park area to check on relatives and friends. Joe Roche, an eighteen-year-old LDF member, always had his bike well oiled and ready for duty. His mother, beside herself with worry over her three sisters, who lived over there, told him to speed over and check on his aunts. "So I went up on my bike to see how things were. Two houses were flattened and debris all over the road." His aunts were quite safe, but shaken. On his way home with the good news he encountered a flow of curious people trudging towards the scene.

After Paddy Walsh and his comrade had rescued the elderly woman trapped in her bed they began assisting with the removal of debris at another house. Suddenly, behind him, he heard the smashing of glass. Swinging around, he saw ARP men throwing stones up at the street lamps. For a few seconds he couldn't think what in the world they were doing. Then he heard the plane's engines and looked up:

> I'll tell you, I *did* get frightened when the bomber came back. 'Cause when he came back the second time, to the point where he had dropped the first one, we thought we were the targets, the rescuers.
>
> Oh, yeah, we could see him. He circled around, evidently trying to get his bearings. And all the street lights were on. So, some men went to break the lights along the avenue, throwing stones to get the lights out. He didn't drop any more bombs—but we were expecting it!

———

2 January 1941, Co. Kildare

Horses heard them first. Their ears pricked up at the first drone of the engines. At 6:30 a.m., twenty minutes after planes had visited Dublin, they appeared over Co. Kildare and released between thirty and forty bombs onto the countryside, a combination of incendiary and explosive bombs. It was seemingly a random pattern. One incendiary bomb landed on James Cox's farm, setting fire to about 100 tons of hay and straw.

The Curragh was Ireland's prime horse country. Prized thoroughbred race horses with delicate temperaments and as pampered as royalty were stabled throughout the area. The great fear of owners and handlers was a stable fire, which could destroy a fortune in horseflesh in minutes. Within seconds of hearing the blasts, every stable hand was running towards their wards to calm them. Some horses were already wild-eyed, pushing hard against their stalls. Though the bombs were peppered widely across the landscape, three fell on the Curragh racecourse itself. Three others exploded on a 200-acre stud farm at Ballymany, the property of the Aga Khan, damaging a water pipe and upsetting some of his finest racehorses.

After the planes dropped their bombs they promptly departed. The military were soon swarming over the countryside in search of evidence. They found that not all the bombs had detonated. That afternoon the Department of Defence announced that "an incendiary bomb picked up at the Curragh was identified as German."[19] No-one was surprised.

What *was* surprising was that nearly forty bombs had fallen without any deaths or injuries. With one exception—"out in the fields a rabbit was killed."[20] Local people could only marvel at their good fortune.

2 January 1941, Co. Wexford

The same night planes were again heard in the skies over eastern Ireland. Shortly before 8 p.m. military observers detected aircraft heading north over Co. Wexford. Some residents who had not read a newspaper or listened to the wireless that day did not even know yet of the earlier bombings at Knockroe, Dublin and the Curragh and when the planes flew over they took it as a normal occurrence. This time, however, they dropped three bombs on Ballymurrin, between Enniscorthy and Wexford, causing no injury or damage.

——

3 January 1941, Dublin

On the third morning of the new year the main headline in the *Irish Times* read "BOMBS FALL ON FIVE IRISH COUNTIES". The *Irish Independent* noted that it had happened on the 491st day of the war—for Dubliners it was the first real day of the war.

Earlier that morning, before Dubliners had even a chance to awake, have tea and pore over the dramatic events of the previous day in their newspaper, trouble struck again. Planes were back above the city, this time to drop just one bomb. Senan Finucane and his colleagues at the Garda barracks in Kevin Street were awakened at 3:55 a.m. when "we heard the '*whizz*' of the bomb falling from the sky. And the next thing, the bomb exploded. We weren't used to that." The barracks quickly cleared as men rushed to the point of impact.

It had landed in Donore Terrace, off the South Circular Road. The *Evening Herald* got a jump on other newspapers, as one of its staff lived in the street. He was immediately roused by the "terrific thud". In a flash he was outside, making notes and interviewing people. It was described as a very "low-flying aircraft" that had dropped its single bomb on the attractive row of red-brick houses, completely toppling numbers 91 and 93. Other properties were damaged as well.

Nick Harris, now ninety-one, an LDF member living nearby in Dufferin Avenue, was dressed within two minutes and out on the street, running past people who "had their dressing-gowns on them. I got to Donore Terrace and saw some houses damaged, and one woman was crying. They got her out." Garda Bill Nolan from Kevin Street was already surrounded by a crowd of shaken local residents. He was explaining to them that it had indeed been a bomb but that they needn't panic. It was best to go back home and stay out of the way of the rescuers.

The bomb fell at the rear of the two houses, its blast causing them to crumple. Number 91 was occupied by George Day, who awoke to find "a ton of masonry lying on top of himself and his wife."[21] With one of his arms he was barely able to make a "passage to allow the air through." Otherwise, he later said, both surely "would have smothered."[22] A large piece of plaster lay across his legs, pinning him to the bed. ARP men freed the couple, and they were rushed off to Mercer's Hospital.

An astonishing story was that of the Plant family, whose home at 93 Donore Terrace was demolished. They had previously lived at 25 Rathdown Park, which had been severely damaged the day before. Both of their residences had been struck by bomb blasts within twenty-four hours.

A few houses down lived Harry Lazarus and his family of nine, as well as his mother, who had just returned from London, where her own home had been destroyed in the blitz. She came to Dublin for safety and peace of mind. She had just arrived the night before and had refused to go to bed, giving no reason. Perhaps she was still nervous from her London experience, or simply savouring the security of neutral Dublin. She chose to sit downstairs by the fire until the small hours of the morning. Then the bomb struck and the house shuddered. No-one in the house was injured, but it was not easy to calm her down.

At 113 Donore Terrace lived Dr James Smyth. Unhurt, he looked around to assess the minor damage to his house. He was struck by the fact that "all the pictures on one wall had fallen, except an illustrated copy of Yeats's poem 'A Pity Beyond All Telling.'"[23]

One of the first doctors to assist on the scene was Dr T. V. O'Donnell of South Circular Road, whose house was almost opposite those bombed. Though his home had also suffered some damage, "I grabbed my steel helmet and rushed out, arriving on the scene in about one minute. People were screaming in their houses and running out into the streets."[24] Over the next few hours he treated about thirty people, mostly for minor injuries and bad nerves. There were no deaths—with the single exception of a pet parrot found in one of the houses. It was thought he had died of fright.

Considerable physical damage was done to two religious buildings, Donore Presbyterian Church and the South Circular Road Synagogue. At the church, stained-glass windows were shattered and pews overturned. Umbrella holders in many pews were torn off and Bibles and hymn books scattered and covered with dust. The clock was blown off the wall onto a pew some distance away, and "when picked up, it was still ticking away, although the minute hand was missing."[25] Damage was also done to the vestry and the adjoining school.

Nonetheless, in the morning, when a reporter from the *Irish Times* dropped around he found "the Rev. Thomas Bole, the minister, and his wife cheerfully make the best of things," despite some destruction to their own home next door.[26]

The bomb did not directly hit the synagogue but was close enough to have caused considerable damage. Flying debris crashed into the façade, smashing windows and breaking religious emblems. One observer described the exterior looking "as if it had been attacked by a machine-gun fired from ground level, so greatly was the white-faced stone pock-marked."[27] Inside, plaster fell from the ceiling but the pulpit was unharmed. Fortunately, the synagogue, built in 1924 with steel joists at the hefty cost of £14,000, proved to be extremely solid.

Much was made by local people of the bomb striking a Jewish community and despoiling their synagogue. Newspapers were discreet in their coverage. The *Irish Press* simply noted that "most of the injured and those whose houses were damaged are members of the Jewish community who have resided in that district for generations."[28] It was part of the area known as "Little Jerusalem", in which about five thousand Jews lived at that time. Nick Harris, born in 1915, was long a leading member of the Jewish community and in his eighties wrote a book about the history of Dublin's Jewish settlement. He was troubled by the talk that the Luftwaffe had deliberately aimed at Jews in Ireland. Many people, he recalls, were going around saying that "Hitler had it in for Dublin's Jews." To him it was nonsense.

The first three days of the new year had seen German bombs fall on several counties in Ireland. The pattern appeared random, and the results remarkable for their improbability. At the Shannons' farm in Co. Carlow three people had been killed. Thirty to forty bombs plummeted onto the Curragh area and not a person or a horse was scratched. In the heart of Dublin, a residential district had been bombed on two consecutive days, with no fatalities, major damage or serious injuries.

It is not possible to say how many Dubliners put the incidents down to Providence, how many considered it plain good luck. The *Irish Times*, however, made a cogent point about the bombs that had fallen on the capital:

> Owing to the fact that they fell on comparatively soft ground in all instances, much of their force was spent in the earth.[29]

Fortunately, they were also all of relatively small calibre.

The bombings had an ironic effect on many people. Rather than making them more fearful, it instilled in them a belief that bombings were "quite survivable." After all, there had been two days of bombs falling on Dublin, with not a single death or serious injury. As long as their city was not blitzed by waves of German bombers raining large bombs down on them—which, of course, "could not happen" to a neutral city—people could get through a few mishaps now and then.

In retrospect, many Dubliners admit that the incidents of early January 1941 actually reinforced their complacency.

Chapter 3 ∿

"SUBURB OF A CITY ON FIRE"

All around us cataclysmic things are happening. There are still amongst us people who speak and act as if the war was being fought upon another planet … who expect us to be immune from the effects of it.

(SEÁN LEMASS, *Sunday Independent*, 26 January 1941)

Ireland is a suburb of a city on fire. It would be foolish to think that we are not in danger.

(*Irish Press*, 7 February 1941)

January 1941

Within forty-eight hours, unexploded bomb parts and fragments from the Curragh, Julianstown and Duleek were proved conclusively to be of German origin. Evidence in Dublin showed the same. Yet in Ireland there were no public outbursts of anger, and no protests against the German transgressor. By contrast, Americans of Irish heritage were fighting mad. In heavily Irish-American cities, such as New York, Boston, and Chicago, there were angry outbursts and protests against Germany. According to a despatch from the Associated Press on 3 January, "the dropping of bombs on Eire has caused a tremendous sensation in New York City where thousands of Irish natives and immigrants live."[1] Irish districts and Irish bars were abuzz with the details of what had happened. Real anger was expressed. Telegrams and letters flowed to relatives and friends in Ireland.

Two days after the bombing incidents a formal protest and a condemnation of Germany's violation of neutral Irish soil was arranged by the Irish community in United States:

The American Friends of Irish Neutrality, an association which represents some 200 Irish organizations in the U.S., has telegraphed the German Embassy in Washington to protest against the "unwarranted invasion of Ireland, which is a neutral country". The Association was voicing the sentiments of many millions of Americans.[2]

The term "invasion of Ireland" was powerfully emotive. Irish-Americans saw it as grave, even if many Irish people did not.

In Dublin the official reaction was mild. De Valera issued no formal statement but instructed the Irish chargé d'affaires in Berlin to lodge a protest. It was politely phrased so as not to offend Hitler, part of the diplomacy of maintaining good relations under difficult circumstances so that neutrality would not be jeopardised.

The German response was a haughty denial:

An Associated Press message from Berlin says that an authorized spokesman, commenting on the raids on Eire, states: "Those bombs are English or they are imaginary. Our fliers have not been over Ireland, and have not been sent there, so someone else will have to explain these bombs."[3]

The dismissive statement, casting blame on the British, was consistent with earlier German claims that Churchill would use clever ploys to draw Ireland into the war on Britain's side. The Germans had actually predicated a scheme in which the British would bomb Dublin and make it look like an act of the Luftwaffe. This allegation would be heard again.

If the Government was essentially mute, Dublin newspapers were determined to have their say, even if constrained by official censorship. They did not have to be as polite and diplomatic as de Valera. The *Irish Independent*, reminding readers of the three young women killed at the Campile creamery the previous summer, challenged the facile assumption that all the bomb incidents had been merely a "mistake":

The public has reason for grave disquiet. It is difficult to conceive that these happenings have been due to a series of mistakes. We should like to think that they are not deliberate attacks on our country. It may be that there is no real ground for undue uneasiness. But we are passing through a period in which it would be foolish to feel too confident of the security of our position.[4]

The editorial in the *Irish Press* concentrated on the two questions foremost in everyone's mind: *how* and *why* the bombings had occurred:

These grave happenings seem to the layman inexplicable. The main boundaries of this country are as clearly defined as it is possible for boundaries to be. To reach us, aircraft have to fly over broad stretches of sea. It is hardly conceivable, therefore, that any experienced airman could mistake our soil for belligerent territory. Should a mistake in navigation under bad weather conditions lead any aircraft over our soil, there are still lights of our cities, visible from directly overhead, to indicate our neutrality.

What can be the possible explanation? That question is being asked in thousands of homes in Ireland today. It would be madness for our people … not to take every step for self-protection and for dealing promptly with every danger.[5]

Public protection depended on the system of sirens and shelters, neither of which had been used when bombs fell on Dublin on 2 and 3 January. The sirens had not been activated, and the citizens did not head for shelters in which they had no faith. The *Irish Press* was openly critical. "No warning of any kind was given in the presence of foreign aircraft over the country … the siren system should have been in operation."[6] At the *Irish Times* the legendary and fiercely independent editor, R. M. Smyllie, was so angry and frustrated by this failure that he despatched one of his senior reporters to the headquarters of the Air-Raid Precautions Service to get a direct explanation. The next day a now-fuming Smyllie shared with readers what his reporter had been told:

The reporter who put this query to the A.R.P. headquarters was informed that there was no information on this subject at the moment.[7]

The mounting exasperation of both citizens and press over the siren debacle forced the Dublin city manager, P. J. Hernon on 5 January to meet reporters anxious for his explanation. His convoluted rationale left most wondering if they had heard it correctly:

If this country were at war, a situation might conceivably exist whereby at least some notice might be given of the approach of hostile aircraft, and in such a case, if bombing or attack were foreseen and expected, it is believed the sirens would be of immense use.

[But] we are not at war, and we do not consider it wise policy to be constantly alarming all the citizens over the wide area of Dublin because of what perhaps is an isolated incident.[8]

Reporters and citizens alike found Hernon's statement illogical, if not preposterous. How could people be "unduly alarmed" when bombs had actually been dropped on the city? "What then," they asked one another, "are our sirens *for*? What *would* warrant their use?"

No-one was more irritated by Hernon's feeble explanation than Smyllie, who decided to take him on directly in the *Irish Times* on 7 January:

> We decline to concede our original case—that sirens ought to have been in operation, if not on the morning of the Terenure outrage, at any rate on the following morning, when bombs were dropped on the South Circular Road. Mr. Hernon seems to imply that it is wrong to waken and alarm many thousands of citizens for the sake of "what is, perhaps, an isolated incident."
>
> Public shelters are useless without a system of warning. The ordinary citizen is not awakened by the drone of a single aircraft; the first indication he receives is the crash of the bomb itself. If he is unlucky, it is too late by then to bolt for shelter.
>
> A bomb might fall upon a household of people who, if a siren system were in operation, would have had just enough time to rush for safety. Is it not worthwhile to alarm Dublin if life thereby can be saved?[9]

Smyllie concluded his commentary by stating: "Happily, no life has been lost in Dublin so far, but who knows if similar fortune will attend another of these incidents should it occur."[10]

Hernon also found himself under fire over the air-raid shelters and the black-out policy, or lack thereof. Most citizens had no faith that the above-ground concrete shelters would protect them. The few who had sought refuge in them reported that some were padlocked, at which the *Irish Times* railed: "This is outrageous ... the public shelters must be opened at once, and far more (better) shelters constructed."[11] When Hernon was informed that at Rathdown Park the ARP men had to run along the street tossing stones up at the lamps to black-out the area for their safety, it again ignited the debate over lighting policy. Which was better, a complete black-out that would conceal the city or full illumination so that it could be easily seen and identified as neutral? Proponents on both sides were hounding Hernon to come up with a firm policy. So far, only large advertising signs around College Green and O'Connell Bridge were prohibited at night. On 4 January Hernon announced that he was seriously considering extending the Lighting Restrictions Order and imposing a "stricter black-out", as he called it, on the city. He promised to make a decision on the matter within a few weeks.

Apart from the failure of sirens and shelters, some Dubliners were asking why the German planes had not simply been shot down. This prompted the military correspondent of the *Irish Independent* to explain the realities of night bombing to readers:

There is no effective defence against the night bomber ... bombers must be brought within the beam of a searchlight and held in it for an appreciable period, in order that height and speed may be reckoned and shell fuses adjusted.[12]

What chance had Irish gunners, with little firing experience and limited ammunition? And, considering the potential military consequences and the political risks to neutrality, perhaps some citizens were thankful that Irish gunners had not brought down any Luftwaffe planes.

The January bombings stirred a surge of patriotism around the country. The Government, seeking to exploit this before it waned, held recruitment drives for new ARP wardens and LDF and LSF volunteers. Teenagers not long out of short trousers stood in enlistment queues next to grey-haired veterans of the 1916 Rising, the Civil War and the trenches of the Great War, all equally anxious to defend their country. It was inspiring, wrote the *Irish Times*:

Not only young men, but men of age, not usually associated with soldiering, came forward. Men who had fought in the wars of twenty years ago joined up once again. In the new defence force, every class and creed were represented.

Ireland is proud of these men, as proud as she was of other men who volunteered their services in the War of Independence. That they will carry on a gallant tradition if the final call comes, there is no doubt.[13]

Despite their noble intentions and the extravagant praise, enthusiasm again declined once the volunteers realised they were not to be made into real soldiers with real weapons. Morale further sagged when they were not taken seriously by the citizenry. The writer of "An Irishman's Diary" in the *Irish Times* poked fun at LDF members, telling how one group leader tried to get his men to wear their caps at a uniform angle so as to look more professional:

Everybody wears his cap at a different angle. Some almost horizontally, others bolt upright. Some tilted so forward it almost obscures the right eye; others hung precariously at the back of the head.[14]

When the leader called his men to attention, "half the caps went flying off their heads." For the LDF volunteers even such mild derision eroded pride in their role. As morale sagged, numbers dwindled.

The Government and the Air-Raid Precautions Service, having endured a barrage of criticism from public and press for the siren failure and the padlocked shelters, wanted to bolster citizens' confidence. On 19 January they staged a large mock air-raid drill in which they could display their rescue skill. It was held in a street just off St Stephen's Green. The selection of such a prominent site showed they wanted a large audience for their exhibition. There was plenty of prior publicity to inform Dubliners of the show, as described in the *Irish Press*:

> Between 10 and 11 o'clock tomorrow morning high explosives and incendiary bombs will plaster a large block of buildings in St. Stephen's Green vicinity, trapping inmates of two buildings and setting rather serious fires ... such is the hypothesis upon which the exercise will take place.[15]

A crowd began gathering more than an hour before the event. ARP officers did not disappoint them. There were simulated bomb blasts, fires, smoke, trapped victims, ladder rescues, stretchers and ambulances. It had the look of a real air raid, people said on their way home. Very entertaining.

Not long thereafter, Oscar Traynor, Minister for Defence, sought to further fortify public confidence in Ireland's security. He sounded positively cocky when he stepped before the Dáil to give assurances about the readiness of the Irish army:

> The morale of these officers, in my opinion, is at the highest possible peak and the general feeling throughout the army is that the freedom of this nation, if assailed by any other nation, will be defended in a way which I believe will surprise the aggressor.[16]

Tough talk. While it may have pleased members of the Government, others worried that such boasts would only contribute to complacency and a false sense of security.

On 25 January Seán Lemass decided to candidly present his views on Ireland's precarious position in a world at war. He selected the perfect forum: the annual dinner of the Institute of Journalists, held at the Royal Dublin Hotel. In a packed room, he sounded his own siren alert. Page 1 of the *Sunday Independent* had a headline that summed up his speech:

TIME OF THE GREATEST DANGER TO OUR NATION
War Crisis Near

The paper considered it important enough to print the essence of Lemass's message:

During the first three days of 1941, German bombs fell on five Irish counties.

Three members of the Shannon family were killed in their farmhouse at Knockroe, Co. Carlow, on 2 January 1941.

EVENING HERALD

DUBLIN FAMILIES' ORDEAL
Agonising Scenes Follow Bomb Havoc

MANY INJURED: TROOPS RUSH TO AID VICTIMS

Greeks Report Mo Successe

THE GOVERNMENT INFORMATION BUREAU HAS ISSUED THE FOLLOWING STATEMENT ON BEHALF OF THE DEPARTMENT OF DEFENCE.

"At 3.55 a.m. an unidentified aircraft dropped two bombs in Donore Terrace, South Circular Rd., Dublin, and destroyed two houses, seriously damaged a third, and did slighter damage to other houses in the area. Some twenty people were injured, but none seriously.

"THE BATTALION OF THE DEFENCE FORCES STATIONED AT GRIFFITH BARRACKS TURNED OUT WITHIN A FEW MINUTES OF THE EXPLOSION AND WENT TO THE AID OF THOSE WHO HAD BEEN AFFECTED BY THE BOMBING."

Three bombs fell between Enniscorthy and Wexford last night.

"Herald" Man's Vivid Story of Early Morning Horror

On the night of 2/3 January 1941, Dublin experienced its first bombings.

THRILLING RESCUE SCENES IN DUBLIN SUBURBS

Narrow Escapes In Shattered Houses

BOMBS SHAKE SUBURBS

The first German bombs on Dublin shattered several houses but took no lives.

"TIME OF THE GREATEST DANGER TO OUR NATION"

WAR CRISIS NEAR, SAYS MR. LEMASS

"FREE PRESS ESSENTIAL"

WITHIN a few weeks, or a few months the crisis of this war will come, and with it the time of greatest danger to our nation.

So said Mr. Sean Lemass, Minister for Supplies, responding to the toast of "Our Guests" at the annual dinner of the Institute of Journalists (Dublin and Irish Association District) at the Royal Hibernian Hotel, Dublin, last night.

Mr. Lemass, Minister for Supplies, with Mr. J. W. Kelly (left), Chairman of the Dublin and Irish Association District, Institute of Journalists, and (on right) Mr. R. F.

Seán Lemass, Minister for Supplies, scolded the public for their complacency in time of war and warned of dangers to the country.

Newcomen Bridge on North Strand Road, only yards from where the big bomb fell on 31 May 1941.

Corcoran's was one of the most prosperous shops in the North Strand village. (*Courtesy of Dublin City Archives*)

The Lynches' 150-year-old cottage at right, next to the Royal Canal lock and showing Croke Park in the distance.

The basement of Charleville Mall Library served as a shelter during the night of the bombing.

St Agatha's Church in North William Street survived the bombing but lost its magnificent stained-glass windows and suffered damage to the roof and exterior.

Agnes Daly (*standing, front centre*), who was nearly killed by a flying section of tram track.

Una Shaw still lives in the house in Rutland Street that was damaged by the bombing in 1941.

Maureen Lynch was knocked unconscious when the bomb exploded close to her cottage beside Newcomen Bridge.

Within a few weeks, or a few months, the crisis of this war will come, and with it the time of greatest danger to our nation. More than at any time in our history ... our people should be made to take our national position realistically. Our position is very grave indeed ... all around us cataclysmic things are happening. There are still amongst us people who speak and act as if the war was being fought upon another planet instead of within sight of our shores, and who expect us to be immune from the effects of it.

We in this country have a right to be neutral in this conflict if we so decide. We have a right to expect that the belligerents will take care to ensure that of the thousands of bombs falling from the skies around us, none will fall upon our territory. We have thousands of rights, but rights alone are poor protection for small states when great Empires go to war.

What the future will hold for us no man can tell. In time of war, the unpredictable, the unforeseeable event is the only certainty.[17]

Public reaction to the speech was mixed. While some appreciated the candour of Lemass's realistic warnings, others thought his words exaggerated, if not alarmist. Only time would tell.

———

January had been a bleak and distressing month, with bombs, frigid temperatures, fuel shortages, wet turf, dwindling stock of tea, cigarettes and other commodities, followed by dire warnings of the "greatest danger" to the nation and a "war crisis" looming. Dubliners were in real need of some diversion.

They found it in cinemas and on the stage. By good fortune, late January saw the release of some cheery films. Two were especially popular, real "escape" films, offering singing, dancing, romance and comedy—marvellously therapeutic for anyone with the mid-winter blues. Showing at the Capitol was *Lucky Partners*, starring Ginger Rogers and Ronald Colman, two Irish favourites. At the Savoy, *Spring Parade* was showing, featuring Deanna Durbin. Coming off a frigid January street into a warm theatre to watch *Spring Parade* made one feel that spring and the Whit holiday were not so far off.

Dublin's talented stage performers always did their best when times were tough to lift spirits and make audiences laugh. No-one was better at comic sketches than Jimmy O'Dea, Dublin's beloved comedian. In January he was starring in a new presentation of *Babes in the Wood* at the Gaiety Theatre. O'Dea had a special way of poking innocent fun at the "Emergency", Hitler, even the LDF and the ARP wardens. In this production, wrote the theatre critic for the *Irish Independent*, "as an air raid warden Jimmy finds ample scope for his wit."[18] His impersonation of a bumbling warden only followed the bombings by a few weeks, but it was a perfect role for the moment. It brought howls of laughter from the audience—especially from the real wardens among the crowd. Those who saw his humour and high jinks on stage liked to go home and share it with family and friends. In this way, he lifted spirits all over the city. He included no jokes about the silent air-raid sirens.

The month that had begun with bomb blasts ended with the bitter blast of a winter snowstorm. Cold and snow blanketed the land as a ferocious blizzard roared across the country. Newspapers called it a "killer snowstorm", because it took lives in both the countryside and towns. People were caught unprepared as "buses were marooned in country districts and drivers and conductors and passengers had to seek accommodations in country cottages."[19] Roads were blocked and people were isolated, without proper clothing, food or shelter. In places, blizzard winds whipped snow into ten-foot drifts. A number of deaths from exposure resulted. It took a full week to dig away the snow and begin returning to normal life.

Dublin survived the dangerous snowstorm without mishap. In fact Dubliners were having difficulty even imagining the ten-foot snowdrifts they read about in the newspapers. They talked about how fortunate they had been to have escaped the "killer" storm.

———

February 1941

February began with an alarm. On the second day of the month citizens were startled to hear explosions again. But it was daytime, and no planes had been heard or seen above the city. Inquiries streamed into Government and newspaper offices. People were relieved to learn that it was "ascertained that the explosions took place during LDF manoeuvres in the northern part of County Dublin ... as demonstrations in the handling of explosives were being given to members."[20] Why hadn't the Government placed advance announcements in the newspapers to inform citizens of the demonstrations, so they wouldn't have been unnecessarily alarmed?

For weeks the beleaguered city manager, P. J. Hernon, had withstood blistering criticism over the air-raid siren failure. At a meeting of the city council he now faced critics who condemned the shelter system as utterly inadequate. He began by presenting the holding capacity of the city's various shelters, in the hope that it might assuage worries:

Basement shelters:	11,466
Trench shelters:	6,836
Above-ground shelters:	5,050

No-one seemed impressed. The total was slightly over 23,000 persons who could be accommodated. Hernon then assured the council that shelters under construction would bring the total to nearly 34,000. Still, councillors were not satisfied. Then he inadvertently threw gunpowder on the already-inflamed tempers by stating that the cost of the trench shelters was £34,000. There were immediate outbursts condemning the trench shelters as archaic, useless, ridiculous relics of the Great War, a shameful squandering of money and abominably poor judgement on the part of the Government.

Fintan Burke rose to demand the "immediate construction of adequate *underground* shelters."[21] These would be of the British type that would provide real safety from bombs. He further asserted that the "existing shelters are a failure so far as the preservation of public morale was concerned."[22] He was followed by Councillor Jim Larkin, who drew both nods and smiles when he stated that "existing shelters are unsafe even to put a hen in—they're elongated hat boxes!"[23]

Hernon then presented his case against the British-type shelters, citing the realities as he saw them. For a neutral country, he argued, they were prohibitively expensive and therefore unjustified. Again, rather than defusing displeasure he raised tempers. The consensus rebuttal of his words was "how could a city already bombed *not* afford safe shelters for its citizens?" Discussion became particularly sensitive when the matter of class and wealth came up. Privileged members of official and business circles had access to deep, well-fortified basement shelters near their offices. And affluent citizens could afford to build their own Anderson shelters in their back gardens.

The debate was focused on hard economics and speculation about whether Dublin, with its policy of neutrality, would ever be seriously bombed. Who in the room was such a prophet? It was just a gamble.

As with every wartime issue, some humour eventually came out of it. Air-raid shelters and gas masks were always fair targets for mockery. In an unusual twist, a serious lecture brought some amusement—if not incredulity—to many Dubliners when they heard about Mr H. McDowell's unique suggestion. McDowell was no crackpot but an esteemed member of the Dublin Society for the Prevention of Cruelty to Animals. Following the January bombings he was motivated to present a lecture entitled "A.R.P. For Animals". Because of petrol shortages there were now many thousands of horses on the city's streets. The speaker had two concerns: the protection of the animals from bomb-related harm and the "protection of humans from panic-stricken beasts":

> Horses should be protected from the effects of aerial bombardment. Gas masks have been manufactured for horses, but only in limited quantities As an alternative, gas-proof stables should be built. Or existing stables should be made gas-proof.
>
> These methods might prove effective against gas attacks … [but] what is to be done with horses during an attack with high-explosive or incendiary bombs? One cannot comfortably accommodate a horse in an Anderson-type shelter.
>
> The only way to prevent such an occurrence would be to construct air-raid shelters especially for the use of horses. It may be argued that it is a sheer waste of time and money on air-raid precautions for animals … but when petrol shortages have rendered the horse so necessary to everyday life it should be protected from the possible effects of the air raids.[24]

He had not yet worked out the economics of his scheme. Nor is it recorded by the society how his address was received by the audience. And what did P. J. Hernon think of McDowell's novel ideas about gas masks, gas-proof stables and air-raid shelters for horses? Regrettably, the record does not tell us.

The city manager's battles with critics were not the only ones being waged on the Dublin scene during the early months of 1941. Several other social struggles and even physical conflicts were taking place. One was particularly conspicuous and violent. The *Irish Times* called the city a "battlefield" where enemies clashed in bloody skirmishes. The notorious "Animal Gang" ran rampant, fought with other gangs and terrified ordinary citizens. People ended up getting killed. Many Dubliners were more fearful of the gangs than they were of German pilots.

John Joe Kennedy, now eighty, who lived in tough Engine Alley in the Liberties, was a member of one of the most vicious gangs. He participated in gang wars in which as many as two hundred combatants brawled with knives, lead pipes, knuckledusters, even hatchets and old swords. After one brutal clash at the Baldoyle racecourse Justice Hanna determined to teach the gangs a lesson. On 26 February he sent a number of them to prison for terms of from four to eight years. Some citizens thought a better idea would have been to ship the ruffians up to Belfast for mandatory enlistment in the British army; let the hooligans take out their hostility on the Germans.

On another Dublin battle front, temperance reformers were fighting against rising insobriety. With the outbreak of war, drinking increased in many circles, no doubt partly because of the wartime woes of unemployment, shortages of food, fuel and cigarettes and worry about relatives abroad. Drink was an escape. Temperance reformers contended that during the war years men especially needed to be sober and responsible. At its meeting on 1 February, Fred Eason, chairman of the Irish Association for the Prevention of Intemperance, said that "soldiers of temperance" must set the example. As war was being waged throughout Europe, they pledged to combat with renewed vigour the widespread drunkenness in their own city.

Women too were combatants in the winter months of 1941. Members of the Women's Social and Progressive League were waging a battle to end discrimination against women and to demand equality and justice. In February they "expressed indignation at the Government's attitude towards women," who were receiving lower wages than men for doing the same jobs.[25] They alleged blatant discrimination, documenting one case after another. They cited a current advertisement for school inspectors in which men were openly offered a "much larger salary for doing the same work."[26] Though they occasionally won a skirmish, theirs was to be a long war. The radical feminists of their day, they were accustomed to defeat but were determined to carry on with their campaign for just and equal treatment.

A lesser but equally lively struggle was being enacted at this time between traditional music purists and modern revisionists. A group of determined "anti-jazz enthusiasts" mounted a campaign to see that "no jazz should be broadcast from any Irish station."[27] The two sides waged their battle by writing letters to the newspapers and arguing in public forums. Jazz opponents wanted only "respectable" music broadcast, meaning "opera, oratorios, symphonic, chamber and instrumental, Irish music and modern dance music." Purists even condemned all contemporary dance music as "jazz". Jazz, they contended, was debasing to Irish Catholic values. To them, this was an honourable fight for the morality of the nation's listening audience. To the public it was mostly an amusing episode during a difficult time.

_____

March 1941

On 17 March, St Patrick's Day was celebrated quite differently in Dublin and New York. This year New Yorkers were more demonstrative and spirited than ever, as "75,000 Irish men assembled on South Street and paraded ... they marched with bands, pipes and banners through the city."[28] Huge crowds cheered them along the way. Their Irish patriotic fervour was at an unprecedented pitch following the German bombing of their homeland a few months earlier. Among participants and onlookers there was much talk of the German "attack" upon Ireland's sacred soil.

In Ireland, the American-style St Patrick's Day parade had not yet been introduced. A military parade was held annually in Dublin from 1931, later augmented with commercial floats; but the parade was suspended for the duration of the war. The *Irish Press* reported:

> Ireland probably celebrated St. Patrick's Day more quietly than the rest of the world ... there was no army parade. Dublin, though crowded, was more subdued than usual.
>
> Perhaps it was thinking of other St. Patrick's Days when carefree friends over the earth were caressing shamrocks from home on their coat lapels.[29]

Perhaps in the chilly midst of March they were also thinking wistfully about the Whit weekend, which would arrive in only ten more weeks and with it, hopefully, sunny skies, warm temperatures and outdoor activities. *Spring.* Then June—and summer. Never had the Whit holiday been more anticipated.

Chapter 4

⏐ BELFAST ABLAZE

For eighteen months of war the people of Ireland have watched from afar. They had "ringside seats" until a few days ago. Then Belfast experienced an air raid. Modern war, in all its stark reality, was brought within less than half-an-hour's flight from Dublin.

(*Irish Times*, 19 April 1941)

The firemen clung to their open vehicles thundering at 60 mph through the chilly morning on a journey of the brave into the unknown.

(TOM GERAGHTY, *The Dublin Fire Brigade*)

I remember Lord Haw-Haw warning us that Dublin would be bombed because the Irish, though we were neutral, had interfered—because they sent fire brigades up to the North to help, and then accepted refugees from the North.

(BERNADETTE PIERCE, 75)

Dublin, 14 April 1941

Dubliners had been awaiting Easter Monday with great anticipation. It was the twenty-fifth anniversary of the 1916 Rising, and a military parade was planned for O'Connell Street. People began arriving early to make certain they secured a good view. Young lads and older fellas tried to climb atop the concrete air-raid shelters for prized balcony seats but were promptly chased off by the Gardaí, who had strict orders to keep them clear. The authorities knew that the unfortified concrete roofs could easily collapse with the weight of a crowd of onlookers. A collapse, on this day and in full public view, not from a bomb but from the weight of parade-watchers, would be mortifying to the defence authorities.

When de Valera, other members of the Government and the military brass arrived to take their places on the reviewing stand, people strained to see whom they could identify. The *Irish Independent* reported:

Dense crowds lined the streets of Dublin to witness the largest and most spectacular military parade the city had ever seen. Over 20,000 trained men and women—troops, L.D.F. and non-military units—took part in the parade which took 2½ hours to pass the G.P.O.[1]

If Dubliners had been reserved on New Year's Eve and St Patrick's Day, they let loose today. They cheered enthusiastically as seemingly endless waves of uniformed soldiers, volunteer forces and military bands passed before them. It was indeed an impressive sight. The Irish military was displaying its strength and its readiness to face any adversary. It was enough to make one feel that the Irish army could indeed stand up to German invaders.

Belfast, 14 April 1941

In Belfast, Easter Monday had been considerably more calm. People had enjoyed the racing in Celtic Park and shows in the Opera House, the Empire Theatre and the city's cinemas, enjoying the peace of the Easter season.

Only one week before, on the night of 7/8 April, six German bombers had dropped bombs on the docks, causing some damage to a section of the Harland and Wolff shipyard as well as a number of fatalities and injuries. But people essentially saw this as an isolated incident.

The government at Stormont, as well as ordinary citizens, had felt relatively secure, confident that they would be spared any attack from Germany. This feeling of safety rested on three assumptions: firstly, that Belfast was too distant and "isolated" to be a target for a long, round-trip air raid; secondly, that the city did not qualify as a significant strategic target for German bombers; and thirdly, that de Valera's declaration of neutrality, as well as the fact that the Constitution of Ireland regarded the North as part of its territory, would be respected by Hitler. As Tony Gray explains, "they reckoned that Hitler would not want to risk endangering Eire's neutrality by a blitz on a city which de Valera regarded as part of his territory."[2] In short, most people believed that the North was "off limits" for German pilots.

Nonetheless, it was "strange that Belfast was not better prepared" for at least the "possibility of an air attack," as people went about their life in quite a normal way after the war started.[3] The city's dance halls, cinemas and theatres remained open, and people freely crowded the streets and open parks. Many failed to take the air-raid precautions, shelter drills or black-outs seriously. As a consequence, Northerners were ill-prepared, both physically and psychologically, for a real attack upon their city.

Belfast's air defence depended on twenty-four heavy and fourteen light anti-aircraft guns. The city was woefully short of firemen and fire engines, with a full-time fire service of only 230 men.[4] The underlying premise was that it was unlikely that greater resources would ever be needed.

Unfortunately, Belfast's assumptions of security were faulty. Especially naïve was the belief that Belfast was not a worthwhile military target. It had not only the huge Harland and Wolff shipyard, one of the largest in the world, but other large factories turning out a steady line of aircraft, tanks and other war material, as well as engineering works and linen factories. In reality, Belfast was a prime—and predictable—target. And with the fall of France in June 1940 it now meant that the journey for German pilots from continental Europe to Britain and Ireland was considerably shortened. Belfast was easily reachable.

At the outset of the war, the assumption that Germany would not touch the North because of the Irish constitution's claim to the Six Counties may have seemed logical. But having witnessed the German invasion of neutral Belgium and the Netherlands, Northerners surely should have been uneasy.

On Easter Tuesday night, at 10:40, the comfortable assumptions were suddenly shattered. Air-raid sirens began shrieking as squadrons of German aircraft appeared without warning. They began bombing runs that were barely impeded by the inadequate anti-aircraft defences. Many of the bombs were incendiary, igniting conflagrations throughout the city. "Hundreds of Belfast firemen, augmented by auxiliary fire fighters, worked feverishly all through the night to bring the fires under control."[5] But their efforts were insufficient, and fires raged out of control. It was a desperate situation, not only for the city's fire brigade but for political decision-makers as well. They needed firefighting assistance, and urgently.

Shortly before 4 a.m., with Belfast still ablaze and firemen becoming fatigued, a telegram was sent to London asking for assistance. Forty-two fire pumps with four hundred firemen were promised; they would be despatched by destroyer from Liverpool and by Admiralty ferry from Glasgow.

But firefighting help was needed *immediately*.

At 4:20 a.m. a "momentous political decision was made": Dublin would be asked for assistance.[6] "An urgent message was sent by the Belfast Commissioner of the Royal Ulster Constabulary to the War Room in Stormont," seeking approval to ask for firefighting aid from Dublin.[7] John MacDermott, the Minister of Public Security, immediately approved the request.

A telegraphed request was sent at 4:35 a.m. to P. J. Hernon, Dublin city manager. It had to be sent by telegraph because the phone lines between Belfast and Dublin had been severed by the bombs. At about 5:10 a.m. de Valera was awakened and informed of the request. He replied that he would immediately consult his advisers and make a swift decision. There was scant time to contemplate the political ramifications of a decision made so hastily and under such stress.

Close to 5:50 a.m., de Valera gave the "go ahead", committing his Government services to crossing the border and providing firefighting and ambulance assistance to Belfast. To British citizens.

By 6 a.m., full responsibility for carrying out the mission had been placed in the hands of Major J. J. Comerford, superintendent of Dublin Fire Brigade. No man in Ireland was more capable of responding to the crisis. He was experienced, quick-thinking, resolute, and hugely respected by his men.

In 1936 there had been a fire in Pearse Street in which three firemen had lost their lives. Later there were questions about mismanagement of the brigade, followed by inquiries and the dismissal of officers. A new superintendent was needed to shake up the force, from top to bottom. Comerford was the man selected to undertake the job. Jack Conroy, a 22-year-old recruit under Comerford's new leadership, recalls the impression he made on the men:

> This army man took over as chief, a Major Comerford. Oh, he was a spit-and-polish merchant. He had us marching up and down in the barrack square. Oh, God, yes. He had an ex-sergeant in the army come in twice a week to drill us, and teach us how to salute. I enjoyed it, but some of the older men didn't like it. But it made us *fit*. Comerford turned the place inside out. A *good* man. His word was law!

Within a few months Comerford had transformed what had been a rather lax force into a disciplined, highly skilled fire brigade. Jack Conroy recalls: "He used to time us with his stopwatch and we had only one minute to be out after the fire alarm bell rang. We *wanted* to get out and do our stuff." In April 1941 Dublin's fire brigade was at its peak of physical condition, skill and morale.

By 6:30 a.m. Comerford had all his men assembled before him in Tara Street fire station. Among them was Paddy Finlay, who had joined the brigade in 1938 at the age of twenty-two. He was stationed at Rathmines fire station at the time, but shortly after six o'clock he and his colleagues "got a phone call to proceed immediately to Tara Street station. We assembled in the appliance room and were addressed by Major Comerford." The superintendent informed them that Belfast had been severely bombed and that they had sought help.

Comerford, he remembers, looked every man directly in the eyes, speaking in clear, concise terms. He stood perfectly erect with his military bearing and laid it on the line. He was asking for volunteers. No man should feel obliged. Comerford said that the request had come from the very top, Dev himself. The duty carried risks, because the city was ablaze and German bombers still lingered around. He could make no promises about how long they would be gone, and could offer no guarantee of their safety—or even if they would return. But he needed their decision—on the spot.

Were there any questions? Several men asked about their pension cover in the event of their being killed. Would their families be provided for, as this was volunteer duty in a different jurisdiction? "We were assured that if anything happened to us our families would be taken care of," Finlay recalls. But this assurance was verbal, not written. They would have to take Comerford's word for it. To a man, they did. There were no more questions. Then Comerford called for volunteers.

Paddy Finlay's hand shot up and he stepped forward.

At the same time, over in Buckingham Street fire station Jack Conroy and his six mates were hearing similar words from their station officer. One of the reasons why he admittedly joined the force in his early twenties was because "there was a certain amount of glamour attached to it." When the call came for volunteers he and several other men came forward:

> I was pleased to go … didn't know what was facing us, just "things are bad up there." And we accepted that. I was twenty-two years of age, you know, there was a spirit of *adventure.*

His brother, a fireman over in Dorset Street fire station, was also ready to volunteer. But Conroy quickly informed his station officer that his brother was married. Thus, he was the one chosen.

Comerford arranged to recruit volunteers from fire brigades in Dún Laoghaire, Drogheda and Dundalk as well. In each place most men were eager to sign on—but not all, Finlay explains. Each man had his own reasons.

By about 7:30 de Valera was informed of Comerford's progress. He had six fire engines ready to go, three from Dublin and one each from the other towns, as well as several other vehicles. According to Hernon's official memo, a total of seventy-one men had been selected.[8] However, as Finlay recalls, there were probably "over a hundred of us" altogether. It is possible that the official record of the number of men despatched north was reduced for political reasons.

Comerford's final words to his men on leaving Tara Street station were that he "hoped the men would not disgrace the great tradition of the Dublin Fire Service." When Conroy and his mates were pulling out of their fire station, the local officer shouted his final words to them:

> We made up a crew of five of us—and off to Belfast! And when we were going out the gate our station officer says to us, "Well, you're *out*—and God knows when you'll be back!"[9]

It was the ride of their life: fast, cold, and swervy, sometimes holding on for dear life with numbed hands. When they roared out of their stations it was exhilarating, fraught with uncertainty. As they sped north on the open engine their faces and hands were exposed to the chill and wind and they felt as if they were freezing. Drivers had to sit on one hand while they kept the other on the wheel, then switch. At high speed on unfamiliar roads, with plenty of curves and bad patches, the journey was perilous. The other men had to keep some sensitivity in their hands in order to hold on safely, stuffing one hand inside their jacket while clinging to the shaking vehicle with the other, and having to balance themselves when the fire engine swerved and bumped. With almost no traffic on the road, the engines reached 60 miles per hour on open stretches.

Conversation was virtually impossible except for a few shouted words from time to time. Each man was left quite alone with his own thoughts. Neither Finlay nor Conroy recalls giving a thought to the possible political ramifications of their act, which was technically a violation of the neutrality policy. To Hitler and von Ribbentrop it could be regarded as aiding one of the belligerents. Instead, the firemen thought about what might lie ahead, about their families at home, warmth, a mug of hot tea, their next meal.

Most of the men had never been to Belfast before, and they didn't really know what to expect. About half way there, Paddy Finlay was struck with an unsettling thought. "For some extraordinary reason, I was of the opinion that Northern firemen would not protect Catholics. You see, it was bred into us here. But did I learn a lesson!"

When they reached the Killeen border post they received an escort of British military motorcycles, which guided them towards Belfast. Petrol stops were a welcome break from the paralysing chill. The men had a few minutes to warm their hands, feet and face, walk around a bit to limber up their body and get their circulation flowing again. Conroy especially remembers one petrol station:

> We were told to fill up with petrol at any station going up, 'cause we were short on petrol. We crossed the border and stopped in Newry and filled up. Got off to stretch our legs. And this woman came up and said, "Where are you from?" And we said Dublin—and she said "*Dublin*?" She couldn't believe, it, that we had come up from the Free State, as they called it then, to help them out.

As they got closer to Belfast they began to receive cheers along the way from people recognising who they were. It gave them a different kind of chill.

As they approached the outskirts of Belfast they made a quick stop to thaw out once more and try to get a bit of nourishment before they were cast into the uncertainty that awaited them. As they spotted an open pub, the drivers geared down and pulled in. Conroy smiles:

> We went into the pub—and they shouldn't have been open, but they were—and we hadn't got a penny in our pockets. And the barman said, "What are you having?" And whatever you wanted, they gave us.
>
> And there was this old Belfast chap, sitting by himself in the corner drinking his whiskey, and he said, "*Up de Valera!*"

Minutes later, on the road again, they got an idea of what faced them. They smelled smoke and in the distance saw massive flames. It looked as if all Belfast had been turned into an inferno. They began to encounter bedraggled people shuffling along the road. It left a lasting impression on young Finlay:

> On our open vehicles I could see the flames in the sky and the flashing. The last of the planes were still there and you could see them firing at them. And, funny thing, fear never occurred to me.
>
> We had an idea of what we were going to encounter when we met the refugees coming along with handcarts and walking, with anything and everything. It reminded me of the pictures I saw of refugees in Belgium and France.

Many of the homeless were women and children, pulling carts and pushing prams, their faces expressionless, dazed. They sat along the road or in fields to rest, a pitiful sight to the firemen from Dublin. Then it struck Conroy and Finlay that they were heading right into the hell that these people were fleeing.

They arrived in the city shortly before 10 a.m., already weary and hungry. Their muscles and joints ached from hanging on tightly to their vehicles during the journey. But when they saw the devastation and distress of the people who needed their help they felt rejuvenated. Before they could plunge into firefighting or rescue, however, they had to receive official orders from Belfast Fire Brigade headquarters in Chichester Street. Finlay and several mates hopped off their engine, rushed into the station and asked to see the chief fire officer:

> I enquired from a junior officer, "Where's your chief officer?" His name was Smythe. And he was *in under* the table—and he wouldn't come out! In front of his own men! Oh, the blitz was on—and he *wouldn't* come out. So I dealt with another man.

After receiving orders, they were led to their sites. Some men concentrated on residential districts where people were still trapped. "You'd go around to see if there was any people injured, and I found several. And we worked on any fire where there was any chance of saving anything." He and Conroy both had close calls. As he puts it, "I nearly met my Waterloo!" He was descending from a high ladder that rested against a shaky brick wall: "I sneaked down the ladder, careful not to disturb it." Only seconds after reaching the ground, "the whole wall came down! Wasn't *that* luck? I was standing looking at it." Some distance away, Conroy was fighting a ferocious blaze in a flax mill when "an oil pipe burst and hit me with hot oil. Luckily enough, it hit the backside of my helmet, ran down the back of my long rubberised slicker, and the heat of the oil lifted the coating off."

Every person they helped heaped thanks on them, some surprised to find that their rescuers spoke with a "foreign accent." One terrified woman, just dug out of the ruins of her home, heard an unfamiliar tongue and asked if she was being captured by Germans. When her rescuers assured her that they were not Germans but Dubliners she cried, "Oh, my God, I've been blown down to Dublin!"[10]

After about five hours of unrelenting work they were famished, growing weak. No provision had been made for feeding them. Then, Conroy recalls, a godsend appeared. "Soldiers came along with their mobile kitchens and gave us big cans of tea and sandwiches and hard-boiled eggs." They gratefully accepted the food, sagged to a sitting position on the ground and devoured it. Meanwhile, "soldiers were all sitting down with us, telling us of their experiences, that the Germans came down and machine-gunned the streets."

By evening, after nearly ten hours of duty, the men were fatigued, and a halt was called. They returned to Chichester Street station, a welcome sight to Conroy. "We got a meal, and they had mattresses laid out for us on the floor. We were grimy and dirty and washing ourselves." After which all fell immediately into an almost comatose sleep.

Only one hour later they were shaken awake. It was now about 10 p.m. The order had come from de Valera to get the men out of Belfast as quickly as they had come in. He didn't want them there during the night, when the Luftwaffe might sweep over again. He was taking no chances of fatalities, which could be a personal loss and a possible political disaster. Conroy remembers: "Word came to *pack up*, we're going home."

How the fatigued, sleepless firemen were able to pull themselves aboard their engines, hold firmly and stay awake during the return trip they can't recall. The trip south, in the dark this time, was even more hazardous than the first. Headlamps on the fire engines were not fitted with black-out covers, so they had to navigate the road in the dark, guided only by the rear lights of a motorcyclist. To try to stay awake they sang lustily, shouted anything into the night air to retain alertness. Mercifully, they received refreshments and a few minutes' rest in Banbridge and Newry. Finally, in the middle of the night they arrived back home in Dublin—returning heroes, though not yet aware of it.

Their mission of mercy had lasted about twenty hours. It seemed more like days. No-one was more relieved with their safe return than de Valera, who had found himself in a position of having to sit nervously on the sidelines awaiting the final outcome of their journey. Only when he received word that all the men were back safely was he able to relax. It had been about twenty-four hours since he had made his decision. He did not find himself regretting that decision, but he was now wondering about the possible consequences.

He had never had to make so important a judgement in so short a time, and at that hour of the morning, with less than one hour in which to reason it out and decide on a course of action. He knew, of course, that it was technically a breach of neutrality to despatch firefighters to the North, thereby assisting the British during a wartime crisis. But humanitarian considerations outweighed the political in this case. He had followed his instincts and his heart:

> De Valera showed the true colours of his sympathies for the democracies and the one-nation concept when he dispatched fire brigades to succour the stricken Belfast. The "niceties" of neutrality did not deter him at a time like that.[11]

Even the German Minister, Hempel, later said that he "understood the emotional and political reasons behind the act."[12] Sensitive to de Valera's personal feelings and the predicament he confronted, Hempel told an Irish journalist: "It was a deed of sympathy for your Irish people, and we fully understand what you felt. Your own people were in danger."[13]

Hempel was expressing his personal sentiment—not that of his boss, Hitler.

By dawn the next day, de Valera had another crisis on his hands. Thousands of refugees from the North were streaming south towards the border, seeking asylum in neutral territory, also needing food, shelter and medical assistance. De Valera knew that a humanitarian act of accepting the refugees could be construed as another violation of neutrality. Nonetheless, once again he acted from his heart. He also gave approval for the Great Northern Railway to make special night runs up to Belfast to bring refugees down to Dublin.

Dublin's relief agencies, most notably the Red Cross Society, responded quickly to the crisis, making arrangements for the refugees to be met at Amiens Street railway station, to be medically examined and then sent to shelters. Dr T. A. Hayes, city and county medical director, personally took charge of seeing that they received whatever medical attention they needed. Those appearing weak from hunger were promptly taken over to the GNR buffet and well fed. Touched by their plight, citizens offered their own homes, taking in strangers. As the *Irish Times* wrote, "as the day wore on, Dublin's kind heart went out in sympathy to the sister city in the North."[14]

By the evening of the 17th more than three thousand refugees had arrived in Dublin. Compassionate crowds stood outside, watching them emerge from the station. And a pathetic sight it was: men, women and children looking lost and frightened, carrying small parcels, baskets, items hastily wrapped in paper, mothers barely able to manage lugging babies while looking after other little ones. Nine-year-old Maura O'Toole was among the crowd of onlookers at the bottom of the station steps as the refugees shuffled past. "They came with little or nothing, their clothes in tatters, no luggage or anything. Just refugees. But *we* were very safe." Many Dubliners observing so closely the misery of their neighbours to the north were doubtless thinking the same thing. As the *Irish Times* commented:

> The sight of trainloads of destitute refugees arriving at Amiens Street station brought home to the people of Dublin, as no story of Coventry or Glasgow ever could have brought home, the appalling tragedy of the present war.[15]

They were not watching a wartime newsreel in the cinema this time: these refugees were Irish. For the first time, they were *seeing* the human consequences of war.

The perceptions and emotions of the refugees from the North were no less profound. Upon arrival in Dublin they were overwhelmed by the outpouring of kindness and genuine friendship of the people.

They had not expected it. Many had never been to Dublin before; but from the moment they stepped off the train they were made to feel welcome. The *Irish Independent* captured the sense of kinship created by the dire circumstances:

> Many of us have already come in contact with the refugees … who have thrown themselves on the generosity of their fellow-countrymen. With the generosity and welcome of the people of Dublin it can never be said that any Irishman abandoned those of his own race and kin in need.

If anything further were needed to demonstrate the utter unreality of the artificial border that divides our country, the welcome that has been given to the refugees from Belfast provides it.[16]

Heroes all. That's the way Jack Conroy, Paddy Finlay and the other firemen were greeted the next morning when they returned to their normal life. Everywhere they went, the *Irish Press* reported, "crowds cheered them."[17] Says Finlay, "Oh, the *praise* we got!" By mid-morning, everyone in the city had heard about their dramatic dash north to Belfast to help put out fires and rescue victims.

Their story of courage and generosity also hit the headlines of newspapers not only in Ireland but in Britain, on the continent, in the United States and beyond. And in Germany.

When de Valera forged his policy of neutrality he had doubtless considered exigencies that might arise to threaten the agreement. It is not likely, however, that he envisaged having to send fire brigades across the border, or take in thousands of Northern refugees. Having done so, he would probably have preferred that it remain little known beyond Ireland.

The opposite occurred. The big story about the heroic Dublin firefighters was of great human interest in other countries, probably to de Valera's dismay. He could never have imagined how widely the story would be spread abroad. Articles in Irish and British papers not only lauded the bravery of the firemen but praised de Valera for his courage and judgement in approving the action. The *Belfast Telegraph* stressed the good-neighbourliness between South and North:

> The people will remember the magnificent spirit which prompted fire brigades from Eire to rush to the assistance of their comrades of the North. This is the good neighbour policy in action, worth months of speeches and assurances. Suffering can be the great leveller, cutting clean through all petty prejudices.[18]

The *Irish Press* called "the part played by the Fire Brigades in the 6 Counties … a grand show … highly praised,"[19] while the *Irish Times* hailed it in near-poetic terms:

> Humanity knows no borders, no politics, no differences of religious belief. Yesterday, the people of Ireland were united. We are all of the same stock, flesh of one another's flesh and bone. Fundamentally … the heart and soul of the North and South are as one.
>
> Has it taken bursting bombs to remind the people in this little country

that they have a common tradition, a common genius, and, above all, a common home?[20]

John MacDermott, Minister of Public Security in Northern Ireland, extended his heartfelt thanks to de Valera, to the firemen and to the people of the South, as did the Lord Mayor of Belfast, Crawford McCullagh, who cited the firemen's "professional assistance and humanitarian work."[21]

Under other circumstances de Valera would probably have glowed in the light of such praise at home and abroad. But any satisfaction he was feeling must have been tempered by his concern over what Hitler had thought of it all.

Many Irish people believed that the answer came through the words of William Joyce, "Lord Haw-Haw", in his radio broadcasts. For it wasn't long thereafter that Bernadette Pierce was sitting beside her granny in their cottage in Shamrock Terrace listening to the radio when they heard Lord Haw-Haw (whom her granny professed to despise, though she never missed one of his broadcasts) come on the air "*warning* us that Dublin, particularly Amiens Street station, would be bombed." He asserted that it would be in retribution for de Valera's breach of neutrality in sending fire brigades north, and then taking in refugees. Over in Rutland Street, Una Shaw heard the same broadcast, as did thousands of other Irish people. His words were perfectly clear: there would be a penalty for "interfering." Many members of the Government and the military surely listened as well. But did they give his words any credence? After all, Lord Haw-Haw was always full of bluster and bombast.

Following the blitz of Belfast, new realities emerged. De Valera's hope—or illusion—that the neutrality blanket would cover the full thirty-two counties had been shattered. Bombs were now falling "just up the road" in Dublin's sister city. As the *Irish Times* candidly contended, for the first eighteen months of the war "the people of Ireland have watched from afar. They had 'ringside seats.'"[22] Now, Luftwaffe bombs were being dropped "less than half-an-hour's flight" from Dublin. In an editorial on 17 April headed "A Terrible Beauty," Smyllie criticised the public's previous complacency and noted the sudden enlightenment:

When parts of Belfast were bombed recently, little more than an almost academic interest was aroused in the South of Ireland. Public opinion had become so much inured to stories of bombings in Great Britain and elsewhere that the fact that a few more bombs had been dropped on Belfast's docks and ship yards hardly caused the citizens of Dublin or Cork to pause in skimming their morning newspapers.

Yesterday told a vastly different tale. When the news reached Dublin yesterday morning the people seemed to have been stunned by it. For the first time since the outbreak of war, the people of Ireland have been able to realize what it means; for previous bombings have been trivial affairs.[23]

As Smyllie summed up, the "stark reality ... of modern war" now stood at Dublin's doorstep.[24]

On 20 April (Hitler's birthday) de Valera took the opportunity to publicly express sympathy for the North when he spoke before the Conference of Parish Council Representatives in Galway. His remarks were brief and sincere. After first noting that the people of the North and South did not always "see eye-to-eye politically," he stated:

But they are our people, their sorrow is our sorrow, and I want to say that any help we can give them will be given whole-heartedly, believing that, were the circumstances reversed, they would also give us their help whole-heartedly.[25]

It seemed to be an affirmation that he felt he had made the correct decision. Indeed, he seemed to be saying that he would do the same again if the need arose. As the *Irish Times* succinctly put it, "when all is said and done, the people of the Six Counties are our own folk; and blood is stronger than the highest explosive."[26]

In the wake of Belfast's tragedy, Dubliners began writing to newspapers with ideas about how citizens might be better prepared for a real bombing in their own city. Some of those with genuine merit were printed, such as the following:

One of the most horrible necessities of the Belfast Blitzen was the identification of bodies ... [Should not] identity discs be worn by everybody, man, woman and child, in Dublin? A metal disc bearing his or her name and address. It will not keep off the bombs, but it will save a very great deal of trouble and mental anguish.[27]

To most Dubliners it still seemed very far-fetched that they would ever have to identify corpses at a bomb site or in a morgue. More sensible, many thought, was wearing a religious medal around their neck, to ward off bombs in the first place. One citizen wrote to the *Irish Independent's* "Readers' Views" column offering his novel idea about the power of piety and sacrifice in saving the city:

Would it not be a splendid act of reverence if all places of amusement—theatres, cinemas and dance halls—remained closed and all sports fixtures were cancelled for one day. It would mean a genuine sacrifice for many people, but, *oh*, would it not be worth it if, by refraining from pleasure and giving our thoughts completely to God for just one day, we secured the priceless joy of peace?

I am sure the poor people of Belfast would refrain from amusements not only for one day but even for one year, to avert a similar ordeal as that which they endured on the 15th and 16th.[28]

He made no mention of closing the pubs.

On 22 April the Dublin city manager, P. J. Hernon, announced that he had finally made a decision about the city's black-out policy. Under the Emergency Powers Order, banned in Dublin would be all illuminated signs, shop fronts and advertisements during the hours of darkness, as well as all lights on premises and hoardings for the purpose of advertisement or display. It was also decreed that during the hours of darkness there could be no lights outside cinemas, theatres or other places of public resort. Furthermore, lights could be on in shops only while they were open to the public. This dousing of bright lights dramatically dimmed the mood of night-goers as well as the cityscape. As the *Irish Independent* observed, "the streets of Dublin presented a gloomy appearance last night ... the lights most missed were around College Green and O'Connell Bridge."[29]

There was still no prohibition of home lights, meaning that it was really a partial or "half-way" lighting ban, leaving citizens befuddled. Proponents of different lighting policies were equally dismayed, those who favoured full illumination to identify the city as neutral and those who wanted a complete black-out to hide the city from aerial detection. Though Dubliners were about equally divided, most agreed that the partial black-out policy was illogical.

De Valera had a plan of his own to present. It had been ten days since the bombing of Belfast, and he had given much thought to Dublin's vulnerability. He was also concerned that many citizens still did not fully grasp the perils facing their neutral territory. He chose 25 April, at a meeting in the Gresham Hotel, Dublin, to share his concerns and to suggest a plan. His opening statement sounded dire: "I hope nobody will think I am trying to create a panic."[30] No-one in the audience could recall ever hearing him use such a phrase. He continued:

In modern war there is no notice given; the first notice we would get of an impending attack is when the attack is already here.[31]

He proceeded to explain that "Dublin was the weakest point" in the country, having by far the largest population and yet only a minimal defence system. The city must be prepared, he asserted, by having a "scheme for evacuation." He spoke in terms of many tens of thousands. There were, he went on, "few people in Dublin without relatives in the country" with whom they might stay in time of crisis. The *Irish Independent* summed up his final thoughts:

> It was reasonable to think that the Almighty, who had so far brought them safe, would continue to see them safe to the end; but if optimism went to the point of neglecting things which they were bound to do, then they are blame-worthy.[32]

Had the speech been motivated by his personal observation of bedraggled Northern refugees streaming into Dublin and his wish that Dubliners would be spared such an experience? In any case, he gave no details of how such a mass evacuation might be carried out. It seemed more a quixotic concept than a definite plan.

Towards the end of April the *Irish Times* offered a more positive outlook on the future:

> Happily, we in Dublin have been spared the terrors of nocturnal attack. Twice, since the war began, bombs have fallen on our city; but there was no loss of life, and the great majority of our citizens have no first-hand experience of the bursting bomb.
>
> We in the South may thank God ... and we pray that Eire will continue to be left in peace.[33]

Chapter 5 ❧

THE MERRY MONTH OF MAY

Most men consider that knee-length skirts are the limit to which a girl should reach.

(MALE LETTER-WRITER, *Evening Mail*)

May was always a month of merriment and mirth in Dublin. People were drawn out of their winter hibernation by the sunshine and warm days. It was a time when both nature and social life began budding again. Doors and windows were flung open; people dallied on footpaths, chatting and bantering. Streets were packed and lively, the market dealers out in full force. On 8 May a cargo of oranges and lemons arrived at the docks. People hadn't seen their likes in nearly eighteen months. Word spread as they flocked to the markets just to look at them. But these were now luxury items, affordable only by the well-to-do. For those feeling a bit of springtime luck, a new sweepstake for the benefit of the Irish Red Cross Society was launched, the first prize set at £10,000.

May saw Dublin inundated by a sea of bicycles. Many of the cyclists aspired to one day owning a motorcycle when the war was over, of course. At this early stage many people believed the conflict would not last long, that one side or the other would soon prevail. In May the *Irish Times* journalist Harold Brown buoyed the hopes of those fantasising about a motorcycle by speculating optimistically about what he felt would soon be the fruits of a short war. "Thousands of bargains in motor cycles should be available when the war ends, when Army machines are turned over to disposal boards."[1] With minor alterations, he explained, they could be made suitable for "touring and general use." For avid cyclists it was a good reason to hope for a quick end to Europe's war.

Part of May's gaiety was showing off the new spring fashions before the public eye; and in 1941 Dubliners got an eyeful. When stylish shops such as Clery's, Brown Thomas and Switzer's introduced their "daring" new line of above-the-knee skirts it raised many eyebrows as well. With younger women they immediately became the rage, setting off a lively social debate in which almost everyone had their opinion about whether they were pretty—or pretty indecent. As leggy young women paraded up and down Grafton Street and strolled through St Stephen's Green, onlookers cast a discerning eye. Most men were unabashedly transfixed. Older women had differing reactions. While some saw them as innocently sexy and perfectly acceptable, others condemned them as scandalously immoral. To the women who wore them they were liberating, some flaunting their abbreviated skirts just to get the amusing reactions.

The spring season was enlivened by the continuing debate over the exact "limits of decency". Some skirts were quite noticeably shorter than others, which of course heightened the controversy. When citizens began submitting their opinions to the readers' views columns of newspapers, the topic could be elevated from amusement to hilarity. As it turned out, some of the most severe critics of short skirts and exposed legs were men. When one man righteously wrote to the *Evening Mail* that "most men consider that knee length skirts are the limit to which girls should reach," an offended woman replied in print:

> Well, girls, I hope you'll not hesitate to give him it, and put a stop to these milk-and-water types of men interfering with the apparel of the fairer sex—"Up, girls, and at him!"[2]

Letters from critics were typically stodgy and unimaginative; by contrast, those from women wearing the short skirts were amusing, even impassioned. One woman seemed to have the last word on the subject in the *Evening Mail*:

> Sir—Allow me space in your paper to remind all the hags and goody-goodies that we are now living in the year 1941! A girl can wear whatever clothes she likes. These critics should mind their own business. Now, girls, don't pay any heed to these old-fashioned growlers, and remember, life is very uncertain nowadays, so make the most of it.[3]

It was more uncertain than Dubliners realised.

The charms of May not only delighted Dubliners but drew visitors from the North and from Britain. Following the blitz, Belfast residents found Dublin a desirable destination. For those with bad nerves, the South offered calm and security. Most came by train through Amiens Street station, and as soon as they emerged into the streets they felt it was "another world," they said. They enjoyed the city's fine hotels, theatres, restaurants and shops; but more than anything else they savoured the simple normality of life. One of their greatest joys, they said, was hearing the tintinnabulation of the city's church bells on a Sunday, a seemingly small pleasure yet one much missed at home:

> The people of Northern Ireland have not heard the church bells rung for over a year, and at the present time they certainly do not want to hear them, for the peal is now a summons to arms against invading troops or parachutists.[4]

British people willing to risk the perils of crossing the water were greatly attracted to Dublin, especially those from bomb-riddled cities, such as London and Manchester. Apart from the food and entertainment, some were drawn by a passion for horse-racing. John Ryan recalls:

> The best steaks in the world were grilling over charcoal at the Dolphin Hotel, there was racing in the Phoenix Park and white ties and tails at the Shelbourne, while whiskey poured niagarously in the Pearl and Palace bars.[5]

The greatest luxury, however, was sleeping in peace and security. Having seen the tragic newsreels of destruction and death in Britain, Dubliners heaped sympathy upon war-weary visitors. At the Shelbourne Hotel chambermaids were given orders to treat Londoners as casualties of bomb shock. "Voices and footsteps were accordingly muted, soft ministrations were many, and in no night nursery could one have been more fondly, soothingly tucked up in bed."[6]

By mid-May the social season was in full swing. Among the middle and upper classes, parties and other social functions were held, and theatre-goers attended new plays. The Dublin theatre crowd anticipated the much-touted play by Moss Hart and George Kaufman, *You Can't Take It With You*. A theatre critic stirred enthusiasm by reporting that American audiences "have gone wild about it."[7]

One troubling aspect of Dublin's spring flings was that some parties and drinking were getting out of hand, not only in pubs but also in homes, where private drinking parties were increasingly being held. These "bottle parties", as they were called, had become a feature of social life among the more affluent. The report of the Temperance Committee, published in May, concluded that Irish people were seen increasingly by outsiders "as a drinking and gambling nation," while countries all around them were struggling for freedom and survival,[8] one more sign that people in Ireland were woefully out of touch with the realities of wartime suffering. It was disgraceful, and should be curtailed.

May always saw the city's streets filled with volunteers collecting funds for one good cause or another. The Irish Red Cross Society, St John Ambulance Brigade and St Vincent de Paul Society counted on filling their coffers in springtime. This year the St John Ambulance Brigade made an especially big appeal for funds. Marjorie Lyndon wanted to do her part, so she and her dance students put on a special matinée at the Gate Theatre to raise money. The money was needed because the organisation had just acquired a new mobile canteen, at a hefty cost of £600, the first of its type in the 26 Counties. Hot stew and soup prepared in cooking centres could be taken in five-gallon insulated containers to the canteen, as well as tea, Bovril and sandwiches. It could serve as many as three or four hundred people per hour. Brigade officials explained that it could be used in another emergency if more Belfast refugees arrived. However, it was emphasised that "it is hoped that the canteen will not be required for wartime purposes" for Dubliners.[9]

During May there was a significant increase in activity by the German air force over the east coast of Ireland. German pilots, following their usual northerly route over Dublin, began heavily striking targets in the south and west of Britain. On 4 May, "Liverpool was stunned [by] the ravages of the Luftwaffe in a night-long savage assault." Many Dubliners had relatives and friends working in factories there; they now wished they had remained safely at home in Dublin.

The following night German bombers again flew north over Dublin. But instead of veering off towards Britain they kept a due northerly course, then struck Belfast again. It was not nearly as intense or destructive as the Easter Tuesday raid and the city was better prepared this time. Nonetheless, Belfast firemen once again needed assistance with extinguishing fires and rescuing victims. De Valera too was better prepared. On 15 April he had had only minutes in which to make his decision: he had now had three weeks during which to consider what he might do should the same situation arise again. Once more he would send help.

On this occasion, however, his orders were more specific, and more restrictive. Fifty-three men were to be sent, with six pump vehicles and two ambulances.[10] The Irish Red Cross sent another three ambulances and the St John Ambulance Brigade two. Firemen from the South were to "confine rescue activities to private homes rather than military objectives."[11] De Valera realised it meant that more refugees from the North would soon be arriving in Dublin again. As before, they would be welcomed and helped.

This action constituted a repeat breach of neutrality. It also came at a time when news had just been released that for the past several weeks Dubliners and relief groups had been collecting and sending to Belfast large consignments of clothing to help the homeless. This might also be construed by Germany as assisting the enemy.

During the attack on Belfast on 5 May a significant incident was reported by the pilot and crew of at least one plane:

> The Luftwaffe crew recorded despondently that there was "total interference with the radio navigation system," adding that since last December the precision of the target-finding had suffered extremely from British radio jamming.[12]

For months the Germans had been using new technology to transmit navigation signals on intersecting lines to guide their planes to cities in Britain. But British scientists had devised a system for countering this by jamming or distorting their signals. Some called it "bending the beam" of the German directional lines. This technology would become famously controversial and is still discussed and debated two-thirds of a century later.

On the same day in early May that Belfast was being bombed for the third time the Irish Minister to the United States, Robert Brennan, was the guest speaker at the annual dinner of the American-Irish Historical Society in New York. His audience was noticeably more serious than in past years, and he was peppered with questions about Ireland's neutrality and security. What had the January bombings of the South meant? Why had Hitler failed to respect the North, as de Valera had requested? Was Dublin now imperilled? After answering the questions to the best of his ability—stating candidly that he did not have the explanations for the motives behind it—Brennan told the audience what they wanted to hear: "The Irish would defend their country against any attacker."[13] The remainder of the evening was more relaxed.

Belfast refugees gradually ended their sanctuary period in Dublin. On 22 May, after a stay of about five weeks, a party of four hundred refugees assembled at Amiens Street station to depart by special train for Newry. Included were six babies born to Belfast mothers while in Dublin. All talked of how well they had been treated by the Red Cross and the people of Dublin. They confessed to being "afraid of further bombings" in Belfast. Many sobbed, saying they did not want to leave but felt they had to go back home and face the risks. There were tears on the cheeks of well-wishers as the train pulled out of the dim terminal into the bright daylight, heading north.

On Sunday 25 May—one week before the Whit weekend—the ARP service carried out what was called its most realistic mock air-raid ever. This one was staged on the north side, only a few streets from the North Strand. Those who relished street theatre showed up in great numbers to take it all in. They weren't disappointed. For realism, the ARP wardens set fire to two three-storey houses in Little Denmark Street that had been marked for demolition. Black smoke billowed above rooftops as the fire brigade arrived, set out hoses and put up ladders. Firefighters broke through doors for rescue, and "arranged casualties" were placed on stretchers. In what was declared the ARP service's biggest test, a scene was created where there had been "high explosives dropped ... and citizens subjected to the terrors of an enemy air-raid."[14] This time the ARP wardens even arranged to have a few "looters" rounded up and hauled off. There was attention to almost every detail.

On its conclusion it was proclaimed that if the real event ever struck—though highly unlikely—the rescue services would not miss a step in carrying out their duties. Of this the ARP wardens seemed absolutely confident.

For the next three days the rapt attention of Dubliners was fixed on the thrilling naval battles involving the behemoths of the British and the German fleets, the *Hood* and the *Bismarck,* the mightiest warships afloat. It was inconceivable that either could ever be sunk.

Dubliners had closely followed naval events since the beginning of the war. Furthermore, many had relatives and friends serving on British ships, which were always in danger. So, the headline in the *Irish Times* on 26 May stunned them:

H.M.S. HOOD WAS SUNK IN "MILLION-TO-ONE CHANCE"

It seemed as unfathomable as the sinking of the *Titanic.* The *Hood,* a battle-cruiser with a displacement of 42,100 tons, was the world's largest warship and the crown jewel of the colossal British fleet, carrying a complement of 1,341 men, some of whom were Irish. The British had regarded it as virtually unsinkable, for no enemy ships stood a chance against its power.

Paddy Launders, a Dubliner, had joined the British navy early in the war, at the age of nineteen. Already he had seen ships in convoys only two hundred yards from his deck "blown into oblivion" before his eyes by German submarine torpedoes. It was a horrible thing to see. Yet even he could not have imagined the mighty *Hood* going down; but the article in the *Irish Times* confirmed its fate:

An "unlucky hit" during the big battle with the German naval forces off the coast of Greenland caught the *Hood's* magazine and the ship blew up. Shells from a well-directed salvo from the *Bismarck* must have scored a direct hit on the vulnerable spot—almost a "million-to-one chance". It is feared there will be few survivors.[15]

The *Hood* was not just a huge warship but a symbol of Britain's strength and its invulnerability to defeat. Its sudden sinking was a psychological blow to Britain's morale as well as a tremendous military loss. To redeem pride and confidence, the score had to be settled.

What ensued over the next forty-eight hours was an unprecedented sea drama, as daring and dramatic as any that had ever taken place. The world was watching. And Dubliners were more entranced than most, as the drama was being played out in the seas to the north of Ireland. The only way the British navy could fully exact retribution was to go after the *Bismarck* itself, and send it to the bottom.

The *Bismarck* symbolised nearly as much to Germany as the *Hood* did to Britain. At 35,000 tons, it was built so solidly that its crew believed that, at worst, it might be crippled, but never blown up and sunk. The British sent every type of attack vessel they possessed in a search-and-destroy mission against the *Bismarck*, from destroyers to aircraft carriers. For nearly two days the British ships sped, manoeuvred, and stalked their prey. They were willing to lose other ships if necessary. Finally, after a pursuit of incredible distance in so short a time, they caught up with the ship that had dealt the *Hood* its death blow. On 28 May the *Irish Times* told quite a different story.

BISMARCK SUNK AFTER CHASE OF 2,000 MILES

The *Bismarck*, 35,000 tons German battleship which sank the H.M.S. *Hood* on Saturday, was sunk yesterday after being chased for nearly 2,000 miles by battleships, cruisers, destroyers and air-craft carriers of the British navy.[16]

The score had been evened. As the *Bismarck* was settling on the North Atlantic seabed, one of the British officers who had taken part in the battle commented coolly that it had been "a good scrap ... eight or nine torpedoes hit her before she finally keeled over ... the Germans fought with great bravery."[17]

The *Hood-Bismarck* drama had captivated Dubliners for three days. When the excitement was over it left a feeling that the war had been stepped up. On the same day that the *Bismarck* was sunk, President Franklin Roosevelt announced in a broadcast that "we will not hesitate to use our armed forces to repel attack ... what started as a European war has developed into a world war for world domination."[18] To add muscle to Roosevelt's words, within hours of his address the US Congress approved a bill for the production of forty thousand new warplanes.

There were already many more warplanes in the skies over Dublin. During May alone it was estimated that nearly 2,700 German bombers passed directly over or near the city.[19] Everyone heard them and many saw them, sometimes at astonishingly close range. When Paddy Walsh and his mates at Tara Street fire station were bored late at night they liked to climb up to the tower and watch the aerial activity. "They used to come over regularly, up the coast from Wexford and follow the coast line, 'cause it was all lit up. Fly over Dublin and later veer over towards Britain."

Often there were dogfights between British Spitfires and German planes right over the heart of Dublin. Nan Davis was living in Chancery House, a block of flats by the Four Courts. One night she and her father were out on their balcony watching. "The British pilot was chasing him across our flats—it almost hit the top of the roof! You could see the pilot in it they were so close, so low passing over."

One morning at about nine o'clock Agnes Daly and her pal Kathleen Reid were walking along Summerhill when they heard engines and looked up. "We saw a dogfight between a Spitfire and a German fighter plane. We could see the planes as clear as anything."

Occasionally Irish gunners at different posts fired a few warning rounds from their anti-aircraft guns to remind pilots that they were over neutral territory and should depart immediately. Fragments of these exploding shells could be dangerous if they hit anyone below. Dubliners had been warned about this before but paid little heed. In May, with the increased number of planes overhead, the issue was raised again. The *Irish Times* decided to publish a public-service notice to warn careless citizens, those foolish gapers who instinctively cocked their head skywards to watch passing planes under warning fire:

> Many necks have been strained to locate fliers. No doubt this astral gazing is a very natural reaction to aero engines overhead, but inquisitive citizens might not realize its dangers.
>
> Planes passing overhead are liable to be fired upon by our ground defences ... a large, ugly, dangerous mass of metal is hurled skywards, but the law of gravity inexorably insists that what goes up must come down—even the exploded fragments of an anti-aircraft shell. There is no need for panicky rush to shelter, but "rubber-necking" may well lead to unnecessary danger.[20]

More than a few citizens pointed out that Smyllie himself was often caught in the act of "rubbernecking."

People had grown so accustomed to the sound and sight of belligerent aircraft that it was taken as a normal event. Many Dubliners paid no attention at all to planes. However, on the night of Wednesday 28 May a most unusual incident occurred in Dublin's skies. Many citizens noticed it, and it surely caught the full attention of military observers.

It was around midnight. It began normally with Air Defence Command spotting about fifty German planes flying over the south-east coast, heading towards Dublin. The planes flew up the Wicklow coast, passing over Dalkey at one end of Dublin Bay, then onwards toward Rush. Then, however, according to the Air Defence Command plotting map, one plane "turned around when it reached the border at Cootehill, while another was recorded by ground observers almost 80 miles to the south at Mountmellick."[21] Some other planes seemed to be in disarray, no longer flying in tight squadron formation. Next, coastal observers reported seeing "lights, flashes and explosions."[22] At first, military spotters thought they were anti-aircraft fire from the battery at Collinstown, Co. Dublin. Similar explosions were soon heard elsewhere along the coast.

Military officers quickly determined that some of the planes appeared disoriented. Apparently, crews began jettisoning some of their bombs into the sea in order to lighten their load and preserve fuel. This was a common Luftwaffe practice that Irish observers had witnessed on previous occasions. What greatly concerned them on this night was why the Luftwaffe pilots were flying erratically, completely out of normal character and routine. There was a striking resemblance between what the German pilots had reported, in great frustration, during the raid of 4/5 May on Belfast—that some interference with the plane's navigational system had caused locational confusion—and what Irish military observers were witnessing on the night of 28 May. Highly trained, disciplined pilots did not suddenly break squadron formation and fly haphazardly without good reason.

By the next morning, Air Defence Command officers were wondering if the strange incident they had witnessed could possibly have been caused by the new British counter-technology that "bent the beam" of German navigational signals. Irish experts probably knew little at this time about Britain's scientific technology in this new field, but they had certainly heard about it.

Did it mean that the British were now capable not only of interfering with the Luftwaffe's guidance system to throw them off course but also of directing them *towards* other targets instead?

Chapter 6 ~

A LITTLE VILLAGE UNTO ITSELF

It was a little community; they were as close-knit families as you could ever find.

(ALEC KING, 82)

People on the North Strand, they were like one large family.

(MARY DUNNE, 76)

No Dubliners felt more remote, or more safe from the war, than Northstranders. For, as local people were fond of saying, theirs was "a little village unto itself." It was an old-fashioned community, delightfully "behind the times"—a charming anachronism on the Dublin cityscape. Rural in appearance and provincial in outlook, it was more like a small town in Connemara yet was within easy walking distance of the heart of Dublin. It was only two streets from Amiens Street station, through which the refugees from Belfast had arrived.

The North Strand had a picturesque character that enchanted local people and visitors alike. Small family-owned shops dotted the cobblestoned streets where the old gas lamps were still tended by lamplighters. Down lanes were dairies and piggeries. Animals were seen everywhere: horses, ponies, donkeys, goats, hens, their sounds and scents detected streets away. Most of the houses were vintage red-brick Georgian or Victorian and small artisans' dwellings; there was even a scattering of stone cottages, centuries old. In the centre of the village stood an ancient arched stone bridge, beneath which flowed the Royal Canal. It had fresh water, grassy banks and tree-lined groves. Men fished as children swam among the ducks. The gentle sound of the water spilling over the canal locks added a special tranquillity to the setting. Its rural charm was treasured by all.

But even in 1941 some said it was too good to last.

Villagers' roots ran deep. Generation followed generation, in the same streets and even in the same houses. Like other inner-city communities, they retained the old customs and traditions pertaining to births, christenings, weddings and wakes. The old ways were comforting, Maura O'Toole remembers, especially "always helping one another," no matter what problems arose. A needy neighbour was never let down. Says Dermot Ring—who, at the age of eighty-one, still lives at 17 Clonmore Terrace, not only in the same house but in the same room in which he was born: "The old community was *very tight,*" like an extended family. Some older women wore shawls; and the North Strand and Ballybough area is believed to be the last part of Dublin to relinquish the speaking of Irish. Reasons for pride.

Northstranders saw their area as a distinct enclave, geographically and socially detached from the rest of Dublin. This created a strong provincialism, evidenced in the phrase of women who, when venturing only a few streets away to Talbot Street for shopping, said they were "going into town." However, the area was so self-contained that there was little need to stray beyond. It had its own grocers, butchers, chemist, tailors, pubs, dairies, cinema, post office, church and undertakers. Some inhabitants, such as Margaret Ladrigan's mother, hardly set foot outside the village. "My mother was reared there, lived there, never left it. Her whole life was there … she knew nothing else."

The local shops, pubs and post office were the social meeting-places where people would congregate to chat, exchange good news and bad. Village life was lively, and intimate. Shopkeepers who lived above their shop were lifelong friends. They knew every customer, all about their families, and willingly extended credit when it was needed. Local pubs, such as Fagan's, Crowe's, Creighton's and Maguire's, were *really* local. Regulars had their own coveted chairs and stools. Here, in their sacred "Men only" refuge, they shared all in life—"everything under the sun" was their term. Pub mates could be as close as blood brothers. Publicans were respected pillars of the community, often strong paternal figures. In time of need the publican could be counted on for helping out with everything from a christening gown or First Communion outfit to funeral expenses.

Small, quirky shops contributed to the village's unique character. As a girl, Bernadette Pierce frequented them all:

I can remember *all* them shops. There was Ma Gainor's, a small sweet shop, and we'd get little liquorices if you had a penny. Then there was Maud Gallagher's, a bacon shop—back when *bacon was bacon,* you know? At Roddy's shop I'd get a candy, a "ducky lump", a penny for it. Candy like rock, with pink sugary stuff over it. And me granny'd say, "It'll cost me more to get your teeth fixed!"

Diffney's shop stands out, well stocked with books. She'd encourage you to save up and get your book, just ha'pennies and pennies. God love her, she was *so kind* to us. And Salvese's was an ice-cream shop. A big fat man, and he had a round scoop and he'd give you a wafer. Now Dirty Dick's—oh, a horrible, dirty old shop. And the dirt of *himself!* But he sold second-hand comics.

Everyone liked Corcoran's provisions shop and its van with the slogan on the side, "Here comes Corcoran's." But the shop was best known for its large clock outside, the village timepiece. People counted on it, especially to get them to Mass on time. "What would we do without Corcoran's clock?" it was often said.

No shopkeeper was more liked or respected than Richard Fitzpatrick, the butcher. He was a beloved paternal figure who had served generations of villagers, listened to their problems, offered gentle advice from time to time—and discreetly handed over a "wrap-up" of meat parings for those in hard times, from which they could make a hearty stew or soup. Never would he see anyone go hungry. In his sawdust-sprinkled shop, wearing a soiled apron, cleaver in hand, he always had a welcoming smile.

Above his shop, at number 28 North Strand, he lived with his wife, Ellen, daughter Margaret, and sons Noel and Gerry. The Fitzpatricks were pillars of the community, the most "lovely people" you would ever find, says Jenny O'Brien, now seventy-five. She knew the Fitzpatricks well, because her brother Charlie Connell worked as a messenger-boy for the butcher. "He was more like Mr Fitzpatrick's son than a messenger, it was such a close relationship."

His son Noel, who had gone into the theatre, was popular both locally and on the stage. Gregarious and entertaining by nature, he loved performing, whether before a theatre audience or before local people on the street. He was already making quite a name for himself in Dublin, especially at the Olympia Theatre. The *Irish Press* called him a "well-known variety artiste" who had gained considerable acclaim at a young age.[1] Kind and charitable like his father, he was a dedicated member of the St Vincent de Paul Society and the Sunshine Fund. Whatever the good cause, he "regularly gave his service for charity."[2] Around the North Strand he always had a cheery greeting, humorous quip or entertaining story. Everyone in the village immensely liked him and enjoyed watching his steady rise in the theatre.

The centrepiece of the area was Newcomen Bridge, an ancient-looking arched stone structure beneath which flowed the Royal Canal. Villagers who had to pass over it habitually paused to place their hands or elbows on the wall and peer down at the lock, or the water, or just take in the panoramic view. There was no better spot at which to rest for a few moments, reflect, or chat with friends. It was a natural meeting-point for villagers of all ages.

Just beside the bridge, only about fifty feet away, on the bank of the canal some ten or twelve feet below the level of North Strand Road, stood a unique feature of the village: a perfectly kept 150-year-old whitewashed stone cottage of the Co. Galway variety. It was nestled on the grassy bank and surrounded by rose bushes, flower gardens and vegetable patches and with animals all around. It was known as "Lynch's cottage", owned by Michael Lynch, who worked for CIE. His daughter, Maureen, relished her upbringing in the idyllic setting:

> Ah, it was *lovely* here. We had a pony named Molly, and a nanny-goat. And about fifty fowl here, chickens, and fresh eggs every day. And pigs. We always had two or three horses that belonged to the bargemen, and we'd put them up at night. And we used to have cabbage and rhubarb and potatoes up on the banks, and lovely flowers ... Oh, a good life.

Nothing better exemplified the village's rural character. Local people took pride in the cottage as visitors marvelled upon discovering it. Directly in front of the cottage was the canal lock, tended by the lock-keeper, who lived on the other side of the bridge. As the water gently cascaded over the lip it created a most restful sound, day and night—another reason why people enjoyed standing on the bridge for a few moments of repose.

A particularly fascinating feature of the canal was the bargemen who halted there for the night. By the early 1940s they were already a dying breed, their antiquated activities of great interest to local folk and to outsiders. Now ninety-five, Michael Lynch reflects on the men and their horse-drawn barges, which hauled a variety of cargo between country districts and Dublin. "There were eleven barges on this canal, all cargo and corn, coal, timber, Guinness barrels." The most prominent barge families were the Leaches, Caffreys and Metcalfs, all strong, hard-working men—and great characters, he swears. When they halted at the lock for the night they turned their horses over to the Lynches for keeping and grazing.

Saturday nights were always the most entertaining, as the bargemen would sit atop the wall of the old stone bridge, smoke their pipes and sing till the wee hours. Their favourites were "The Old Bog Road", "I'll Take You Home Again, Kathleen" and "Come Back, Mavourneen". The men virtually adopted young Maureen Lynch and always invited her aboard to join them for meals or chat. They were always happy to converse with local people, who delighted in stopping on the bridge, leaning over, and talking for a spell. On Sunday mornings, Maureen remembers, they'd walk over to St Agatha's Church in fine suits, "round soft hat and snow-white shirt and tie, with Rosary beads" in their large, calloused hands, and always wearing a gold watch and chain, then return to their barges and fry rashers, sausages, eggs and maybe black pudding with brown bread. And "you'd *smell* that!" all over the village. After their meal they liked to sit on the bridge again to read the Sunday paper or play cards on the grassy canal banks. The bargemen's presence always enriched village life.

An especially exotic event along the canal was the regular arrival during the summer months of pleasure boats or "fancy boats". They carried wealthy people from such places as Dalkey and Greystones, who had parties on board, sometimes with a small piano and with the finest food and drink. And always elegantly dressed. Local people would cluster on the bridge to look down at them. But the best fun for Maureen Lynch was when film stars would show up on the fancy boats—the likes of John Huston, Tyrone Power, Gene Tierney and others. She met every one of them.

———

Country folk moving to Dublin, a huge city to them, were understandably drawn to the North Strand area as a comfortable place of first settlement. Its small-town way of life was familiar and manageable, yet it was close to the centre of the city. This was the case with the Browne family from Edenderry, Co. Offaly. Harry Browne was born in Edenderry in 1904, where his father was a master coachbuilder. Next door to the Brownes lived the Corrigans, whose daughter Molly was four years younger than Harry. As children they played in the same little mob and rather fancied one another. After leaving primary school he followed his father into the trade, getting a good job in the local Aylesbury factory.

Childhood friendship with Molly blossomed into romance, and in 1930 they were married. Both families thought it a perfect match. Harry was making a good wage, and soon children came along. But when the Aylesbury factory shut down it was an unexpected blow. Harry moved his young family to Castlereagh, Co. Roscommon, where he could continue his trade. But it wasn't the best job, and he knew his chances for better employment were to be found in Dublin, though the city's size was daunting. But his family was growing and he wanted to provide well for them.

In 1937, after much deliberation, the Brownes decided to move to Dublin. Here, in the "hungry thirties", he could secure steady work and a living wage. Harry's father and mother had moved to the city two years earlier and seemed to be adjusting nicely. Harry had gone in advance to reconnoitre the North Strand area, about which he had heard many promising things. When he later brought Molly to have a look she was equally smitten with its country flavour and its hospitable people. It would be the ideal place in which to raise their family.

Harry was fortunate to be offered a good job as a coachbuilder in the bus department of the Great Southern Railway. So he, Molly and their young daughters, Maureen and Ann, and son, Edward, moved into number 25 North Strand, above Nally's shop. The residence was clean, spacious, with large windows and welcoming neighbours, and the rent was reasonable. They found themselves in the very heart of the village. The children were delighted with the variety of shops, the canal and bridge, and the little Strand cinema just a few paces from their door. It seemed a good decision—and wonderful luck.

Neighbours took a liking to the Brownes straight away. After all, they were a striking-looking, most engaging couple. He was a handsome man, with chiselled face, thick, dark hair and winning smile. Molly, with her cherubic face, curly hair and sparkling eyes, could easily have appeared in a magazine advertisement for Pond's cold cream. And every one of their children took after them.

When the war came and the Local Defence Force was formed, Harry wanted to serve his community. He immediately joined the local LDF unit, attended every drill, took his service seriously. If there was ever any trouble in Dublin, he could be counted on. Northstranders, however, weren't much concerned about the faraway war. They hardly looked beyond the world of their own village. Indeed they were not highly informed about international matters and war events; many couldn't afford newspapers and didn't possess a radio. They knew, of course, about the "big events" but were not inclined to follow politics or military struggles in detail. As regards any perception of ever being closely touched by the war, the North Strand might as well have been the North Pole.

———

When Dick Eyres was appointed ARP post warden for the North Strand district he chatted with people on his daily rounds about every matter in life—except war worries. But if trouble ever should arise, he was the man to deal with it. Employed by Dublin Corporation, he was reliable, quick-thinking and decisive. Everyone liked and respected him—a "real man of action," they always said, when anything in the community needed attending to. As post warden he was directly responsible to the local army commander, Captain McDonagh, and took his job most seriously. Always interested in aircraft, he could identify every type of British and German plane by engine sound and specific features. Whenever they passed over he always listened, looked up, strained to spot them. It was also his duty to get to know the residents of his district, for identification purposes in case of any emergency. He always assumed this meant in life, not in death.

Just across from Dick Eyres's house in Shamrock Terrace lived two wardens, Annie Waddick and May Stanley, on whom he could immediately depend if ever a crisis arose. At the end of the terrace the corporation had a depot with large arches, where they kept lorries. They allowed Eyres to keep his ARP equipment there, such as stirrup pumps, ladders, hatchets, shovels and the like. Most importantly, the depot had a telephone, which could be used as an ARP message centre in an emergency. Bernadette Pierce, then eight years old, remembers his strong character but calm manner in the face of any trouble that arose in the village. He was the person to whom everyone turned—always on the spot when needed. She was quite fond of Mrs Eyres as well, especially when she gave her some of her delicious apple jelly and jam. Sometimes Dick Eyres let Bernadette and a few of her pals play under the depot arches. Whenever she was around him she was fascinated by his unique habit:

> Dick had this habit—a Woodbine cigarette just dangling from his lip. Nobody ever knew how he could smoke that cigarette without ever touching it. He'd just leave it, on his lip. It'd just dangle, and *stay* there. Many a man would try it, but they'd just burn their lip.

In the days leading up to the Whit weekend of 1941 villagers' thoughts were about tidying up their homes and making their holiday plans. Nowhere in Dublin were people more house-proud, and it was a tradition that days beforehand women were outside, scrubbing their steps or pavement, polishing windows till they gleamed, washing their white lace curtains, or putting a fresh coat of paint on the door. Windowsills were dusted off and brass knockers and knobs polished with Brasso. Shopkeepers did the same with their shop fronts and windows. The Whit weekend always brought visitors to the area, and local people wanted to show themselves at their best. The Lynches pruned their rose bushes for admiring eyes.

Richard Fitzpatrick knew his butcher's shop would be packed full of women on the Friday and all day Saturday. He would have to stay open later than usual on Friday night, possibly to ten o'clock or later. He could be on his feet for fourteen straight hours. He'd sleep well that night, that was certain.

The Brownes had now been settled in the North Strand for nearly four years. Little Angela, born two years after their arrival, was regarded as native-born. About that time tragedy struck when Harry's father was killed by a vehicle while crossing the road at Newcomen Bridge. Harry and Molly arranged for his mother to live with them above Nally's shop. Being with her family afforded security, and having the little ones on her lap was the best tonic for her sorrow.

They were a young family, Harry thirty-seven and Molly thirty-three. Maureen was seven, Ann five, and Edward four. Two-year-old Angela was the baby. Margaret Ladrigan remembers how the Brownes always seemed in good spirits, "the *whole* family." Mary Dunne, now seventy-six, who lived near them in North William Street, had immediately befriended all the children and played with them daily. "I knew *all* the whole Browne family. I used to play with the children down the back lane." She was close friends with Maureen and Ann, with whom she played chainies and picky-beds. And, of course, "relieve-io". Before long, she says, they were one of the most popular families in the village.

No-one knew what the Brownes had planned for the Whit weekend. Perhaps they had planned a trip to the seaside or a picnic in the Phoenix Park; maybe a matinee for the children at the Strand cinema. Relatives may well have been coming from Edenderry for a holiday visit. The Brownes liked to show off their lovely, peaceful village, tell how blessed they were to have found such a perfect home, where their children would grow up, and grandchildren be born.

"Little did the Brownes realise that their Dublin house would one night be their tomb."[3]

Chapter 7 ～

WHIT WEEKEND

It was Whit Friday night and we were all going somewhere—oh, delighted with life.

(ANN LEONARD, nurse, 84)

Father Jackie Masterson had a presentiment that something sinister was going to happen and he had his holy oils ready.

(75th ANNIVERSARY REPORT, St Agatha's Church)

I have this sixth sense, and I was possessed by the feeling of something terrible about to happen. I can still remember the feeling of foreboding—I just knew there was going to be a disaster in Dublin.

(ALEC KING, chief rescue and demolition officer, 82)

Friday 30 May 1941

The Whit weekend had finally arrived. Spirits were up on Friday morning as people hurried about, collecting their weekend provisions and completing holiday plans. Streets were clogged with buses, trams and horse-drawn vehicles, and cyclists zigzagging everywhere. Pedestrians stepped more quickly and chatted louder than usual. Everywhere people smiled with the excitement of the holiday weekend just ahead.

Scores of Dublin children, however, began their day glumly rather than gleefully. They dreaded getting their diphtheria inoculation that afternoon. Dr M. J. Russell, medical officer of health for Dublin, had scheduled some 35,000 children for Whit Friday. Kathleen Martin, then thirteen, remembers waking up that morning "feeling very sorry for myself" because of the injection she faced. Mothers were told by the doctors and nurses that their children might sleep restlessly that night because of a sore arm. "Be ready to get out of bed and comfort them."

Many excited young lads were looking forward to Whit Saturday, when they were to receive their first Holy Communion. By custom, they were sure to get a good few shillings pressed into their hands from relatives and friends.

Their happy Whit holiday seemed assured. Everyone was telling them it would be a big day, long remembered.

Mary Cooke, one of seventeen siblings living in a tenement house in Lower Gardiner Street, had something to look forward to as well. The 31st of May was her birthday. It was one to be imprinted for ever in her mind.

By midday on Friday it seemed that everyone was out and about. Along every street people were heard saying to one another, "Whereya goin'?" Sharing holiday plans was part of the fun. Patrick "Dixie" Dean of St Joseph's Mansions, now eighty-three, explains:

> It was the Whit holiday, people going out to Dollymount or to Malahide. Or out to Howth. Had their bikes out, fixed for a holiday—people were *happy*, you know.

Everyone had plans of one sort or another, says Stephen Loftus. "It was Whit—and *everything* was going on!" A great variety of activities and entertainment for Dubliners of every class: park picnics, seaside trips, visits to the zoo, excursions to resorts; going to the cinema, dance halls, or the theatre; sporting events, including handball, football, golf, tennis, sailing and horseracing; or just gardening and visiting friends. Something for everyone.

Weeks in advance, announcements in the *Irish Independent* assured holidaymakers that there were "plenty of excursion fares by ordinary trains from all parts of the country, to run to Whit Monday."[1] The Great Southern Railway was putting on special trains to Cork, Killarney, Limerick and Tralee. It also offered low-cost tickets to popular centres in Cos. Wicklow and Waterford. The International Travel Bureau in Dame Street was promoting "Whitsuntide Week-End Tours" to Killarney and Galway for those who wanted to "get out of the city" for the weekend. The Bray Amusements Committee was boasting that when their season opened on Whit Monday visitors would find a "more attractive series of amusements on the sea front than has obtained hitherto."[2]

The Baldoyle Races were always a big event during the Whit holiday. This year there was particular interest in a horse named Balinter, which had great promise but had got off to a bad start at the Curragh, because of some "bad luck", it was claimed. Baldoyle offered the opportunity to show the horse's true talents. It was to be an interesting challenge, drawing a huge crowd.

Filmgoers couldn't have asked for a better choice. At the Savoy, Betty Grable and Don Ameche were starring in *Down Argentine Way*. But the film reviewer for the *Irish Times* swore that Carmen Miranda, the "Brazilian Bombshell", really stole the show, as she "sings deliciously and wiggles her hips"—in full Technicolor.[3] Over at the Adelphi, *Second Chorus* was showing, featuring Fred Astaire and Paulette Goddard, with "good, clean fun and a laughable plot." The film had been setting records in America and London, and Dubliners would need to queue up early. The Regal Rooms was showing *The Marx Brothers Go West*, and, as one film critic quipped, "the West has not been the same since."

People around the North Strand didn't need to "go into town" to see a good film over the Whit weekend. Their own little Strand cinema was showing *Hold That Ghost*, with Bud Abbot and Lou Costello. Local mammies assured their children that if they weren't able to get in for Saturday's showing they could see it on Sunday or Monday.

While the serious theatre crowd had *Macbeth* at the Gate Theatre and *Cathleen Ni Houlihan* at the Gaiety, the Theatre Royal put together a terrific entertainment for the Whit holiday crowds, featuring musical numbers, dancing by the Royal Violettes, and Mervani, an "illusionist performing some very unusual tricks." Indisputably the most extraordinary act in the city over the Whit weekend was that of the amazing Rolando at the Olympia Theatre, described by the *Irish Times:*

> Rolando eats fire and thrusts pins nine inches long into his tongue, chest and arms ... he walked among the audience with three pins projecting from his flesh. Everybody was relieved when Rolando withdrew them, and he was applauded.[4]

Dance halls drew huge crowds. The La Scala was putting on "Three Holiday Dances" for each night of the holiday. The Adelaide Hall competed by offering its "Grand Whitsuntide Dance", featuring the popular Jim Bacon's Band. Every dance hall boasted some type of Whit extravaganza.

For sheer Whit whimsy, nothing matched the fun of the contest put on by one of the cinemas. It offered a "film star look-alike contest," encouraging everyone to have a crack at it. And many crackpots showed up. The best story must be the one about the "young woman who approached the adjudicator and argued for herself as follows: 'I look like Boris Karloff and sing like Mae West—what about it!'[5]

Happiness and frivolity were contagious. Everyone in Dublin was hopping.

Well, not quite everyone. Some people, mostly elderly and "old-fashioned" in their beliefs, were highly wary of Whit. To them, Whit weekend was a time for staying at home, indoors, and being cautious. It was still an old superstition around parts of the city in 1941. Margaret Pringle, now eighty-eight, tells that her Granny and her Da took it very seriously:

It was an old superstition. They thought that Whit weekend should be the "three cross days". And they wouldn't go away. My father wouldn't go *anywhere* on Whit weekend, and my grandmother.

They were *afraid* to go out, that something would happen to you. Yeah, it wasn't *safe* to go out. My grandmother, she'd say, "Oh, *I'm* not going anywhere on Whit!" And she'd say to me, "You *daren't* go out—you're *not* going out on Whit." *Very* superstitious. So we didn't go anywhere on Whit.

Some Dubliners had no choice: they were on duty over the Whit weekend—firemen, gardaí, hospital and newspaper staff. Publicans and barmen. Lamplighters. Morgue attendants. The city's hospitals had pruned down to a skeleton staff so that most doctors and nurses could enjoy their much-deserved holiday. Whit weekend was normally slow—the usual babies born, minor accidents, heart problems. Hospital corridors were typically quiet and duties uneventful.

The same at newspaper offices. Ordinarily there was no big news over the holiday, with government and business shut down. Drawing duty in the newsroom over Whit was a bore. On Friday 30 May twenty-year-old Tony Gray had lucklessly—or so it seemed—been assigned to night duty at the *Irish Times*. Everyone in the building had seniority over him: he was merely a "junior writer", a title below that of real reporter. But he didn't mind working that night: in fact it gave him an opportunity to relax with other staff members, talk, and learn from them. The editor, R. M. Smyllie, would also be staying late that night. Gray could learn much from him. The lordly Smyllie would make his nightly pilgrimage across the street to the Palace Bar "surrounded by the literati of Dublin and distinguished foreign correspondents from London, Washington and New York."[6] After he had held court for a few hours he would toddle back the few paces to his office. Perhaps, thought Gray, I might be able to engage the legendary editor in some meaningful conversation during the long night ahead.

Nor did lamplighters, by now a dying breed, get a reprieve over the holiday weekend. Frank Wearen, born in 1898 and destined to be one of the last of the real lamplighters in Dublin, was on duty and had to make his full rounds along Gardiner Street and up around Summerhill and the North Strand. At forty-three he was fit from walking miles each night with his long malacca cane with which to light the globes. On warm summer nights a lamplighter might clandestinely sneak into a pub along the way for a quick pint, but if the roaming inspector caught him he was in trouble.

Dick Eyres also had to dutifully make his rounds with his ARP partner, Nicholas Quirke, carrying out general surveillance, scanning the sky, making notes about passing planes, their approximate number and type. Dick prided himself on being able to recognise the sound of every type of British and German aircraft. When conditions were overcast, he made his best estimate. This evening, however, was so clear that he thought he would probably even see the pilots in their cockpits.

Gardaí Senan Finucane and Maurice "Mossie" Walsh, both on night duty, had their rounds to walk as well. Being younger members of the force, they had to work most of the holiday weekend. Finucane was stationed in Kevin Street barracks, while Walsh was in Rathmines station. The Whit weekend always saw a lot of heavy drinking and often brawling, but it was nothing they couldn't handle. When Finucane made his rounds beside his legendary mate James "Lugs" Brannigan, few dared give them any trouble, lest Lugs teach them a lesson on the spot.

Over on the north side, Garda Byrne from Store Street station, known simply as "123" from his number, was sure to have his hands full with unruly intoxicated men. And women. He was as tough and fearless as his Liberties counterpart Lugs. His nightly beat included Quinn's Cottages near the North Strand, three lanes where the "poorest of the poor lived," as Agnes Daly puts it, better known as "Heaven, Hell, and Purgatory." During weekdays it was peaceful enough. In fact the air could be suffused with operatic song. One woman, she recalls, was "a most beautiful singer, like a trained singer. She looked like somebody who had been very well off and had crashed." Down on her luck, she would amble the lanes and sing as pennies and ha'pennies were tossed on the cobblestones around her.

On weekends it was just the opposite, as drinking, shouting, cursing and fighting erupted. On Saturday nights the battling Byrne sisters would take centre stage. It was considered regular weekly entertainment, according to Agnes Daly:

> The two sisters were terrible fond of the drink. Alcoholics, yeah. And on a Saturday night the two of them would fill themselves up with beer and there'd be *murder!* The two of them'd be rolling down the lane boxing one another. And everybody'd run out and "*Ruggy up! Ruggy up!*" Just stand watching. *Every* Saturday night. They'd throw off their shawls and, oh, they'd be *really* fighting, pulling out bunches of hair and everything. Oh, they'd *kill* one another.

Firemen had to fully staff their stations over the three days of the holiday weekend. Jack Conroy was not on duty that night at Buckingham Street station, but other men with whom he had gone to blazing Belfast a few weeks before were working. They expected a calm night. With warm weather, people didn't need their fireplace, which was the major source of tenement blazes in the inner city. The firemen planned to pass the night as usual playing darts or rings, or most likely cards, or perhaps listening to the radio they had rented. At some point during the evening they might fall into conversation again about their recent experiences up in Belfast. It would have been a satisfying topic. Conroy had just bought a new bicycle, for which he had long saved, and he intended to cycle over to the station on Friday evening to show it off to his mates. Over the weekend he had plans for some serious cycling on the roads outside Dublin.

Ann Leonard, a St John Ambulance Brigade nurse in her early twenties, was not on duty either. She and her best pal, May, were going to kick up their heels at a big Whit Friday dance: "I bought a new pair of shoes that day." She was proud to show them off and keen to break them in on the dance floor—but careful not to scuff them. She remembers never feeling happier—"oh, *delighted* with life!"

Seventeen-year-old Dermot Ring was going to stay at home in Clonmore Terrace, a stone's throw from Newcomen Bridge. He had studying to do over the weekend. "I wasn't going to do anything on Whit because the next week I was doing my final Leaving Certificate examination." He took his studies seriously and wanted to devote the full three days to preparation. Clonmore Terrace was beside the restful Royal Canal, just across from Charleville Mall Library, a quiet setting in which to concentrate on studies.

Over the weekend, far from Dublin, two men would also be staying at their favourite retreats. Hitler was to be in his mountain sanctuary above Berchtesgaden in Bavaria, the setting in which he best relaxed, and planned. Roosevelt would be at Hyde Park, New York, where "he was preparing a secret and highly important document" for the US Ambassador to Britain, John Winant, to deliver personally to Churchill.[7]

At the end of the work day on Friday, Dubliners collected their wage packets and headed home to enjoy the holiday. Along the way, many picked up an evening newspaper. War news from Britain was mixed. While Londoners were grateful for having had the past three weeks free from German bombs, the battle front in Crete looked grim as the German High Command reported that the "British are in full retreat."[8] British people feared that thousands might be killed or taken prisoner.

A world away from the bloodshed in Crete, Dubliners sat on their front steps with the *Evening Herald* in hand, chuckling at the shenanigans of Mutt and Jeff.

The weather was on everyone's mind. A Whit weekend was only as good as the conditions outdoors. So far, nature was co-operating. The morning had been mostly clear and the afternoon turned sunny and quite warm. But this didn't mean the next three days would be good. Because of wartime censorship, no weather forecasts could be announced on the radio or in the newspapers. People had to rely on their own natural barometers—and hope.

By 7 p.m. the curtain was drawn on an exquisite evening in Dublin. A perfect spring evening. An incandescent sky, the scent of spring flowers and freshly mowed grass cast a spell over people. After supper, everyone wanted to be outside until bedtime. In every street people were inspired to do a bit of evening gardening. Many stood by their door, railing or front pathway, chatting with neighbours, even engaging passing strangers in friendly conversation. Children frolicked about the streets, shouting gleefully. On a night like this windows were open wide, and from inside tunes could be heard from "Step Together", a popular radio programme by the Radio Éireann Symphony Orchestra.

Evening faded surreptitiously into early nightfall. Darkness revealed a starry and moonlit sky, remembered by all who saw it that night. Stephen Loftus, now eighty-five, a painter who was living in Buckingham Street, was walking home from a late job, pausing along his way just to gaze up and take it all in. "It was a *lovely*, summery night ... a *brilliant* night." It was a stunningly "*clear* night," recalls Colleen Heeney, then twelve. In the perfectly cloudless sky was a canopy of glittering stars for as far as one could see. People described the night's extraordinary beauty as "gorgeous", "dazzling", "majestic". A "*very, very* bright moonlit night," says Una Shaw. "Ah, you could see all the way to heaven," some moonstruck admirers gushed. Even the lamplighter Frank Wearen, who saw every night sky in Dublin, couldn't resist halting from time to time to glance up at the spectacular luminosity above.

Not everyone was captivated by the beauty and serenity of the night. It would later be verified that a number of Dubliners were beset by troubling feelings of unease, or outright worry, that night, what Diarmuid Hiney confirms as "an uncanny amount of personal premonitions of impending disaster."[9] This is a common occurrence reported after some great disaster. What particularly validates those in Dublin on the night of 30 May is that the forebodings were expressed explicitly by prominent individuals, among them a priest, a chief rescue and demolitions officer, ARP wardens and LDF members, as well as a host of other mature and reliable citizens. At first they merely felt "unsettled"—on a perfectly *settled* night. Then came a sense of impending trouble of some sort—a most strange feeling on a night so tranquil. For it seemed so unnatural amidst the calm and beauty of the night.

Father Jackie Masterson lived at 595 North Circular Road, a few streets from the North Strand. He was a beloved member of the community, not only for his role as a caring priest but also for his personal traits of friendliness, good humour, and ability to interact with people of all ages. Everyone was drawn to be around him, seeking his attention. Grannies were charmed by his courtly manner and wit, and, as Margaret Pringle saw, "Oh, the kids loved him, and he'd bring all the kids for a drive in his car."

And it didn't hurt that he was also a handsome man, catching the eye of every woman in the parish. "A very tall, dark man, a lovely big man," says Pringle, "and he used to wear a black coat with a black fur collar." As Jenny O'Brien unabashedly confesses, women just liked looking at him, whether on the street or the altar:

Father Masterson, he was a beautiful-looking man. A lovely man. And I shouldn't be saying this, but when we were young I think we girls went to Mass not for the sake of the Mass but to see Father Masterson. He was a *gorgeous* man.

On the evening of Whit Friday he had been standing outside taking in the glory of the night and chatting amiably with those hovering around him. About 10:30 he felt it time to retire. As he was preparing for bed the feeling first came over him—a prescience that something was out of order, not right. A man of high intellect and reason, he was not given to imaginary musings. Despite his rational mind, he could not ignore the persistence of "having a feeling that something was going to happen," as he would later put it. At about eleven o'clock he put out the light and climbed into bed. He would try to work out the nagging sense of looming calamity the next morning. Though tired, he couldn't sleep.

Miles away in Milltown, Alec King was wrestling with his own sensations of trouble brewing. At twenty-one he had undergone, and barely survived, a difficult brain operation. The surgery began at ten to six in the evening and was completed at twenty to two the next morning. The doctor was soaked in perspiration. Nurses nearly passed out. "It was a hammer-and-chisel job on my skull … it was only touch and go. I could have been brain-damaged for life." At one point, he remembers, "I saw what I thought was Heaven … I was dead." Instead he survived to discover that he had inexplicably acquired what he calls a "sixth sense", the perceptual ability, at certain times in life, to detect disturbances in advance—not identify them, just see that they are on the horizon. His prescience became well known to his family and friends. Too bad he couldn't use it at the bookies, his mates joked. He didn't experience this power often, but once he had the feeling that the universe was out of proper alignment it was always proved to be correct by events.

Now twenty-eight, he held a good job at Crampton's, the big building firm. In 1939, when the war broke out and the Air-Raid Precautions Service was created, he joined. Before long, his intelligence and leadership qualities were recognised and he was selected to attend the "anti-gas school, to learn about gases if an air raid came." It was an intensive five-month course, in which he excelled. He was then made chief air raid warden for the Ranelagh district. Within a year he was promoted to chief rescue and demolitions officer in Number 6 Dublin Area. "I had eighty men under me. We had a blue helmet with 'R&D' on the front of it, a type of boiler suit, Wellington boots and an axe—I *still* have it!" He was highly respected by the men under his command. Crampton's allowed them to meet and train on their premises and store in the depot all their gear—planks, ladders, crowbars, welding equipment, shovels, picks and the like. They could even use the firm's lorries in a real emergency.

On Whit Friday afternoon Alec King came home weary, looking forward to the long weekend ahead. He intended to have his evening meal, relax, read a bit, then go to bed early. But the majesty of the night and the warm temperature enticed him into some late gardening. Then, without warning, his sixth sense kicked in:

> At times I have a sixth sense, and it worries me. On this Friday, I came home from work, had my evening meal, and went out in the garden. I started to dig around for the spring, sew seeds and plant things. I can *still* remember that feeling of foreboding when I was out in the garden digging. Like I was reading the fellow's mind, the German's mind. I just *knew* there was going to be a disaster in Dublin, and the rescue squad would be needed. I didn't know it would be a bomb, it could have been anything. I just had this awful sense that *something terrible* was about to happen.

Around the North Strand, people were still about the streets, making last-minute purchases in shops that were soon to close. By ten o'clock Richard Fitzpatrick had been on his feet in his butcher's shop for nearly fourteen hours and hoped to get the doors shut soon. An hour or so earlier he had released his messenger-boy, Charlie Connell, so that he could go home, change clothes, and head out with his pal, Sniggy, to a big Whit Friday dance. Jenny O'Brien recalls her mother telling her brother Charlie to have a good time but to get home at a reasonable hour.

Close to eleven o'clock Richard Fitzpatrick was finally bolting the doors for the night. He was exhausted; and he knew the next day would be a madhouse of customers as well. He needed a good night's sleep.

A few streets away at 584 North Circular Road, Mrs Grice was just as eager to close up her small provisions shop. The problem was that the late-night crowd from the cinemas, dance halls and pubs habitually stopped by her place for some last-minute cigarettes, sweets or other "necessities". On Whit Friday night she was reluctant to turn them away. She'd stay open a bit longer on this lovely night.

By now, Alec King had finished his evening gardening, had cleaned up and was ready for bed:

At about eleven my wife went up to bed while I put out the milk bottles and locked up. Then I went upstairs to bed. But I just couldn't settle down … there was something *wrong*. This sixth sense *took over!* I was *possessed* by the feeling of something terrible about to happen.

I made several attempts to sleep, in between trips to the kitchen, the bathroom, and back to bed again—all to no avail. Finally, I gave it up, dressed and went downstairs to listen to the radio.

There was a couple of planes buzzing around … but I didn't know what it was.

It was approaching midnight, the moon having risen higher in the sky above Dublin. Most Dubliners had gone to bed. But a good many late-nighters were still milling about the streets. Several were standing on Newcomen Bridge, gazing down at the serene moonlit water.

Only a few paces away, Corcoran's clock struck midnight. It was now Whit Saturday, 31 May 1941. The village clock would soon mark history with deadly accuracy.

Chapter 8 ~

FAIRY LIGHTS AND
"FLAMING ONIONS"

Long, eerie fingers of light from the searchlights swept
backwards and forwards searching for the planes, and anti-
aircraft shells and flaming onions could be seen bursting in
the clear, cloudless vault of the sky.

(*Evening Herald*, 31 May 1941)

It was like fairy lights—all lit up. Oh, it was lovely!

(AGNES DALY, 81)

The Whit holiday had barely arrived. At two minutes past midnight, throbbing engines were heard above the city. Ann Leonard was walking home from the dance with her pal May, her new shoes by now hurting her feet. "I knew *immediately* they were German planes, the 'dock, dock, dock, dock.'" Every Dubliner knew the sound of the Heinkel 111 and Dornier bombers, heading north to strike British cities. Their repetitive "thump, thump, thump" was like the thrashing of an old washing-machine. It could get on one's nerves. But normally the planes passed over within minutes.

This night was different.

As recorded in the log of Air Defence Command, searchlights were exposed at 00:04. This was standard practice whenever belligerent aircraft were detected overhead. The huge searchlights began their rhythmic crisscrossing pattern against the city's starry canopy. Those Dubliners still awake gazed up. Young Tish Martin peered out of her window in Gloucester Diamond and said to her mother, "They must have got new searchlights." The beams seemed brighter and more penetrating in the clear sky.

At first, Air Defence crews casually watched, waiting for the planes to clear Dublin's air space, as they ordinarily did. Normally, German pilots flew in tight formation on their course towards British targets, politely responding to flare warnings that they were over neutral Ireland. But on this night, ARP spotters along the coast were reporting the same alarming observation: "Large numbers of aircraft proceeding northwards and southwards along our East coast."[1] *Southwards?* This flight pattern was completely contrary to the usual routine.

Not only were they flying in different directions but they were breaking out of their squadron formations. This made it impossible to determine accurately how many planes there were. Military observers reported that they could do no more than "hazard a guess" under such confusing circumstances. According to Lt-Col Padraic O'Farrell, "the numbers of planes in the air seemed considerable," producing what he called "a heavy drone" above the city.[2] Captain A. A. Quigley estimates that "as far as could be ascertained from Air Defence Command, there were twenty planes, some grouped in fives."[3] Other witnesses placed the number considerably higher, possibly twice as many. All agreed that many of the planes were not grouped uniformly in squadrons but rather flying independently in a curious meandering manner. According to Quigley, several "kept circling."

The strange behaviour made Air Defence Command nervous, if not yet worried. It couldn't help but remind them of the similarly scary incident over Dublin two nights before, on 28 May, when several Luftwaffe planes clearly appeared confused and disoriented.

Whenever it was determined that belligerent planes overhead—be they German or British—might actually pose a threat, there was a prescribed procedure they were to follow:

> Three flares were sent up, representing the national Tri-Colour, to inform the aircraft they were over neutral Irish territory. After which red ones were also sent up to warn them that they would be fired upon. They were then allowed fifteen minutes "to clear", after which the ground defences opened up.[4]

This action was not implemented lightly. Firing shells towards heavily armed belligerent aircraft was a most serious decision, one reluctantly and cautiously made.

Minutes passed. As Air Defence Command intently watched the erratic behaviour of the German pilots directly over the city, tension mounted. Finally, at 00:18, the order was given to send up three tri-colour flares to clearly identify neutral Irish territory below. At 00:20 several red flares, or "flaming onions", were lofted skyward. Then began a period of nervous waiting and watching.

Air Defence possessed only minimal firepower to back up their warnings to the mighty Luftwaffe. Anti-aircraft batteries in the Dublin area, at Clontarf, Collinstown, Dalkey, Stillorgan, Ballyfermot and Ringsend, were manned by gunners with little firing practice, as shells had to be carefully rationed. The presumption was that they did not need to be sharpshooters, as their role was simply to fire warning shells to prod planes away, not to strike them and bring them down. "Thank heavens," it was added.

At their disposal were several types of anti-aircraft guns. The Clontarf and Ringsend batteries had 3.7-inch guns, classified as a heavy anti-aircraft weapon. There were also 3-inch guns, a medium anti-aircraft weapon, at Stillorgan and Ballyfermot, capable of reaching altitudes of 6,000 to 8,000 feet. The small Bofors gun at several sites was a 40-mm weapon with a range of 1,500 to 2,000 feet. In a close support role at several batteries was the Hotchkiss gun, a medium machine-gun firing .303-inch rounds. In reality these weapons, with limited ammunition, were more of a warning device than a defence system.

As the minutes ticked away, officers smoked and cast silent glances at one another. The drones overhead told them that the flare's message had not been heeded. They did not want to have to resort to shooting. But military men obeyed orders.

After the mandatory fifteen minutes a number of German bombers remained above, still flying in their haphazard pattern. At 00:35 the order was given to commence firing, and "ground forces first came into action when Clontarf fired four rounds."[5] The total number of shells fired that night would be exactly documented, though it was not possible to record the sequence of firing from the different batteries. It was, however, importantly noted in the Air Defence Command log that the first anti-aircraft volleys included some shells of heavier calibre. Why were lighter shells not exclusively used at first to nudge the German pilots away? This would have seemed more prudent under the circumstances.

The Luftwaffe aviators recognised immediately the size of the shells bursting around them. These first warning shots may have been aimed only in the general vicinity of the planes, not intended to bring them down. However, German pilots could not interpret intention. They only knew that shells from the 3-inch and 3.7-inch guns could destroy their aircraft if hit. At the very least, they were probably surprised, and displeased. The question is, were they also angered by the unexpectedly heavy barrage?

———

Meanwhile, Dubliners found it all quite exciting. In the clear sky, brightly moonlit, the sweeping searchlights, multi-coloured flares and bursting shells created a captivating extravaganza of lights and sound. From streets, gardens and windows, viewers across the expanse of the city responded as if they were an audience, calling it "sparkling", "magical", even emitting "oohs" and "aahs" at moments, as if they were at some happy fireworks celebration. The *Irish Press* wrote that the entire "sky was lit up … by the anti-aircraft barrage, flung-up shells, tracer bullets and 'flaming onions'."[6] From the window of her home in North Clarence Street, thirteen-year-old Agnes Daly watched entranced:

> I opened my eyes and the window was facing me and I saw *all* these lights … they were like fairy lights. Now we never saw a Christmas tree and we never had a birthday. There was nothing like that. But I saw *all* these searchlights going, and flares going … all these lovely lights. Oh, it was *lovely*, it was beautiful—*all lit up*. Lovely! And I wasn't a bit frightened.

Nor were other Dubliners, apparently. For in their thousands, they nonchalantly stood outdoors and peered through windows, taking in the colourful sky pageant, completely ignoring Smyllie's warning about the danger of "rubbernecking" when all sorts of debris was falling downwards. The *Sunday Independent* would scold citizens for their naïve behaviour:

> Thousands of citizens stood at their windows and many fool-hardy people ventured out into the streets or their gardens to watch the spectacle as they listened to the 'pom-pom' of the anti-aircraft fire.[7]

The city's ARP wardens, who had the responsibility of alerting citizens to the danger of an air-raid attack, seemed no more alarmed than other Dubliners. They acted more as spectators, enjoying the show of lights and the excitement of it all, as if they had no active role to fulfil. The "wardens can have felt no great sense of apprehension," as not one of them in any part of Dublin saw fit to activate the siren system, alerting citizens to the possibility of danger.[8]

If the ARP wardens seemed unfazed by what was taking place, some others were by now quite worried. Two who were highly apprehensive were Father Jackie Masterson and Alec King. From the outset, King knew that planes continually "buzzing around" overhead rather than moving away were cause for real concern. It kept him awake. At 12:35 a.m., when the anti-aircraft firing began, his wife sensed his agitation:

> My wife said, "I can't sleep with you shifting around." So I put on my boiler suit and got into my Wellington boots. Got up, and off on my bike I went—headed down to my rescue service depot to see if everything was all right. It was a warm night, so I didn't need a coat, as I would not be away

long ... little did I think I would not see home for a few days.

By now Father Masterson was also up and fully dressed. Convinced that his premonition must have something to do with the German bombers, he "had placed the holy oils in his pocket and he was pacing the floor of the presbytery," pausing every few moments to peer out the window.[9] The two men, as well as a number of other astute observers, realised that the abnormal behaviour of German pilots could well portend real danger. The vast majority of Dubliners, however, were still far more curious and entertained than worried by the "show" they were watching.

Like many of the other children who had received their diphtheria inoculation on Friday afternoon, Bernadette Pierce had a sore arm and was too restless to sleep. "My arm started to pain me and I was crying. So my grandmother brought me downstairs to give me something to ease the pain." The orphans over in the Sisters of Charity convent in North William Street were also awake with the noise of the anti-aircraft guns, sitting up in their beds. Only the very young ones remained deep in slumber. Sister Louise and Sister Philomena, as well as several other nuns, were calming their worries and making certain they didn't go near the large windows. Just in case.

Frank Wearen was running a little late on his rounds around Gardiner Street and Summerhill. When the sky lit up with flares and shell bursts he began shuffling along at a slower pace so that he could follow what was going on overhead. Also out on the street around Summerhill was an LSF man by the name of Adamson who was on patrol with a comrade. Both were strolling along, taking in the flurry of anti-aircraft activity and smoking one cigarette after another out of nervousness. Adamson decided he had better try to find some more cigarettes to get him through what looked like a long night. Though it was well past midnight, he knew just the little shop that would probably still be open, serving the late fish-and-chips crowd:

> He purchased a packet of cigarettes at the shop owned by Miss Catherine Slater, 44 Summerhill Parade. It was probably the last time anyone ever bought a cigarette there, for that shop was in a few minutes doomed to be flattened like a crunched match box on top of its owner.[10]

It was now approaching 1:30, and the searchlights, flares and anti-aircraft fire had been going on for quite a while. The novelty of the spectacle was wearing off, and people were growing tired. To many, the chattering guns were becoming bothersome as they tried to get back to sleep. Twelve-year-old Colleen Heeney was in bed. "I was getting tired of listening to it ... *annoyed*, really." There had been enough excitement for one night. People needed to get a decent sleep to be ready for the holiday weekend ahead:

> It was about half-past one on the morning of 31 May, and Dublin was about to have her first experience of what her sister Blighty across the water had endured for so long.[11]

Chapter 9

"GET UP, QUICK! WE'RE BEING BOMBED!"

People were just sleeping, and the next thing there was a "boom!" Everybody was out on the street. People didn't know what to think. Oh, we all got out of the house and ran up to Summerhill. There was a barber's shop on the corner, full of people kneeling down and saying the Rosary.

(SALLY BURKE, 84)

At 1:28 a.m. a strange sound was heard in the night sky. An unfamiliar sound, high-pitched, quite distinct from the coarse noise of droning engines and anti-aircraft guns. To most ears it was a "whining" or "whistling". To a reporter from the *Evening Herald* it was "a *peculiar* whistle."[1] It caused people to slightly cock their heads, straining to identify it.

To Dubliners who had recently spent time in London or Manchester, however, it was all too familiar.

Fifteen-year-old Louis Robinson of Synnott Street had been warned by his older brother, James, an ARP warden, exactly what to do should he ever hear such a sound: "Open the windows and then hide somewhere, like under the stairs." Just as instructed, the moment he heard the whistling he threw open the windows and crouched beneath the stairs with the rest of his family.

Then it struck. The whistle abruptly ceased. The bomb fell at the junction of the North Circular Road and North Richmond Street, and the "flash lit up the sky." The explosion shook the ground and rattled buildings all around. Windows were shattered and slates ripped off roofs. Chimney stacks tilted or toppled as bricks were dislodged. Several houses that took the brunt of the blast collapsed completely or partially. It caused a power failure and started a small fire.

The bomb struck close to Father Masterson's house at 595 North Circular Road, where he was still pacing the floor. The jolt immediately confirmed his premonition. "Three windows were open, which is probably the reason they were not broken, but the force of the explosion threw me across the room, and the lights went out. I went out immediately."[2] Just outside he found Brother McKenna, who had been standing at the bottom of the stairs of the Christian Brothers' monastery in North Richmond Street, watching the aerial display, when suddenly "he was flung on the stone steps" with great force.[3] His face was injured seriously enough to require treatment at the Mater Hospital.

The bomb had landed in front of 582 North Circular Road, the home of Lilly Byrne, and 584, Mrs Grice's shop, above which there were several occupied flats. Father Masterson was on the scene in a flash. He found both buildings badly crumpled, people trapped beneath the bricks and timbers. He was quickly joined by members of the ARP and LDF, one of whom was Mary Dunne's father, who had sprinted up from his home in North William Street:

> With the bomb, the shutters rattling woke me up. I was surprised to see my father in his LDF uniform. He said to my mother, "Get the children down to the basement!" Then Dad said to us, "Be good till I come back, I have to go to duty." There was a lot of noise and banging in the distance. Mam asked him what it was, and he said "bombs."

Father Masterson, Mr Dunne and other rescuers worked side by side to free several people not seriously hurt. Meanwhile, firemen had arrived and were extinguishing the small fire.

Then attention turned to extricating a man described by the newspapers as "buried alive." And indeed he was—up to his very chin. His body was packed in debris as tightly as a wrapped mummy. He couldn't move a limb. Had he been buried three inches deeper he could not have breathed. Fortunately, he could both hear and speak. Seeing his predicament, and realising that further collapse of the building might doom the man, Father Masterson knelt beside him and administered the Last Sacrament, after which he spoke to him in reassuring words.

During his entrapment the man's mind recalled an article he had read recently about a girl buried during the London blitz who had been rescued alive after 107 hours. For some reason, that exact figure had stuck in his mind. The thought fortified him. Father Masterson recalls the end of his ordeal. "I was helping to extricate the man who was buried up to his head, and when workers finally got him up a bit the first thing he asked for was a cigarette— and they gave him one."[4]

When he had been completely dug out, head to toe, it was calculated that he had been buried for 107 *minutes*.

Only a few feet away, at 582 North Circular Road, lived Lilly Byrne, her niece Gene Fortune, and a friend, Michael Carroll. When the bomb exploded just outside their front door the house first shuddered, then just collapsed around them. All three were trapped. At that moment, directly across the road, Bill O'Rourke and Mick Bulger stood at their window, horrified to watch Miss Byrne's house topple down before their eyes. They leapt into action and were across the road as the bricks were still settling:

> Climbing up a mound of debris, Mr. O'Rourke tripped over the twisted remains of a bed, and heard from below a feeble cry. He shouted down, and received an answering moan from a man. Climbing through a window, he found two relatives—the Misses Lilly Byrne and Gene Fortune. Both ladies were badly shaken with fright.
>
> One of them told Mr. O'Rourke there was a man in the next room who should be taken care of. When he opened the door he nearly walked into space. For that room was blown into dust, and the man living in it had fallen down with the floor. It was his cry that Mr. O'Rourke had heard.[5]

O'Rourke and Bulger worked with other rescuers to free the three trapped victims. Michael Carroll and Gene Fortune were slightly injured. He was taken to Richmond Hospital and she to Jervis Street. Lilly Byrne was uninjured but a nervous wreck.

Agnes Corrigan was among the ARP wardens working to dig out Lilly Byrne and the other two. Before the explosion she had been out on patrol, when suddenly "she was thrown to the ground by the blast, sustaining cuts on her knees and right hand."[6] Undeterred, she threw herself into the rescue of others. When some ARP men noticed her injuries and urged her to care for herself, she politely ignored them and continued working to free Lilly Byrne and Gene Fortune. She lived close by, at 15 Summer Street. Seeing the emotionally fragile state of Miss Byrne, she invited the trembling woman to stay in her home, an invitation gratefully accepted. However, the warden found that "at first she would not go to bed, and spent most of the night under the stairs."[7] Eventually exhausted, she was assisted into bed, where she immediately fell into sleep.

Meanwhile, neighbours had their own harrowing experiences. At Nellie Maryone's home "a large paving stone came through the roof where one of her sisters and two children slept."[8] It landed right on the bed. Fortunately, the "occupants of the room had left it only minutes before." Then her small son, who had been "standing at the landing window looking out, was blasted *into* the room where the stone was."[9] But unhurt. Mrs Maryone called it "good luck."

A close neighbour and friend of Father Masterson, Joseph Dempsey, a postman, lived at 578 North Circular Road with his parents, four brothers and two sisters. He was in bed when awakened by "a heavy thud. I switched on the flash lamp and saw a gaping hole in the ceiling above my head."[10] His brother

Thomas, who slept in the same room, had pieces of masonry fall on the pillow beside him. His mother, downstairs and panic-stricken, called up to see if they were safe. "She had looked outside and, seeing all the debris in the street, she thought we too had been blown out with it."[11] The whole family then took refuge under the stairs. Despite the scare and little sleep, Joseph was on time for duty the next morning at Fairview Post Office.

——

On the very heel of the first bomb a second had fallen. It exploded at 1:29, just around the corner at Summerhill Parade. Like partners in crime, the two bombs had apparently been released from the same plane; during their descent they drifted only slightly apart before striking earth. They were of the same size, it was later determined, and produced remarkably similar results. Both demolished two structures, damaged others and left craters that looked as if they had been shaped by the same ice-cream scoop.

If the bomb explosions were similar, people's reactions were not. At her home in 21 North Clarence Street, Agnes Daly's mother was frightened out of her wits by the nearby blasts. She "shouted to me, 'C'mon, Agnes, get up, quick! We're being bombed!' The whole family jumped up, got dressed, and we all went out." They were met by the sound of doors being thrown open all along the street as neighbours spilled out onto the path in confusion, mothers shouting orders to their children.

Over in Synnott Street, Kathleen Martin's mother was decidedly cooler under pressure:

I remember Mother coming over to me in bed, and all the commotion outside. And she looked out the window and she said, "What's wrong?" And they said, "A bomb has fallen on Summerhill." And I always remember my mother said, "It's only a bomb. Go back to sleep." It's only a bomb!

It had exploded just outside Catherine Slater's shop at 44 Summerhill Parade and that of her neighbour, Jane Fitzgerald, at number 43, leaving a large, chunky mound of rubble beneath which at least nine victims were reportedly trapped. Living with Mrs Fitzgerald were her 21-year-old son Noel and 24-year-old daughter Edna, as well as her mother, aged eighty-seven, her sister, Mary Malone, and Thomas Lowth, their nephew. When the missile hit, Mrs Fitzgerald had been standing outside in front of Miss Slater's shop, chatting with neighbours. "Suddenly my house was blown down! I was struck on the head from behind and knocked down, but I managed to free myself."[12] Her courageous mother somehow struggled her way out of the debris. Next, Noel was pulled out safely. Then, Mary Malone and Thomas Lowth were retrieved. None of the five were seriously harmed. Then they looked around, only to realise that Edna had not yet been found.

When rescuers were informed that Edna was still missing they began feverishly digging out the debris in search of her. Then Dick Eyres arrived at the scene. He had trotted all the way from Shamrock Terrace with his patrol colleague, Murphy. "We ran up the street towards Mrs Fitzgerald's house. The complete roof had just sat down on the house."[13] It was an apt description. Noticing some apertures where timbers had crossed, the two men dropped to their knees and began crawling, "under the roof ... and we were talking to a woman in the basement of the house. The house was down all around her. She was saying, 'I'm all right.'"[14] They had found Edna. But digging her out was going to be tedious and dangerous. The two men, now almost on their bellies, clawed their way towards her, continually talking in a reassuring voice, wishing they felt so certain themselves. Their patience was tested by a frenzied dog down in the basement, barking its foolish head off. To Eyres and Murphy it was at first annoying, then maddening, making it more difficult to converse with the distressed woman. Finally she was reached and carefully pulled out. Eventually, all the Fitzgeralds and the other residents were standing up and were dusted off. None required medical treatment. There is no record of what happened to the barking dog.

Next door, at 44 Summerhill Parade, Catherine Slater had been buried when her shop completely crumbled. Noel Fitzgerald tried to help rescuers by telling them, "I was standing at the door talking to Miss Slater when I heard a whistling sound. I shouted to the others to run indoors. Just then, the bomb struck."[15] She disappeared, having taken only a few steps into her shop. She *must* be close by, Noel insisted. Yet rescuers were having no luck finding her.

By this time Adamson of the LSF, who had bought his cigarettes from her and had a bit of a chat only thirty-five minutes earlier, showed up. When the bomb exploded he had been several streets away. He swung around to look in the direction of Summerhill. As the *Irish Times* reported, seeing "flames flare up from the shop he had recently left, he raced back towards the shop and it was gone—*flattened*."[16] He stood there in disbelief. He had *just talked* to her. With plenty of other rescuers on the job, his services were not needed. He was left with nothing to do but stand among the onlookers, and hope and pray.

She was finally found, pinned firmly under rubble and apparently in bad condition. Freeing her would be precarious. After about an hour of intense digging she was accessible enough for Father Flynn of Portland Place to edge his way close and anoint her. She may or may not have been aware of this. The St John Ambulance Brigade stood by with a stretcher to whisk her away to hospital. Finally, "after an hour and a half of frantic digging," wrote the *Irish Times* reporter on the scene, "she was lifted from what was once her home and taken, critically injured," to the Mater Hospital.[17] When the crowd saw she was alive there was audible relief. They all knew and liked Miss Slater. At the Mater, everyone agreed, she'd get the best of care.

Miss Slater's next-door neighbours, Peter Purdue and his wife, at number 45, had better fortune. They too had been standing just inside their doorway looking up at the lighted sky. Deciding to return to bed, they went back inside and began climbing the stairs. Then they heard a plane. "It looked bad to them, so they started *out* again. As they opened the door there came a whistling, then a bomb blast which hurled them both backwards."[18] Peter Purdue (variously described by newspapers as a "bootmaker" or "bookmaker"—probably the former) conjectured that their open door, through which they had been so cleanly thrown back, had "lessened the effect of the blast on them."[19] Their home, however, was so "badly shattered" that they were unable to remain there that night.

The next morning he would return home to assess the damage. He also did a bit of measuring and determined that his front door was "only about three paces to the right of the crater."[20] For the rest of the day he enjoyed telling friends and reporters how the bomb had fallen so close to his door that he could nearly have reached out and touched it.

Just on the other side of the crater, at number 41 Summerhill, lived 28-year-old Patrick McLoughlin, his wife, and their two-year-old son, William, and two-month-old baby, Vera. Their home had suffered damage similar to the Purdues', rendering it temporarily uninhabitable. But they were in luck, because his mother-in-law lived just a few streets away, at number 157 North Strand. Following the blast, Peter and his wife calmed their two children, grabbed a few items of clothing and set out towards her mother's home. Along the way they both said how doubly fortunate they were, firstly to have survived unharmed and then to have her mother's home open to them. She met them at the door, greatly relieved to see that all were well. As his wife was settling the children into their granny's, Peter decided that he should hasten back to their damaged house and fetch more clothing and other items. He realised that the next day the street would be cordoned off and impassable even to local residents.

As he was going out the door he called back to his wife that he would return shortly. Around two o'clock.

Meanwhile, people living in the vicinity but not yet knowing exactly what had happened were reacting in all sorts of ways. Most were out on the streets, shouting, asking questions, milling about and running in every direction. Over in Portland Row, twenty-year-old Sally Burke, her parents and four brothers sprang out of bed on hearing the explosions. They pulled on clothing and lurched out into the street, into a mass of confusion and running. Sally saw two streams of people, some heading *towards* the bomb scene, others running *away* from it. No-one seemed sure in which direction they should go: they just felt the need to run somewhere. As Sally Burke stepped out her door she and her parents found themselves swept up in a current of humanity that carried them towards Summerhill:

> Oh, we all got *out* of the house and ran up to Summerhill. *Everybody* was out on the street. Now there was a barber's shop on the corner, and that door was open, and it was *full* of people, sitting on the floor and lying on the floor. *All* squeezed in the barber's shop. And they were kneeling down and saying the Rosary. Oh, God, yes, they were frightened!
>
> And my mother nearly *walked* on people in the barber's shop, she was that frightened. I was outside with my father. We couldn't get into the bloody thing! There was so many people crammed in, if he dropped another bomb on *there* there'd have been a massacre!

People's instincts were to herd together, like sheep, for security, whether it was barging into a shop or a home, or gathering in the streets. Everywhere, they sought refuge together—except in the concrete "hat-box" air-raid shelters.

People living in the complexes of flats poured out onto their balconies and then down the stairs into the open courtyards. This is what happened at St Joseph's Mansions, where eighteen-year-old Patrick "Dixie" Dean lived. By the time he had scrambled down the stairs into the crowd there was already a heated argument under way. "I ran down into the square, and the caretaker, he wanted to put the *lights on*, in the square. And it kicked up a row—'cause he was *supposed* to keep the lights *out*! But *he* wanted to put them *on*." Some residents were frightened at being in the dark, while others were fearful of putting the lights on. A lighted courtyard, they argued, would provide German pilots with a perfect target. Dean, a young LDF man, sided with the "sensible" fellas—"we got them put out, anyway."

Dubliners living beyond the city centre could only watch from afar and imagine what had happened. Noel Brady had been standing outside his parents' home out on the Naas Road, watching intently, when the bombing had occurred. With him were several of his mates, fellow-members of the St John Ambulance Brigade. They determined right away what had happened. "We heard the planes coming over, and we *seen* the planes. Then we saw the flashes in the sky." But there was no way of knowing how serious the damage had been. Should he head to the scene right away on his bicycle, or try to get some sleep and await being called to duty the next day?

Clear across the city in the Phoenix Park, the sound of the two explosions had been muted by distance and foliage. Nonetheless, owing to their highly sensitive hearing and nervous system, ears of zoo animals pricked up at the noise and tremors of the blasts. Some stirred, lifting their heads; others, more alert, stood up. A general jitteriness prevailed among the zoo's population.

Park keepers and zoo staff had worked hard during May to have everything looking its best for the large Whit weekend crowds expected. Lawns were mowed and manicured, flower beds cultivated, shrubs neatly trimmed, walkways patched up and swept for elderly visitors and mothers with prams. Lakes and ponds cleaned out. Zoo personnel scrubbed down and freshened up the animals' stalls. Where possible, those animals that were special attractions were bathed and groomed for viewing. Dubliners loved their zoo, and those responsible for maintaining it took great pride in their work. During the war years, when life could look bleak, visiting the Park and the zoo was more important than ever for lifting spirits.

No zoo resident was more popular, or more pampered, than Sara (whose full Indian name was Sarawathi), the cow elephant. She was the darling of zoo-goers, from toddlers to grannies. Her friendly nature, gentle disposition and endlessly entertaining antics made her everyone's favourite. To her zoo minders she possessed almost human qualities, being sensitive, responsive, obedient and always well behaved. No-one went to the zoo without visiting her. For the Whit weekend she had been bathed and groomed to meet her admirers. She even seemed to know it.

At 1:31 a.m., when the zoo was as quiet as it ever gets, a third bomb fell, landing in the Phoenix Park near the pumping station. Joseph McNally, who worked at the station, lived just beside it with his eleven-year-old daughter, Winifred. Both were sleeping soundly when the bomb fell "within 20 yards of their home which collapsed as if it were made of cardboard."[21] It gouged a deep crater, estimated to be about fifteen feet deep and eighteen feet in diameter. The blast "tore away trees around the McNally home and top-dressed almost every yard of the grounds of the Phoenix Cricket Club nearby."[22] Margaret Foley, who resided in the club, was removed and taken quickly to the Rotunda Hospital for observation. Joseph McNally, the newspapers reported, came away with only "a scratch on his forehead, and his daughter with a slight scratch on her right foot." The bomb had also burst a water main and had broken windows in Áras an Uachtaráin and the American Legation.

Most distressed were the zoo's animals. The first two distant explosions had stirred them, but this one, so close, terrified them. Many began crying or bellowing incessantly. Most audible were the elephant-trumpeting and the shrieking of monkeys, which carried through the entire zoo, spreading a sense of fear. Some animals became aggressive in their attempts to bolt free.

One of the zoo's most massive and muscular beasts was crazed with fear and began thrashing about. The huge "bull bison ran completely amok with panic ... stampeded and broke his railings ... and almost succeeded in breaking bounds."[23] He was on the verge of charging madly through the park and then possibly onto the city streets. As the *Irish Independent* described the scene, "the dangerous bull bison had actually broken down the iron railing around him in a desperate attempt to escape, but was beaten by the blast" at the last second.[24] Apparently, delayed shock or stress dropped him in his tracks, just as he had "beat the bars" and was ready to charge away.

Sara was just as frightened. Her instinctive response was to run away and hide; but she was far more intelligent, and more capable, than the other zoo residents, who howled and hurled themselves again their bars. Rather than expending energy, she sought another way out. She proceeded to execute a Houdini-style escape that astounded even those who knew her best. The *Irish Independent* described her feat, surely deserving of recording in the annals of pachyderm lore:

> "Sara", the cow elephant in the Zoological Gardens, had a remarkable display of animal instinct and performed a rare jail-breaking feat by opening four iron padlocks and unbolting three gates en route to her conception of safety.
>
> The inner gate of her stall had two padlocks which Sara continued to shake with the little "finger" on top of her trunk, until they opened. She then removed them with the same "finger" and pulled back the two bolts—one underneath and one on top. She dealt similarly with the lock on the second gate, unscrewed the shackle in the outer gate, crossed a fence, and moved down to the edge of the lake where she lay down among the bull-rushes, which she possibly regarded as the best available imitation of the jungle thicket.[25]

"Grace under pressure", in the best Hemingway tradition.

As Sara was carrying out her great escape, the curator, Cedric Flood, the windows of whose home had been shattered, was rushing towards his wards. When he found out about the bison's attempted break-out he said, with great relief, "I believe if the blast had not stunned him he would have broken away."[26] He knew the temperament and habits of every animal in the zoo. And he was known for his ability to talk to them in his own way, coaxing and comforting when it was needed.

When informed of Sara's escape and disappearance he immediately went in search of her. He knew she would seek to hide herself in some cover. Logic led him down to the dense reeds around the lake, all along the way calling out to her. Sure enough, he tracked her down to the lake's most dense thicket of vegetation, into which Sara had wedged herself. She immediately responded to his voice. He later explained to fascinated reporters how he had spoken to her. "I had only to shout at her, 'What are you doing there, Sara?'—and she started to return to her stall immediately."[27] When her huge form was seen lumbering towards home there was immense relief by the zoo staff. Everyone found themselves smiling at Sara, who acted a bit sheepish at her behaviour. Her "break-out" adventure was to become great zoo lore.

Their feeling of happy relief was short-lived. It was still the middle of the night, and planes remained overhead. Cedric Flood was worried about more bombs falling and dangerous animals getting loose. All Dubliners had seen the danger caused by runaway horses or cattle being driven to the market or the docks. They often caused damage, even death. Flood had heard about other bombed cities in Europe, where dangerous zoo animals had broken free to run wild among the public. He also knew about cases in which such animals had to be shot as a precaution. But it always seemed to him to have no relevance to neutral Ireland.

Only six weeks earlier this unfortunate act had to be carried out in blitzed Belfast. Thirty-three exotic and valuable, but dangerous, zoo animals were shot, not because they had escaped but because they *might* break free during another bombing. No chances were being taken. Included were some of the zoo's most treasured residents, including nine lions, two tigers, five bears and one puma. Now Cedric Flood found himself on the spot. A decision had to be made. Public safety was paramount.

Shortly thereafter, he issued his dire order; "attendants stood by, ready to shoot the animals should the need arise."[28] The "firing squad" were handed weapons. Every man dreaded the thought of having to carry out the act if it became necessary.

———

While fear and drama surrounded the three immediate bomb sites, most Dubliners were quite calm. To southsiders, a few bombs had fallen "somewhere over there," on the north side of the city. Probably another minor mishap of the January type. As no sirens had been sounded, there was no cause for serious alarm. Even northsiders living beyond the immediate scenes,

The three lanes at Quinn's Cottages, near North Strand Road, were better known locally as "Heaven, Hell and Purgatory."

The German blitz of Belfast in mid-April 1941 led to the Irish Government despatching firefighters across the border to battle the conflagration—a possible breach of neutrality.

Men at Buckingham Street Fire Station who volunteered to dash north to help blazing Belfast. Jack Conroy is second from the right.

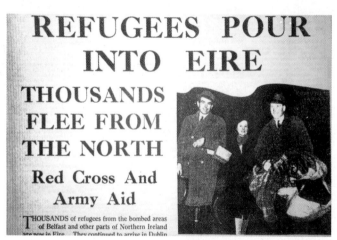

REFUGEES POUR INTO EIRE

THOUSANDS FLEE FROM THE NORTH

Red Cross And Army Aid

THOUSANDS of refugees from the bombed areas of Belfast and other parts of Northern Ireland are now in Eire. They continued to arrive in Dublin

The Irish Red Cross Society sheltered and fed most of the Belfast refugees, but many ordinary Dubliners sympathetically took them into their homes as well.

rish Press

oo Cum Slóipe Dé Azup Onópa na h-Éipeann

FRIDAY, APRIL 18, 1941. P 7 **PRICE THREE-HALFPENCE**

er / Of

orces

r

Belfast Refugees Arriving At Amiens St. Station, Dublin

3,000 Refugees Arrive In Dublin

UP to last night approximately 3,000 refugees from the Six-Counties had arrived in Dublin, the majority of them being women and children from Belfast. About 300 came yesterday, amongst them a family from Derry on their way to relatives in Cork.

Mr. Seán Moylan, Parlia-

Within three days of the Belfast Blitz, more than three thousand refugees from the North were welcomed in Dublin—another possible breach of non-involvement in the war.

Jack Conroy (*right*) had to race on foot from his fire station to the nearby North Strand bomb site, encountering a headless man along the way.

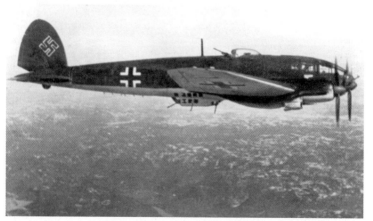

German Heinkel HE-111 bomber of the type which carried out the Dublin bombing.

Bread and Flour · Made by · JOHNSTON MOONEY & O'BRIEN

The Irish Press

Bo Cun Mbon Bó agur óráig na b-ɖeann

CITY SPECIAL EDITION

Vol. XI. No. 128. The Truth in the News.   SATURDAY, MAY 31, 1941.   PRICE THREE-HALFPENCE

EVERY FARMER NEEDS A SILO
EVERY FARMER CAN AFFORD
WEATHERWELL SILO
WEATHERWELL LIMITED CLONTARF

BOMBS ON DUBLIN: MANY DEAD IN WRECKED HOMES

Fires Follow Big Explosion

Damage In 4 Areas: Heroic Rescue Work

AIRCRAFT WERE OVER DUBLIN EARLY THIS MORNING. THE ANTI-AIRCRAFT GUNS WERE IN ACTION. BOMBS FELL IN FOUR DISTRICTS.

An explosion, believed to be that of a land mine, wrecked a block of houses in the North Strand area, and large numbers of people were buried under the debris.

It was estimated early this morning that some 30 or 40 people had been killed and the injured number 100 or more.

A bomb demolished a house in Summerhill and. An old woman was rescued and it is believed that a girl is buried in the ruins.

In the North Circular Road, nearby, another house was demolished and it is believed that, here also, people are buried in the ruins.

A bomb dropped in the Phoenix Park and exploded, the shock broke windows in the President's residence and in the American Legation.

Buried To Neck In Debris

Another eye witness reports happenings from this morning's midnight air attack on Dublin from an A.R.P. first-aid worker said it was not then possible to ascertain the full position of casualties.

"I have just seen the rescue of

VIEW OF THE DAMAGE IN THE NORTH STRAND AREA

An IRISH PRESS photograph taken at the North Strand shortly after the explosion

Crete Battle Nears End

British Trapped,

FLOODS HOLD UP DRIVE ON BAGHDAD

(PRESS ASSOCIATION)

BRITISH forces in Iraq have made a further advance from Khan Nuqta, which they captured on Wednesday, though their progress eastwards has been delayed by floods on the River Abhi Abhi mains.

In London it is stated that damage to the "Tara Bridge"—almost eight miles west of Baghdad—is the obstacle. Troops advancing up the Euphrates from Basra have occupied Ur, a rail junction west of Kala Hammar.

The heaviest thrust in Baghdad is that of a British mobile force, which is only five miles away in the north-east.

Reports received in London said that Rashid Ali has crossed the frontier only from (Persia) accompanied by Amin Beg, his Chief of Staff, and Rashid Ali, when he reached Rugom in place of the Emir Abdul Illah.

A Baghdad despatch to Vichy says that to-day gives "towards Mosul for last-ditch," taking with him the

On Whit Saturday, 31 May 1941, in the middle of the night, four bombs fell on Dublin, one of which was an extraordinarily powerful weapon.

The destruction at numbers 23 to 29 North Strand Road. (*Courtesy of Dublin City Archives*)

While some buildings were blown into rubble heaps, others were left standing as dangerous empty shells, which had to be quickly demolished.

Very few possessions could be salvaged from buildings still standing. (*Courtesy of Dublin City Archives*)

SATURDAY, Irish Independent MAY 31, 1941. 5

BOMBS ON DUBLIN THIS MORNING
Many Killed And Injured

DESTRUCTION ON NORTH SIDE OF CITY

People Buried In Wreckage Of Their Homes

BOMBS WERE DROPPED ON DUBLIN EARLY THIS MORNING. THEY CAUSED WIDESPREAD DAMAGE AND MANY CASUALTIES, AND IT IS FEARED THAT THE DEATH ROLL IS HIGH.

The destruction was confined to the North side of the city where bombs which fell in the North Strand area demolished dozens of houses and many people were buried in the wreckage.

Many shops and dwellinghouses on the left hand side of North Strand from the Five Lamps to Newcomen Bridge were demolished by a high explosive and burned out afterwards.

A.R.P. workers clearing debris in the search for victims at North Strand Road, Dublin.

HOW BISMARCK AND HOOD SANK

Crete Battle Nears End, Germans Say

BRITISH ON "DELICATE" SITUATION

CRETE'S garrison is trapped, and the issue of the battle is decided, Berlin asserted last night. The British are in full retreat, the German News Agency reported, and while German troops on forced march are nearing the South coast town of Sphakia, Italians are advancing from the East.

LICENCE FOR SALE OF COAL

New Orders

No Escape, Berlin Says

Newspapers reported that the North Strand, from the Five Lamps to Newcomen Bridge, was "virtually wiped out."

Damage at Rutland Place, showing children behind the barrier at the rear and a Ford Model B in the foreground. (*Courtesy of Dublin City Archives*)

Soldiers, LDF wardens and others standing at the edge of the North Strand crater. (*Courtesy of the* Irish Independent)

on hearing that "only" a few houses had collapsed, with few injuries and no deaths, were not particularly worried.

What no-one could have appreciated at the time was the sheer good fortune of the three bombings. All had landed on relatively soft surfaces and were of small calibre, once again leaving the same impression as in January, that bombings were not necessarily catastrophic events. Frightening, but survivable.

Over at the *Irish Times* office in Westmorland Street, when the first bomb had exploded at 1:28 a.m., Tony Gray, Alec Newman and R. M. Smyllie dashed "down the stairs and through the front office and out into the street" to see if they could pinpoint where it had struck. When the second one detonated they fixed their gaze in the direction of Summerhill. There they stood, watching as the minutes passed. But, as Gray admits, they were quite nonchalant about it all:

As none of the previous German bombs which had dropped on Ireland had done very much damage, we didn't take this raid very seriously.[29]

Chapter 10

┃ "HE'S COMING BACK!"

Oh, we seen the plane—coming straight over!
(CHRISSIE BYRNE, 88)

We were looking up at that pilot with our mouth wide open!
(AGNES DALY, 81)

Following the Phoenix Park blast at 1:31, minutes passed and no more
bombs fell. People began to breathe more easily. Gunners at anti-aircraft
posts sat back and lit cigarettes. But Air Defence Command officers
were baffled, and worried. After the third bomb explosion within four
minutes, some of the German planes had drifted away, but others remained
above the city, flying in seeming disarray. Why were they still hanging around?

Many residents of the North Strand, seeing explosive flashes up around the
North Circular Road and Summerhill, headed straight over to find out what
had happened. It was only a few streets away. Upon arriving, they said to one
another, "We were lucky, all right … ah, it *could* have been us!" Others
gathered on Newcomen Bridge, which offered a good vantage point from
which to see into the distance. Their babble just outside her open cottage
window made it difficult for young Maureen Lynch to sleep. Nearby, Richard
Fitzpatrick, who had closed his butcher's shop a few hours earlier, wasn't
about to get out of bed. He was probably unaware that his seventeen-year-old
son Gerald was not home yet from the Whit Friday dance, having probably
stopped at the chipper and then headed over to the bomb scenes.

A few doors down were the Browne family. Harry, a dedicated LDF
member, had immediately put on his helmet and armband and gone to
Summerhill to assist with rescue efforts and crowd control. His wife, Molly,
was trying to get the children back into bed after they had been aroused by all
the excitement outside. "It's all over now," she told them, "so back to bed it is."

Some time between 1:35 and 1:38 a.m. Air Defence Command observers
were struck by a strange and disquieting occurrence, recorded in a report that
was classified in Military Archives as "secret" for the next sixty years. They had
been watching a few more German planes finally head north again, out of

Dublin's air space:

> One plane proceeded north only as far as Collinstown, and when engaged
> by the anti-aircraft battery there, turned south again. The aircraft seems to
> have been hovering around, as if awaiting instructions.[1]

This abrupt reversal of direction by the plane, just after being fired on by anti-
aircraft gunners, caused some observers to wonder at first if the aircraft had
been struck; or possibly the pilot was provoked by being fired on as he was
departing. In any case, he headed his bomber back over the heart of Dublin
and began a bizarre and unnerving pattern of aerial behaviour for the next
half an hour, to be remembered for ever by all who witnessed it.

At first the soaring plane appeared like a lazy gull, making easy loops on
air currents above the city, generally flying in a circular pattern, as if awaiting
something. People watched what was now becoming a one-man show.
Occasionally the pilot would drop down and make low sweeps over the city.
From his home in Seville Place, Louis Robinson saw it all clearly. "The plane
was going away and coming back, as if he was going around in circles."
Gradually it began tightening its circle over the north of the city, focusing on
the Amiens Street station area, a couple of streets from the North Strand.

After ten minutes or so Air Defence Command determined that the pilot
was not merely "hovering," as if "awaiting instructions," but was now
swooping very low, apparently in *search* of something.[2] Orders were given to
anti-aircraft gunners to increase their fire. According to the *Evening Mail*, the
"Ak-Ak guns opened up a fierce attack on the aircraft" with a combination of
light and heavy shells.[3] When the pilot descended within range, gunners could
let loose with their rapid-fire Hotchkiss machine-gun, perhaps hoping to
wing the plane and drive it away.

Dubliners now viewing the spectacle were fascinated with the cat-and-
mouse contest, as the German aviator skilfully eluded searchlight beams and
gunners' shells.

It was now the "mystery plane". Everyone in Dublin was wondering,
"What's the fella up to?"

According to Captain Quigley, the plane "kept circling for approximately
half an hour", an astonishingly long time under the circumstances of being
fired on, often at low altitude and close range.[4] The pilot must have been well
aware of the risks he was taking. A few minutes before 2:00 he began
dropping, making extremely low passes over rooftops. What may have been
thrilling for people to watch suddenly became chilling for those around
Amiens Street and the North Strand. No longer like a gull, the plane now had
more the look of a hawk hunting its prey. To those directly in its path it felt

menacing. Chrissie Byrne and her sister watched the spectacle from their open bedroom window in North William Street, becoming more frightened as the plane drew nearer:

> We were in bed and there was a little window, and Sheila was beside me. And I said, "*Quick, quick,* look up at that plane—it's coming *straight over!*" Oh, we seen the plane, as plain as anything, the two of us.

The experience was most frightening to those who actually saw the face of the pilot in the cockpit, just above their heads. Agnes Daly was at the corner of North Clarence Street and the North Strand, standing with several other girls, all still jabbering excitedly about the first bombs, when suddenly the mystery plane appeared right above them. She recalls her disbelief:

> It was a clear night, a *beautiful* night, and we could see everything. We saw that plane as clear as if we were *sitting in it!* We were looking up at that pilot with our mouth wide open. Then we said, Oh, Jesus, Mary and Joseph, *he's back!*

Unimpeachable eye-witnesses would later give similar accounts of having seen the pilot's face as the plane swept low over them, seemingly within reach. Dick Eyres's wife and her neighbour Annie Shaw were among those to give such testimony. Hearing the loud drone of the bomber as it skimmed over rooftops in Shamrock Terrace, the two women darted out the door to look upwards at the precise moment it passed over their heads:

> As sure as God, I could even see the *men* in the plane. The thing was over my head, and the two of us went down on our knees. We couldn't move; stuck to the ground, we were.

Jack Conroy and his fellow-firemen were so immersed in rescue work at Summerhill that they didn't have a second to look skyward. Then "one fella says, 'They're *still up there!*'" Dick Eyres was still in the midst of extricating Edna Fitzgerald from her mother's collapsed house when, above the barking dog, he heard someone scream fearfully, "*He's coming back!*"[5]

Still no air-raid sirens were sounded.

The only warnings heard were the shouts of terrified people on the streets, telling others to "get *down, hit the ground!*" At the Summerhill and North Circular Road bomb sites, wrote the *Irish Independent*, "while firemen and other services worked frantically by the glow of lamps to get to the injured, a warning cry was raised and people flung themselves on the glass-strewn streets."[6] Along Guild Street, Colleen Heeney remembers, one woman had recently returned from visiting relatives in London, where she experienced the blitz. She was familiar with all the sounds. "And she's *running* along the street, shouting, '*Get down, on your stomachs, get down*—he's *releasing*, he's *releasing!*' That was her way of putting it." A number of people tell of actually hearing the plane's bomb bay mechanism opening in the last seconds. Cissie O'Brien recalls, "We could hear what I can only describe as like the gears of a car jamming, then we heard the whistling."[7] Others said it sounded like creaky doors on the back of a van being opened.

Everyone remembers one sound, for it sent awful chills through them. It was not the whizzing or whistling of its three predecessors; instead it was a hideous screaming or screeching whistle. "I remember the *terrible* whistle," says Kathleen Martin, "a *dreadful* whistle." From Dermot Ring's house in Clonmore Terrace, about eighty yards from Newcomen Bridge, "Oh, I could hear it *screaming!*"

There was nothing for people to do in those final seconds but wait. From their cottage in Shamrock Terrace, Bernadette Pierce's granny knew it was coming:

> It was whistling, and she knew it was going to fall. And she thought we were goners! So my grandmother held me close, I remember that. And then she put her hands over my ears and *pressed* them real hard so I wouldn't hear the bomb falling.

Like others, their only defence at that moment was to muffle their ears with their hands.

The mystery of the mystery plane had been revealed. No-one needed any longer to wonder, "What's the fella up to?" He had come in for the kill.

The large hand on Corcoran's clock was nudging 2:05 a.m.

————

At that very moment, two men were running madly towards the North Strand. As others were hitting the ground or scrambling for cover, they tore frantically through the open streets, the bomb screaming down above their heads. One was headed for number 157 North Strand, the other towards number 24. Both men were young, strong, fleet of foot, actually trying to outrace the bomb in hopes of reaching their families in the nick of time. Conceivably, they may have even noticed one another in their homeward dash.

Harry Browne was headed for his home at 24 North Strand, from which he had departed about thirty minutes earlier to carry out his LDF duties at Summerhill, assuring his wife that he would be back shortly. When the mystery plane began zeroing in threateningly around the North Strand, he decided to return at once. He must have been "within a half a block" away when he heard the screaming bomb descending. He raced the rest of the distance, and got as close as humanly possible. His hand firmly grasped the door knob at the split second of explosion. There it was to remain, frozen in death.

The second sprinter was Patrick McLoughlin. He had just collected a few more items of clothing from his bomb-damaged house in Summerhill Parade and was walking back to his mother-in-law's home at 157 North Strand, where his wife and two young children were settling into bed. On the return trip he had felt no need to rush. More probably he was feeling thankful that his family were unhurt and safely ensconced with the children's granny.

When he saw the plane drop low, then heard the bomb shrieking, he broke into a run. He reached the door only seconds before impact—just enough time to plunge inside and probably shout out a warning to his family. As the *Evening Mail* poetically wrote:

He must just have arrived back at the North Strand house ... when death came hurtling from a star-lit sky.[8]

Chapter 11 ~

"WHEN DEATH CAME HURTLING FROM A STARLIT SKY"

There was a blinding flash and a deafening smash, followed by stillness.

(*Irish Times*, 31 May 1941)

It blew up *everything and we went* flying ... *like an earthquake.*

(MAUREEN LYNCH, 78)

It knocked down houses like a pile of snow. Oh, it was dreadful.

(FRANK WEAREN, 91)

A t 2:04 a.m., Tony Gray, Alec Newman and their editor, R. M. Smyllie, were standing outside the *Irish Times* building in Westmoreland Street, where they had been since about 1:30, when the first bombs fell. As they were not taking it "very seriously," as Gray put it, their talk was cheery. People were drawn to stay out on the streets. Smyllie was in a jocular mood after his nightly sojourn across the street in the Palace Bar. He had even been clowning around. From his office he had seized a steel helmet kept for air-raid purposes and a broom beside it. Out on the street he adopted a mock-military posture with the broom over his shoulder, posing as the soldier ready for action. His two subjects no doubt gave him the approval he was seeking. It was harmless enough, Gray recalls, noting that Smyllie "had, inevitably, some drink taken, as they say."[1]

At 2:05 their mood abruptly changed. Like other Dubliners, they had been watching the mysterious plane make its repetitive sweeps and dips over the north of the city. But when the pilot released his screaming cargo, says Gray, they stiffened:

There was a huge flash and the whole sky lit up with a sort of fiery flame, followed by an almighty "crump" sound, the kind of explosion you feel as pressure against your chest as well as hear.

Smyllie, who knew what bombs sounded like, turned white, took off his helmet and said, "Gentlemen, they are not joking. That was a very big one."[2]

The thunderous explosion rocked the city. Smyllie understood its seriousness better than most, having been a civilian internee in Ruhleben camp in Berlin during the First World War. When the fourth bomb violently shook the ground beneath them, he became all business. There was a big story to cover. Immediately, Gray recalls, "we went back into the office to discuss what should be done."[3]

The mighty blast was the grand finale of what had been a two-hour tragic drama, beginning at 12:02 a.m. with the drone of engines followed by searchlights, flares, and anti-aircraft fire. Then the three bombs and the increasing tension of the menacing mystery plane, like a theatrical production in which the sequence of acts first engages, then captivates, the audience, ending with a sudden, apocalyptic climax. A drama perfectly scripted and choreographed for the entire Dublin audience, as reported by the *Irish Times*:

Suddenly the throb of engines sounded, presently growing into a savage crescendo. Pencils of searchlights slowly plotted arcs in the night, hovering now, as like callipers, they seemed to hold the humming menace in their grip. Now anti-aircraft fire split the skies in solemn peals and sharp cracks, and the aeroplane hum rose, and then there was a blinding flash and a deafening smash, followed by stillness.[4]

For observers it was a frightening finale, with hell-fire sky, trembling earth and doomsday cast—as if the "end of the world had come," some said. For many, it had.

———

The bomb struck with a blinding flash, lighting the sky magnificently. "A *big* light," recalls Louis Robinson, "a *flash*, like *fire*." It created a reddish-crimson sunburst effect that threw a terrible beauty over the cityscape. "The sky was like a big sunset," says Nan Davis. People gushed over its splendour, calling it "beautiful", "gorgeous". At first the crimson colour was intense in the clear night sky, but as rising clouds of dust and smoke thickened, its beauty was veiled. Through the haze, it eerily became "a sky lit by a dull red glow," reported the *Irish Times*, an aura of Dante's Inferno.[5] Fires from houses and shops would keep the skyline red and alive for hours to come.

A stentorian noise accompanied the flash. A "deafening explosion," the *Irish Independent* called it.[6] Many times louder than a sonic boom, it penetrated one's brain. Like the "most *dreadful* heavy thunder," says Maura O'Toole. It jolted people's entire body, left them quivering as if they had received a powerful electric shock. Many, like Mrs Eyres, tell of also feeling great pressure in their head, on their temples, like a tight vice. "*Unmerciful*," says Margaret Ladrigan. "Loud enough to wake the dead," people swore. Or "stop your heart," said others. For some, it had done just that. Its deep roar and rumbling swept outwards across the city, through suburbs and beyond.

Buildings of brick, stone and timber shuddered, then toppled into mounds of rubble. Some disintegrated, dissolving like a sand castle caught by a rogue wave. Tremors radiated outwards, causing a vast landscape to tremble. The "explosion echoed right across the city," affirmed Lt-Col Padraic O'Farrell, "and reverberated beyond to parts of Wicklow, Kildare and Meath."[7] Inhabitants of Enniskerry were awakened to feel their houses vibrating and windows rattling.

It all happened within seconds.

As roofs were ripped off, walls crumpled, and windows smashed open, occupants were sent lurching and sprawling about their rooms, colliding with furniture, walls, one another. At St Joseph's Mansions, Dixie Dean, a fair-sized man, was catapulted the full length of his room. "Oh, God, it *threw me* out of the bed … *unbelievable!*" People on staircases and landings found themselves bouncing around and somersaulting down the stairs like awkward circus acrobats. Some were ejected through windows and open walls out into the street. As they were being bashed and bruised, limbs could be heard snapping, followed by cries and moaning. And praying aloud.

At number 4 Gloucester Diamond, Tish Martin had been "looking out the window, and I was sent *flying* across the room. My granny came in in her nightdress; she had a Rosary in her hand, saying, 'Mother of God, pray for us!'"[8] Many tell of being lifted up and flung about as if weightless. Cissie O'Brien—whose father had recently been killed when his British ship was torpedoed by a German submarine and whose two brothers were fated to die similarly in 1943—was beside her mother, trying to get back to sleep after the excitement of the first three bombs:

I was in bed with my mother and we could see the big red flash—and then the big explosion. I thought I was going to be killed. The bed *lifted off the floor* of the house. I threw my arms around my mother as the bed went up *in the air*, and everything came down around us.[9]

Over in North William Street, Mary Dunne saw her mother and baby brother scooped up and carried airborne. "My mother was sitting holding James, the baby, and there was a *huge* big bang! And she was *blown* right across the room! And we were crying and screaming." Seconds later, her granny appeared at their hallway door, screaming, "Oh, my God, my God!" Then the "top landing window came in and she was bleeding with cuts."

Tempests were raging within the rooms, as every object, from heavy furniture to thimbles, was set in motion. Bulky cabinets, beds and tables shifted, lifted, toppled and broke into pieces. Smaller objects, such as lamps, religious statues, mementoes, fell and smashed. Glassware, cups and plates quivered and jitterbugged around before sliding over the edge onto the floor. With everything in the room knocking about and sailing around—including the occupants—some would later liken it to the tornado scene in *The Wizard of Oz*.

The scenes outside were just as turbulent, if not more dramatic, and deadly. When buildings were annihilated by the blast, the bricks, slates, wood and glass were sent flying at high speed in every direction. Chunks of chimney stacks and roofs passed overhead. Poles and beams snapped like matchsticks, as bricks and heavy setts were fired like cannonballs great distances, some crashing through roofs, onto beds, striking people. Entire brick walls cracked, swayed, then toppled over like dominoes on whatever was below. Physical structures left standing were dangerously destabilised.

Nor had the bomb any respect for steel, for, as the *Irish Times* told readers, "tramway lines were twisted and thrown up in the air."[10] Tram rails were crudely coiled upwards seven or eight feet high. Other sections of track were snapped off and tossed airborne, as Agnes Daly can attest. She and her pals were standing in North Clarence Street when suddenly "this piece of tram track, about two feet in length, came *flying over* and landed here. It would have killed someone if it had struck them." Lampposts fared no better. Seemingly immovable objects, they were plucked out and knocked down like bowling pins. Frank Wearen saw, to his astonishment, his lamps uprooted and misshapen:

When the bomb dropped I was in Gardiner Street. I got the blast and I nearly collapsed. *All* my lamps were gone, *blown out* into the middle of the road. And there was no gas. See, the gas main was blown up on the North Strand. Oh, it knocked houses down like a pile of snow.

Brute force that could snap heavy timber beams and bend steel showed little mercy to people caught out on the open street near the point of impact. They were wildly thrown horizontally and vertically, blown along cobblestones and pavement, scraping off skin, slamming into walls and objects in their path, sometimes ricocheting around. Maura O'Toole's father and cousin were going down North William Street when the blast erupted, "and there was only one motor car in the street and it *threw them right under it!* The *force* just *pushed* them under the motor car." As it turned out, "it saved them, because the windows all around them shattered." It uprooted large trees and rolled some cars over as if they were toys. It even knocked an occupied ambulance seventy-five feet down the road. John Doyle, a St John Ambulance Brigade driver, and his orderly, John Maguire, were speeding towards the Summerhill bomb site along Gloucester Street when the big one detonated. A shaken Doyle later gave his account to the *Irish Times*:

> As the ambulance was being driven by John Doyle the bomb struck the North Strand, literally blowing their car twenty-five yards down the road. The radiator burst and the top of the ambulance was struck, the windows smashed, and mudguards splintered with bomb fragments.[11]

As most people caught out in the open were pummelled about, some were thrust upwards and deposited feet or yards away. Often injured, even killed. Several were sucked high up, in tornado manner, above lampposts, even into trees. "The first thing I took note of," remembers Maurice Walsh, "was a huge tree near the bridge, and there was a man's jacket hanging from this great tree … the man was never found." Nearby, however, the *Evening Herald* reported, there was a discovery. "On a roof near Newcomen Bridge a body was found, it is thought the victim was standing on the bridge when the bomb fell and was blown on to the roof."[12] A few days later, Una Shaw recalls, when the authorities were searching other rooftops for missing people, "they found a man's body on the roof of the Strand cinema. It had been blown up there."

Body parts were widely found on roofs, ledges, windowsills, in streets, in gardens. "It was *terrible* to see the pieces of bodies," says Senan Finucane. Rescuers and reporters soon to be arriving on the scene would be horrified to see such gruesome sights. Even veteran firemen and doctors were sickened by people "blown into bits," as many put it. Newspapers would have to be discreet in their coverage. It was not an age in which they printed photographs of dead bodies, or described victims in graphic terms. Nonetheless, even the conservative *Irish Times* told of people "horribly mutilated."[13] Several newspapers wrote of decapitations. The *Evening Herald* described the awful fate of one person. "The headless body of a man was found on the footpath of the North Strand. The head was found one hundred yards away."[14]

Those near the point of impact experienced typhoons of flying fragments and particles—brick, mortar, gravel, slate, wood splinters. And glass, which pelted the skin and eyes, causing countless injuries. Large chunks of brick and mortar blew furiously as if they were dry flower pods caught in an autumn gust. Some tried to outrace the storm of fragments, dodging behind walls or beneath bridges. Most were caught. An *Irish Times* reporter told of one man who "had taken cover near the railway wall near the bridge, but, even so, the blast hammered his back with a hail of gravel."[15] The high velocity of the flying fragments easily cut and embedded themselves in flesh.

Scores of people were caught in blizzards of broken and pulverised glass. In a split second, thousands of windows had simultaneously shattered. Large glass windows in shops and pubs blew out as easily as small panes in rooms. Clara Gill, in her bedroom above her father's pub on the North Circular Road, was startled by the crashing noise of the large window just below her shattering into a million pieces. With so many people still out in the streets and multitudes of foolhardy sky-watchers pressing their noses to windows, it was inevitable that countless injuries, and some deaths, would result.

Flying glass was murderous. Larger pieces mutilated victims, even decapitated. Dagger-sized shards sliced limbs, heads, throats. No sooner had Nurse Ann Leonard arrived at the bomb scene than she was handed her first case, a small boy with a piece of glass deeply embedded in his forehead. Another boy would be found "nearly cut in two" by a large, jagged glass sheet. Smaller glass slivers spun like free-flying scalpels, while particles the size of peas could rob one of one's eyesight. In the wake of the blast, streets were carpeted with sparkling, crunchy glass. Around St Agatha's church was an exotic carpet of brilliantly coloured stained glass from the huge windows— later to be collected and coveted by local children for their games of chainies and "shop."

The bomb's reach and its pattern of destruction mimicked that of an earthquake. From its point of impact shock waves radiated outwards in concentric circles, creating a primary and a secondary blast-force field. The primary zone, affirms Captain Quigley, was readily observable, as "the streets of the North Strand took the most dreadful punishment of the high-explosive bomb."[16] Within a radius of about two hundred yards damage was total or severe, as structures were either demolished or largely collapsed. The secondary zone extended to about half a mile, stretching radially to include Ballybough, Summerhill, Gardiner Street, Seville Place, and Portland Row. Within this district the majority of buildings suffered significant damage to roofs, walls and windows. As Garda Maurice Walsh made his way towards the North Strand he observed how the bomb damage was "scattered out," as he saw that "glass from *all* the shops in Talbot Street was shattered a half a mile away." With each street closer, it became worse. Powerful reverberations extended clear out to Co. Wicklow, to Mullingar and Enniskerry, where houses trembled and some walls and windows cracked.

People some distance away felt the bomb blast in different ways. Some, like Tony Gray over in Westmoreland Street, felt a "crump" sensation on their chest. Like a tight leather strap, some said. Others experienced pressure in their head or on their face, or a blast of warm air. Detective-Sergeant Scully was cycling along the North Circular Road nearly half a mile away when "the bomb fell and he felt a *swish* of air and was lifted off his bike and flung against the wall of a house ... the glass of windows fell on him."[17]

Alec King was miles away at the time, outside his rescue and demolition depot, awaiting the arrival of his men:

> There was a *tremendous* "bang"! And about ten seconds later there was a terrible "*whoof!*" and I got a puff of air on the left side of my face. And I thought, that's no ordinary bomb.

Meanwhile out in Clontarf, about a mile from the North Strand, 22-year-old Muriel Godden and her two sisters had been sleeping in their sturdy Georgian house. Her bed was directly beside a large window. Suddenly, "oh, a terrific explosion, a *terrible force*. It was like a giant hurling himself against the window casement. It was *really* terrifying." The pressure visibly pushed the window in like a balloon about to burst.

After the first three bombs, hundreds of frightened citizens had raced to seek refuge in Garda stations and fire stations around the city. They saw the thick brick structures as safe bunkers, as well as finding security in the presence of uniformed men. Many people around the North Strand pushed their way into Buckingham Street fire station, just around the corner. Though not on duty that night, Jack Conroy had pedalled furiously over to the station on his new bike after the commotion began. He found it already "filled with civilians who got scared and came in for help." Shortly after, when the huge bomb exploded, the entire crowd was lifted clear off their feet and tossed in a mound like turf:

> We were trying to calm the people down. And *with that* the North Strand bomb came down. Only a few hundred yards away. All I know is that whatever percussion there was, we were thrown in a *heap* on the floor. *Thrown down!* Every bell in the place went off and *clouds* of dust came down from the ceiling. It was so near that we all thought the bomb fell in the back yard.

Though damaged, the building stood. No-one inside was injured seriously.

In the wake of the seismic explosion, people would struggle to find an apt description. Most grasped terms from nature's wrath—earthquake, hurricane, tornado. In the Lynches' cottage beside Newcomen Bridge, "it *blew up everything* and we went *flying!*" recounts Maureen Lynch, "like an earthquake in a foreign country." Those within, or near, buildings hammered by the blast told of avalanches of bricks and slate, which trapped and buried some victims. To Bill O'Rourke, who was up on the North Circular Road helping to free the moaning man trapped in Lilly Byrne's basement after the first bomb fell, the big one "seemed to make the whole street go up and down in waves, just like an earthquake."[18] As the ground oscillated, tremors began their outward journey, rumbling along like a train over bumpy track. Those caught flush in turbulent gales of flying debris and glass, like Dermot Ring, drew a different analogy: "It was like a *hurricane!*" Others likened it to being caught unexpectedly in the throat of a tornado or typhoon.

All around the North Strand and environs, people told stories of how their placid world had been shaken violently and cruelly, as if by the hand of an angry God.

———

The deed, however, had been wrought by the hand of man. And with no ordinary bomb.

In the aftermath of the tragedy, military investigators would comb the bomb crater and surrounding ground for evidence of what caused such physical destruction and human carnage. Their findings were conclusive, and astonishing, even to Air Defence Command officers. In air-raid exercises, military officials had not envisaged an event in which such a highly explosive device would be used against neutral Dublin. Yet the proof, readily collected within forty-eight hours, was irrefutable.

It was identified as an extraordinarily powerful 500-pound landmine, one of the most destructive weapons in the German arsenal at that stage of the war, specifically "designed to smash through metal defences and pre-stressed concrete of industrial targets," its sensitive fuse activated instantly by impact.[19] This was to "prevent penetration of the ground so that maximum blast would be obtained … the bomb tore down whole streets, blowing them into dust."[20]

The Luftwaffe used them sparingly, for heavily fortified strategic targets. During the blitz of Belfast in April, hundreds, perhaps thousands of bombs were dropped, of which only seventy-six were of this devastating type.[21] Belfast residents were awed by their horrific destructive power, which took not only a great physical toll but a psychological one as well. Indeed, their "existence was not publicly acknowledged by the British Government until 1944."[22] It was such a bomb that, at 2:05 a.m. on 31 May, screamed down upon the softest of targets: men, women and children sleeping in their beds, in the heart of neutral Dublin.

The bomb's performance depended on a complex set of variables: striking velocity, angle of impact, fuse setting, type of case, nature of filling, charged-weight ratio, and the character of the contact point. Effectiveness was determined by their interaction, but the most critical variable was the density of the impact point. This largely determined the crater's size, depth and adjacent destruction. Bombs falling on earthen, relatively soft or collapsible surfaces penetrated more deeply, their explosive force being partially absorbed, or smothered. This was the case with the first three smaller bombs dropped in Dublin, especially at the Phoenix Park, where it embedded itself in the soil. Conversely, bombs detonating on a hard surface cast outwards their full explosive energy, radiating great distances.

At the North Strand there were two parallel tram tracks running into and out of the city centre. Between these steel rails were thick stone setts. No surface in Dublin was more hard and dense. The 500-pound bomb struck directly on steel and stone, triggering instant detonation at ground level. "It fell on the tram-tracked roadway," verifies Lt-Col O'Farrell. "This means the device did not penetrate unduly, so its blast force was considerable in the built-up areas."[23] Observers on the scene clearly saw the evidence. When Garda Maurice Walsh arrived he immediately noticed that "the bomb dropped *right* in the middle of the tram track. Hit the hard surface, didn't go very far in the ground. Oh, and blasted all the houses." When Louis Robinson wriggled his way through the crowd and stood beside the crater to get a good look, he drew the same conclusion:

> The landmine was a big *huge* thing. It hit the metal tracks and blew *quicker*. If it would have gone deeper, it would have dulled the impact, been a deterrent ... wouldn't have been as devastating on the buildings around it.

It was not, however, solely the explosive burst that wrought such destruction. It was also the powerful *implosive* force, for which German landmines were noted, and feared, a reverse energy thrust resulting from the great "suction created by the explosion seconds later."[24] This cyclonic reflux inhaled mightily across the site just ravaged by explosive power. The implosive suction knocked down, pulled over, peeled away whatever remained. The combined explosive-implosive energy acted as a "one-two punch": what the first blow didn't knock down or tear apart, the second was likely to.

The interaction of the forces created the angry vortex of flying debris and glass, as if a hurricane had followed an earthquake. People witnessed how implosion toppled still-standing houses and walls, sucked up floorboards and linoleum and peeled off wallpaper. In her home Mrs Eyres saw how the "lino on the floor had been sucked up off the ground."[25] Only a few houses away, in Shamrock Terrace, Bernadette Pierce and her granny watched in amazement as "the floorboards were kind of coming away under our feet, like splinters coming up."

To Joe Roche, it was the implosion, more than explosion, that had delivered the knock-out punch. An ARP member living on the south side, he mounted his bike when the bomb fell and headed for the North Strand. In his ARP training he had learnt about the dual destructive forces of certain German bombs. Upon arrival, he scanned the evidence, concluding that it exactly fitted the profile of the landmine:

> The landmine that was dropped there, it exploded *above* the ground—it was designed for that blast effect. It wasn't the blast *out* that caused the trouble, it was the *implosion coming back in again. That* was what did a lot of the damage.

A Department of Defence document later verified that the bomb had "exploded after very little penetration … the resulting cone of the blast was very flat and therefore had maximum effect."[26] A flattened cone was ideally conducive to expansive destruction. As a consequence, affirms Robert Fisk, unimpeded it clearly "deflected the blast into neighbouring houses."[27] Evidently, all the critical variables had integrated exceedingly well for paramount performance. Striking the steel-stone surface had created the optimum detonation for unleashing the bomb's full fury.

In short, the Luftwaffe pilot could not have planned it better. He had delivered the "perfect bomb."

Chapter 12 ✆

| PANDEMONIUM

Fear seized an entire city.
(LT-COL PADRAIC O'FARRELL)

Hysterical *some people were ... with the fright of it.* Panic!
(SALLY BURKE, 86)

There were shrieks and cries of people who rushed on to the street ... there was pandemonium.
(*Irish Times*, 31 May 1941)

Immediately following the terrifying explosion a hush blanketed the North Strand. A great "stillness", the *Irish Times* called it.[1] To many, it was more frightening than what had preceded it.

Mute and motionless, few *dared* to stir. "I just *couldn't* move," they later said. The quiet was eerie. Then, suddenly, it was broken by a weird sound, captured by the *Irish Times*:

> Some seagulls reacted ... after the flash and rumble of the bomb they made the night hideous with their harsh cries and screams. Hundreds appeared as if from nowhere ... and turned erratically in the sky.[2]

Crazed, shrieking seagulls circling above like vultures added to the doomsday cast of the sky.

Survivors were stupefied, their senses numbed. As some would later put it, "the old brain shut down." "You weren't thinking sensibly, or *clearly* or *normally*," explains Louis Robinson, "with something coming out of the sky and blowing the whole thing apart! People totally shocked." Sally Burke, returning home from Summerhill, where her mother was huddled in fear with others in a barber's shop, was caught out in the open street by the blast, stunned and disoriented. "I didn't know *where* I was ... you couldn't think properly. *Confused.* Your *brain* wouldn't move."

People inside their homes, in beds, in basements or crouched beneath tables or staircases, were frozen with fright, with fear that the plane would return any second to drop another bomb. Actually *expecting* the next jolting explosion. Afraid to lift a finger, they dared not move; so they waited.

Many remained motionless for practical reasons, worried that if they shifted even slightly it might disturb something that could bring down a wall or a ceiling upon them. Those pinned down or surrounded by rubble remained still, listening to things ominously settling around them, afraid not only of trying to wriggle free but even to call out for help at first. For those like John McDonald of 158 North Strand it was an agonising predicament. "He was in bed when planks and debris started falling on top of him," wrote the *Irish Times*, "he was only slightly hurt. But the floor held. He remained there for minutes, thinking he was going to be buried alive."[3]

For many people, in those awful seconds, feeling suspended between life and death, praying was comforting. It seemed the only thing one could do, as mothers whispered to their children, "Be *still* now, and *pray!*" Some dared not even reach for their Rosary beads. When the blast struck their cottage in Shamrock Terrace, recalls Bernadette Pierce, her granny was sure "we were goners!" As her granny prayed and feared the worst, young Bernadette felt an inner peace, even joy:

> She didn't know I wasn't afraid of death, and that I thought I was obviously going to Heaven. Now honestly, I *remember* as a child, I always wanted to die before I was seven—or *at* seven. Because you were always told that if you died after you made your Holy Communion you would go *straight* to Heaven.
>
> Now I had made my Communion two weeks before that. So I thought I was getting lifted up to Heaven! I *really*, *honestly* thought I was going to Heaven.

Out in Clontarf, the Goddens were preparing to make their heavenly journey as well. When the first bomb blasts shook their sturdy Georgian house it sent a frightened Mrs Godden and her three daughters—Betty, Muriel and Aileen, aged nineteen to twenty-three—clambering down into the basement beneath the massive granite front steps. Mr Godden had served with the British in the First World War. Every evening he listened to the BBC war reports, and he hung on Churchill's every word whenever he gave a radio address. War was quite real to the Goddens. So, when the big explosion sent tremors through their house, Mrs Godden firmly believed they were in for a blitz—and wouldn't survive. As she held her young son in her arms she readied all the children for Heaven by singing to them. Betty remembers:

I remember *exactly*. It was *quite clear* to us that our mother thought we'd got into a war—and we were all going to be killed! That's why she was singing "Safe in the arms of Jesus ... sweetly my soul shall rest." It was *obvious* she didn't expect us to survive this. She thought we were all going to Heaven.

The hush, the stillness, the soothing hymns and prayers—the proverbial "calm before the storm".

————

The storm of emotion struck when people emerged from their shocked or dazed state and regained their senses. It was then that the full horror of what had happened hit them. Suddenly, says Lt-Col Padraic O'Farrell, Dublin became a "city seized in fear." To Muriel Godden "it just seemed like all your body and soul were taken away with the terror of it." Around the North Strand there erupted what the *Sunday Independent* called mass "havoc."[4] Colleen Heeney saw it as sheer "bedlam".

Emotions broke down. "*Everyone* was crying," recounts Dixie Dean. "People were *terrified!* You could *hear* people crying, *see* them crying ... it was like rivers coming out." All were gripped in the fear that more bombs might fall at any moment. It was a logical assumption, as the four bombs already dropped had the essential character of the start of a real attack, as verified by the Department of Defence:

> These four bombs formed an incident which had all the features of a major air-raid on a small scale; searchlights, anti-aircraft fire, bomb explosions, and fires, with the rise in terror as the tempo of the attack increased.[5]

What else were Dubliners to think? "I thought it was only the start" of a Belfast-type blitz, Eileen Pugh remembers. "We were all under a big round table," Margaret Pringle recalls, "and we all thought he was going to come back—*fear!*" It created a terror even worse than the sudden, unexpected bomb blast itself. As Una Shaw remembers, "you were *waiting* for it, to *happen again!*"

During these moments of awful tension people gradually became aware of unnerving discordant sounds all around them, which heightened their trepidation—buildings still cracking and settling, walls crumbling, glass smashing, slates sliding down and crashing. Snapped electrical wires and tram cables were crackling and sparking; fires were hissing; people were crying and moaning, men shouting, mothers calling out for their children. Children were screaming pitifully for their mammies. Dogs were howling; and the infernal seagulls were still shrieking.

People's first instinctive reaction was to get out of their building. *If* they were able. Winnie Brennan heard the voice of Sammy McIntyre booming throughout her tenement in Mountjoy Place from the hallway door below:

My father leaned over the bannister and said, "What's wrong, Sammy?" Sammy was the ARP man, and he was *shouting* up the stairs, "*Get up, ye lazy sods!* Do you not know a war's on!"

As occupants scrambled down pitch-black stairs they tried not to tumble over one another. Children—crying, trembling, half-awake and some still sound asleep—had to be carried or tugged along, as adults shouted out to one another in desperation.

As people flowed from their houses out onto the streets, partially illuminated by fires, panic could set in when they saw the horrific sights. Winnie Brennan was dumbstruck. "The people, their bodies were *blown out* the walls, and the beds were hanging out, dangling. We could see that." The *Irish Times* described the ensuing scenes:

On the footpaths people in their night clothes, covered with blood, lay moaning, and stretchers with the injured and dead passed to and from the scene of destruction. People trapped in the debris were crying for assistance, little children shouting for their mothers, and mothers who did not know the fate of their families.

From the interior of shattered houses could be heard the faint shouting of men, the screaming of women and children, and the rumble of masonry as it fell. There were shrieks and cries of people who rushed on to the street … there was pandemonium.[6]

Once outside, they faced mass confusion. "People didn't know *what* to do," says Dixie Dean, "so they were running *all over* the place … shouting, crying, looking for their own, trying to help people. There was *chaos*."

Feeling frantic, people had an overwhelming compulsion to run—anywhere. As they tore madly in all directions, Kathleen Martin saw many who were hysterical. Many were in their night attire, some with a coat, shawl or blanket slung over their shoulders. Slipping and stumbling in streets littered with glass, sharp objects, and heaps of debris, they carried infants and dragged children along. Throngs fleeing the scene streamed down Amiens

Street towards the city centre; others went out the North Circular Road. Many headed to Fairview Park and the open spaces, perceived as safer from German bombers. When Jack Conroy and his mate from Buckingham Street fire station ran headlong into the sea of humanity churning down Amiens Street he saw delirium in their faces—"*mobs* of people, all running away! *Hysterical* ... shouting and screaming."

Many of them, Margaret Pringle recalls, were running aimlessly, "running *here*, running *there* ... from fear." Like sheep, they could get caught up in a flock of panic-stricken runners and be carried along. Others ran alone in their fear. Una Shaw's father dashed out of their house in Rutland Street to see about his brother Joe, who lived down in Portland Row:

> A poor unfortunate woman, dressed only in her night clothes, came *running* and *screaming* hysterically, in the centre of the road. He grabbed her and flung her down, and held her there until an ARP warden came and took her away.

Just down the street, Sally Burke was trying to keep pace with her father. The two of them were heading home to Portland Place from the Summerhill bomb site when the big explosion quaked the ground beneath their feet. Her father, wide-eyed with fear, broke into a full gallop:

> We heard the big "*booom!*" The bomb hadn't fell very far from us—and he *ran*. He said to me, "*C'mon!*" And I was *running* down Portland Row, trying to hold on to my father's jacket. He forgot about me 'cause he had such a fright.

Meanwhile, havoc reigned in "Heaven, Hell and Purgatory" as the three lanes became jammed with scared souls, many no doubt believing they were facing ascension or descent to their final destination—or an eternal reservation in Limbo. Quite a number had been drinking heavily on Whit Friday night, not thinking clearly even before the bomb blast. When the cottages burst into pieces and flames shot up, the lane-dwellers, in a fit of terror and muddled confusion, herded against one another, stumbled, fell, cursed. With everyone out on the cobblestones scurrying frantically about, it was like an ant colony under attack.

On the other hand, some survivors ran purposefully to specific destinations, most often to see about other family members nearby, or to seek refuge in their home. This sometimes meant having to temporarily leave behind their children, who were already frightened enough. When Margaret Ladrigan's mother burst out the door of their house in Synnott Street, headed for her sister's house, young Margaret was determined to follow:

> My mother had a sister, Maggie, up on the North Strand, with three
> children. And she cried out, "The North Strand is bombed! I'll have to get
> up there!" So Mammy goes out *quick* as she could. And I was crying,
> "Mammy, Mammy, please don't go!"
>
> And I'm *running after* her … "Mammy, please come back!" And I
> remember walking on the glass, all crunchy under my feet, and the noise.
> The place was *littered* with glass. And I was running, and she'd turn and
> say to me, "You go back, *go back*; you *can't* come with me!" "Mammy, no,
> don't go, don't go!" I *tried* to catch her.

Amidst the commotion, other family members were sometimes inadvertently
left behind. Over at number 21 North Clarence Street following the explosion
Agnes Daly, the youngest of eleven children, had crowded with her brothers
and sisters "up against the hot wall of our house—the fireplace was at this wall
and it was always hot." At first they felt secure together; then, realising that
their house had been seriously damaged, "we *ran* up this lane into Walkers'
house for safety." In the turmoil of the moment they forgot and left one
behind: their cat, named Hitler.

One man, by the name of Boyle, ran forth, then back. He lived at number
127 North Strand, and on hearing the first two bombs he ran over to see about
his mother, who lived in Richmond Street. While he was gone the big
explosion hit. He tore back homewards, only to find "his house was
completely demolished, and he had no news of his wife and child."[7]

A number of men ran directly to the most unlikely of spots—the edge of
the bomb crater. Not out of curiosity but for safety. Their rationale was based
on the old belief about lightning never striking the same spot twice. Lt-Col
O'Farrell explains their folly:

> A typical pishrogue of the [London] blitz was faithfully observed in the
> capital of the land where superstition was weaned—the belief that "they
> never bomb the same building twice."[8]

And there the men remained until the police and LSF showed up to push them
behind the cordons.

———

As pandemonium reigned in the streets, there was tumult within the damaged houses. The meanly combined explosive-implosive forces tore apart roofs, walls and window frames, leaving dwellings in perilous shambles. Hundreds of occupants who had been injured, trapped or partially buried were struggling to escape, or awaiting rescue. Some situations were desperate. Victims groped about in dark rooms with no lighting and with thick clouds of choking dust and smoke. With everything knocked asunder, their own homes felt unfamiliar. Inching their way along, they sought to get their bearings and find doors and staircases. Often only to discover that banisters and staircases were loose or completely missing—all the while calling out fearfully to one another. It was particularly frustrating for those frantically fingering around for their glasses—or teeth. Nothing was in its proper place.

In Synnott Street, thirteen-year-old Kathleen Martin's granny "had cataracts and she couldn't see without her glasses, and she's *roaring* out for her glasses." Kathleen's mother was able to slowly guide her own elderly mother down to safety; then she decided to rush back inside with the help of a fire's glow on the street to retrieve a few personal items. Her arms full, she went running back out of the building, unable to see what was in front of her, and fell into an open manhole and injured her legs. When she was later being lifted into a St John ambulance the orderly seemed oddly delighted. "This lady said to her, 'Isn't this *wonderful*. All our training didn't go amiss, now we're able to *use* our training.'"

At their tenement dwelling in Mountjoy Place, Winnie Brennan's younger brother Paddy was found, "lying *flat out*, with the window and half the wall on top of him. He was confused, saying, 'Who's throwing bricks on top of me?'" A short distance away, in Synnott Street, Margaret Ladrigan couldn't find her missing little brother. The family were frantic. There was "terrible destruction, windows blown in and the roof, our furniture was in bits and pieces." After picking themselves up off the floor, everyone had begun searching for the child. "I kept saying, 'Where's Seán? Where's Seán?'" They quickly found that he had been "blown out and *under* the bed." Their fear was that he had been blasted out into the street, as happened to others. As the *Irish Independent* reported, "many people were blown from the wreckage of their homes and lay injured on the sidewalks."[9] Or dead.

When their houses collapsed on them, injured victims were commonly knocked unconscious or pinned down. When their minds cleared, they sought to regain equilibrium and escape from the dangerous dwelling as quickly as possible. But many found themselves precariously trapped. When the houses had been jolted by the blast, even those still standing were knocked out of alignment, which jammed windows and doors. This impeded their exit as well as entry by those trying to reach them. They could become panicky to escape, especially when hearing the structure still cracking and settling around them. For the elderly, the most helpless, it was terrifying. Trapped residents often had to wait many hours—for some, days—for rescuers to find and free them with crowbars, axes, ladders and ropes.

A remarkable number, however, escaped through their own survival instincts and efforts, or with assistance from relatives and neighbours. At number 26 North Strand, a Miss Dempsey's house had been hammered hard:

> Miss Dempsey was in bed when the walls crumbled in around her. She struggled out and jumped down from her bedroom window. She then secured a roof ladder and placed it against the wall. In this way, she rescued her mother unhurt from the wrecked building.[10]

After saving her mother, she discovered an injury to her knee. Undeterred, she took the risk of going back inside the tottering dwelling to retrieve a precious statue of Our Lady. At about that time, twelve-year-old Colleen Heeney was frightened to find herself cut off from the rest of her family. She had been sleeping when the sky turned a fiery red and their house broke apart. She awoke to hear her mother calling for her to immediately come down to the kitchen, where the rest of the family were gathered:

> I jumped out of bed and *ran*. But I couldn't go down the stairs, because the wall had collapsed between the kitchen and the hall and all the rubble was on the steps. My father and brother had to make a clearing to get me down.

At number 158 North Strand, John McDonald faced a particularly difficult challenge. Having been pinned in his bed when planks and other debris fell on him, he remained stone-still for several tense minutes, fearing a total collapse and possible burial if he so much as moved a hand or a foot. Finally, he realised that he *must* try to free himself before the situation became worse:

> He was only slightly hurt … as he began trying to wriggle free. Roars and cries of pain came to him, especially from the next house where there seemed to be children. Eventually, he struggled free. Then he thought of Mrs. Bryson who was living next door. When he found her there was a heavy beam pinning her down by the legs. He extricated her and, then, hearing the cries of Mrs. Nora Grafton somewhere in the remains of the same building, he found her trapped in a room.[11]

However, he couldn't reach her, because bars on her windows blocked him. Through the dark and the debris he could barely make out her pleading figure. Unable to dislodge the bars, he crawled with the greatest caution to the rear of the building, where he finally succeeded in prying open her back door. She welcomed him with open arms as he dug her free and pulled her to safety. Then, "as he knew everyone living nearby," he remained to assist rescue parties for several hours, despite his own injuries.[12]

What John McDonald could not have known, however, was that directly next door, in number 157, four new residents had temporarily moved in only half an hour earlier, in the middle of the night. The displaced McLoughlin family had just come down from their damaged home in Summerhill to take refuge with Mrs McLoughlin's mother. The "roars and cries of pain" he had heard were in all likelihood from the ill-fated McLoughlins.

As people fled the scene for their own safety, others remained behind, sometimes at considerable risk, to help victims. Outsiders also rushed in to help those injured and trapped. Michael Fox, described by the *Irish Press* as "a variety artiste", dashed to Newcomen Bridge when he heard the explosion.[13] There "he saw a hand sticking up through the debris and rescued a woman alive."[14] Then he trotted up to 161 North Strand and "freed a child, a woman, and an old man." Similar stories of selflessness would later emerge. Most went unrecorded in the press.

Dixie Dean raced from St Joseph's Mansions straight to the bomb scene to try to assist those in need, only to find that there was little he could do:

> I went to the Strand—and there was *chaos*. We run all around the place, *trying* to help the people ... but we couldn't *do* anything. You couldn't actually move the debris ... but you could hear crying. Ah, yes, they were. There was a man there and a sheet of glass went through his leg. But we had *nothing*! People were shouting, they didn't know *what* to do. Oh, it was desperate!

Local women, especially those with nursing experience, opened their homes, if not too badly damaged, as makeshift first-aid stations. They tried to stop bleeding, clean out wounds, do bandaging with what they had at hand, ripping sheets and garments apart. Their on-the-spot treatments, as simple as they were, undoubtedly diminished suffering and may well have saved some lives.

Mary Cooke's grandfather wanted to do his part as well. Without a moment's delay he headed from his tenement in Lower Gardiner Street up to the North Strand. He was in the local ARP and had served with the British forces in the First World War, where he witnessed plenty of bloodshed and death. He thought he had seen it all. But he soon returned from the bomb scene, badly shaken:

I *always remember* him coming back with the story. The *first* thing, he saw a man, a Corporation street-sweeper, out working that night, and this street sweeper had no head—his head had been decapitated. Just out sweeping the streets—and his head *blown off!*

Children had their own fears. During the chaos their greatest dread was being separated from their mothers. They clung tightly. Orphans, however, were deprived of such security. At the Sisters of Charity convent in North William Street there lived ninety motherless children, aged three to seventeen. When the blast shattered the large windows in the middle of the night Chrissie Byrne heard their cries from her home down the street:

The orphanage was just up the street and, *oh*, the *screams* of them children. The whole glass of the orphanage came out into the street. Oh, the children were terrified … the *screams* of them!

They had good reason to be so frightened, explained the *Irish Times*, as the convent was "midway along the path straddled by the bombs."[15] The first two bombs had detonated on one side of them, quite close. Then the large one exploded just on the other side, even closer. Within seconds, Sisters Philomena, Ita, Kevin and Louise rushed into the dormitory to calm their fears. The older children helped to hold the little ones, who could not stop shaking. About an hour later, wrote the newspaper, "when the refugees began to arrive, those older children in the dormitories took the mattresses from their beds and carried them downstairs—without even being told."[16] The convent would accommodate hundreds of homeless people over the coming days, as the orphans were taken over to Mount Prospect convent. The next day the *Irish Times* described the convent children as among the "bravest of all in the stricken area."

But many children were more afraid of entering a convent in the night than of being bombed again, fearful that if they were taken in they might never come out. Children who misbehaved were commonly threatened by parents with being taken over to the convent and "left with the nuns." Una Shaw remembers it as a dreadful threat and one that was much on the minds of children that night as they were led into several convents by their homeless parents in the pitch dark:

So the children, of course, they were frightened—to have to stay *overnight*. Because you always had a fear then, as a child—"You better behave yourself now—or it's around to the nuns!" So you can *imagine* some

children having to go in there that night—thinking they'd *never get out!*
Oh, they were frightened.

Children whose homes were blown apart faced a different sort of harrowing
experience. In the old days, hair from horses and other animals was used in
the plaster mixture for making walls, creating an environment in which
insects nested and bred prolifically. There were countless varieties, from gnat
size to cockroaches several inches long. When the bomb tore open walls and
ceilings, colonies of insects swarmed out in their own state of frenzy,
scurrying across floors, climbing onto people, sometimes biting. Children like
Margaret Ladrigan were horrified by the creatures:

> They were all very old houses, and these big beetles were running across
> the kitchen floor. Big, shiny-black four or eight-legged creatures, running
> around after the bomb. A cockroach! They had nests. *Running* across the
> floor. Well, I was more terrified of them than the bombing. I was saying,
> "Mammy, Mammy!"

In retrospect, more than half a century later, many women avow that they
were more traumatised that night by the fear of convents or insects than they
were by German bombs.

As crowds were fleeing in the streets, others were scrambling down
basement stairs for refuge. Hundreds descended on the nearby Charleville
Mall Library, hoping to squeeze into its cavernous basement. Among them
was Mary Dunne, who was carried over from North William Street through
glass-strewn debris in the strong arms of her uncle, a well-known local
chimney-sweep, Johnny Rooney:

> When we crossed from our house to go to the Charleville Mall, I looked
> down the street and it was all *ablaze,* and a huge big gas main on fire. And
> nothing but broken glass; that's why children were being carried. So we
> went in and I'd say there was maybe two hundred to three hundred people.
> Oh, it was *packed.* Yeah, because they had brought in people who were, say,
> the "walking wounded". There was a lot of praying, and a lot of shouting.

The library basement was being used as a makeshift first-aid centre as well as
a refuge shelter. Injured victims cried out in pain, and babies bawled all
through the night. Nonetheless, it felt safer than being out in the
pandemonium of the streets. But there would be little sleep.

Meanwhile, around Mountjoy Place and adjacent streets, many residents
rushed over to Mountjoy Square, seeking entry to one of the city's few

underground air-raid shelters. As a crowd massed, they found the door padlocked. Assuming that the keyholder would show up at any moment, they waited anxiously. Finally, the local ARP warden arrived, to a show of relief but with no key in hand. Instead, remembers Winnie Brennan, who was among the frustrated group, he made an announcement. "He said, 'We're waiting, trying to make contact with whoever the keyholder is.'" Then he disappeared, leaving the people standing in confusion. "After a while he came back and said, 'The keyholder lives on the North Strand, and that's a no-go—so we want you all to go down to your basements.'" The same predicament was occurring elsewhere with locked above-ground shelters. Near Margaret Ladrigan's house "there were two shelters, but they couldn't *find the keys!*" The Corporation's bungling of the locked shelters would later ignite a firestorm of criticism from citizens and the press.

Winnie Brennan's family and all the other tenants along Mountjoy Place were told by the ARP warden to first gather in front of their buildings before descending into the basement—why, she didn't know. But everyone followed orders. "*All* the houses assembled—a *lot* of people—out on their steps. Some brought a piece of bread in case they got hungry later." Most didn't have such foresight amidst the commotion. Then the warden shouted out orders to march down into the damp, dank basements. As women and children began moving, many men hesitated. Then Winnie's father spoke out:

> I heard my father say—and this is as true as God—"*I'm not* going into any basement!" he says to the other men, "I'm going down to the pub—they'll open up on a night like this." And all the men thought this was a great idea.
>
> And so *all* the men left *all* the women and children and went down to the pub! If it wouldn't have been open, they'd get your man *up!* And they stayed there all night. They *did!* All the women and all the children were left. And all crying.

This scene was being played out along other streets as well, as publicans opened their doors to men with shattered nerves and a great thirst, but little sensitivity. Those men who sought their refuge in pubs during that long, frightful night, abandoning their wives and children, were to be long remembered for their shameful behaviour.

Once down in the dark, stenchful catacombs of Winnie Brennan's tenement, the women and children had to share space with a "spunker" (homeless man) long in residence there, much to their dismay:

> Your man in the basement, he was lying on his rags and sacks. And he had orange boxes all around, so we all sat on the boxes. My sister sat on one

and I sat on my mother's knee. And all the time I'm saying, "Oh, God, leave me alive till I make my first Confession, 'cause I thought I'd go straight to Hell if I didn't make my first Confession.

Anyway, then the Rosary started. And what depressed me was the horrible, damp smells, and your man never washed; he hadn't got a tap. He *never washed, all* his life. His fingers were *black!* Poor man. Anyway, when the Rosary was over the old man got out a brown scapular. I think it was a Franciscan one. But the man probably had it on him since the day he was born! And he took it out, and as he opened his chest—the *dirt!* And the women were *gagging*.

And he said, "Now everyone is to kiss this, and we'll all be safe." So he went around ... oh, and he came to me, and I was trying to keep away from the smell of him. And my mother had to kiss it and he banged it up against her face—and she nearly *gagged*. And the next thing, at the *top* of her voice, she shouted, "Jesus, if the Jerries don't kill us, we'll be poisoned to death!" I swear to God—she just couldn't resist.

In other tenement areas the occupants tended to congregate in the rooms of those whom they trusted in times of crisis. Most commonly it was that of a wise, strong granny who served as community caretaker. In Mary Cooke's tenement room at 91 Lower Gardiner Street tenants flocked to the door seeking security with her granny, who always handled any trouble in the house:

> There was a terrible shake in the old tenement ... there was tremblers. Oh, everyone was awake, and there was ten families, and they *all* come into our room. See, it was my granny's room too, a room that people would go to if there was any trouble. Because people were really shocked that night, very much afraid, and I remember well in the room there was great fear. And some of the men had brought whiskey to be taken ... because of shock.

In many tenement rooms, men supped as women and children prayed.

Virtually no-one sought safety in the overground "hat-box" shelters. "*Nobody* went in there the night of the bombing," testifies Maura O'Toole. Mary Cooke confirms the same about residents along Lower Gardiner Street and surrounding streets. "There was no way" that they would enter them, feeling safer in basements or under tables and chairs and stairways.

This prompted some ARP wardens, having failed to coax people into the shelters, to begin forcibly herding them in, even if they resisted. This created a fear of its own. As the *Irish Times* benignly phrased it, "the ARP wardens and fire brigade prevailed upon people to go into the shelters."[17] The victims—as they saw themselves—tell a different story. Colleen Heeney, her family and their neighbours were rounded up and *forced* in, very much against their will. "The shelter was dirty, and everybody from all the houses around were all *shovelled in*, all huddled together. You know, '*Get in! Get in!*'" Being forcibly crammed into fetid concrete blocks caused people to feel panicky, claustrophobic, even ill. They felt like "dungeons", says Bernadette Pierce. It churned up a desperation to get out. Those who had been pushed to the back walls cried out for release.

Tish Martin was watching the shelter outside her home in Gloucester Diamond being filled up with resisting neighbours. "All you could see were old people being dragged into the shelter … the old people were praying and saying, 'We'll all be blown up!'"[18] Just then her mother called to her to take her own grandmother down into the shelter before it became full. She had no choice. Her granny was "in her nightdress, her Rosary beads in her hands, saying, 'Mother of God, pray for us!'" As she was leading her down the stairs she encountered her cousin Lizzy, rushing up frantically with her new baby wrapped in a plaid blanket. Seeing that Tish was on her way down, "she told me to take the baby into the air-raid shelter." Which she was glad to do. However, she found that she could not assist her frail granny and hold the baby at the same time. "So I put the baby on the table; he was fast asleep." As soon as she had escorted her grandmother inside the shelter she would return and collect the infant.

As all this hubbub was going on—the pandemonium in the streets, people struggling to escape damaged houses, seeking refuge in basements, convents and the library, men heading to pubs, and firemen, policemen and rescue services desperately rushing towards the scene—another drama was being enacted, one not covered by the press.

It was being carried out by a relatively small number of local people, mostly—but not solely—men and boys, who were out on the streets for a different purpose: looting. Many shops and pubs had been blown apart, or at least blown open. Merchandise was strewn about the streets, pathways, shop windows and floors. It was a great temptation for scavengers to scoop up the pickings.

Most looting took place during the first thirty minutes or so, at the peak of chaos, before the authorities had arrived to halt it. For most, it was probably more a quick reflex action than a deliberate moral decision to steal. During those first frenetic minutes normal social order was temporarily suspended, and clear, deliberate thinking was impaired. All sorts of shops were blown open: grocers', butchers', general provisions, clothing, newsagents'. And pubs. Men concentrated on gathering up bottles of drink, women on the food items and clothing, and children on the sweets and toys. Upon hearing the explosion, Gabriel Molony ran from his home in Fairview Strand to Newcomen Bridge in record time, thereupon encountering several scenes of looting:

> I *ran* all the way down, and there was fires in all the shops, particularly a grocery store; it used to sell spirits and everything. And Rafferty's as well, they sold sweets and things. And people went in to get things—to *rob* them. Oh, they *were*. See, it was all debris and flames and smoke all over the place. And fellas taking whiskey—and then they had a late-night session! Then the police were on the scene, and they were all stopped then.

Similar looting incidents were taking place along other streets as even little huckster shops were cleaned out. Sally Burke watched it happen just outside her house in North William Street:

> It was a little shop that was blown to pieces, only a little huckster shop. Stuff *blown* all over the place: tea, sugar and milk, and whatever. And I needn't tell you what was coming out of that shop—they *robbed everything!* 'Cause the shop blew apart and everything went out onto the road. They were *running* away with boxes of sweets and chocolates and bread … robbing everything. Oh, everyone had a hooley!

Even children were faced with temptations, and decisions. At Doyle's shop on Ballybough Road the large front window had been shattered clean out. For eight-year-old Maura O'Toole this posed a serious moral quandary. She had long admired a particular doll in the window. And now there it sat—just waiting to be lifted out. She and her pal Patty stood together within reach of the doll, looking at it, then at each other. "I was going to take it out of the window … and *all* the sweets you could have!" They hesitated for another half minute or so, just long enough for her father to show up beside her and remove all temptation. "He wouldn't *allow* us, told us not to touch a thing—but they were *all* taken!"

What was looting to one man was serendipity to another. When Fagan's pub was blasted wide open, looters began running off with the booty, until their illicit activity was halted by the police. Guards and LSF men were then posted at the pub to keep thieves away. As the night wore on, they grew thirsty; so did other policemen, firemen, ARP and LDF members. Dust and smoke parched their lungs. The publican was nowhere in sight. What harm could there be in having a small sup in the midst of a crisis to soothe a burning throat and treat dehydration—all in the line of duty? Somewhere around 4 a.m. the pub was discreetly opened to firemen, police and rescue forces. Garda Maurice Walsh, then only twenty-one, was on the scene and recalls how men partook of refreshments without a pang of conscience—under the circumstances:

> Fagan's pub was *completely* shattered. The roof came off—no roof at *all*. Shattered ... oh, 'twas open! And the publican wasn't there at all. And you could see all the bottles in there. And so we were all in there, for refreshments, and there was drink, *free* drink, for firemen, ARP men ... And we were in there having a drink and sharing things. I remember there was a fireman serving the drink—and you could have *anything* you wanted. Ah, nothing wrong with it, 'cause the publican was gone anyhow, you know.

To the best of his recollection, not a single man abused the privilege. Nor did they linger. After having a quick drink and a few minutes' break and chat they returned directly to duty. No different from visiting the mobile canteen for a mug of tea or Bovril. And it fortified them for more long hours ahead.

The looting by citizens took place so swiftly, amid such turmoil and before newspaper reporters were on the scene, that it was witnessed only by local people, most of whom were reluctant to talk of it later. The looters themselves perhaps regarded their actions as simply salvaging items blown out onto open streets and destined to be destroyed under foot or under the tyres of rescue vehicles. Those who actually entered shops to steal items could explain their behaviour in the confession box. Newspapers, which later heard a few of the looting stories from reliable witnesses, would have to contend with their own conscience in deciding whether or not to report the incidents in print—for all Dublin to read. Should they bring shame on a community already on its knees?

———

No scene that night was more bizarre than that witnessed by Bernadette Pierce and her granny from the doorway of their home in Shamrock Terrace. Dick Eyres had given orders to his ARP men to be on the lookout for victims who appeared so shell-shocked or dazed that they were drifting aimlessly, unable to seek safety or to care for themselves. They could be identified by their vacant eyes, expressionless face, detached sense of calm, showing no fear or normal awareness. Some stood still, others shuffled along.

Eyres decided that they needed to be rounded up and taken, for their own protection, down to the end of Shamrock Terrace to the large brick arches of the Dublin Corporation yard where lorries were normally kept. This would serve as a temporary first-aid station until the Red Cross could properly look after them. As it turned out, they all had to be led directly past the front door of Bernadette Pierce's cottage. She and her granny stood in perfect silence in their hallway, door wide open, as they watched the eerie procession:

Anyone who was traumatised, they steered them down into the cleared-out arches. All together. I remember *hundreds* of people, walking like zombies, down the terrace, in their night attire. They didn't know *where* they were. They had probably been blown out of their houses, and they were shocked.

They weren't screaming, they were *moaning* and *wailing*, you know, just shocked! Just walking in their night attire down the street. That's one thing I remember, the moaning and wailing … but not screaming. And the terrace was like a scene from a horrible horror film … hundreds of people walking like zombies. Zombies!

In their night garb they seemed to float ethereally past, like druids in shrouds, a ghostly procession against a backdrop of fiery glow, smoke, dust and rubble, a surreal image to be replayed in nightmares for years thereafter.

The ARP wardens who had forced people into the concrete shelters were facing a rebellion after twenty or thirty minutes. People felt imprisoned, desperate to be released into the open air. The rise in body heat, the stagnant, stenchful air and sounds of human distress became insufferable. Women fainted. Colleen Heeney recalls: "We were in the shelter, and it could have been a half an hour later then when they let people come out. And they were addressing each other, 'Oh, *thank God*, Josie!'" Over at the shelter in Gloucester Diamond, Tish Martin and her granny, as well as all the other captives around them, were frantic for freedom. When they finally got word that they were to be let out into the night air, the whole mob burst through the door as if in a jail break.

Once outside, Tish was immediately met by her cousin Lizzy, who was in a state of high anxiety:

Lizzy said to me, "*Where* is the baby?" "*Holy God!*" I said; "I *left him* on the table in the parlour!" There he was, *still* fast asleep. He slept through the entire air raid.[19]

Chapter 13 ❧

RESCUERS UPON A "HELLISH SCENE"

It was like a battlefield*!*

(ANN LEONARD, NURSE, 84)

We were faced by a hellish scene ... nothing left.
Devastation! *Poor unfortunate people blown to blazes. It*
was as if we were in a different world.

(ALEC KING, RESCUE OFFICER, 82)

U pon hearing the almighty explosion and seeing the fiery sky, rescue
services from every corner of Dublin hastily converged on the North
Strand. As they approached the scene from all directions they collided
in the streets with a torrent of humanity headed outwards, resulting in
clogged chaos, as the two groups fought their way around one another, one
desperate to get in, the other desperate to get out. According to the *Irish Press*,
"thousands of A.R.P. workers were on duty within fifteen minutes ... they
received great assistance from members of the L.D.F. and L.S.F." [1] And from the
fire brigade, gardaí, soldiers, Red Cross and St John Ambulance Brigade.
Before long there were too many rescuers on the scene.

As Alec King, chief rescue and demolition officer, found on his arrival, it
created mayhem, because "there was *no organisation* at the North Strand."
Rescuers anxiously searched through the crowds, trying to find fellow-
members of their units and officers in charge to get official orders for action.
For St John Ambulance nurse Ann Leonard and the legion of other "first-
responders" it was "one mass of confusion," creating frustration. She knew
that valuable time was being lost.

The fire brigade and Gardaí, as front-line forces in any emergency, were
immediately despatched from stations all over the city. Thanks to Major
Comerford's rigorous training, the men of Dublin Fire Brigade were in peak
form, racing out on their engines well within their allotted sixty seconds.
Many had been baptised under fire in Belfast only six weeks before. They

knew what they faced. Those already on the first bomb sites at Summerhill and the North Circular Road quickly gathered up their gear and sped down to the North Strand. Support crews were needed as "the on-coming watch in the fire stations joined those already on the scene, and those on leave were called in from their homes to cover the fire stations."[2]

For the first time since the Civil War, the whole of Dublin Fire Brigade was called into action. Their Leyland and Merriwether fire engines, though not the most modern, were well made and reliable. "It was a *good* fire engine," Jack Conroy testifies. The larger pumps could put out 700 to 900 gallons per minute, while the smaller ones had a capacity of 120 to 150 gallons. This, of course, was dependent on the proper flow and pressure of water. In normal fires, water mains didn't break.

At the Tara Street station the fire brigade also had two ambulances, left over from the Spanish Civil War. "Like a field ambulance," explains Paddy Finlay, "You could put six stretchers in them—like bread racks." They were seldom needed, as they were meant for battlefield conditions with numerous casualties. However, they had been useful in several large tenement fires where there were a number of injuries, and even deaths. For firemen back in the early forties, deaths had a double meaning, Paddy Finlay confides:

> When you brought in a BID—that's "brought in dead"—to the hospital you received a pound from the doctor. He gave you a pound note, to the fireman. Because he used to get six pounds for the PM—the post-mortem. They'd often say, "Don't forget now, get as many as you can and bring them in"—they made a bid!

Bringing in dead bodies was always tragic—but profitable.

As firemen were arriving on their engines, policemen were making a beeline to the scene. Most had to walk, but a few had transport. Twenty-one-year-old Mossie Walsh was a raw recruit who lived in Rathmines Garda station. He was still adjusting to city life in Dublin. At 2:06 he heard a loud shout to wake up:

> I had finished my duty that night. There was maybe twenty of us in the station. We were in bed, waiting to go on duty again in the morning. Then we were all called up—"*Get ready to go!*"—to the North Strand, where the bomb had dropped. The truck came from the depot to transport us all. So we donned our metal helmets and off we went!

Senan Finucane and his mates at Kevin Street barracks didn't have the luxury of transport. No buses or trams were running in the middle of the night, and they would have to hotfoot it over from the Liberties on their own. Garda Finucane had not needed to be roused by a bark to "*get up!*": he had heard the screaming bomb descending:

> You heard the bomb falling from the sky, then an *awful* explosion. We were called in, every available man was to go over—"*Everybody out*, get over to the scene of the bomb!" Oh, you'd be inclined to say a prayer, all right.
>
> We were told to have a quick cup of tea, and *off*. We had to walk over, because there were no buses at that time of night. *Everybody* was heading to that scene, walking—the *whole of Dublin* wanted to see. There was so many people it was just like a Saturday in town, same as O'Connell Street during the day on Saturday.

The hurried trek over was made more difficult because "we had steel helmets—war helmets. First time we ever wore them. It was a few pounds weight and very severe on your head; you'd tire wearing that." All along the way, people pestered them with questions, slowing them down. It became annoying.

————

Out on the Naas Road, Noel Brady had been standing in front of his parents' house with a few fellow-members of the St John Ambulance Brigade. They had watched the bomb blasts at Summerhill and the North Circular Road. By two o'clock they had decided to get some sleep and wait for a call to duty the the next morning, if they were needed. A few minutes later they changed their minds. Each raced home, put on their uniforms, grabbed their medical pouches and mounted their bicycles:

> We heard the bomb, and the sky got *all red*. We seen the flash. I figured a *big* bomb had been released. We didn't *wait*: I hopped on my bike and *down to the North Strand!*

He had joined the St John Ambulance Brigade only a year earlier, taking the six-week training course to become an orderly. It included lectures by doctors as well as intensive instructions on "how to treat wounds, bandage, control haemorrhages, treat fractures" and so forth. His medical kit even included a "fits stick" with a rubber piece on it, to place in the mouth of a person suffering an epileptic fit. He enjoyed the training and passed his test with flying colours. Technically, he felt well prepared.

Emotionally, however, he was a bit shaky. When he joined he was chided by mates who knew that, from childhood, he could get queasy and feel faint at the sight of even a little blood. Why had he joined the ambulance brigade, they wondered. Somehow, he had been able to tuck the fear in the back of his mind. Now, as he was cycling through the dark streets towards the bomb scene, he was giving it plenty of thought. "*That* was my main worry going down that night: *blood!* Would I get weak?" He knew he wouldn't have to wait long to find out.

By contrast, Ann Leonard, a young nurse in her early twenties, also in the St John Ambulance Brigade, was supremely confident. Nursing was her calling. Since childhood she had wanted to become a nurse, like her mother. "It came as second nature to me, playing with my dollies, bandaging them up and all—it was *in* me." She had no apprehension about treating people severely injured, in pain, bleeding; no misgivings at all about how she might perform in a real tragedy. "I was never a nervous person. I had nerves of steel."

Shortly after two o'clock she and her friend May, a fellow-nurse, were on their way home from the Whit Friday dance. Her feet were sore from wearing her new shoes for the past six hours. The two young women were talking about the fun of the Whit weekend ahead:

> The next thing, the bomb went off. Oh, God, it was *dreadful*—the *noise* of it. And I said, "May, that's a bomb!" And she said, "Well, he's been going around for the last hour and a half!" We were *panic-stricken!* And May said, "What do you think?" and I said, "Go home and get into your uniform— we're in for a tough night.

Over at Buckingham Street fire station, just around the corner from the North Strand, Jack Conroy and the crowd of frightened citizens who had taken refuge there were struggling to their feet after having been thrown "into a heap" by the blast. As he helped some of the older ones to their feet, he tried to offer reassuring words to everyone around him. But he couldn't remain with them, he explained, because he was needed *immediately* at the scene.

He pushed his way through the mob to grab his slicker, boots and helmet. Then he pivoted around to join his crew on their fire engine—only to realise that neither was there. In the commotion at the station he had completely forgotten that the duty crew of five men and their one engine had already been sent to the scene of the first bombings. Like himself, one other off-duty fireman had shown up at the station on his own. "There were just two of us there, 'cause the engine was out in Summerhill!" With the station bell still clanging and dust covering everything and everybody, he and his lone partner stood for a moment looking blankly at one another. Then they wriggled their way through the crowd out onto the street, their heavy boots making a flopping sound. Without a word exchanged, they began running down Amiens Street, in full firefighting gear, against a tide of frightened people:

> Just the two of us there, so we went down on foot to the North Strand. We had our steel helmets on and we were *running*—and the other fella was seventeen stone! As we were going past the Five Lamps there was *mobs* of people coming up, *running away* from it, in their night attire.
>
> Oh, they were in a shocking state … *shocking* state, all the people and children. I'll never forget all these people *running* down, pulling kids by the hand … *hysterical*, shouting and screaming, "It's *down there*, fireman, it's *down there!*"

ARP warden Dick Eyres was on the scene in a flash, having been up at Summerhill when the big bomb blew. "I ran down into a cloud of black smoke on the North Strand." He then cut straight over to Shamrock Terrace to check on his wife and children. Mrs Eyres had been standing outside her door with her neighbour Annie Waddick, also an ARP warden, as the plane skimmed over the rooftops, allowing them even to see the pilot's face. The blast then bowled them both over. Standing close by was another neighbour, "Fizzer" Keogh—so named for his puritanical language. But the shocking explosion caused a momentary lapse, she recalls. "Fizzer Keogh, he *never cursed* in his life; he always used to say 'Fizz it.' But the *noise* of it! And he said, 'Mrs Eyres, for *God's sake*, go in!'"[3]

She got to her feet and turned to "run and see how the children were, but the lino on the floor had been sucked up and it blocked the door." At first it prevented her entry, then "I tore it up and pushed the door in." The children were safe, but frightened. Seconds later her winded husband arrived, poked his head inside, and "I roared to my wife, 'Are you all right?'" Finding his family safe, he made a dash for the phone in his ARP depot at the far end of the terrace. His recollection is precise:

> I put a call through at exactly twelve minutes past two, to the ARP messenger centre: "A bomb has dropped on the North Strand. I don't know exactly where, but somewhere between Newcomen Bridge and Shamrock Terrace.[4]

Just as he put the phone down the two wardens from down the road, Annie Waddick and May Stanley, showed up at the depot ready for duty. "I told them to carry on with the telephone messages, and I went up to the North Strand." Bernadette Pierce saw how decisive Dick Eyres was under pressure. "Dick said to these two lady wardens, 'Get as many ambulances as you can, notify the gas company and the electricity board, *all* these people. He thought of *everything*, in an *instant*.' For the next twenty-four hours the tiny depot, with its single emergency telephone, would be a madhouse of activity, says Mrs Eyres. "The ARP men were going wild on the phone."[5] Calls were constantly coming in and going out, everyone desperate for information.

———

No-one in Dublin was more eager for information—*plenty* of it, and *accurate*—than R. M. Smyllie at his office in the *Irish Times*, which by now was about as frenetic as the North Strand. Following the blast of the 500-pound bomb he had bolted up the stairs to his office, Tony Gray and Alec Newman close on his heels, to put a plan together. As Gray remembers it:

> We went into the office to discuss what should be done with the Chief Sub-editor and the reporter on night duty. He had already telephoned the Chief Reporter (News Editor nowadays) who lived in Malahide and could not get into Dublin, but suggested that the reporter on night duty should ring Matt Chambers, Deputy Chief Reporter and ask him to get into the office immediately and supervise the reporting of the whole affair.[6]

Smyllie was in a dither. Some of his most senior staff lived far out in the suburbs, and no public transport was running in the middle of the night. Some didn't even own a bicycle. They couldn't reach the office until morning; meanwhile, the biggest story in Dublin in a generation was breaking. Every staff member living within reach was contacted and told to get to the office, on foot if necessary. As it turned out, most were already on their way.

Twenty-year-old Gray knew to remain mostly silent during these tense moments. Smyllie looked as serious as he had ever seen him. But he could also see his mind spinning—facing a story of such magnitude, and short-handed; precious minutes passing away. Then Smyllie flashed an enlightened look in his direction:

> Although I had never done any reporting, Smyllie offered me, as the youngest of the editorial department, as an auxiliary reporter. We had now heard that a bomb had been dropped on the Dublin Zoo, and I was told to get on my bicycle and cycle out to the Zoo, phone in a report from there, and then cycle back to the office via the North Strand, pick up any additional information I could, and get back to the office.[7]

There was no time to glow over his promotion. He grabbed his notepad and mounted his bicycle, then began weaving through the crowds jamming the streets. It was now about 2:20 a.m. as he cycled towards the Phoenix Park—wondering, like everyone else, if another bomb might fall, as planes were still overhead. Yet he felt no fear. Sixty-three years later, at the age of eighty-three (only months before he died), he reflected on those dramatic moments in his young life; "when you are healthy and happy and twenty years old you feel immortal and invincible."[8]

————

Following his premonition, and with his wife's blessing, Alec King had headed out on his bicycle well before the big bomb had fallen. He went straight to the Crampton depot where he and his rescue and demolition squad trained and kept their equipment. After the first bombs exploded, at about 1:30 a.m., his men began filtering in, one by one. Together they began loading their lorry with picks, shovels, crowbars, ladders, ropes, planks, welding equipment, and acetylene lamps. Before long all the men were there, with the important exception of Ned O'Loughlin, their designated driver. Tough and reliable, Ned could always be counted on. Everything was loaded and ready to go. Impatiently, they waited for his arrival. They *had* to get to the North Strand: they could see the huge blaze in the sky. After giving Ned a few more minutes, they determined that something must be wrong. A few hours later, King and his men were to learn what had befallen their colleague:

> Our lorry-driver, Ned O'Loughlin, he was out on the North Strand when the bomb fell, and Ned was fired fifty or sixty yards down the road, and he was *peppered* with glass. And he went "queer". He was a cabbage. He never knew.

Unable to wait any longer, King made the decision to assign Johnny Lawless as their driver. All clambered aboard their six-ton Leyland and tore towards the North Strand at top speed—"sixty miles per hour!"

When they arrived at the periphery of the bomb scene they were halted by a group of armed LDF men. Their orders were to keep *everyone* out. It was a stalemate over who held the higher authority. To King, there was no time for debating—lives were at stake:

> We were eight men and the driver, and we made our way as *fast* as we could go—until we arrived at the disaster scene. At the outskirts we were stopped

by the LDF, complete with rifles. The area was sealed off, and they would let no-one through.

See, we were the first squad to arrive—and there was *no organisation* on the North Strand. And they had orders to let nobody through. I got down and asked for permission to get to the scene—but we were refused! "Nope, our orders is that nobody comes through!" End of story. We said we were the Rescue and Demolition—we were on *orders* to get through, and *rescue* people! But they wouldn't let us through.

I knew they couldn't shoot us. So I went back to the lorry and said, "*Right*, I've got four hefty fellas—and I wasn't small myself—and we took the heads off the picks and took the pick handles. And I said, "With the handles we'll flail our way through!" Because there was *nothing* going to stop us—there were lives to be saved! So we took the pick handles, and the LDF broke ranks—and you talk about *hurling*! We saw the LDF going half the length of the field! Then Johnny Lawless put his foot to the accelerator and the lorry went through like *lightning*. And we were the first there.

As Jack Conroy and his lumbering mate approached the North Strand they had an unexpected encounter too. Huffing heavily from running with the full weight of their gear, they were hit with an emotional wallop:

We ran down as best we could, and the ambulances going back and forth, and you could see a huge cloud of dust as you were coming near the crater. Then we saw a figure lying along the kerbstone. And we looked to see could we help him—and his *head was gone!* The blast blew his head off. Bleeding … just lying there.

They removed their helmets, then walked ahead into the ruins, saying nothing to one another.

The scene awaiting Alec King, Jack Conroy, Ann Leonard, Noel Brady and the countless other rescuers pouring in from all directions was one that would stun them. It immediately struck Nurse Leonard as that of a battlefield, the same as she had so often seen in cinema newsreels of war-torn countries. To King it was "a hellish scene … as if we were in a different world." A reporter for the *Irish Independent*, one of the first to arrive, described the scene:

The area from the Five Lamps to Newcomen Bridge was practically wiped out by a high-explosive bomb … it demolished residences and shops on each side of the street. Burst gas pipes threw an eerie light on the scene of desolation … the roadway was littered with broken glass, slates and other debris while overhead tramway cables were blown down. The left side from North Clarence Street to the bridge was a mass of flames.[9]

Rescuers were walking straight into a highly dangerous environment of live electric wires, dangling tram cables, fire, and what the *Irish Times* called the "menace of gas" floating around and accumulating dangerously.[10] "Smashed electric wires lay across homes and emitted vivid flashes," said the *Evening Herald*, "as fires broke out and badly burned some of the bodies of unfortunate victims."[11] Equally perilous, "as the tramlines were torn down the police feared that the L.D.F. might be electrocuted, the wires being live."[12] Undeterred, rescuers plunged in and "risked their lives in wrecked buildings which were reeking with the smell of escaping gas" and where fires were burning fiercely.[13]

It would not be until the rescuers were able to reach the houses and begin digging among the ruins that they would realise the extent of the carnage wrought by the bomb.

Chapter 14 ∾

"THE DEAD AND THE LUCKY"

There were tales of daring rescue work performed by men who scorned death in a frantic endeavour to reach trapped people … A.R.P. workers, doctors, and priests crawled through openings in toppled buildings to succour the injured.

(*Evening Mail*, 31 May 1941)

In the Jervis Street Hospital, Mater, Richmond and Rotunda hospitals, doctors who have scarcely slept work in relays at the operating theatres.

(*Irish Times*, 31 May 1941)

Our squad collected eleven or twelve that night, dead or alive, maimed … limbs missing. The dead and those who were lucky to be alive!

(ALEC KING)

A few German bombers were still hanging around. Searchlights crisscrossed as the anti-aircraft gunners occasionally fired shells aloft. For nearly two more hours survivors and rescuers would remain under constant threat of more bombs.

There were immediate perils on the ground around them. Most hazardous were the escaping gas and live electric wires and tram cables. When air-raid drills had been held, these dangers had not been simulated. Some unaware rescuers were moving about the site carelessly. It was even a greater danger to local people, who, in their early shocked state, could be completely oblivious. The bomb scene had to be made safe as soon as possible.

Escaping gas was particularly alarming to those aware of its risk for inhalation and explosion. The lives of rescuers and trapped victims were endangered, reported the *Irish Times*:

The menace of gas was present, especially in those demolished houses where rescuers were trying to reach seven people who were reported to have been buried alive.[1]

Meanwhile, gas was accumulating in the air above the site. A cloud of gas could be highly explosive. With live wires sparking and new fires popping up here and there, the danger continually grew.

As firemen attacked the major conflagrations, others sought the source of the gas leaks. Alec King and several other men, who realised its potential for catastrophe, waded through the rubble and smoke, using their torches to try to find the gas line. Local people guided them to where they thought it might be. Within minutes it was found. Distressingly, it was twice as large as the searchers had anticipated. "The bomb blew up the gas main, and it was a *huge* twelve-inch main." And they didn't know how to cap or extinguish it.

By good fortune, a gas inspector—who happened also to be Noel Brady's superior in the St John Ambulance Brigade—lived right beside Newcomen Bridge. He knew instantly how to avert an explosion caused by a ruptured gas main. Noel Brady arrived and dismounted from his bike just in time to see him in action:

My officer in charge, Mr O'Brien, he was a gas inspector too. And he was one of the first there. The gas main had burst, and he put a match to that gas, to save an explosion. 'Cause if the air got full of gas and there was some class of spark the *whole thing* would have exploded! So he just started an ordinary flame coming out of it, to burn it as the gas came out, so there'd be no explosion.

Without his quick thinking, King believes, "the whole neighbourhood would have been gassed."

Conroy and his mate from Buckingham Street fire station, still shaken from the discovery of the headless man, came on the scene just as O'Brien was putting his match to the massive gas main. "There was a big '*puff!*' and the gas main went up in flames. The whole thing then went ablaze, and it provided a giant torch for workers." Eliminating the gas danger so quickly, then having its huge flame provide light for rescuers, was great luck. Luck, both good and bad, would play a part in many lives during the rest of the night at the North Strand.

Shortly thereafter the current in the electric wires and tram cables was shut off. This left the major fires to be extinguished before the scene could be made safe for full rescue operations. Firemen knew their job and had plenty of experience with all the tenement fires around the city, and their recent role in

the Belfast blitz had honed their skills. The urgency of their task was not only
to douse blazes but to rescue survivors and remove the bodies of victims
before they were incinerated by the intense flames, leaving nothing of a
person but ash and bones. At the North Strand the firemen, many of whom
were local people, desperately wanted to retrieve bodies intact so they could
be given a proper burial by their families. This was always a race against time,
said Paddy Finlay, who had faced the situation many times in his long career:

> I had the experience of seeing human spontaneous combustion, where the
> body ignites, burns … oh, it burns to a *cinder*. The skull and bones were
> still there, but the flesh was gone … and we had to use shovels.

Firemen knew they would find charred bodies, but they didn't want to have
to hand over to relatives a skull and a handful of bones.

As fire, gas and electrical hazards were eliminated, another was growing: the
"people menace", as it was called by several newspapers. By 2:15 a.m. crowds
were converging on the scene from every direction. They constituted a major
impediment to firemen and rescue crews, running helter-skelter, stepping on
fire hoses and blocking water hydrants, rescuers' paths, and ambulances.
Amid the mayhem and darkness it was difficult to distinguish between local
residents, sightseers, and rescuers, most of whom had no uniform, only a cap
and armband at best. Some showed up with no form of identification.

In the first hour or so following the explosion the authorities had great
difficulty handling the crowds. "While firemen and A.R.P. worked frantically
extricating the injured, local units of the L.D.F. and L.S.F. turned out in
strength and some of them formed human cordons to keep the crowds back."[2]
They strung themselves out around the site, standing shoulder to shoulder or
clasping hands to form a human barrier, shouting out orders to excited
onlookers to "*keep back now!*" It was especially difficult keeping the crowd
away from the bomb crater, as they kept pushing forward, trying to peer into
the depression.

By 2:30 gardaí, including Senan Finucane and Maurice Walsh, were
arriving in force. The crowds became immediately more respectful, and
obedient, in their uniformed, physically imposing presence. Nonetheless,
Walsh recalls, as the crowds swelled it felt at times like trying to hold back the
tide. "It was dark at the time, and the *crowds!* From *all* parts—but we *had to
keep them back* from the barriers." Only authorised persons were granted

entry. Two were especially welcomed: priests and doctors. When they showed up the crowd parted like the Red Sea, making a clear path for them to get through. Though each had their own duty to perform, they would often find themselves working side by side, either to save lives or comfort the dying.

Before priests showed up, people had fallen into prayer, especially women. As Bridie Byrne exclaims, "Oh, it put the *fear of God* into you!" Paddy Walsh took notice right away: "People were all out *praying* ... naturally. It's the only thing you can turn to in circumstances like that." Some were praying aloud, others silently. "You might even get five or six collected together praying," tells King, "and they'd have their Rosary beads out." Some were so deep in prayer that they seemed quite oblivious of the bedlam around them.

According to Maura O'Toole, Father Masterson "was the first priest there to give the Last Rites to the people, he was on the scene right away." He had jogged down from the Summerhill bombing within minutes. As more priests arrived from surrounding parishes they tried to spread out across the site. They soon found themselves in the role of military chaplains, even medics. People trapped in collapsed buildings were crying out for help. Hearing the voice of a priest brought comfort, and hope. Some were accessible only by burrowing through the rubble. Younger priests, physically fit, did not hesitate, wrote the *Irish Times:* "Many examples of heroism were seen. A young priest crawling, covered in dirt, amid the wreckage, comforting the injured."[3] They rolled up their sleeves and dug through the debris beside rescuers. Some victims later credited a priest's presence and voice with getting them through their life-or-death ordeal.

Almost immediately, however, priests found themselves distracted from their most important duties, as local people began hounding them to hear their confessions. On the spot! With the fear of death hanging over their heads, they were frantic to have their souls cleansed. At first, Father Masterson and other priests politely refused, citing their more urgent duties. However, many simply refused to take no for an answer, tagging along behind a priest like a whining puppy, pleading over and over again for confession, a few even trying to slip a quick confession in sideways by saying aloud to the priest, "Bless me, Father ... " in hopes that he might pause, turn, and sling a saving absolution at them. Being persistently pestered caused some priests to lose patience, become brusque and bark, "Go away now, leave me be!" Tish Martin happened to encounter Father Gallagher as he was making his way through the crowd towards those victims who needed him:

> On the way down I met Father Gallagher. He was making his way down to the people who were killed and injured. When the survivors saw him they ran over to him, saying, "Father Gallagher, please hear my confession." He

was mobbed by men and women. "You can get confession *tomorrow*," he told them. "I have to go to the dead and injured—they need me more than you!"[4]

To those fearful that there might be no tomorrow, his words fell on deaf ears.

By 2:25 a few doctors had arrived. As they were allowed petrol for their cars they could come from distant parts of the city. But they had to make a decision whether they were more needed at the bomb scene or in hospitals to which the injured were being taken. Most determined that it was the latter, realising they could do more to treat serious injuries and save lives with full medical facilities in their operating theatres. Several doctors, however, chose to remain at the scene throughout the night and morning, mostly those who had arrived early and simply couldn't bring themselves to leave. Here they played an indispensable role, not only by treating injuries but advising the Red Cross and other medical services about the seriousness of different cases and to which hospitals they should be sent. Like priests, they sometimes exceeded the bounds of their training by tunnelling through the ruins to reach people critically injured, some dying and in excruciating pain. They were able to offer more than comforting words and cursory treatment, noted the *Irish Press*. "Where people were trapped, believed to be badly injured, doctors were giving them morphia as the rescue squad tried to extricate them."[5] It not only mercifully alleviated the agony of victims screaming in pain but allowed some to die in peace.

Dr Éamonn Keating from the nearby Rotunda Hospital was one of the first doctors there, within about ten minutes. He immediately headed for the collapsed house at number 154 North Strand. Without hesitation, he worked his way inside, where "he found Mrs. O'Reilly and her baby in a heap of rubble. Their house was demolished."[6] He wrapped the infant in his arms and led the injured mother to safety before more sections of the walls fell in. Then he ordered that she and her three children be taken to Dr Steevens' Hospital. Most victims would be rushed to the nearby hospitals, most notably Jervis Street, the Mater, the Rotunda, Dr Steevens' and Drumcondra. Eventually they would be placed in dozens of hospitals.

Dr J. C. Waugh was lauded for his heroism throughout the night, going into one dangerously toppled dwelling after another alongside rescuers to assist the injured and dying. He encountered sights he had never before faced in his medical career. Dr Waugh later took a few minutes to share with an *Irish Times* reporter some of his experiences, gruesome as they were:

Dr. Waugh described terrible scenes … moaning children crying out for their mothers ... children maimed, many of the victims horribly mutilated ... [including] the body of a boy almost cut in two. Dr. Waugh said that in one house two people were completely decapitated.[7]

Such graphic descriptions in the decorous *Irish Times*—coming directly from a doctor who witnessed them—horrified readers.

———

Two particular individuals played an especially prominent role at the scene, providing a feeling of comfort and security to local people: Dick Eyres and Alfie Byrne. Byrne, a publican and prominent anti-Larkinite, subsequently an independent TD was now the popular—and populist—Lord Mayor of Dublin. People looked upon both men as "family". For the next several days their presence was inestimable.

Eyres was the ideal district warden, capable, conscientious and respected by all. He knew the community from top to bottom. As he expressed it, "every blessed person in that area was known to me." They listened to him and followed his directions. But his close ties with people would make it emotionally wrenching to have to identify those seriously injured or killed. The rescue authorities counted on him to carry out such duties. He would receive orders to identify victims on the scene, in hospitals, and later at morgues. And he was not a man to shirk his duty.

Immediately upon arrival at the bomb scene he was hit with personal tragedy:

> I *ran* up to the North Strand, just in time to see them taking out the body of a man named Callely. He lived in the third house going up towards the bridge. Then I was actually standing *over* Diffney's shop, and I knew the family buried there.
>
> I was looking at them taking out the bodies of children that I *knew* ... and the mothers, and grandmother. The father's body was covered in a white sheet. Across the road they were taking out a man named Carroll, and his daughter. Further up the road I saw them taking out the bodies of Mr. and Mrs. Dolan.[8]

All friends. Yet he kept his composure, because he knew that people counted on him. Only when he would be sent to morgues later that morning and afternoon to identify bodies—after no sleep and nearly twelve straight hours of duty—would his emotional strength slightly waver.

Alfie Byrne was already legendary, the most popular mayor that Dubliners had ever known. He was almost one of them, living at number 63 North Strand. He understood local people, spoke their language, knew their worries, helped them with problems in life—money troubles, mercenary landlords, eviction threats, family illness, bullying husbands. He was always there in time of need. People trusted him.

An avid cyclist, he zipped around city streets, amusing children and chatting amiably with adults. Una Shaw and her young friends squealed with delight whenever they saw him coming. "He used to wear one of these wing collars and a bowler hat and a three-piece suit. And a gold chain, and we'd be fascinated looking at it." Best of all, he always had a bag of lollipops that he bought at the Urney factory in Tallaght and handed out to city children by the thousand. "When we were kids sitting on the steps of the old tenement," recalls Mary Cooke, "*never* did he pass you by. He would stop and talk to you. And put his hand in his pocket and give a woman a few shillings. A lovely man." And "a very *good* man," says Una Shaw.

It was said that "he had the charm and charisma which enabled him to mix on equal terms with kings and paupers."[9] No wonder he was proclaimed "the greatest Lord Mayor of Dublin in over 300 years."[10] What better man to have on the scene of a tragedy? Says Chrissie Byrne, "Oh, Alfie was the *first* on the scene. He helped people." Within three minutes of the explosion he was out on the streets assisting. He would remain on his feet for the next eighteen hours, and would become the most ubiquitous figure at the North Strand for weeks to follow. Having him beside them was better than having Dev himself. "Alfie's with us, sure he's the man to see us through this" was the attitude. No-one could lift spirits and instil hope like Alfie Byrne. During the days ahead his legend would grow.

Alec King and his men were confident about carrying out their rescue and demolition duties, exactly as trained. After they had flailed their way past the obstinate LDF contingent that had tried to block them, their lorry roared towards the most devastated area. Men leapt off and began unloading their shovels, picks, axes, crowbars and other equipment. As his first squad of eight men had finished unloading, "then the second squad came up, that was sixteen. Then *another*, that was twenty-four—and I had to supervise the lot." He gathered his men together, distributed equipment, then sent each squad to their first excavation site.

Frustration immediately set in. Collapsed houses left huge mounds of heavy bricks, slates and timbers. People buried beneath could have tons of debris over them. King and his men quickly found that they couldn't possibly "dig" their way through an avalanche of such rubble. Their axes, shovels and picks were of virtually no use. It was, he remembers, a startling realisation for men who had intended to shovel and hack their way through the ruins to save lives:

> Now we had all sorts of equipment with us there when we arrived, but we discovered that the only thing we could do was use what God gave us—our *hands*. So everybody worked feverishly with their bare hands.

Objects had to be lifted and removed, one by one. So, men tossed aside shovels and picks, bent over or dropped down to their knees, and began the gruelling manual work that would take a shocking toll on their hands, elbows and legs. Men with tougher, thicker-skinned hands who worked as coopers, dockers, carpenters and the like fared best; those with softer hands saw their skin shredding within the first few hours. Chunks of broken brick and mortar were rough and jagged, and timbers were splintery. Paddy Walsh felt great sympathy for the rescuers when he saw what they were up against: "*Imagine*, with a bomb like that, working with *hands!*"

Hands may have seemed a primitive digging tool, but their sensitivity allowed rescuers to feel their way towards trapped victims. This proved to be critical, because the surroundings were so unstable that removing a single brick or shifting a timber might bring down a section of wall or ceiling. Under such delicate circumstances, heavy hacking with picks and shovels would have been highly dangerous. But by relying upon hands one could both feel and sense when the slightest misstep might trigger a disturbance, with disastrous consequences. Rescuers thus made their way cautiously, inch by inch, ever aware that the smallest error could endanger themselves and the victims.

There were, however, instances in which certain equipment was both useful and necessary, especially where a house was still partially standing. Sledge-hammers were used to knock down dangerously tottering walls and ceilings. As the blast had thrown buildings out of alignment, doors and window frames were often jammed tightly. This could prevent escape by occupants and entry by rescuers. In such cases pickaxes and crowbars were used to clear the way. Ladders allowed rescuers to reach upper floors. But this could be risky with rickety walls, as King himself found on several occasions:

> I remember, as clear as a whistle, the face of this shop. It was swaying six feet each way, I'd say, and it was going to fall on someone. I put the ladder upright, not quite to the eaves, and I went up. But a couple of the lads held the ladder with guide ropes and kept it from actually touching the wall. Then I put the loop over the top and through the window. It came down with *one* hand, the *whole front* came down. And then we pulled some

bodies out, some dead.

ARP men were assisting rescuers by going from house to house with megaphones calling out to any occupants inside who were in need of help. When they came to number 157 North Strand they heard cries and moans. Rescuers were immediately called over. Within minutes they found Mrs McLoughlin and her two-month-old baby, Vera. Though Mrs McLoughlin was injured she was able to speak to her rescuers before being taken away by ambulance. As the *Evening Mail* reported, "Rescuers with aching backs and blistered hands were given to understand that Mr. McLoughlin and his baby son are buried beneath the masonry."[11] She told them that her husband had just reached the door after his frantic dash to get back from his trip to Summerhill to fetch clothing. Surely, she thought, he and her son would also be found at any moment and brought to the hospital to join her.

In the same house a Mr Fagan was dragged out uninjured, but there was no sign of his wife. He assured rescuers that she had been by his side when the house collapsed, somehow they had become separated during the last seconds. He too was confident that she would be found alive very soon. He insisted on remaining at the site, only a few feet behind the excavators, until she was recovered and they could be together. As the hours passed, his wait would become a vigil, to be unbroken for forty-eight hours.

Nearby, at number 28 North Strand, Richard Fitzpatrick's butcher's shop had been levelled by the explosion. His family's living quarters above had sunk into a mass of bricks. He and his wife were found dead and taken directly to the City Morgue. His daughter Margaret and son Noel, the stage artiste, were missing. Another son, seventeen-year-old Gerry, had gone to a Friday night dance, after which he and his pals headed to the chipper. They probably then went over to the bomb scenes at Summerhill and the North Circular Road to watch. At 2:05, when the sky blazed red and the earth shook, he headed for home, pushing his way through the crowds. By the time he caught the first sight of his father's shop, wrote the *Evening Mail*, there was nothing left of it:

> A tragic home-coming from a dance by a 17-year-old boy, Gerry Fitzpatrick. His home faced the bomb crater in the middle of the tram lines and was beside a house in which ten persons were believed killed. When he got home from the dance he found his home in ruins, his father and mother dead, a sister and brother missing. Broken-hearted, he was taken in by sympathetic friends from the neighbourhood.[12]

He expressed the hope that his brother and sister would be found still alive.

Only a few paces away, over beside Newcomen Bridge, fourteen-year-old Maureen Lynch had just been discovered in their old stone cottage, beneath the roof, which had fallen on her. It was only about thirty yards from the bomb crater. The only reason the 150-year-old dwelling had not been blown to smithereens, like surrounding houses, was because it was nestled safely down in the canal basin some ten or twelve feet below the level of the road. The force of the blast had skimmed across the top of the house, ripping off the roof but leaving the structure essentially intact. Inside, however, everything was thrown wildly asunder, including Maureen. She was tossed out of bed, bombarded with falling slates and knocked unconscious:

> The bomb *blew everything*, the roof come in and we went *flying*. All the stuff come down on top of me and knocked me out. And when I awoke there was a St John man leaning over me. They were after taking all the mortar off me and they didn't know I was there—and they got a shock! "Where's me mammy, where's me daddy?"
>
> Then he took off his coat and threw it around me and carried me out. And they took me around to this house and on this slab there was a little girl, that was *dead*. Only three or something. And her father blown to bits. And his wife killed as well. Oh, I couldn't believe it!

And there they left her, alone and staring at the dead child beside her.

Pedalling in from the Naas Road, Noel Brady at first made good time. Then he encountered the mobs both fleeing from and swarming towards the North Strand. Having to slow down and zigzag his way through crowds delayed him. "When I was going down there I hadn't a clue what I'd get. When I reached the scene everything seemed to be in confusion. I couldn't just go in willy-nilly, I had to look for the officer in charge." As this happened to be also the gas inspector who was busy saving the day by igniting the ruptured gas main, he had to wait. He remembers thinking, "We had practised for this in mock raids, thank God—but we were hoping it wouldn't happen." As he waited he watched the ambulances from the St John Ambulance Brigade already in full action, as Una Shaw describes them, "*flying everywhere, in* and *out—whizzing* in and out." The night air rang with the incessant clanging of their bells, which were on the front of the radiator and operated with a foot pedal.

Finally he received his orders, simple and straightforward. "We were to treat people, on the spot," to handle each case as it came along. He was placed beside an ambulance where victims were being brought out on stretchers. The moment had arrived—blood was in sight:

> When I got there it just happened automatically. When I saw the blood I *hadn't got time* to think about it! I *knew* that I could stop this bleeding— and I didn't get time to worry about it.
>   I got people with breaks, head injuries, lacerated arms and face, bleeding. *Haemorrhaging.* The neck and face would be torn … I got *severe* head bleed cases, and you're so intent trying to get it done *quick*. And I'd stop their haemorrhage—and then get them to the ambulance.

Ann Leonard arrived at the bomb scene shortly after Brady with her pal and fellow-nurse, May. The two had danced away on Friday night and had been heading home exhausted at about two o'clock when the blast stopped them in their tracks. Now in uniform, medical pouches slung over shoulders, they walked right into what she likens to "a battlefield where they were taking out the dead." She was at least glad that they would be working together through the tragedy. After exchanging comments with a few others around her and slipping off her medical kit to check its contents, she turned to look for her comrade. "The next thing, May was separated from me. I don't know *where* she went—but she was *gone*. And I was on my own." She poked her way through a sea of rescuers before she found her officer, who gave her orders identical to Brady's. "I was told to do what I could."

Her first case tested her "nerves of steel":

> My first experience—I'm left with this little boy. Oh, my God, that child, glass was embedded in him! Right across the forehead. I couldn't in my wildest dreams try to take that out. Because I'd want an anaesthetic for a start. He was only five or six and was crying his heart out! I thought, "Oh, my God, *what* am I going to do with this child?

As there was no ambulance immediately available to take the boy to a hospital, he was left in her care. Over and over, he cried for his mammy and daddy. She could only hold him and try to comfort him with words. Then she was able to turn and quietly ask another nurse near her about his parents. She was told, "His mammy had been dug out [dead], but I don't know about his daddy." She turned back to the child and said calmly, "Look, we'll see about Daddy in a little while." About five minutes later "he was carried over to one of the ambulances and they drove off with him." That was the last she knew of the child.

Leonard, Brady and their fellow-nurses and orderlies worked relentlessly under constant pressure, without sleep, on pure adrenalin and sense of duty.

They also found that trying to diagnose injuries and administer emergency medical treatment in a setting of congestion, confusion and filth was far more difficult than in their antiseptic training quarters, as Leonard recalls:

> Oh, you had people crying out for you *all the time*. You had to make sure there were no broken bones, but even if they had every bone in their body broken, you left that if it was a haemorrhage. And with the dirt and dust flying you had to keep the bandages and dressings *clean*, and *quickly* cover up the wounds. Then put them into ambulances and off to hospitals.

There were not enough ambulances, however, nor enough hospital beds as the night wore on. Nor doctors and nurses on duty. Ambulances could not keep up with the number of victims being brought out of the ruins. Several doctors offered their cars. Finally, some thirty commercial vans had to be pressed into service as ambulances, carrying bodies instead of bread. Life-threatening cases were shoved into the rear as the ambulances tore through the streets, scattering crowds in their path and often nearly hitting careless pedestrians. In one ambulance a victim died en route to the hospital; in another, life began: an injured pregnant woman, shocked into premature labour, gave birth in the rear of a speeding ambulance, the clanging bell sounding like a celebration of the wondrous event.

There was no hurry with the dead. They were covered with a sheet or blanket—or shawl or jacket if necessary—and given the dignity of privacy as they waited to be taken to the morgue. Those around them could not help but cast discreet glances at their lifeless forms.

With ambulances overtaxed and hospitals filling to capacity, first-aid stations had to be hurriedly set up. Nurses and orderlies were assigned to duty there to attend to lesser injuries in a clean, safe environment. This took pressure off the hospitals and allowed for a faster turnaround time for ambulances. Brady felt they were a great help:

> Oh, the ambulances were *so* busy. So, over in Portland Row we made a first-aid station out of the church that was attached to Portland Row convent. Then we could bring the less serious cases there. And the nuns were great, they were praying and they'd give them a cup of tea. And in Portland Row the old maids' home, that was used as kind of a half-way house too.

As victims were retrieved they had to be removed from the rubble, then handed over to stretcher-bearers who took them out to ambulances. However, it was often too risky for stretcher-bearers to come close, so rescuers had to bring them out. "In the ruins of the houses rescue workers formed human chains to extricate people," wrote the *Irish Press*, "lifting them from hand-to-hand out to the roadway."[13] In the haste to accomplish this, uncovered victims who were bloodied, mangled, even dead, often came within full view of onlookers. "Sightseers were horrified," revealed the *Irish Press*, "as people were carried out dead."[14] The sight of mutilated bodies could be worse. Paddy Walsh watched as "they were taking bodies out of Shamrock Cottages, and there was a man and the stairs collapsed and a rung went *right through* him!" Onlookers had to turn away when they saw charred remains, as the *Evening Mail* reported that "appalling scenes were witnessed … with badly burned bodies of some of the unfortunate victims."[15] Sights never to be forgotten.

Rescuers, however, *had* to cope with such grisly sights. As the *Irish Times* noted, it was "a gruesome task … but there was no shirking duty."[16] After "digging frantically" for "entombed" victims, they would often discover "horrible mutilations." Even the most seasoned firemen, police and medical workers could find that they had no stomach for it. Senan Finucane remembers:

> They were working with their *bare* hands, taking out bodies, all bloody. We saw pieces of bodies being taken away, pieces of flesh … legs, hair of the head maybe, and hands. And everything else. It was a *terrible* sight to see!

Cissie O'Brien recalls her neighbour, a Mr Farrell, a well-trained and dedicated member of the Red Cross who hastened to the North Strand to do his duty. "He went up to help but did not stay long up there. The poor man was sick with what he saw … and had to come back home."[17]

Nothing took so great an emotional toll on rescuers and bystanders as seeing children taken from the ruins, injured or dead, still in night clothing, a toy sometimes set on the stretcher beside them. When Jack Conroy and his fellow-firemen first came on the scene they had to remove infants from buildings collapsed and burning. They were stalwart men who could confront adult deaths, but the sight of a tiny, limp body could bring them to tears:

> It was *pitiful* looking at the little babies. Quite a few babies killed. Dead. Innocent. Some of them fell, some down from the top floors, on top of the rubble. Like little waxen dolls that we were pulling out.

Brady, who was handling mangled victims and massive haemorrhages, could become emotionally unravelled when he saw a child torn apart or killed. He wept openly:

Seeing the babies was the worst part of it. And men were taking out their toys. I was in *floods* of tears! 'Cause I was thinking that sure it was only hours ago that the children were playing with these toys. And there was this police superintendent and he said to me, "What the *hell* is wrong with you?" But it was *killing* me ... seeing the babies.

There were occasionally happy endings. One *Irish Press* reporter described how "I have just seen the rescue of a little child, *laughing*, from one of the wrecked houses."[18] There were often smiles, and cheers, when a child was seen being brought safely out of the wreckage.

Alec King's early rescue operations were a breeze, at least compared with what would come later. He and his men were making good progress with their hands. Within the first hour they had found and freed several trapped people who were easily reachable:

In a very short time we were getting people out, about fifteen minutes. We tunnelled our way into a cellar where we found two men and two women who were unhurt, but just dirty and scared of not being found. They had prayed harder than ever before. On their way past me I said, "Now when you have cleaned yourselves up, off you go—and thank God." I was promised they would.

Such success may have buoyed his confidence beyond the realities of what lay ahead, when he would be forced to excavate more deeply and more dangerously.

Not long afterwards, he and his squad were digging through a collapsed house when they witnessed a startling resurrection from the ruins. "A man just *appeared* out of the rubble and dirt and dust. It was like one of those things in the horror films, where a person just appears out of the dust like a *zombie.*" They halted their work and watched him slowly emerge, then walk towards them, as if in a trance or hypnotic state, showing no fear. "He had no idea *who* he was, *where* he was. *Nothing.*" Neighbours who recognised him came forward to take him away. "I don't know what happened to him. He may have died ... or he may have been like that for the rest of his life."

———

By 3 a.m. every Dublin newspaper had reporters on the scene, poking around the ruins, writing observations, pestering the authorities for some hard facts. They especially wanted figures on the number of deaths for the morning editions. But no-one had such statistics. They could be compiled only by enquiring at all the hospitals and mortuaries, hardly possible under the circumstances.

Tony Gray, surely the youngest reporter at the site, showed up about an hour and a half after the explosion, having first followed R. M. Smyllie's instructions to cycle out to the Phoenix Park:

> As it was clear that nobody had been killed or injured in the Phoenix Park area, I phoned the office, told them what had happened at the Zoo, and then cycled into town again, heading for what appeared to be a huge fire which was lighting up the entire sky. It was about 3.30 as I drew close to the bombed area. I left my bicycle against some railings and walked the rest of the way. There was an LSF/ARP cordon around the whole area.[19]

He proudly showed his *Irish Times* credentials, gained entry, then began walking about in a sea of turmoil, intending to jot down his observations. But apart from the fire still raging and frenetic rescue operations under way, there was no way to make any coherent picture out of it for newspaper-readers. As a twenty-year-old neophyte in the news business, he hardly had the confidence or the clout to prevail on the authorities at the scene for detailed information. As he saw, even veteran reporters were having no luck:

> In the darkness and confusion, it was impossible to gain any impression of what happened and, understandably, the LDF and ARP men on duty—much less the police and soldiers—had no time to talk to the press, not that they knew very much more about it anyway.[20]

He decided to cycle back to the *Irish Times*, report to Smyllie, and await further orders. As he was preparing to leave the scene he paused beside some of the ambulances to watch the wounded and dead being brought out on stretchers. Though young, he had seen dead bodies before, as Smyllie had once sent him to the City Morgue as part of his apprenticeship to see corpses laid out. This experience, Smyllie thought, would prepare him for dealing with death in the future. But nothing could have prepared him for what he was suddenly looking upon:

> Bodies were being removed from the shattered buildings. I had seen dead bodies before, but not like this. The body on one stretcher appeared to be covered in what looked like a coating of fine ash, though it could have been dust—and everything seemed to be covered in the dust of centuries.
> And when the stretcher bearers passed under a light, there were rivulets

of what looked like purple tar oozing from the ash. The body was obviously smashed beyond recognition, you couldn't even tell whether it was a man, woman, or child.[21]

Disturbed by the sight, he returned to the office and told Smyllie what he had witnessed. But it was not fit for publication.

Nor was the story of what was about to happen to Alec King and his crew. He and his men had now been working for nearly an hour and a half. They had already pulled out a number of people, a few dead but most alive. By now they felt like veterans, ready for anything. Some of the gory experiences that had sickened other rescuers had not fazed King. It was, he thought, due to his own personal ordeal of having undergone the "hammer-and-chisel" operation on his brain at the age of twenty-one, and having seen his father die a slow, agonising death from First World War mustard gas. Whatever the reason, he clearly had a higher tolerance than most for seeing the "blood and guts" of bomb victims. He was about to be tested further.

His squad was digging in a section where it had been reported that several people were buried. He assumed the leading position, with his acetylene lamp. They were slowly dismantling bricks:

Then I put my hand in, and I said to the lads, "*Quiet*, I've found *hair!*" So, we had to do everything very, very gently, lifting each brick.

Eventually, I got the head out of a woman, with long black hair. The neck was severed from the body, *completely*, her eyes *wide open*, staring at me. I can still see her eyes staring at me, as if to say, "What have you done to me?" *Wide open!* See, the eyes won't close unless you put a penny on them when you're dead. It's a muscle reaction. And when I got her out there were white tubes hanging from her neck that must have been her breathing and guts and that sort of thing.

So I took this head down to the first-aid people and they put it on a stretcher. And I said, "Stay where you are, I've got to find the rest of her." So we started to work away, and we discovered the body and started to lift it out slowly. I took the shoulders and open neck, where you could see into the cavity, and a couple of the lads took the legs, and we started to go down to the stretcher. And on the way down *all the blood* that was in the body, in the carcase—it was hot and clammy—it flowed out on top of me. *All* over me. Oh, I can still feel it ... clammy.

And when we brought that woman out a priest came along, a little man, his name was Father O'Reilly, and he was there on his hands and knees, giving the Last Rites—and he was *crying* his heart out.

At about the same time, what appeared to be another tragic case of dismemberment was occurring over at Kathleen Martin's uncle's house. ARP men were responding to the desperate cries of a man who was looking for his missing leg, apparently blown off by the blast. As she tells it, "These rescue fellas were all running around, and they said, 'Oh, there's a man up there that's lost his leg!" Discovering that the stairs were blocked with debris, "they called upstairs, telling him that they were on their way to help him." Then they yelled out the door, "*Ambulance!*" Within several minutes they had managed to dislodge obstacles on the staircase and scramble up to the stricken man:

> It was my uncle, and it was a Friday night and he had gone to bed—and there was a good few drinks on him. And he was duplicated [drunk] when the bomb fell. And he's shouting, '*Where's me leg? Where's me leg?*' He had an *artificial* leg, it was a *wooden* leg! But *they* thought he had lost *his* leg, you know, in that panic that was going. And then he was going around saying, "If I had me leg I'd be going out better than you!"

It drew a smattering of laughter—rare for that night. And left a great story to tell later.

Any bit of relief from the emotional strain was welcome. As Ann Leonard found, the smallest quip or smile from time to time helped fortify spirits. It had been hours since she was handed her first case, of the boy with glass embedded in his forehead. Since then she had been working unceasingly with cases even worse. It was emotionally strenuous, Fortunately, she found herself working beside another nurse whom she liked. Sometimes they exchanged a slight smile or light comment, purely for relief. On one occasion, when she was treating the wounds of another boy, a priest confronted her with criticism. The young nurse stood her ground:

> This nurse, we had a little giggle about something. *Oh*, and this priest came over and said, "This is *no place* to laugh, nurse!" "*Father*," I said, "anything less like laughing is hard to imagine—take a look at this little boy. If he sees me crying, distressed or upset, how do you think *he's* going to react? And there are *others*."
>
> "Child, child," he said, "I never *thought* of it like that." "*No*," I said, "of course you didn't, you never came across this before—*none of us* were ever in this before!"

At 3:50 a.m. a cheer went up. Rescue workers immersed in collapsed buildings burrowing their way through mountains of debris were taken by surprise to hear it, wondering what it was all about. Air Defence Command had finally given the "all-clear", ordered a cease-fire and doused the searchlights. Anti-aircraft fire had begun at 12:35 a.m. at the Clontarf battery. For nearly three-and-a-half hours, shells of light, medium and heavy calibre had been fired into the Dublin sky. Almost a thousand shells had been expended, including the .303 calibre rounds.

With the huge searchlights off and the chattering of the guns finally silenced, people heaved audible sighs of relief. Rescuers and citizens all over Dublin looked upwards to make certain it was true. Then smiles broke out. The engine drones were really gone. And the sky was lovely, radiant and calm once again, just as it had been at the stroke of midnight when Whit had arrived with its promise of a joyful holiday weekend. Only four hours ago.

The threat of more bombs lifted from their mind, people were noticeably less tense. But the intensity of rescue work did not diminish. On the contrary, excavations were now reaching deeper, becoming more challenging, and more dangerous. Victims were trapped—or "entombed," as the newspapers described them—beneath mounds of bricks, slates and heavy timbers in niches where a misstep by rescuers could disturb unstable surroundings and trigger an avalanche of rubble. Many early rescues, close to the surface, had required only pulling away debris and lifting victims out. Now it was reaching a far more physically rigorous and risky stage.

As Jack Conroy and his comrades found when they began work at the North Strand, "they were old Georgian houses and they collapsed like a pack of cards." But many walls were left standing and with roofs and ceilings only partially collapsed. These tottered and swayed, threatening to crumble further at any moment, which is why King and his men were "*always* afraid, because you *never knew* when there'd be five or six tons of rubble that could suddenly collapse down on you."

As the excavations reached deeper it became necessary not only to remove debris from the pocket being dug out, but then to haul it away safely, giving rescuers more space in which to carry on with the operation. Removing the heavy rubble was accomplished by a wicker-basket relay system that King and his men had devised in their training. "We had practised two men clearing the rubble and lifting and then lifting the baskets behind us, while two other men took the baskets away. This was done non-stop." Lifting and relaying the heavily laden baskets was extraordinarily backbreaking work, sapping men's strength.

After about two hours King realised that lifting baskets of bricks and slates was not only fatiguing his men but was a waste of their skill. With some reluctance, he called on strong local men to assist with the baskets:

We'd hand them these big baskets, about three feet high and two foot across, into which we'd put rubble and slates and bricks. And they'd carry it away and dump it in the middle of the road. In that way, they were a great help.

In the rescue process, King discovered something about his own strength and stamina. Under such pressure to save human lives, the adrenalin charge imbued him with a physical power beyond normal limits. Upon later reflection he would liken it to the extraordinary feats of strength and endurance experienced by soldiers in war, or firemen or police in crisis situations, even ordinary citizens suddenly strong enough to lift a car just enough to free someone trapped beneath. He was astonished by his own power:

> I was *not* myself that night, *definitely*. I was somebody else. I did things I never did before. At times like that you get into a frenzy, and every second counts—and it's *unbelievable*. With fright, as well as excitement. I mean, you're sweating with fright and fear … as well as everything else.
>
> And I was three times stronger than the normal man, 'cause you get to be a person who has gone "bats", that's gone *mad*—and they have the strength of three men! You're *not* yourself. You *felt* the strength … adrenalin was up *high*. A hundred per cent—*over* a hundred per cent! I lifted a board of timber eight inches square and fourteen or fifteen feet long to get in to a call or whisper we heard. And I went back there about three days later and *no way* could I move that block of timber. *Impossible!*

Not long after the all-clear had been given, an officer of the St John Ambulance Brigade came over to Noel Brady and told him that he was needed on special duty. Their ambulances were short on orderlies, and he was to fill in at that position for a while. By this time he was happy to do so. It was a great relief from treating severely injured victims. For someone who had worried about withstanding even the sight of blood, he had handled his share of haemorrhage cases. He packed up his medical kit and reported for duty at the waiting ambulance. His job was simply to assist with getting victims in and out of the ambulance and along the way to jot down personal information about the patients, to be handed over to the hospital staff upon arrival. From some victims he was not able to get any information. They remained unidentified. He found it a cushy job and rather enjoyed the rides back and forth. He felt quite relaxed:

> So I was made an orderly on this ambulance for about two hours. And I had been writing down the names of the people I had in the ambulance,

to have a copy to hand in to the hospital to tell them who we had. And I was sitting on the edge of the stretcher, and the ambulance only had a canvas back on it. And it turned sharply and I fell out of the back of the ambulance—and I rolled onto the grass in the hospital. *Out* I went!

He tumbled several feet, rose quickly, slightly embarrassed, and proceeded with his duties as if nothing had happened. Only later did it occur to him how fortunate he had been not to have been tossed out onto the cobblestoned streets.

The scene inside the hospitals was nearly as frenetic as at the bomb site. Pressure on the skeleton night staff was enormous as they tried to cope with the sudden, unprecedented influx of injured and dying patients.

It had begun slowly, at about 1:40 a.m., as the first victims from Summerhill and the North Circular Road arrived at hospitals within ten minutes. Those injuries, however, were minor and easily handled. Then, at about 2:15, the floodgates burst. For the Mater and Jervis Street hospitals, which took the greatest number of serious cases, it was overwhelming for the first four to six hours. "Unimaginable," nurses and doctors would later say. The *Irish Independent* confirmed that "up to 4.00 a.m. over 100 dead and injured had been removed to Jervis Street Hospital, while the number received at the Mater and other hospitals was also large."[22] The procession of ambulances whizzing in and out seemed endless. "It was learned at 4.15 a.m.," reported the *Irish Times*, "that injured were lying on floors and stretchers, and special drafts of doctors were attending to them. One man who was dead was unidentifiable."[23] As there were not enough rooms, victims had to be accommodated in corridors and lobbies, wherever there was space.

Off-duty doctors and nurses were called in as quickly as possible. Many were already on their way. Others were away on Whit holiday and couldn't be contacted. When doctors showed up, the *Irish Press* revealed, they were short on sleep and on operating space:

In the Jervis Street Hospital, Mater, Richmond and Rotunda hospitals, doctors who have scarcely slept since the fatal [bomb] visit, work in relays at the operating theatres.[24]

At Jervis Street Hospital the house surgeon, Dr Danaher, took charge, issuing orders to the staff, organising surgical teams, designating space in which to place patients. At other hospitals, administrators were doing the same, all trying desperately to keep up with the expanding tragedy at hand.

Other than those who may have served in British army medical units, doctors and nurses had never been confronted with so many patients thrust upon them in so short a span of time. However, it was more than the numbers that so distressed them: it was the appalling *condition* of victims, crushed, burned, maimed. Some were visibly shaken when they saw the cases brought into their operating theatres. They had to steel themselves before proceeding. In life-and-death situations, grave decisions had to be made on the spot. Doctors found themselves having to practise medical triage as if they were on a battlefield: immediately treat the most critical cases and hope the others could wait and survive. Decisions on amputations were especially wrenching. Unremittingly, throughout the night, wrote the *Evening Mail*, "Dublin surgeons are battling to save scores of lives in Dublin hospitals."[25] It was a battle that would be waged throughout the morning and afternoon hours as well.

Apart from the steady stream of ambulances and converted vans delivering patients, masses of injured victims were trekking to hospitals on their own, expecting to be admitted and treated. Most couldn't be taken in at the time, yet hospital staffs didn't want to have to turn them away. Most injuries were relatively minor, but some were quite serious. They clustered around the entrance, hoping to be admitted eventually. Many were suffering from glass injuries. The foolhardy window-gazers had paid a terrible price for their prime perch from which they watched the aerial show. Shattering window glass robbed eyesight. "A lot of people were maimed," Bernadette Pierce attests, including one of her close friends, "a lovely person, she lost an eye and had to have a glass eye." Victims left with an empty socket had to wait for their artificial eye, wearing a patch in the meantime, always arousing the curiosity of children.

Doctors saw some uncommon, and inexplicable, injuries. When Eileen Pugh was taken to Jervis Street Hospital the doctor knew how to treat her leg wound but was baffled by how it had occurred:

> As I was coming down the stairs, passing the landing window, the bannister and everything shook. It was as if the sun burst, a huge big blast. When I got downstairs my brother said to me, "You're *bleeding!* Right there on my thigh.
>
> I remember in Jervis Street Hospital the surgeon said to me, "You know, there's not a trace of glass in that—that was the blast." It was a perfectly clean cut. It wasn't glass, it was the *blast*.[26]

Whether by heat or pressure, or both, the force of the explosion had neatly sliced her thigh open like a sausage. She would remain in hospital for the next ten days.

After several hours of gruelling work, rescuers began taking a few minutes'
break. Having inhaled smoke and dust, their throats were parched and raw,
their eyes burning. Hands were scraped and cut and arms and legs bruised.
Backs ached from the incessant bending and lifting. Now they were thirsty
and hungry.

Local women were saviours, coming to the rescue of rescuers with a mug
of tea and sandwich in hand. They stood at the cordons, reached over and
handed hungry, fatigued men food and drink. Some of the men who had
emerged from excavation holes were so covered with dirt, ash, dust and
bloodstains that they looked like coal miners ascending from the pits, only
their eyes and teeth showing white. Onlookers behind the cordons stared at
them, "as some children were frightened" of the men with black faces and
white, glowing eyes. Some of the smaller children asked their mammies if
they were like the "black babies" from Africa that the nuns had told them
about.

Tea was a great tonic for raw throats and clogged lungs, especially if it had
a drop of milk in it. Some rescuers' throats were so sore that they could barely
mutter a "Bless you, woman." Men gratefully took the sandwiches, then
sagged to a sitting position to eat and rest for a few minutes. The food not
only replenished their strength but nourished their spirits as well. The *Evening
Mail* hailed the generosity, "sterling courage ... and spirit" of local women
"during the ordeal."[27] Alec King sings their praises:

> The North Strand women, they were *brilliant*. "You want a cup of tea,
> son?" There was always tea going. We were handed tea in a mug or jam jar.
> It was like a *godsend*, to wash down the filth in your throat. As the tea got
> down to the bottom it got stronger and stronger, and you needed a knife
> and fork to cut it! You could chew it! But *anything* to get rid of that *awful*
> dirt and filth.
>
> And we were handed sandwiches. We ate them—didn't know *what* was
> in them—could have been rats, bits of dead dog or horses, or *humans!* You
> wouldn't know—you just ate them.

There was one indulgence for which many men would have traded not
only a mug of tea but even a creamy pint of Guinness: a cigarette. Despite
their dry, irritated throats they were "mad for a fag," to get that relief and calm
that smokers crave. Men who never uttered a complaint about the strenuous
work, hunger or thirst, mumbled about how they were dying for a smoke.
There were few to be found at the scene, but when they did get their hands on

one it indeed settled their nerves better than anything else.

A single Woodbine was worth its weight in gold. Every now and then a generous bystander might reach across the cordon with a cigarette in his outstretched hand. The weary rescuer's expression of thanks made words unnecessary. King likes to tell how he wangled not only a few Woodbines but an entire packet of Player's from "Tom Logan, an inspector, a droll character, very neat and proper." He handed the packet to King so he could withdraw one for himself. Adroitly, he quickly drew Logan's attention to another subject of interest, slipped the packet into his pocket, then apologised for having to dash back to his work. Unselfishly, he had pulled off the trick for his men, not himself. When he returned to his squad every man was handed a Player's as they lauded his leadership as never before. To a man, they swore it was the best smoke they had ever had.

He and his men needed a relaxing smoke break, because soon they would be facing their most difficult and delicate rescue operations, where nerves would be strained as never before. Between four and six o'clock many of the most challenging rescues would take place. By this time trapped victims had been buried for several hours, gradually becoming more weak and dehydrated, their lungs filled with dust and dirt. Some were slowly suffocating or bleeding to death. As they became more feeble, their voices grew weaker. They could no longer forcefully call out for help. At best they might utter a whisper, moan or sobbing sound. Their survival now depended on the rescuers picking up these faint human signals. Where possible, rescuers tried to snake a tube or hose through the debris to detect any verbal sounds. The constant fear was that the victims might be losing hope as well, the will to hold on and live.

Most of the easier, surface rescues had already been carried out. Spaces now became tighter and the risk of collapse greater. Even slightly dislodging a brick or timber might bring down a slide of debris. "See, if you took *one* brick out, you had to *watch it*," King explains, "that half a ton didn't fall down on you! It was a feat of unknown engineering." Some retrieval operations required the precision of a surgical team.

He and his men had learnt much about the cautious technique of removing obstacles by hand to save lives. Now they were facing the most delicate rescues, which demanded great patience, remaining quiet, and *listening*. Success depended on picking up a faint voice or cry from below. With all the surrounding commotion at the bomb scene, this was exceedingly difficult. To exacerbate matters, there were dogs and cats caught in the ruins, and their sounds of distress could duplicate those of humans. Even when they did verify a human voice or sob, trying to pinpoint exactly where it came from was sometimes next to impossible. They might dig to within a foot or two of a victim and not realise they were there. Inches were critical.

Trying to find a buried person solely by detecting the slightest sounds often meant proceeding at a snail's pace, delicately removing a small amount of debris, halting, then listening; calling out to them, remaining perfectly silent, using the highest auditory powers, then repeating the process. Some men were better at it than others. King believes he had an advantage:

> This is where my sixth sense came in. You'd suddenly stop and say, "*Hush, lads!*"—and you'd *listen*. Everybody with their ear to the bricks. And you'd listen for a faint call or faint cry … or a faint whimper. Or *something!*
>
> Where it came from you couldn't tell, because one echo would bounce off a wall, off a fireplace, or an upturned bed … and you wouldn't know *where* it was! And then you had to go very gently.

For strong men more inclined to rip away at rubble, it was agonisingly slow, trying their patience to the limits. King set the example and led them along the way. No-one had more empathy for buried victims who were in pain and struggling to hold on to life than he. For he had been in their place seven years earlier when he endured his excruciatingly painful brain operation, a touch-and-go surgical marathon in which he was at times barely clinging to life.

Now he understood how others, similarly suffering and close to death, were near to the same point of passage. He found himself the one who might bring them through their life-or-death ordeal. Every second, he was keenly aware of his role. It *drove* him.

Before the night was over he and his first squad of eight men would bring out a dozen or more victims—"the dead and those who were lucky to be alive," in his words.

There had been no more bomb explosions since 2:05. But fears arose that there might be. Rumours were going around about some "duds". An *Irish Times* reporter learnt at 4:30 that "two unexploded bombs have fallen at Summer Street and Fairview. All homes in the vicinity have been evacuated and the area cordoned off."[28] The story spread swiftly. Following the all-clear at 3:50, people had finally felt relief; now they were tense again, wondering if there would be delayed explosions. ARP and LDF men were despatched to comb the area for bombs. Citizens too were told to keep their eyes open for any suspicious-looking devices.

About that time, King made a startling discovery of his own. He had been probing the interior of a partially collapsed house, walking gingerly on the first storey, which was badly damaged and sagging, uncertain whether the floor would hold his weight. Tentatively, he inched forward, using his acetylene torch to see his way, looking for any signs of life:

Then I saw in the corner a wicker chair and a big sheet of galvanised iron on the chair. It must have been blown there by the grace of God, because I lifted it away, and in the wicker chair was a *lovely* little golden-haired child. Now I didn't know if it was a boy or a girl. And it sat up and rubbed its eyes and started to cry out for somebody. And I picked it up in my arms. I'd say he was fifteen months old, roughly.

And I took him up in my arms with blankets and brought him down. And some of the people took him from me and said, "We'll look after him, sir." He was intact. I can *still* see him, a lovely curly fair hair.

Like some other children, he had slept right through the thunderous explosion.

So did at least one adult. It happened at number 63 North Strand, just across from Newcomen Bridge, where the blast was loudest. Here lived an 86-year-old woman who had gone to bed on Friday night at a sensible hour and was sleeping peacefully at 2:05 a.m. That her building took a hard blow from the blast and windows shattered in her room, the glass strewn across her bed, did not disturb her slumber in the least. She was Alfie Byrne's mother. Her hearing loss had spared her any upset.

Chapter 15 ∾

| DAWN AND DEAD CATS

At 6.00 in the morning, the milkman came around and told
us half of Dublin had been wiped out … we were aghast.
(EDITH NEWMAN DEVIN, *Speaking Volumes: A Dublin*
Childhood)

I've never seen *so many dead cats—and not a mark on*
them! The blast*! Like they were sleeping in the sun.*
(DERMOT RING, 81)

No Dublin dawn had been so welcome. As the first faint light crept across the city's rooftops it brought a great sense of relief, a feeling of having "made it through the night." With the disappearance of darkness, fears subsided. People felt safe once again, at least for the time being.

The light of dawn enticed people to come and see for themselves what had really happened over at the North Strand. Rumours, many grossly exaggerated, were already swirling around the south side of the city where citizens were too distant to have reliable information. Edith Newman's milkman was going on his rounds, telling customers that half the capital had been wiped off the map.[1] How were they to know otherwise?

Comforted by daybreak, throngs crossed the Liffey by bike and foot to view the bomb scene. Gardaí Walsh and Finucane, on their feet manning the cordons for more than five hours without a break, saw the crowds swell with the rising sun. New onlookers arriving from other parts of the city exhibited a different attitude from that of local people who had rushed to the scene just after the bomb exploded. Louis Robinson watched them amass, "*huge* crowds, all around, and all *gawking! Excitement!*" Their unabashed curiosity and excitement offended many, including one writer to the *Evening Mail:*

> People came to gape at the North Strand holocaust … this is not civilian folly but purely morbid curiosity … these people should stay at home and thank God for having been saved from such appalling havoc.[2]

They pestered Finucane, Walsh and the other policemen along the cordons by peppering them with endless questions about every aspect of the bombing, which, of course, they couldn't possibly answer. "Wait for the newspapers!" they were told.

There was naturally a great fascination with the large crater that had been gouged out. In the early morning light people were finally able to gaze down into its depths. Parents hoisted children onto their shoulders to gain a better view. Adults stood on tiptoe. It was indeed a very alien-looking feature in the heart of Dublin and subject to great exaggeration as "gawkers" returned to their localities with eye-witness accounts. "How deep does it go?" everyone asked about the "great crater". Some people went away saying that it was large enough to throw a pile of cars into, or a house or two. Some compared it to the craters on the moon. "Even bigger!" children gushed. In fact, it was quite small, considering the huge bomb that had carved it out. Had it fallen on a softer surface it would have been far larger. The *Irish Times* gave what was probably a reasonable estimate: "the crater is about eight feet deep" and roughly thirty feet in diameter.[3]

Whatever its precise dimensions, it would not have been large enough for a mass grave to hold all the people killed.

As the sky brightened, the landscape came into better visibility. "In the daylight we were looking in *awe*," exclaims Louis Robinson, "saying, '*How could it happen?*' Just *unbelievable!*" Everyone was awed by their first panoramic view of the destruction, including firemen and other rescue workers who had been concentrating their work in small, dimly lit spaces. When, for the first time, they paused and surveyed the North Strand—or what was left of it—in full light from end to end, they were dumbstruck. People were seen putting their heads in their hands.

The entire landscape looked strangely unfamiliar. "We went down to have a look," recalls Mary Cooke, "and it was *devastation* ... houses *gone*, whole tops off them, bits of walls here and there ... bricks everywhere." To Mary Dunne it looked "like a jagged edge of an eggshell," exactly like the images she had seen in cinema newsreels of the London blitz. Houses and shops had simply vanished, some so obliterated that it was as if they had never existed. Uplifted, twisted tram tracks, bent lamp-posts and uprooted trees gave a tortured appearance to the whole misshapen landscape. The thick layer of dust and earth covering the entire bomb site made "everything grey and desolate," Maura O'Toole remembers. It was as if Vesuvius had erupted and spewed tons of ash over the land.

On Whit Friday evening the little North Strand village had been one of the tidiest places in all Dublin, with houses, shops and pavements proudly scrubbed, polished and decorated for the holiday weekend. Now it was a hideous, ravaged wasteland. The white lace curtains fluttering in the slight breeze through shattered windows looked like flags of surrender being wanly waved.

Once it became light enough, Una Shaw's mother gave her permission to prance over to the scene with a few pals—so long as they were careful not to get in the way of others. Upon arriving, "you just *couldn't believe your eyes!*" Heeding her mother's words, she moved carefully through the crowds, overhearing how different people were describing the destruction: it had been "blown up," "blown down," "blown to high heaven," "blown to smithereens." Then she paused by a few women and heard a unique phrase:

> There was a couple of women standing beside me looking on, saying, "Dear God, isn't it *terrible!*" And one of the women around beside her says, "Just imagine," she said, "they were *blown into maternity!*"

As this was a term with which she wasn't familiar, she asked her mother when she returned home what it meant. The explanation was followed by a slight smile.

With the rising of the sun, details of the damage could be better discerned. Onlookers were focusing much attention on those houses that were still partially standing. In some cases the roof had been neatly stripped off and the front wall completely collapsed, leaving a skeletal structure that looked like a doll's house with every room exposed and baring personal details within. Crowds were fascinated by being able to peer into private chambers and see the remains of furniture, bedding, cooking utensils, clothing and personal items of every sort, all now on glaring public display.

When one focused on a single room it was as if the curtain had been drawn at the Abbey Theatre, the stage arranged for the opening scene. The audience could study the wallpaper, pictures on walls, items of clothing and furniture, curios, a kettle still set in place. All that was missing was the cast.

Though it was a tragic sight to witness, it was undeniably intriguing. Especially if there were "freakish" sights, as one newspaper called them, and there were many:

> One of the strange effects of the bomb is a dresser remaining in place, with some of its delft intact, although the entire floor of the room, with two of the walls and roof, had been blown away. In another room one solitary framed photograph remained on the chimney breast although the mantel piece had been destroyed.[4]

Larger objects, completely smashed, could stand directly beside small, delicate items perfectly intact. Glass, delph, religious statues and picture frames survived in the midst of devastation. A man's coat remained neatly hung on a wall rack when all else was gone. Beds and furniture were tossed up, standing perfectly vertical. Mattresses were sucked up, sticking to walls and ceilings. Flowered wallpaper curled into delicate spirals like decorative icing on a wedding cake. Gawkers could hardly be blamed for marvelling at the amusing and bizarre features of some damaged houses. One sight particularly fascinated Tony Gray because it seemed to defy gravity:

> One of the collapsed houses had an open piano seemingly clinging to the wall of the third-floor room, except that there was no floor, and no room … it just hung there as if suspended from a picture hook, with an open sheet of music still propped up in the music rest, an unforgettable sight.[5]

Dermot Ring was baffled by one freakish sight he encountered: dead cats, strewn all around the streets and lanes, without so much as a mark of injury on them—as if they were napping peacefully in the warmth of the new day's sun. Or perhaps they were stuffed toy cats that had been hurled out of children's rooms. Confounded by the mystery, he walked past one dead, unmarked cat after another:

> I've *never seen* so many dead cats. In my life. You were going around and there were cats here and cats there … two cats, three cats. An *awful* lot of cats. I couldn't say the number, it'd be—"There's another one, there's *another* one!"
>
> And not a *mark* on them! You wouldn't see a damaged cat, but they were all lying dead. The *blast!* Whether they suffered much trauma … I suppose they could suffer trauma as well as anyone else. No dogs! Always cats. Amazing, isn't it? And *quite* a few. Sometimes six or seven *together*. And then two or three, and then a few more. I didn't see *any* damaged cats at all. Like they were sleeping in the sun.

Others puzzled over it as well, but no-one could explain it. Upon closer observation, it looked as if the blast had petrified the cats in a perfect state.

No mention was made in any of the newspapers of the "dead cat mystery", but a number of articles referred to the plight of other animals, especially pet dogs injured or trapped. Some had been sent into a frenzy of fear by the blast, whimpering and crying incessantly, causing distress to those hearing it. The *Evening Herald* wrote that "a pathetic sight was a white cat and terrier going through what was left of a house, searching through the debris looking for their owner."[6] They told readers that the two frightened animals "ignored all inducements to get them away." Rescuers, sometimes at personal risk, retrieved dozens of injured and trapped animals, turning them over to local people in the hope that they could be reunited with their owners. A few newspapers even told stories of birds being rescued.

———

When 21-year-old Denis Dunne of South Cumberland Street drowsily walked through his back garden shortly after dawn, an object on the ground caught his eye. Whatever it was, he knew it had not been there the evening before, because he had swept that patch of ground. Bending down to inspect it, he found a white enamel plate bearing the mysterious inscription NOTBREMSHAHN. He picked it up and showed it around to some neighbours, a few of whom assured him it might be an important piece of evidence related to the bombing. He promptly took it down to the local Garda station and handed it over to the officer in charge, for which he received thanks and a promise that he would be notified of its meaning, and possible importance, once it could be deciphered.

Close to the same time Mary Twomey made another early-morning discovery. She lived in the Royal Canal lock-keeper's cottage, where her father was keeper employed by CIE, just beside Newcomen Bridge and across from the Lynches' cottage on the other side. Their house, like the Lynches', had been largely protected by its sunken position in the canal basin, though the roof and windows suffered considerable damage. At dawn, she ventured out to look around. Within a few seconds, flecks of pinkish-grey matter caught her eye. When she went closer to get a good look, shivers ran through her body. "Pieces of flesh were found in our garden ... where people were blown to pieces,"[7] probably those caught out on the bridge at 2:05.

Shortly after dawn, Dick Eyres marched forth with a surprising find of his own. When he strode down the centre of debris-laden Shamrock Terrace holding it gingerly in both hands it drew amusement from all those watching. It was about the last thing one would expect to see in the midst of dirt and devastation. It brought a smile to Bernadette Pierce and her granny when he passed before them with the lovely white embroidered treasure cradled in his two palms, like a newborn baby:

He came down Shamrock Terrace and he had the top of a *wedding cake* in his hands! Somebody had been married and the wedding was in the house, and during the bombing everything was destroyed—but he recovered the wedding cake. He brought it home and gave it to his wife.

Dawn's visibility brought an awful racket. Daylight allowed heavy demolition and roadwork to begin. Demolitionists began knocking down dangerous tottering buildings and standing walls, as road crews started using their chattering, ear-piercing pneumatic drills and hammers. To the sensibilities of people sleepless and emotionally fragile, the harsh sounds were barely sufferable. Meanwhile, large lorries were being brought in to begin the gargantuan task of hauling away mountains of rubble. For days to come, the grinding clamour would continue from dawn to dusk.

Dawn also brought a welcome vision. Spirits were lifted by the sight of the shiny new mobile canteen, the pride of the St John Ambulance Brigade, as it was rolled onto the site:

> Shortly after dawn we turned out a mobile canteen from which ARP workers and civilians were supplied with tea, Bovril and sandwiches ... the Brigade came to the service of rescuers who were weary and heavy-eyed after a night of ceaseless work.[8]

Needy local residents, as well as rescue crews, were welcomed at its counter as it began dispensing food and drink, which it would supply to thousands over the coming days. The canteen also importantly provided a central gathering-point for everyone, a sort of community centre on wheels. It nourished morale as well as appetite.

Fuller daylight made it possible to undertake some rescue efforts that had not been safe in the dark. The dangers could now be better assessed in unstable buildings where a slight disturbance of the wrong type might bring down walls, ceilings, even entire floors. Good visibility allowed rescuers to be more exacting, and innovative, in their extrication process. A number of injured and trapped victims had been waiting hours for daylight to arrive so that rescuers could finally begin to safely try to free them.

Two tricky cases involved women stuck in precarious conditions. In the first, "a woman and child were rescued unhurt through a hole knocked in an eighteen-inch masonry wall, and then cutting through the head of an iron bedstead."[9] In the darkness, rescuers would never have dared the surgical procedure. The second rescue was equally challenging:

> A woman was rescued by cutting upwards through the wire mattress of a bed on which she was trapped by debris. The bolt-cutters and wire-cutters of the rescue kit were not suitable for this job, and a pair of garden shears were pressed into service. The woman was then lowered to safety through a hole in the floor.[10]

Both operations had to await daylight. The women's patience had paid off.

The LSF man Adamson had been on duty around Summerhill the entire night. He had anxiously watched the ordeal of Miss Slater, the shopkeeper from whom he had just purchased cigarettes, as she was dug out of the ruins seriously injured. Finally, "he went home at 5 a.m. to catch an hour or two of sleep," after which "he went to work in a plumbing job at 8 o'clock."[11] Like Adamson, thousands who had toiled throughout the night had jobs requiring them to work a half day or full day on Saturday. Each had to decide whether or not they could make it, considering their sleepless, fatigued condition. And what might be the consequences of not showing up? Would their employers understand? It was to become a controversial issue in days to come.

At dawn, Jenny O'Brien's parents had a decision to make as well. Their son, Charlie Connell, was still not home. He had gone out on Friday evening, after finishing his duties as messenger-boy for Fitzpatrick's, with his pal Sniggy to the Whit Friday dance. He was a very responsible young lad. Indeed, Richard Fitzpatrick had regarded him as a son as much as a dutiful employee. With all the hubbub in the streets it was understandable to his parents that he might stay out late. But *all* night? Having fretted for several hours, constantly peering out the window in hopes of seeing him straggling home, they decided at about 6 a.m. to venture out in search of him. They couldn't have imagined the massive crowds they would encounter in the streets around the North Strand.

Meanwhile, fourteen-year-old Maureen Lynch was waking up. She had been unconscious when the ARP men found her in her stone cottage, beneath the collapsed roof. She had been carried to a building and placed directly beside the dead body of a young child, then covered with a man's coat. At some point she fell into sleep—for how long, she doesn't know. When daylight came and loud noises were heard outside, she stirred, sat up and looked around. She felt bruised but not injured. The dead child had been removed. Suddenly, she remembered all that had happened and became frantic to find her parents. She darted out of the house, a bit wobbly on her legs at first, towards their cottage beside Newcomen Bridge, then burst through the police cordons before anyone could stop her. Reaching home, she found her parents and brothers and sisters all gone:

I got up and run screaming through the barriers. And when I got back here, I couldn't get in, it was that bad. I couldn't find my mother—for nearly six or seven days!

They took her away unconscious. We didn't know if she was alive or not. Everyone was scattered ... and I couldn't find *anybody*. And so I sat there.

Denis Dunne was impatient. He wanted to know the meaning of the white enamel plate he had found in his garden bearing the word NOTBREMSHAHN. Gardaí at the station had told him he would be informed, but little more than an hour later he decided to trek back and ask if they had any information yet. Sure enough, it had already been translated. (It was, after all, only a single word.) It was a German term meaning "emergency tap or cock", similar to that displayed on trains in Germany. It was concluded that such a plate could well have been affixed on German bombers as well. He was told that he had delivered an important piece of evidence pertaining to the bombing. He felt pleasantly important as his pals tagged along home with him talking about it all.

At 6 a.m. sharp, Dubliners owning a wireless tuned in to the early morning BBC news broadcast in hopes of hearing details of the tragedy in their city. In essence, it was reported that "bombs had fallen in Dublin … and lives lost." That was all. Hardly a big story in embattled Britain.

Dubliners would have to wait for the first editions of the morning newspapers to hit the streets.

Chapter 16 ❧

| # THE MORNING AFTER

> Everybody was buying papers—to find out what really
> happened!
>
> (GABRIEL MOLONY, 83)

> See, we thought de Valera would let nothing happen to us.
> We felt safe. Really. Like "We're neutral, they couldn't do
> anything on us!" So it was a shock.
>
> (COLLEEN HEENEY, 79)

> In the morning people all assembled out in the streets,
> waiting for the churches to open ... everyone wanted to go
> to confession that next day.
>
> (AGNES DALY, 81)

> Distraught relatives called at the City Morgue and city
> hospitals seeking news of missing family members.
>
> (TOM GERAGHTY, *The Dublin Fire Brigade*)

Morning brought its own dramas and agonies.

The day broke brilliantly—exactly the sort of Whit Saturday that Dubliners had longed for. Bright sunshine in a clear sky, with warm temperatures, promising to be hot by afternoon. "Oh, the weather was beautiful," Margaret Pringle remembers. "The sun was shining ... *gorgeous!*" But at the little North Strand village the sun shone over a scene of appalling destruction and carnage.

Sunrise brought out flocks of children. They ran about, pushed through the crowds and seemed everywhere to be under the feet of adults. Their mammies, of course, had turned them loose with orders not to interfere with activities at the bomb site. To the children it was an adventure, gallivanting about with pals in unbridled excitement, maybe getting a scolding or a quick clip on the ear from an annoyed adult for their rambunctious behaviour. Among them was Mary Cooke, up from Gardiner Street with a few friends.

"Being city kids, we were *curious*. Of course, the men'd shoo you away, but you'd *come back*." For Clara Gill and her pals there was great fun and banter. "I remember one of the young lads saying what a rotten aim that German pilot had—that he had not bombed O'Connell Schools!"

Other children shouted aloud that they wanted to see some of the "dead bodies", just like the ones they had seen in scary Boris Karloff films. It would be "fun", they screamed, to see the *real* thing. Clara Gill recalls how her father, a publican and an ARP warden, headed out to do his duty. "After the bomb dropped he was helping digging for the bodies in the rubble. Of course, as children, we went down to see the bodies." So too did twelve-year-old Cathal O'Shannon, later to become a well-known *Irish Times* journalist and television presenter:

> I remember the night well, the flares, the ack-ack and then the blast from the bomb—which nearly shot us back from the windows out of which we were hanging to see the fun. My next door neighbour, Paddy Ennis, was in the LSF and we, as kids, followed him to the bomb site on the morning after the raid—but we got chased away because we only wanted to see the corpses.[1]

Those children who actually saw a body being removed found that it wasn't much fun after all, especially if there was blood or excretion on the sheet or stretcher. Most, like Una Shaw, were repulsed, particularly when seeing body parts being dug out and removed:

> Oh, I couldn't *wait* to get out! But I wasn't prepared for what I saw when I got there. A horrible thing for us was seeing them digging out the bodies. With *bare hands!* We *saw* them doing it. It was *dreadful* ... there were arms, legs, feet from bodies. But we stayed looking at it, you know, and kind of not believing this. And while we were looking, somebody said, "There's a body!" But the *minute* we heard that we got back—because we didn't *want* to see anybody coming out dead.

Everyone was mad to get their hands on a morning newspaper. Smyllie and his competing editors at other papers were working under great pressure to get the huge story out. There had been three big news events in Dublin over the previous twenty-five years: the 1916 Rising, the Civil War of 1922 and the 1932 Eucharistic Congress. But these had unfolded over days and weeks. The German bombing, with its destruction, death and pandemonium, had occurred in a matter of hours—in the middle of the night, on a holiday weekend. Adrenalin had been running almost as high in editorial offices and newsrooms as on the bomb scene itself. As Tony Gray recalls, "we were all so excited about it," every person hurriedly trying to do their part in piecing together the comprehensive story.[2] He returned from the North Strand on his bike somewhere between five and six o'clock carrying the news he had jotted down and found the office in a frenzy of activity. Reporters were excitedly surrounding the deputy chief reporter, each trying to feed him their accounts:

> I went back to the Reporters' room, where Matt Chambers, the Deputy Chief Reporter, was sitting at his typewriter, surrounded by other reporters who were dictating to him what they had been able to discover about the events of the night. The reporters had been in different areas of Dublin and around to the hospitals. Chambers was trying to type them out and was then handing them to a sub-editor who was collating the various accounts into a coherent article.[3]

The pressure felt by everyone, Gray remembers, was palpable, because the circumstances of the tragedy and time constraints did not allow for the normal careful verification of accounts and cross-checking of facts. Most challenging, and frustrating, was trying to obtain figures for the deaths and injuries that were reliable enough to be printed. Readers would look for the death count straight away. But a newspaper's reputation rested on accuracy, and so caution had to be exercised, as evidenced by virtually identical headlines:

BOMBS IN DUBLIN THIS MORNING: MANY KILLED—*Irish Times*
BOMBS ON DUBLIN: MANY DEAD—*Irish Press*

Neither newspaper would commit itself to a hard figure. The *Irish Independent* was similarly restrained, reporting that "it is feared that the death roll is high … and many people were buried in the wreckage."[4] The *Evening Mail*, whose reporters had more time during the day to probe, confirmed in its late afternoon edition that *at least* "eleven bodies were taken to the City Morgue."[5]

Smyllie was clever. As the editor of Dublin's most respected newspaper, he felt he had a special responsibility for accuracy. Other newspapers might put out differing estimates of the number of deaths; Smyllie chose to quote respected sources about *their* estimates. Dr J. C. Waugh had been on the bomb scene since about 2:25 a.m., in contact with all the rescue and medical services who carried out the dead and injured. His relationship with *Irish Times* reporters was good. In a "stop press" morning edition, Smyllie decided to print Waugh's statement that "the death toll might be as high as thirty to forty."[6] In this, he had scooped his competitors—and played it safe at the same time, because it was acceptable for the doctor to be wrong.

Most newspapers printed conservative headlines, but ran articles with tantalising titles.

BURIED TO NECK IN DEBRIS
HUGE CRATER: HOUSES CRASH
RESCUERS FORM HUMAN CHAIN
FIRES FOLLOW BIG EXPLOSION
HEROIC RESCUE WORK
DARING ESCAPES SEEN

One headline stood dramatically apart from all the others, both in size and phrasing. The *Evening Herald* had its compositors dig out their largest type, dusty from disuse. Their headline blared across the city:

NIGHT OF HORROR

To keep pace with continually unfolding events, newspapers printed updated "stop press" editions. "The presses were constantly stopped throughout the morning," recounts Tony Gray, "constantly updated until about eight or nine o'clock, to incorporate the latest version of the story."[7] Generally, the reportage was excellent and the photographs of high quality. Under the strain of circumstances and time, some errors were inevitable. Most were of minor importance. The *Irish Times* printed the most blatant error when it stated that "three bombs were dropped in Dublin early this morning."[8] All other newspapers correctly reported four bombs. Had Smyllie's staff forgotten about the explosion in the Phoenix Park?

The presses had been humming at full speed for so long that when the last copies of the final edition flew off they were nearly smoking. Throughout the morning, newspaper carriers and Dublin's newsboys had been waiting in fits of anxiety to grab all they could carry. Just behind them were crowds of people waiting to snatch a first copy on the spot. The newsboys, mostly from the tenements of the north side and Liberties, stuffed papers under both arms and ran through the streets like savages, shrieking, "Big bomb falls on Dublin." In the flurry of handing out papers as people grabbed for them, newsboys couldn't take the time to count the pennies and ha'pennies being thrust into their hands or tossed into the box on the ground. Some customers, so eager to begin reading the news, didn't even bother waiting for change. Within minutes their newspapers were sold out and they were tearing back like marathon runners for their next load.

As trams and buses from the suburbs arrived in the city, anxious passengers cried out to newsboys as they thrust their arms out windows to get a copy. Christy Murray, who began selling papers as a lad of eight, saw people wildly waving their arms out of passing trams:

> I was like a hare, I'd dodge the horses and traffic. *Jump* up onto the trams and sell the papers, dash downstairs, then hop off. And then onto another tram. Then *fly down* and bring more back.

He had no idea how many newspapers he sold that day—more than he could count, that's all he knows.

People bought newspapers who couldn't even read what was in them. They relied on others to read the words for them, after they had stared at the shocking photographs. This was especially prevalent among the city's tenement-dwellers, many of whom were barely literate. A single newspaper could be passed from hand to hand, read by so many that it was eventually in tatters. In Mary Cooke's tenement house in Lower Gardiner Street one woman read the news to all the occupants:

> Not everybody in the tenement could afford a paper, though it was only a penny and a ha'penny. But there was a woman at the top of the house and she used to come and sit with us at night and she'd read her *Herald*. So, she was reading out the stories of what had happened. *Everyone* was interested.

In pubs it was the same scene: men either leaning over one another's shoulders to look at a copy spread out on the table or bar, or one man reading it aloud to others. In the city's public houses there was talk of nothing else. Indeed, says Mary Cooke, "*everywhere* you went in Dublin, people were talking about the bombing; it was on everyone's lips."

———

Government officials began arriving at the bomb scene at about nine o'clock. One after another, their black cars pulled up beside ambulances as sombre-faced men stepped out into the bright sunshine, now fully exposing the ravaged landscape around them. When Éamon de Valera showed up with members of his Government, even rescue workers halted for a moment to glance over, everyone awaiting his reaction. Behind were members of the Dáil and Seanad, along with Lieut-General Daniel McKenna, chief of staff. Also there was the Archbishop of Dublin, John Charles McQuaid. Stony-faced, de Valera led the entourage into the ruins, still smouldering, with flare-ups here

Stevens' cycle workshop at 171 North Strand Road, with a penny-farthing bicycle in the background. (*Courtesy of Dublin City Archives*)

Damage at numbers 153 to 164 North Strand. (*Courtesy of Dublin City Archives*)

The *Evening Herald*'s headline, "Night of Horror," captured interest and sold newspapers at a record rate.

Numbers 24 to 27 Richmond Cottages were left standing but badly ravaged. (*Courtesy of Dublin City Archives*)

Members of the St John Ambulance Brigade carrying out a victim on a stretcher. (*Courtesy of Military Archives*)

Noel Brady was a young member of the St John Ambulance Brigade in his early twenties. He is shown here in the late 1980s.

William Grice's tobacconist shop on the North Circular Road, which suffered damage from the first bomb that fell on 31 May 1941. (*Courtesy of Dublin City Archives*)

Various types of bomb damage between numbers 153 and 164 North Strand Road. (*Courtesy of Dublin City Archives*)

Children outside numbers 5 and 5A Newcomen Court whose houses survived. (*Courtesy of Dublin City Archives*)

Gardaí and soldiers had to patrol the ruins to watch for looters and for distressed residents trying to gain entry to their condemned houses. (*Courtesy of the* Irish Independent)

One of the lanes at Quinn's Cottages. (*Courtesy of Dublin City Archives*)

Numbers 1 to 3 Summer Hill Parade, close to where one of the smaller bombs fell. (*Courtesy of Dublin City Archives*)

Jenny Connell, whose brother Charlie was missing and feared killed following the bomb blast.

and there. They passed stretcher-bearers coming out with victims. Reporters and photographers tagged along behind at a discreet distance.

As the procession of officials was led towards the crater, they were largely silent, some noticeably tight-jawed, slowly shaking their heads. Several were visibly touched. A reporter for the *Evening Mail* who managed to get close to the official party observed that "Mr. de Valera looked very moved as he watched the terrible destruction wrought upon happy homes," adding that he also saw "tears in the eyes" of Alfie Byrne as he "comforted persons who had lost many of their dear ones."[9] De Valera quietly praised the rescue squads while "heartily commending the pluck and cool-headedness of people who had been bombed out of their homes."[10]

Photographers stepped forward to take pictures whenever possible. One photograph was particularly telling. De Valera stood at the lip of the crater, his head bent slightly down, as if he were at a graveside. The photographer positioned himself perfectly, directly across from de Valera on the opposite side of the crater, at just the right moment to capture his expression. The Taoiseach looked utterly bewildered, peering into the depression as if seeking answers.

For a man seemingly in command of every situation, on this early Whit Saturday morning he looked decidedly less commanding. Some said he looked shaken, uncertain—less sure of himself. Citizens worried when seeing *him* worried. It didn't instil confidence at a time when Dubliners were fearful of being bombed again that night. "People were *flabbergasted*," Mary Cooke claims, "because everybody thought de Valera was so pally with Hitler that he wouldn't even *breathe* near Ireland." He had convincingly stood up to both Churchill and Hitler in forging his neutrality policy, and it had seemed to be working. "We thought de Valera would let nothing happen to us," says Colleen Heeney. "We felt safe, 'we're *neutral*,' they couldn't do anything on us! So it was a *shock!*"

Upon completing his official visit, wrote the *Irish Press*, "An Taoiseach went to each house, in turn, and spoke to homeless people who were still waiting to hear of news from relatives."[11] He extended his condolences to victims but made no public pronouncement before departing. Nor did other politicians, with the exception of the leader of the opposition, W. T. Cosgrave, whose sentiments were printed by the *Evening Herald*:

> Mr. Cosgrave, T.D., who inspected the damage, expressed deep sympathy with the victims of the bombing, and said it was a shocking thing that innocent people should be subjected to such an outrage.[12]

Most members of the Government did not stay long; nor did some of them ever return to talk to Northstranders, or supervise recovery efforts. As Una

Shaw flatly claims, "De Valera and the others, they just came and went." The exception was Alfie Byrne, the most ubiquitous figure on the scene, day after day, week after week. Many local people preferred his presence to that of Dev himself.

Shortly after nine o'clock, Maureen Lynch was still sitting alone on the front step of her parents' roofless, windowless cottage beside Newcomen Bridge. With her mother, father and siblings missing, she could think of nothing to do but sit and wait. Only a few feet in front of her the water was still spilling pleasantly over the canal lock. It seemed like the only natural, peaceful feature of the village left. Fifty years later she can't recall what she was thinking about at that moment, whether she was afraid, or crying. Just sitting.

The sight of a young girl, so conspicuously forlorn in the midst of destruction and havoc, caught the eye of just the right person. This she remembers perfectly:

> As I was sitting there, Alfie Byrne, the Lord Mayor, he came down and he had the medal on him, and he was a great gentleman. And he put two and sixpence into my hand and said, "Go and get yourself a gur cake."

As mayor, Byrne championed children's rights and fought to get them playgrounds and swings and open spaces. He held parties for deprived children in the Mansion House, sometimes inviting "up to 2,000 children to face up to 5,000 cakes, 3,000 apples and a ton of ice cream!"[13] Who better to happen upon the sad and lonely figure! He asked about her parents, reassuring her that they would be reunited soon.

Her spirits revived, she found a shop a few streets away that was damaged but open, selling the most delicious gur cake she had ever tasted. Upon finishing the last morsel, she decided to try to find her best friend, who lived just across the road, where some tenement houses had taken a fierce battering. Maybe they could stay together and play until her parents showed up:

> So my pal, Mary, lived over there, and she just scratched her leg and she was sitting in the parlour—the other half was gone. So I said, "C'mon, let's go gallivant!" And when we were going down the stairs didn't we fall three flights *down*! Because the banister broke, and we were nearly killed. We landed in the back yard and couldn't get back up to come out the front. And we had to climb out.

Just as they reached the street, a shop that sold paraffin oil was ignited by embers and broke out, "just *blazing*. There was a huge crowd, but everybody had to get back." For the remainder of the morning and afternoon the two girls stuck together. For the moment, at least, they had found company in one another.

As the officials had been making their visit, and Maureen Lynch munching on her gur cake, lamplighter Frank Wearen had still not returned home. He was now hours late and his family were sick with worry. They knew that his nightly rounds took him along Gardiner Street and Summerhill, right up around the North Strand. When the bomb exploded he had joined the crowd of onlookers. At about seven o'clock, after fretful waiting, his wife and two sons decided to go in search of him. Along the way they would ask people if they had seen Frank, a figure known to all. When he finally headed home for some breakfast he found his wife and sons still out looking for him:

> I didn't get home until after nine that morning, and my wife was out on her bike and two of my sons searching for me. They didn't know *where* I was. And I says to my little ones, "Where's your mammy?" "They're out looking for you, Da, they thought you were blown up!" They thought I was blew up ... but I wasn't. So she was delighted when she came home, I'll tell you.

By now the atmosphere in the reporters' room at the *Irish Times* had become somewhat more relaxed. The critical first editions had been pieced together, printed and distributed throughout Dublin. Several reporters were assigned to remain on the bomb scene and at hospitals and mortuaries throughout the day to collect news for the next day's edition. Smyllie gave Tony Gray, Alan Bestic and other reporters permission to go home and get some sleep. But the adrenalin was still too much for some to do so. As Gray explains, they were still "too excited" to leave the story, and "since it was too late to go home, Alan Bestic and I went back to the North Strand to collect more material for the next paper."[14]

As the two reporters cycled back to the scene they noticed throngs gathered at every church they passed. People frightened that they would be bombed again that night flocked to the one place where they could find some solace—and Absolution. "*Everybody* wanted to go to confession that next day," says Una Shaw. Those who had been unable to halt a priest on the street or at the bomb scene were particularly desperate. Once inside a church they were reluctant to leave, Dixie Dean remembers. "People were *terrified*, and they went in and just *sat* there." By early morning, churches were completely filled, with people outside on the steps and pavement waiting to get in. "Oh, *every* church in Ireland was packed," says Sally Burke. "My mother couldn't *get into* the church." With every priest busy at the bomb site, hospitals or refugee shelters, it would be a long wait until confession boxes would be "open for business" in the afternoon. In the meantime, the multitudes lit penny candles, said the Rosary over and over, and prayed hard.

Other church affairs had to be postponed under the circumstances. At St Agatha's Church, only about forty yards from the bomb crater, the boys of the parish were to have made their first Holy Communion that morning of 31 May. It was the tradition in Dublin that girls made theirs in mid-May and the boys followed two weeks later. It was always much anticipated, for monetary reasons as well as religious. It was always a big day in their lives. They would race home, tear off their Communion outfit, then head to the nearest sweet shop.

Though St Agatha's Church survived essentially intact, all its large stained-glass windows were shattered, and damage was done to the roof and exterior. The building was not safe to enter on Saturday morning, nor would the authorities allow people on the site for days. To the boys, at their age, the postponement was as devastating as the bombing. "The children were *so* disappointed," recalls Bernadette Pierce, "'cause your Communion was the only day you'd get some money, and they were looking forward to that." Other local churches proceeded with their plans. Up around Mountjoy Square and Mountjoy Place, Winnie Brennan recalls, the boys benefited from sympathetic sentiments, even though their area had not been directly bombed:

> The boys making their first Holy Communion, people were *so sorry* for them … "Oh, they never got a night's sleep last night!" And where they [usually] got sixpence they were getting two shillings, or half a crown! They made a *fortune*, and they were delighted with themselves.

When the boys from St Agatha's got wind of the generosity being heaped upon lads in other parishes, they were less than delighted. But when their big day would come a few weeks later, they would profit handsomely.

On Saturday morning countless other decisions had to be made. Whit holidaymakers who had made all sorts of plans for the three-day weekend had to decide whether to proceed or to cancel. Some were only jaunts to the seaside or to parks, but others were expensive excursions by train to Galway, Killarney, Sligo and elsewhere. The sunny weather was alluring, and many felt they needed to get away from the tensions in Dublin. By all accounts, most holidaymakers stuck with their plans—a decision that would later bring some criticism. It was not their departure from the city or their need for enjoyment that drew criticism but their exuberant mood and seeming insensitivity to the tragedy of fellow-Dubliners.

By mid-morning, crowds had gathered at all the city's transport terminals, in cheerful spirits, anticipating the weekend's fun, as described by the *Evening Mail*:

Dublin's Whit week-end saw a great trek from the city, and at railway stations and bus terminals happy throngs were rushing to sea and country. The exodus began on Saturday and continued to Whit Monday.[15]

Many in the crowds laughed and bantered as if everything were normal, while a few streets away bodies were still being removed from the ruins and others remained buried or missing. Holidaymakers standing outdoors waiting for buses and trams could see the curls of smoke still rising from the North Strand and ambulances tearing past them with their bells clanging.

"Happy throngs" in a city stricken with tragedy and grief seemed an awful incongruity to many Dubliners.

Thousands of other Dubliners had a decision of a very different sort to make on Saturday morning—whether or not they should show up for work. In 1941 many shops, factories and offices were open on Saturdays for at least half a day. Thousands of employees were members of the ARP, LDF, LSF and other emergency services who had no sleep and were fatigued from physical and emotional exertion. Were they required to show up for work, or would their bosses grant them leave to recuperate? Many of them feared their bosses and worried about losing their job or having their pay docked. While some employers were understanding and lenient, others were tyrants. On the morning of 31 May each employee had to make their decision, take their chances. Dixie Dean, who worked at the foundry in Hammond Lane, had a boss with a heart, who would surely excuse his absence under the circumstances. But he knew many others who might face a stiff penalty or even dismissal if they failed to show up on time. It was a weighty decision.

Those who lived close to the bomb site and who went to work as usual on Saturday morning found themselves the centre of attention, surrounded by workmates from other parts of Dublin who wanted to hear all about their eye-witness accounts. Twenty-two-year-old Bridie Byrne of Rutland Street was up the entire night, but she dutifully headed off to work at the Rowntree chocolate factory out in Inchicore. So too did Margaret Pringle, who worked at Woolworth's in Henry Street. Both were treated like celebrities when they reached their work-place, where everyone first expressed relief to find that they had survived; then came an avalanche of questions. When they told those huddled around them about the terrible destruction, people killed and buried alive in the rubble, they were agog. Even their managers stood by, listening intently.

Chrissie Byrne went to work as usual as a domestic servant in a private house on the North Circular Road. When she boarded her regular bus, "*everyone* was talking about it—and I was in the centre of it. Yeah, 'cause they knew I lived there. And they wanted to know how did we get out." She told them the full story—at least as much as the journey time allowed. But not every work-place hummed with talk of the bombing, as Muriel Godden found when she arrived for work at the Bank of Ireland in College Green. Then twenty-three, she was from a well-to-do family living in Clontarf and had attended Alexandra College. She held a good position at the bank and liked her fellow-workers and bosses. The bank atmosphere was very professional, but staff members at all levels were warm and friendly. However, on this morning she found the lofty Bank of Ireland to be a world apart from the reality just beyond its doors.

When she entered the bank chambers it was a silent world. No talk of the bombing, no excitement, no upset. Nothing even *unusual*. As she proceeded to her desk, others greeted her in the ordinary manner. Not a single utterance about the tragedy. Business as usual! As if the staff and management had never *heard* about the bombing, or read anything about it in the newspapers. She was flummoxed:

> Next day I went to my job in the Bank of Ireland; we had to work Saturday mornings then. The most *extraordinary* thing when I got to work is that there wasn't *one word* about the bomb. Not a word! I thought *everybody* would be talking about that terrible night, with these bombs. I was shocked … it would have been a relief to have somebody say, "Oh, that was dreadful last night," you know? But the work of the bank went on just as if *nothing* had happened. It's *extraordinary!*

She settled in to work at her desk, then discreetly glanced around to try to detect whether any others were feeling the same sense of puzzlement and discomfort. But there were no signs. So she too remained silent, all the while wondering why her colleagues had so sympathetically discussed the London and Belfast blitzes. Why not Dublin, their own city? Sixty-three years later, in 2004, it still confounded her:

> I think there was a kind of *taboo*, a silent taboo, over it. That *nobody* said a word about it. You would think that nothing had happened. A taboo over it … like we weren't *supposed* to say anything rude about the Germans. *Why* did they not talk of it at *all*? I never did understand that.

By ten o'clock every hospital bed in Jervis Street and the Mater was filled and hallways jammed with victims on beds or trolleys awaiting treatment. Many were in great pain, moaning and calling for attention. But theirs were not the only voices of suffering, for the hospitals were now being besieged by relatives desperately searching for missing loved ones. As the *Evening Mail* phrased it, "the ominous word 'missing', applied to so many of the victims of last night's bombing, has given rise to many pathetic incidents."[16] Reporters stationed at hospitals hoping to get updated figures on deaths and injuries, as well as some human-interest stories, wrote of the frantic despair of relatives searching for the missing. As many of the injured had not been identified, the situation was frustrating for both hospital staff and relatives. The *Evening Mail* addressed the growing problem of missing and unidentified persons:

> It was stated in many circles that a number of persons were either walking or standing on the North Strand when the bomb fell. A number of badly mutilated and unidentified bodies are in city hospitals, and it is suggested that they might have been these people.[17]

Some frantic relatives wanted to go from room to room in the hospitals, looking at victims, to see if they could personally identify the face of a mother, son, or granny. It was difficult for staff members to explain to them why this was not possible. Thus, wrote the *Irish Independent*, "tragic scenes were witnessed at the hospitals as distraught people sought for missing relatives."[18] The situation would grow worse throughout the latter part of the morning and afternoon as more unidentified victims were brought to hospitals and mortuaries. The missing list steadily climbed.

At the bomb scene and in hospitals, refugee centres and mortuaries, the agony of family members was painfully apparent. It was said by some to be even more pitiful than that of losing a loved one by death. For death, at least, was conclusive, while the ordeal of seeking missing loved ones could be torturously prolonged for hours, days, even weeks. At the North Strand, reported the *Irish Press*, "many children were crying for their mothers, who could not be found."[19] It was nearly impossible to console them.

From the moment Garda Finucane arrived at the bomb scene, people began approaching him about their missing relatives, "a terrible lot of agony and crying and weeping, 'cause no-one *knew* about their missing"—where they were, whether they were dead or alive, or possibly still buried beneath the rubble, struggling to hold on to life.

Verification of death was at least mercifully final. But the agonising suspense of not knowing could become nearly unbearable. The longer a person was missing, the greater the torment. There were many like Maureen Lynch who were unable to find her mother, "for nearly six or seven days." After a while, when emotions frayed, distraught relatives would approach *any* authority—rescuer, policeman, fireman, hospital staff, ambulance orderly, Red Cross nurse—blurting out a description of their mammy, daddy, son or granny and pleading for help in finding them. Noel Brady recalls how, one after another, relatives would approach him. "They'd come looking for their sister or 'me brother'," even if he was in the midst of treating a serious injury. Some even asked if they could climb into the back of ambulances to look at victims waiting to be taken away—which, of course, they were not allowed to do. Nurse Ann Leonard felt immense sympathy for such desperate souls, because they seemed to be at their rope's end. "People were killed, and there was *no-one* to identify them. And some could be lying in the hospital unconscious, and people looking for them—that was the *awful* part of it. They could be *anywhere*."

Relatives, therefore, had to search everywhere. They normally began at the North Strand, then proceeded to hospitals, first-aid stations and eventually the refugee shelters. Mortuaries were the last, dreaded resort. Around dawn the Connells had begun their search for their son Charlie at the bomb scene. They had not realised how congested and chaotic the site would be, as they tried pushing their way through the crowds, looking for Charlie's face. "Having no luck" and feeling overwhelmed, their daughter Jenny recalls, "they headed to Fitzgibbon Street police station. Given the panic that was there, the police directed my parents to the morgue." They were stunned to hear the term used in reference to their missing son. It was the last advice they wanted to hear, and they were not about to follow it. Instead they would begin making the rounds of hospitals. They began with the Mater and Jervis Street, which by this time had a total of nearly two hundred new patients, many of whom had not been identified. They quickly found that there was no way to obtain information from busy staff members. So they went outside for a while and watched ambulances as they pulled up, to see if Charlie might be on one of the stretchers. No luck.

Finally returning to the North Strand, they were surprised to find that Charlie's older brother Richard, who was in the army, had been sent to the scene with his unit to help with digging through the rubble. They told him that Charlie was missing. At once he became fearful that with every brick and timber he removed he might see his younger brother's face beneath. His parents did not mention to him the advice they had received from the police at Fitzgibbon Street.

——

By 10 a.m., the shelters for homeless people were filling up fast. Refugees came not only from the North Strand but from surrounding areas as well, their homes having been damaged too seriously for safe habitation. The Red Cross headquarters in Mespil Road accommodated the largest number, already in

the hundreds and steadily growing. Several convents, most notably the Sisters
of Charity convent in North William Street, were taking in hundreds more.
Among the other shelters were Baggotrath Hall in Baggot Street, Charleville
Mall Library, the YMCA hall in Middle Abbey Street, An Óige Hall in Mountjoy
Square, and St George's Hall in South Great George's Street. Homeless victims
were even taken into the Mansion House, the Theatre Royal, and the
Municipal Art Gallery in Parnell Square. Who would have thought to look for
their missing family members at an art gallery, a theatre or the Lord Mayor's
residence? And, as reported by the *Evening Herald*, many local residents took
needy refugees into their homes:

> Local residents, whose homes, though damaged, were still standing …
> forgot their own troubles in the face of the disaster that had befallen their
> less fortunate neighbours and offered shelter for the homeless and cared
> for frightened children.[20]

As homeless people were widely dispersed in shelters throughout the city,
there was no central registration system through which they could be traced.
Many people officially listed as missing, and feared dead, were eventually
found in shelters, but this could take days or weeks. The situation was made
all the more confusing because many people were shifted from one shelter to
another, especially during the first forty-eight hours. During this process
families were often split up. This occurred when many of the frightened
Northstranders who had scrambled down into the basement of the
Charleville Mall Library during the first minutes following the blast were sent
over to the convent in North William Street a few hours later. Then, on
Saturday morning, some of them were transported once again across the
Liffey to Baggotrath Hall. This was Mary Dunne's experience:

> In the morning the big army lorries came and took us from the convent,
> all the women and children, and we went to Baggotrath Hall. It was a
> Protestant hall. I don't know where the men were put. And we were
> sleeping on mattresses on the floor, a lovely polished floor, and they would
> feed us down in Mespil Road, at the Red Cross. Huge big army cooking-
> pots and big kettles for the tea. And there was bread and jam.

Most of those in shelters were women and children. Men were generally
sheltered separately.

Scores of shaken men chose a different kind of shelter: the public house.
This was their refuge. "Men only." The majority of local men behaved
honourably when the bombs fell, remaining with their families or hastening

to do their duty in rescue work. But it is verified by oral history, both from their families and from others, that too many men did not. They essentially deserted their wives and children after the terrifying explosion and fled to public houses for their own security and companionship. If women instinctively turned to prayer, these men instinctively turned to drink.

Most pubs around the North Strand had either been blown up or at least blown apart, with smashed windows and damaged roofs, some with ceilings and walls cracked or crumbled. But they were functional. With the explosion, every publican within a mile was awakened and was up checking on his premises. Within minutes they heard the voices of men gathering outside— men suffering from fear, bad nerves, and a great thirst. Drink, they reasoned, would stabilise them—and it would take a heartless publican to turn them away in the midst of such a tragedy. Where publicans did not promptly open up, men banged loudly on the door and shouted up to their living quarters above. Many pubs were thus opened for business in the middle of the night. As Winnie Brennan explains, for both publicans and patrons "the attitude was 'there's no guards going to come around and arrest us on a night like this!'" They were quite right, as policemen indeed turned a blind eye. A few in fact were known to have stepped in themselves to grab a quick sup to steady their own nerves. As fathers and husbands were drinking the night away in their sanctuaries, their families were huddled in basements and shelters, left to survive on their own.

Brennan's father and his mates from around Mountjoy Place were typical. When the ARP warden had ordered everyone along the street to seek safety in tenement basements, he and his friends declared they wanted no part of it: the pub was their preferred destination. And *off they went*—leaving their families behind to fare for themselves. Once ensconced in a pub they could drink all night long, as publicans were glad to extend credit; just "put it on the slate." Many stayed not only all night but the next morning, afternoon, and the following day. Some went on a drinking binge for days and were counted among the missing. Late on Saturday morning, Winnie Brennan's father traipsed home, without a hint of remorse or apology. In fact, Winnie remembers, her father's attitude was quite smug:

Now my father, the next day he comes in and he's sitting there thinking. And he said to my mother, "You know something, I was thinking of the lot of youse down in that basement last night when I was having a few jars." "Oh," says she, "and we had *nothing*, not a cup of tea nor drink of water."

"Ah, well," says he, "that's the way it is. But I was thinking of youse all and was thinking, sure if a bomb lands on that house the *whole thing'd* fall on top and we'd have never got you out of there—and you'd have been smashed with the top in on top of you. And I was terrified thinking of that." And she said, "You'll frighten the child, talking like that." And he says, "She's *alive*, isn't she, she's there!" And he was *laughing! Imagine*, he thought it was hilarious.

It was lovely that a crowd of men could go to the pub and sit drinking all night—when they *should* have been *helping* their families! But that's the way life went in those days.

———

Noon was approaching, as the sun rose higher. The afternoon was sure to be a scorcher. Some firemen, policemen and rescue crews had been relieved by fresh reserves. But not Senan Finucane and Maurice Walsh, now into their ninth hour of duty. "It was *very* hot," sighs Finucane, "and there was no hope of getting us any relief." He and Walsh had dry, sore throats from the smoke and dust and continuous talking to people behind their cordons. They had hours yet to go.

Dick Eyres had also worked relentlessly since 2:05, helping with rescues and comforting people. Shortly after eleven o'clock he received a new order: "Captain McDonagh, our area chief warden, turned up. I was asked to go around to the local hospitals and assist in identifying people who had been killed."[21] He spent most of his time at Jervis Street and the Mater, where "I did identify some of them."

By late morning every hospital mortuary had bodies. Of the first eleven taken to the City Morgue, only one had so far been identified.[22]

Jack Conroy and his comrades from Buckingham Street fire station remained on the job because small fires kept popping up out of the smouldering ruins. When burning embers found something flammable, such as paraffin oil or dry timber, they could suddenly erupt into a blaze. As the morning grew hotter and drier the firemen used their hoses to spray down the dust at some rescue sites, leaving pools of dirty water and mud. They joked among themselves about how their local publican would be giving them a free pint for their good work. Which, indeed, many did later.

Noel Brady and Ann Leonard were finally relieved as reinforcements were sent in from the St John Ambulance Brigade. For nearly nine hours they had been on the "battlefield", as Leonard called it, and they were filthy, with blood-stained uniforms. The fresh nurses and orderlies paraded past them in immaculate uniforms, with clean face and hands. Brady packed up his medical pouch, mounted his bicycle and began slowly pedalling home, out to the Naas Road. Along the way he found himself thinking just the opposite

thought to that which had been locked in his mind on the way to the North
Strand, about his terrible fear of blood. "Now," he said to himself, "I'll never
worry about blood again."

Leonard was as weary as she had ever been: "I wouldn't stop to get a drink
of water, *didn't* stop till that morning." She slung her medical kit over her
shoulder and began the walk home, across the Liffey and through Merrion
Square. She was surprised to find how people along the way were so
appreciative for what she had done:

> I was coming up Merrion Square on my own and I had my white helmet
> on and the whole lot, and people were coming over and saying, "Nurse, can
> I carry your case?" But I knew that I had morphine tablets in it, so I said,
> "Sorry, it's not heavy." *Everybody* wanted to help me.

It wasn't until she got home and looked in the mirror at her bedraggled
condition and soiled uniform that she understood why people were so
sympathetic.

By eleven o'clock, the St John's mobile canteen that had been brought to
the North Strand at dawn had served more than a thousand people. Now they
began providing lunches in the form of hearty soup and stew brought in large
drums. It was hot, fresh and greatly welcomed by famished rescuers. It
brought people together for a few minutes where they could relax, even smile.
Those who could finish off their break with a quick smoke were especially
contented.

At 11:45, the crowd that was gathered around the canteen turned to look
when they heard a commotion over at one of the digging sites. A reporter
from the *Evening Mail* was on the spot to cover what was happening, as "two
women were rescued, having been trapped beneath tons of debris on their
homes for nearly ten hours ... medical men had fed them through a tube."[23]
Within minutes the news spread from one end of the North Strand to the
other, lifting everyone's spirits and giving fresh hope to Mr Fagan and others
who still had loved ones buried under the rubble.

Only ten minutes later there was another happy scene:

> Begrimed and tired, rescue men were still continuing their work in one
> area when they were attracted by the singing of birds. Going into the
> debris, they found two cages in which a Bull-Finch and Linnet were
> chirruping gaily. The birds were at once removed to a safer place.[24]

By late morning surely everyone in Dublin had seen a copy of one of the
newspapers. They knew *what* had happened, and *where*, and saw the

photographs of destruction. But information about deaths and injuries was vague. Readers wanted the *details*, and more eye-witness accounts and stories of survivors and "daring rescues". The morning papers had whetted their appetite for more coverage of the bombing; they now eagerly awaited the appearance of the evening newspapers with updated news and fresh stories from the scene.

They especially wanted to know more about what the *Sunday Independent* would call the "Two Family Tragedies", those of Harry Browne and Richard Fitzpatrick, who were "wiped out", as the paper bluntly worded it. A third family, that of Patrick McLoughlin, would be added later. The unfolding drama of these three families would, for the next week, captivate Dubliners. The more details they learnt, the more people would come to feel they personally knew members of the three families, and the more deeply they would grieve at their funerals.

Richard Fitzpatrick and his wife had been found early on Saturday morning in the ruins of their butcher's shop at 28 North Strand. Both were declared "dead on admission" at the Mater Hospital, then taken to the City Morgue. Their seventeen-year-old son, Gerald, had arrived home just as his parents' bodies were being removed. The Fitzpatricks' son Noel and daughter Madge were still buried somewhere in the rubble. The hope was that they at least would soon be found alive. Noel was scheduled to appear in the Olympia Theatre's new production, beginning in only two days.

The death of Richard Fitzpatrick was immediately surrounded by conflicting accounts of how he was killed. Several grisly stories were going around. "Weird things happened," contends Dermot Ring, "like with Mr Fitzpatrick, the butcher up there. The story is that a pane of glass took his head off." As other cases of decapitation had been verified, it was credible. On the other hand, Cathleen Roche got the version that he darted into his vault-like cold room for protection, "went into the freezer and was killed" when the door jolted shut and suffocated him. Noel Brady heard a similar account: "He went into the fridge for shelter, then the blast knocked it down and he was asphyxiated. And the *cold*." Others claimed he died of shock or a heart attack. Local people hoped that the City Coroner would clear up the matter on Tuesday, after the post-mortem examination had been carried out.

By far the most tragic case was that of the Browne family. All seven lives were snuffed out in the huge blast. There would be no speculation about how they had died, for the autopsies would provide the awful evidence quite convincingly.

Throughout Saturday morning talk of the Browne family tragedy was heard everywhere. It was the details of their fate that wrenched the hearts of Dubliners. Witnesses came forward to say how they saw Harry Browne sprinting towards number 25 North Strand in those last seconds, arriving just in time to reach out and grasp the doorknob. Local people came forward to tell how everyone in the area was immensely fond of Harry, his wife, Molly, and their children, Maureen, Ann, Edward, and little Angela, who had been born there. By all accounts the Brownes were happy with their decision to leave Edenderry and adopt the North Strand as their new home. They loved the people, the setting, the close community feeling. And the children were delighted being by the canal, Newcomen Bridge and the Strand cinema. Harry and Molly wanted them to grow up there and hopefully raise their own families. All their grandchildren would be "native Northstranders".

They all died violently. "Their bodies crushed, burned or torn asunder," it was written, their home completely "demolished ... beams left sticking up like broken human bones."[25] Rescuers saw that they had no chance. Removing their mangled and charred remains was too much for several to bear. When they found Harry it was verified that he had reached his door precisely at the second the bomb detonated:

> Harry Browne made it to his front door, for when the rescuers reached his body which was buried under the debris he had the door-knob in his hand. Inside were the bodies of Harry's mother, wife, and children.
>   Molly's body was found with the youngest in her arms, as if she had got out of bed to see what was happening.[26]

Dubliners wept openly when reading the details.

Back in the early 1940s, most Irish Catholics accepted that every event in life, large or small, was the result of "God's will", part of "his plan". Some would have difficulty comprehending the cruel fate of the Brownes, especially when they read that Miss Nally, another resident in the same house, escaped not only death but injury by "being blown into the basement," where she found enough air to survive until rescuers found her.[27] Where was God's justice and mercy? There would be much about the bombing tragedy that would cause people to reflect deeply upon their faith in the days ahead.

The parallel between the heroic efforts of Harry Browne and Patrick McLoughlin was widely commented upon. Both men had raced back from Summerhill to reach their families as the bomb descended screaming above their heads. Each had just reached the door, Patrick McLoughlin managing to plunge a few feet inside. But the similarity of outcome was yet unknown, as McLoughlin and his two-year-old son, William, were still buried beneath the debris at 157 North Strand. Possibly alive. Late on Saturday morning there was still hope, especially with the rescue of the two women at 11:45 after their ten-hour ordeal.

Patrick McLoughlin's wife and their two-month-old baby, Vera, had been pulled out of the crumpled house injured. As the hours passed, she waited in the hospital for news of Patrick and little William. Over the coming days, all Dublin would be waiting with her. The continuing drama of the "entombment" of father and child would be reported in every edition, even when there was no fresh news to report. It generated great interest on streets and in trams and buses, where one stranger might ask another who was reading a newspaper, "What's the latest on the McLoughlins?" Towards the end, it was simply "What's the latest?"

The three stricken families—Fitzpatricks, Brownes and McLoughlins—would deeply touch the emotions not only of Dubliners but of Irish people throughout the country. Ultimately they would become part of the enduring history and folklore of the capital.

With the expansive coverage of the bombing filling the newspapers on 31 May 1941, other topics received little attention. Some that would normally have been of considerable interest were probably only scanned or ignored altogether. For example, the *Irish Independent* published a fascinating article about the recent great sea battles involving the British battle-cruiser *Hood* and the German battleship *Bismarck*. There were riveting descriptions from British naval officers who had taken part. Another feature told about the "Battle of Crete", telling how the "British are in full retreat."[28] Normally big news to Dubliners but probably little noticed on this day.

One small piece in the *Irish Press* was probably missed by most readers. It was based on an official communiqué issued at Stormont, revealing that "during the hours of darkness last night some enemy aircraft passed over Northern Ireland ... no incidents have been reported." However, it went on to confirm:

> German raiders attacked Liverpool and other parts of the Merseyside this morning. Raiders were also over the West of England, and bombs were dropped in a Southern English town.[29]

These incursions over Northern Ireland and the bombing of western and southern Britain had occurred in a period close to that when the four bombs were dropped on Dublin. Was there any connection?

Chapter 17 ∾

| "STREET OF SORROWS"

There was not a single smile to be seen anywhere along that bomb-straddled path of havoc, which I, in company with sad thousands, toured on Saturday afternoon.
(*Irish Times* reporter, 31 May 1941)

Even the hard men who were supposed to be afraid of no-one, they were all there for Confession—it took the German bombs to get them to go!
(TISH MARTIN)

Distraught relatives made a sorrowful pilgrimage to the City Morgue, where many unidentified bodies lay. Sobbing men and women coming from the mortuary told the story that they had at last found the remains of their loved ones.
(*Evening Mail,* 2 June 1941)

It was noon, and already it was a scorcher. Mortuaries were about the only cool places in Dublin.

Every day at twelve o'clock at "Daddy" Egan's pub on the corner of Smithfield and North King Street when the Angelus bells rang, the eccentric publican barked out orders for all the men to kneel down and pray. His regulars were a mix of tough cattle-drovers, horse-dealers, dockers and Travellers. But they followed his orders—or they were barred. Christy "Diller" Delaney, a regular for more than half a century, explains that Egan was "an old failed priest, and he was religious mad. At noon time he'd walk out with a Rosary beads, and you *had* to join in with the Angelus." At noon on Whit Saturday, 1941, when the bells sounded, every man dropped to his knees, most bowing their heads, and began to pray—*before* they heard "Daddy's" dictate. On this day, they *wanted* to pray.

Across town, Ann Leonard had just arrived home and was met at the door by her mother who had been anxiously looking out the window, waiting for her figure to come into view. She slipped the medical pouch from her shoulder, sagged into a chair, and put her feet up:

> I just went in and said, "Ah, Ma …" And she said, "Is it very bad?" and I said, "Yes, it is." "Well," she said, "you'll have a cup of tea now and you'll be okay in a little while."
>
> Then she said, "Did you know any of them?" and I said, "I believe one of our nurses was killed." And she *was*, bless her. She *was* killed. She was going home over near the Newcomen Bridge, and that's where the damn thing "banged". Yes, wrong place at the wrong time.

Beyond that, she said little. Her orders were to remain silent on the subject, even with family. "We were told by our officers that we kept it under our heart. My Mam, she didn't know *how bad* it was—and I wouldn't tell her." No mention of children with glass embedded in their heads, or nearly cut in two. Her mother made her a light meal with her tea. Then she noticed her shoes:

> The new shoes that I bought the day before—by God, they were *cut to ribbons!* And they were *thick*-soled. If you *saw* that pair of shoes! And I said, "Look at my shoes, Mother." And she said, "Oh, thank God it wasn't your feet!"

Inspectors' shoes were taking a beating as well, as they had to trudge through the worst rubble carrying out their duties. By afternoon, inspectors from the military, Dublin Corporation, gas company, health board and Electricity Supply Board, among others, were probing around, nearly bumping into one another, searching for their own findings. Some brought bad news to hundreds of residents who hadn't expected it. They were told that their damaged houses were beyond repair and would have to be demolished, some that very afternoon, as they posed immediate danger to rescuers and others. It was tearful news, wrote the *Evening Herald:*

> Crowds of people gathered to watch the work of demolition and some shed tears as the last remains of their house toppled into the dust on the roadway.[1]

They could do nothing but stand by and watch as demolition squads finished off the deed begun by the Luftwaffe.

Many other occupants were informed that their damaged homes could, in time, be repaired, but they were not at present fit for habitation. They would have to be condemned and abandoned—*at once*. This news came as a shock to many residents who were quite prepared to live with damaged roofs or cracked ceilings and walls.

When the inspector showed up at the Dalys' door he was blunt, Agnes recalls:

> That afternoon they were going around inspecting the houses for damage. When they examined our house they said the walls had opened and it would fall in like a pack of cards—these are the *very words* he said to my father. My mother said, "What are we going to do?" "Well, missus," he said, "You *can't* go in there!" And a big notice was put on the door warning people that it was a dangerous building.

Within hours, the two parents and their eleven children were split up and sent off to different shelters. Agnes and her sister Jenny got the best "digs" when they were taken over to the Mansion House. Throughout Saturday afternoon more and more people were hit with the news that their homes were condemned and they were to be evicted. They packed up a few parcels of belongings, then walked out into the streets as refugees.

Meanwhile, health inspectors were going from house to house delivering their own upsetting news. Regarding sanitation—and insects. Walls were ideal nesting and breeding places for an array of very nasty insects, which, when left undisturbed, kept mostly to themselves. But when the bomb blast pulverised the plaster walls it set them loose, swarming everywhere, biting hapless victims, causing awful itching, rashes, sores and infections. Some were so small they could barely be seen, as they easily worked their way beneath clothing; others were large black beetles that scurried about and frightened children. With the hot temperatures, human perspiration and dirt, the swarms of insects became a real health menace, both for local residents and for rescuers, who, like Alec King, might not realise the damage they had done to their bodies until they got home hours or days later and went to undress and bathe. In an effort to combat the insects and treat bites and sores that might lead to infection, many people splashed themselves with Jeyes Fluid, which stung as much as it disinfected. Others used Sunlight soap or other carbolic soaps, with little effect.

Health inspectors who were seeking to combat infection and disease stemming from the combination of open wounds, dirt, insects and lack of proper sanitation, confronted people with the solution: they needed to bathe in steaming hot water and to be properly disinfected. They issued orders that those in need should proceed to the public Tara Street or Iveagh Baths, to be scrubbed clean and disinfected. While many people were delighted to get a free hot bath, some of the elderly women fretted, even cried, over having to face the immodesty of being "scrubbed down" naked in view of others. Some puritanical grannies flatly refused to expose themselves in such an indecent manner. Others endured it, but not without tears and trauma, such as Bernadette Pierce's aunt:

> People all had to go to the Iveagh Baths to be washed down because of the scabies and lice and other things they got. And they *scrubbed*. An aunt of mine had to go, and she was *crying*, saying, "I have to stand *naked?*" And they just got a big scrubbing brush and then swept people down with this white stuff.

After they survived the trauma, the "disinfectees" were glad they had complied with orders.

No news was more painful to have to deliver to people than that of loved ones killed. This task ordinarily fell to ARP wardens and to priests, none of whom had been trained for such a duty. At the North Strand, Dick Eyres and Father Masterson assumed the burden in most cases. Sister Louise from the Sisters of Charity convent in North William Street also played a prominent role. These three, who "knew every soul" in the community, also had the responsibility for going to mortuaries to identify the dead.

From the moment the bomb burst, Sister Louise had been assisting those in need: first her convent children, then refugees taken into the convent, and finally local people in distress. She volunteered to go to the morgue with distraught relatives as they searched for missing family members. Without a flinch, she would even pull back the sheet herself. Winnie Brennan remembers her as saintly:

> She *ran* to everybody, to be a counsellor to everybody. And there were some dead she identified. And at the City Morgue if someone came and identified their child or whoever it was, Sister Louise was there to console them, to put her arms around them to give them some comfort

By Friday afternoon, people's emotions were becoming fragile from lack of sleep, physical fatigue and emotional strain. It was sometimes difficult even for ARP wardens and rescuers to maintain their composure. The *Evening Mail* revealed that "one warden, who had been over 11 hours on duty, cried when he had to tell a young woman that her sister was dead."[2] As the hours passed, emotions would grow even more frail as even priests and doctors would be seen weeping.

A far easier chore for Dick Eyres was that to which he was assigned at about two o'clock. Rumours still persisted about two other bombs having fallen but not having detonated As it continued to unnerve both local residents and rescuers, ARP headquarters decided to try to put the rumours to rest by carrying out a complete search of the area. "I was told to go along the canal as far as Clonliffe Road," says Dick Eyres, "to see if I could find evidence of another bomb that was missing."[3] He was hunting for an unexploded missile, oblong in shape, probably four to eight feet in length and two or three feet in diameter, which could explode at any second and blow him to smithereens. Yet he didn't mind the assignment, as strolling along the canal with its cool water and lush grass was calming. It temporarily got him away from the horrors of the bomb scene. Upon completing his search, he reported back to headquarters—"We found nothing."

While Eyres was finding solace in nature, throngs were seeking it inside confession boxes which finally "opened for business" on Saturday afternoon. People had been waiting for nearly seven hours. In such a predominantly Catholic country, Saturday confession was a weekly ritual. Confession queues were normally modest. This Saturday, however, records were set at churches packed to absolute capacity with people, all waiting anxiously to have their confession heard. Queues stretched out the doors and out along the streets. Even grannies and young children who were beyond real "sin" determined to wait as long as it took. When priests arrived they were as sleepless as everyone else and weary from their duties at the bomb site, in hospitals or at shelters.

Everyone sought one thing: *complete* absolution. "People went to Confession in *droves*," testifies Una Shaw. "They were all afraid and didn't want to die without having their souls nice and clean." Because, adds Sally Burke, "everyone thought the planes were going to be there that night, *again*." Among the flock were many sheep long gone astray, some of whom hadn't been seen inside a church for more years than anyone could remember. Their presence drew mutterings, raised eyebrows and some disdainful looks. "*Bloody hypocrites!*" it was heard muttered. As Ann Leonard saw it, "Ah, a lot of *heathens*—'cause if the bomb was coming down again, they were going *up!*" Their fear-driven return to Mother Church did not hoodwink priests who recognised their identity. As Cissie O'Brien recalls, pious people waiting outside the confessional got an earful:

I was sitting in this church with my sister, and this man who was in front of us went into the confession box. Well, we could *hear* the priest *shouting* at him, "You're only here because the Germans dropped the bombs on the Strand! Otherwise, you would not be here—you would not show your face inside this church, or any other church, only for the Germans!"[4]

Elsewhere in Dublin, legions of men were heading towards the Phoenix

Park race-course, where the much-heralded "Ballinter" was featured in an event that could show his greatness, or disappointment. He was a horse with real potential, everyone agreed. But he had run into some bad luck in a recent race at the Curragh, apparently having to do with poor course conditions. This was his day for redemption, and punters were excited about his prospects. The sunny day and dry track would give him a shot at fame. As the *Irish Times* described it, from the sight of the happy crowd one would never have imagined that not far away bodies and mangled victims were still being dug out of the ruins:

> Despite the fact that most people in Dublin had gone through a sleepless and disturbed night, there was no trace of any uneasiness about the big crowd at the Phoenix Park on Saturday. The excellent programme of racing was being followed in the usual enthusiastic fashion.[5]

On the perfect afternoon, many other sporting and recreational events were under way. The high temperatures drew hordes to the city's parks and to nearby seaside destinations. Cyclists whizzed through the streets, heading for the countryside or the Dublin Mountains. Golf courses were filled, many offering special Whit holiday competitions. There was also a wide variety of tennis, handball and bowling competitions being held around Dublin. As the Leinster senior cricket matches were being played, yachting races were taking place in Dublin Bay. At Croke Park, just next to the North Strand, the Dublin handball senior semi-final match had been scheduled for three o'clock. The Dublin lawn tennis inter-club competition proceeded on Saturday afternoon with five of its six scheduled matches—only that between Dublin University and Bective was postponed, out of respect for the victims of the bombing.

The city's billiards parlours were abuzz with news from Melbourne, where Walter Lindrum had just set a new world billiards record by running to 3,752 before his break. Trying to fathom that feat got men's minds off German bombs for a while.

There was one unscheduled event on Saturday afternoon, and well attended. It was a hastily organised tour for newspaper reporters and photographers covering the scene, sometimes creating a nuisance and getting in the way of rescue efforts. The authorities decided it would be best to simply corral them together for a collective tour, during which they could get a close look at the destruction, ask questions, and take photographs. They could stand at the crater's edge, even peer into some of the collapsed houses. For those who had arrived after the cordons had been established, this was their first close-up view of the devastation. A poignant article was written by a reporter from the *Irish Times*:

There was not a single smile to be seen anywhere along the bomb-straddled path of the havoc, which I, in company with sad thousands, toured on Saturday afternoon. But neither was there a whimper anywhere to be heard; and depressing as was that pilgrimage along Dublin's Via Dolorosa, the memory that persisted was not one of those pulverised homes, with their blood-splattered thresholds, but, rather one of all those little stories everywhere of the courage, self-sacrifice and good neighbourliness which alleviated the tragedy.[6]

If readers were moved by this prose, they found hard facts sobering, such as the list printed by the *Irish Independent* of only some of the shops and establishments no longer there:

—M. Fagan, family grocer
—Mrs. Nally, tobacconist
—M. Dempsey, draper
—G. Jordan, butcher
—R. Fitzpatrick, victualler
—F. Fitzpatrick, jeweller
—W. Grenville, general stores
—North Strand Mission Hall
—L. Lynch, grocer
—J. A. Pattison, chemist
—R. Roche, hairdressers
—Mr. J. Roddy, confectioners
—North Strand Post Office

These were premises only on the west side of the North Strand. Readers saw that the commercial heart of the village had been plucked out, along with some of their proprietors who were pillars of the community.

One reporter from the *Evening Mail* summed up his coverage of the destruction and loss of life along the North Strand by dubbing it the "street of sorrows".[7]

———

The Connells still had not found Charlie. Having combed the bomb scene for hours and visited several hospitals, they were weary and about at their wits' end. They could put it off no longer. The last resort: they'd investigate the City Morgue.

The "death house", as it was commonly called, was a dreadful place. By Saturday afternoon on Whit weekend, 1941, conditions were unprecedented in their disarray and gruesomeness. The place was always cold, clammy, dismally grey. It had the look of death, feel of death, smell of death. Everyone passed it countless times during their life—and always hoped they'd never have to set foot inside.

In the early 1940s, home wakes were still the custom in many parts of Dublin. Bodies were lovingly prepared by grannies or local "handywomen", then placed on snow-white sheets in a room decorated with crepe, ribbons and little wreaths and lit by candlelight. Rosary beads were arranged in folded hands. The deceased, who ordinarily had died from natural causes, looked as if they were peacefully sleeping. It was a natural, serene, homely setting, in which the departed was surrounded by loving family and friends.

The sight of a body laid out in the City Morgue was the cruel antithesis of a home wake.

On an ordinary day, a body or two might lie in the City Morgue. Attendants calmly escorted visitors for identification purposes, everything always orderly and discreet. By Saturday afternoon there were between twelve and fifteen bodies, most of which were unidentified. And more were on the way. The bright sunshine and heat outside made it feel more chilled and bleak than normal. Most of the bodies had been taken directly from the filthy rubble of the bomb site to the morgue, without the opportunity to clean them, to make them presentable for viewing. Some had been brought in crushed, charred, blood-soaked. Nor were some of the bodies beneath the sheets even whole: they were missing arms, legs, hands, even heads. Relatives sometimes couldn't recognise their own kin. It happened to "a friend of mine," confides Bridie Byrne. "May, she lost her husband; he worked in Findlater's. He wasn't expecting to be blown to bits ... and all unrecognisable."

It was to this setting that "distraught relatives made a sorrowful pilgrimage," wrote the *Evening Mail*, "sobbing men and women seeking the remains of their loved ones."[8] They were unprepared for what they might find when the attendant pulled back the sheet.

Neither were the morgue staff prepared for what they had to face. A trickle of timid visitors began showing up late in the morning. By afternoon, as the list of missing grew, it had become a stream, far too many for the few attendants to handle in the usual slow, deliberate manner. As relatives inside were escorted from slab to slab, others outside grew impatient for their turn. At some point they began pushing their way forward, through the door, as the attendants lost control of them. Things became disorderly, then out of hand.

People began shuffling about on their own, removing sheets to have a look at the bodies beneath. At first they might draw it down reverently, but as they moved fearfully from corpse to corpse, some began whisking it down quickly to see. Going from slab to slab, lifting sheets—like some perverse shell game.

Many viewers did not respond well to what they saw, for it was not the peaceful, sleeping expression of a waked person. The bodies had not been properly washed; they were bruised and discoloured, their hair, eyes, nose and mouth matted with blood. Some remained locked in the expression of fear at death. Dismembered bodies were hideous to uncover. People felt sick, faint. The *Irish Independent,* which had a reporter posted at the City Morgue, wrote discreetly of the "tragic scenes as people visited the morgues in search of missing relatives or friends."9

Into this nightmare walked Jenny O'Brien's parents in their search for Charlie, an experience vividly remembered by their daughter:

> When my parents arrived at the death house it was crammed with people—*crammed!* There was so much confusion and fuss in the death house, with people *themselves* going in—'cause they weren't waiting for anyone to assist them. Because everybody, naturally, was all excited and frustrated, wanting to know—like, "I *want* to find me son! I want to find me daughter!" *Desperate!* With *grief!* And they didn't wait for any attendants to do anything, they done it *themselves.* Oh, they went *around* looking, they were pulling back the sheets, looking for people. To see was it their mother, was it their father.
>
> At the morgue there were bodies *everywhere.* My father said he never in his life witnessed anything like it. To him it was like a battlefield, what you see in a battle. You know, bodies lying all around. And people were crying, screaming, *shouting* out names. He said it was terrible to go over and look. Sheet after sheet, they uncovered young and old, some strange faces, but some familiar too. Mr and Mrs Fitzpatrick lay there. There were other people on the slabs that they *did* recognise. There was one person there, God help the poor unfortunate man, and his legs were blown off. There were some people who were unrecognisable, they couldn't recognise them.

When a drawn sheet revealed the face that the person had been looking for, fits of crying and screaming could erupt. Some women collapsed on the floor. Everyone would turn to look.

The Connells managed to wriggle their way through the crowd, reaching all but the last two sheet-draped figures. From where they were standing, these two forms looked small, more like women than a lad like Charlie. But they wanted to be certain, and they decided to wait patiently until they could manoeuvre their way over to the last two slabs.

On Saturday afternoon Dublin Corporation decided that it should assume the responsibility for providing a proper burial for all the victims. There should also be a public funeral, at which all grieving Dublin could participate. It was up to the corporation to select the firm, or firms, to handle the big job.

There were dozens of long-established undertakers' firms in the city, many dating back centuries. It was a traditional business in which families, generation after generation, loyally stuck with the same firm, a business in which reputations counted for everything.

Undertakers were renowned for their independent and competitive character, proudly providing their own hearses, drivers and coffins. They were also known for their unwillingness to help one another out. On learning that the corporation was to provide a large public funeral for all the bomb victims, the most prominent undertaking firms in the city must have presumed that they had the best chance for the job. It would not only be profitable but would be great for public relations, as all Dublin would be looking on.

Over near the North Strand, McCarthy's Undertakers had been badly bomb-damaged. And the firm of J. J. O'Neill had been destroyed by the explosion. But there were a few other small local firms still intact. Nearby, in Fairview Strand, was little Kirwan's Undertakers, "Established 1923," a mere upstart in the business. Tom Kirwan was eight in 1941; he would join the family firm when he reached eighteen. His grandfather had started the business, but his father was now in charge. It was a small, local firm, easy to manage, with a modest staff and several hearses. Mr Kirwan hardly had any hopes of being chosen to participate in the most important public funeral in the last quarter of a century.

When the phone call came informing him that his fledgling firm had been selected to handle the mass funeral, he was elated. All he knew, says Tom, was that "we got the job from the Dublin Corporation." That's all. Nothing was explained to him about the selection process. His father did not ask questions, just gratefully accepted the offer. Kirwan's would be getting the lion's share of business, some twenty-two funerals.

Once his elation had subsided, Mr Kirwan found himself confronted with the realities. At first, he and his small staff glowed over their good fortune. Now they were concerned about how exactly they were going to pull it off. For such a big job they were short on staff, hearses and drivers. Fortunately, from their own stock they could find twenty-two coffins of the right sizes, including small white ones for children. They possessed only five hearses, but they were very good Chrysler motor hearses. However, they would need at least twelve for the large public funeral. They were short not only seven hearses but the drivers that came with them. The first, smaller funeral was scheduled for Wednesday, the large public one for the following day. Time was short, and their task was challenging, because they would have to ask—or plead—for help from other undertakers who were probably flushed with anger at having been passed over.

It was soon apparent that other firms were not about to come to Kirwan's assistance. Tradition was tradition. They all knew that Kirwan's had only five of its own hearses with drivers. This left them with no choice but to turn to their country cousins, small undertakers in towns outside the capital—to appeal to their charity, sense of public responsibility, even patriotism if necessary. With no time to waste, Mr Kirwan began making phone calls, determined that he could make the deadline and have twenty-two bodies prepared for burial, coffined, and carried in top-quality hearses for the funerals only a few days away. When he and his staff would find any time for sleep, he didn't know.

———

Back at the City Morgue, the Connells had finally reached the last two sheeted bodies. Up close, the forms still looked considerably smaller than their son, so there was little apprehension when Mr Connell reached over the first slab, pinched the sheet and drew it back slightly. It wasn't Charlie. With only one left, "My Da said to my Ma, 'There's a remains over there on that slab. I'll go over and have a look to see.'" His wife stood beside him, slightly back:

> So Daddy pulled back the sheet and saw on the slab what was the remains of a woman. And the woman was an *image of his own mother!* And my father dropped the sheet and *ran* out of the morgue. *Ran out!* And my Mammy couldn't understand, of course, what was wrong. So she went over, thinking it was *her son!* And when she saw the woman, she *knew* it looked like her mother-in-law. And when she went out, my father was the colour of milk. And she says, "C'mon, we'll go home now, there might be some word at home."

One shock followed another. For when they walked through the door of their house, there stood Charlie in fine fettle, calm as could be, wondering what all the fuss was about. Some time during his parents' absence, when his little sister Jenny had dozed off, he had come home:

> Charlie had come in and went up to bed—and I knew *nothing about* this.

And when my Mammy and Daddy come in, very upset, with this loud talking, Charlie comes down into the room. And when my mother seen him she didn't know whether to *hug* him or *flatten* him! With the *fright* they got, you know.

About an hour later, Charlie's brother Richard was relieved of his army rescue duty and stopped by the house to see if there was any news. He was equally surprised and relieved to see Charlie safe and quite nonchalant about the whole matter. Then the family sat down for tea and a meal, rejoicing in their reunion, even finding some humour in it now. Then, Jenny recalls, her father, sleepless and emotionally drained, who was in the ARP, "put on his uniform and went *right back* to work at the North Strand! To do his duty. Because he was grateful to God that *his* son was safe."

Throughout Saturday afternoon, pubs in Dublin were packed to the walls, clusters of men standing outside drinking, putting away more than usual. The combination of the Whit weekend, the shocking bombing and shattered nerves made their need for drink greater than ever. The hot weather increased their thirst. Frothy pints cooled them down and replenished bodily liquid. As drink flowed freely, voices hit a high pitch. By late afternoon Mr Gill had to ask for a bit of hush among the crowd at his pub on the North Circular Road to announce some bad news: his whiskey had run out. The men were heartened, however, when he immediately assured them that the stout and porter would continue to flow.

The roar that erupted from the Phoenix Park also told of good news. Ballinter had won his big race, as "he made his due amends," wrote the *Irish Press*, "by an all-the-way success," taking away the coveted Brooke Plate.[10] Happy racing fans began flowing back into the heart of the city, destined for their local pubs. Some found they couldn't squeeze in, so they stood at the door and shouted out their orders to the barmen.

Meanwhile, the seven bodies of the Browne family had been taken to two morgues, the City Morgue and the one at the Mater Hospital. From the records it is not possible to determine why the decision was made to separate in death a family so close in life. To John Corrigan, father of Molly Browne, fell the grim responsibility of visiting the morgues to identify the remains. With a steely composure, he looked squarely upon the faces of his daughter, her children, her husband, and his mother. After giving positive identification for the coroner's record, he said little, leaving without a spare word.

By late Saturday afternoon the morning newspapers' news was stale. New developments had been unfolding every hour of the day. People were anxious for updates and fresh stories. They knew that reporters from the *Evening Mail* and *Evening Herald* had the whole day to get the latest death and injury figures, more eye-witness accounts, and photographs. Readers were not disappointed, as both papers had a bounty of new material. These evening papers were known for their sometimes embellished human-interest stories. In this case, both essentially produced coverage that was accurate and discreet. Because of the great drama of the tragedy and horrific details of death and destruction, there was no need to embellish or sensationalise coverage. The facts spoke for themselves.

The *Evening Mail* reported that up to that afternoon "rescuers were still busily digging out bodies," as the death count was sure to rise over the next twenty-four hours.[11] The *Evening Herald* was confident enough to cite a specific early figure: "Up to the present, 18 persons were killed." It added that a number of seriously injured victims in hospitals were barely clinging to life and would probably soon be shifted to the death column.[12] The newspaper's bold, eye-catching headline, "NIGHT OF HORROR", ensured that copies sold out soon after reaching the streets. The list of missing was growing by the hour, as the *Evening Mail* revealed that "no news has been received of a family named Delaney, numbering five, in number 52 North Strand."[13] Nor was there any trace yet of Noel and Madge Fitzpatrick, or of Patrick McLoughlin and his son, William, or of Mrs Fagan. Mr Fagan continued to stand statue-like in his vigil at the ruins where she was still buried. On the other hand, reported the paper, there was the good news that J. J. Newcombe, secretary of the Mount Street Club, and his brother Peter, both of 153 North Strand, who had earlier been listed as missing, had shown up late on Saturday afternoon. It turned out that they had been away from home, visiting friends for the Whit holiday. In days ahead, people would carefully follow the names of all those officially listed as "missing" in every newspaper.

As Dubliners spent Whit Saturday retrieving their dead and injured, it was a day of loss for the British as well. Five of their large ships "were sunk during a mass u-boat attack on a convoy taking American supplies to England." The attack occurred about 450 miles east of Greenland. It was likely that some Irish seamen were on board.[14]

After Dubliners finished their supper and reading the evening newspaper they began to feel nervous with the approach of nightfall. The returning darkness was not welcome.

Chapter 18

NIGHTFALL AND SUSPENSE

None of us could sleep, because, you see, you were waiting for it to happen again. That was the awful fear that you had ... "He's going to come back!" We were absolutely terrified.

(UNA SHAW, 75)

Many people on Saturday night did not get any sleep after the bombing, suffering agonies of suspense wondering would it start again.

(*Evening Mail*, 9 June 1941)

It was to be the most eerie night of their lives. As nightfall neared, anxieties and fears rose. The day that had dawned with radiant sunshine was soon to turn dark and brooding, once again frightening the wits out of a city already suffering from shattered nerves. Many Dubliners would later report that they were more fearful on Saturday night than they had been during the bombing the night before.

Most people went ahead with their Whit Saturday evening plans, although in a subdued form. The city's cinemas and dance halls were again packed. But attendants noticed that crowds were not as happy-go-lucky as usual. In the cinemas, laughter at Laurel and Hardy and Joe E. Brown was not as uproarious as in evenings before.

Wherever dances or parties were held throughout the city there were collections to raise funds for the bomb victims. From small parish halls to grand hotel ballrooms, people placed coins or pound notes on a plate or in a bowl. At a gala held at the Royal Hotel in Howth some three hundred people showed their generosity, as did dockers and coalmen in quayside pubs, putting their pennies into a brown sugar-bag being passed around.

As Dubliners faced nightfall they prepared as best they could for the unknown of the dreaded "next night". Garda headquarters had assigned men to the cordons around the bomb site to block looters and any local residents determined to sneak back into their dangerous dwellings to retrieve possessions. Dublin Fire Brigade was placed on alert. Firemen were either on active duty or on call, while a crew with their engine stood by at the scene to keep watch for any delayed flare-ups from the ruins. The Red Cross and St John Ambulance Brigade were also in a state of readiness. The director of the Red Cross Society, Rory Henderson, was working beside his staff of sixty, who would be on continuous duty throughout the night at their head office in Mespil Road, attending to the needs of hundreds of refugees now in their care. By late evening the Red Cross had served more than 1,200 meals. The next day they would have to serve more, and more again the following day. Henderson was worried about how quickly the Red Cross's resources had been drained in a single day, and how depleted the city's blood supplies were becoming. If more bombs fell, he knew, they were in serious trouble.

Hospitals prepared for the coming night. Full staffs were on duty and medical supplies replenished. Relays of doctors continued their surgery in operating theatres. Hallways were still full of victims on beds or trolleys. During the day, windows that had not been blown out were covered with wire to prevent shattered glass from flying in the event of another bombing. At the City Morgue, doors were finally closed for the night. Inside lay bodies now as cold as marble, some still unidentified. At the Mater Hospital there were three unidentified bodies, a man, a woman and a child. The small figures of unclaimed children and babies at the mortuaries were the most heart-rending—for little ones should never be left alone at night.

Priests and pastors spent Saturday evening preparing their Sunday morning sermons. Every house of worship in Dublin was sure to be filled.

Ordinary citizens could do very little to prepare for the night ahead, whatever it might bring. They gave virtually no thought to air-raid shelters or to gas masks stuck away in niches. If more bombs fell they would once again head for cover under stairs or tables or down in basements. Some beds had been pushed away from windows, and delicate glass or delph items removed from mantelpieces. A number of people prepared a bag with essential clothing, some small valued items and perhaps bread or biscuits to take with them if they had to flee their home. Many decided to sleep with their clothes on, in readiness to rush again out into the street.

Many concentrated on being religiously prepared, having made it to Confession and saying especially sincere bedtime prayers. Never would so many Dubliners go to bed with Rosary beads twisted in their hands. Some would end up lying awake the entire night, saying prayers over and over. Gabriel Molony remembers that when people bade goodnight to one another on Whit Saturday there wasn't that comfortable certainty of seeing them the next morning. The phrasing was tentative and the tone unusually sincere: "I'll always remember them saying, 'Good night and God bless you—see you tomorrow, *please God!*'"

The hundreds of homeless refugees placed in various shelters would find the greatest difficulty in sleeping. The majority were women and children on mattresses and makeshift bedding on the floor. Away from home and frightened, they couldn't settle down. There were many discordant and disturbing sounds in the shelters: praying aloud, singing, crying, muffled sobbing, moaning from minor injuries. At Baggotrath Hall, Mary Dunne and her family were given mattresses on a lovely polished floor, but there was little chance of sleep, mostly because of the unrestrained excitement of children:

> Of course, *all* us kids would be singing the song "Bless them all, the long and the short and the tall." Oh, the kids was in their element, to be honest with you. Once mothers were reassured that their kiddies didn't have any injuries it was just a matter of looking after them.

Being in shelters, particularly in the Theatre Royal and Baggotrath Hall, was a lark for children—singing, clapping, playing games, running around and staying up late. The communal setting was exciting. Mothers generally allowed them to express their exuberance, as it released tensions and fear, wearing off energy, in the hope that they would eventually fall into sleep. It was better than having them crying and trembling with fright.

Agnes Daly was one of the "lucky" ones sheltered in the Theatre Royal. Like everyone else, she was starry-eyed the first night, looking around in awe of the grandeur of the setting. Being placed on the stage to sleep on mattresses was every bit as thrilling for grown women and grannies as for children—the same stage upon which Jimmy O'Dea and famous film stars appeared. It was exciting, at least for the first night in residence. But when bedtime came, it was the discomfort and noise Agnes Daly most remembers:

> We were put up on the stage and there were mattresses on the stage and a lot of people down in the stalls. And *all* night long there was a child crying, and this one woman was singing hymns to keep him quiet, trying to soothe the baby that was crying. *All night* long! It was pretty noisy. So we slept over there, but we didn't like it—we couldn't sleep.

It was the same story over at the convent, the YMCA, An Óige and all the other shelters. The Municipal Art Gallery in Parnell Square had never been so cluttered and noisy.

As the night grew later, not all homeless people were in shelters. There was still a scattering of refugees out on the streets who had no place to go. Many ended up being taken in by sympathetic citizens. This situation prompted Patrick Belton TD to write to the *Irish Times* a few days later, criticising the

Government for not having done a better job of finding accommodation for all the homeless bomb victims. "The other night in Dublin people were going about inquiring of one another, 'Will you take someone in?' That was a condition that should not be."[1] He even took in an old woman in one of the houses he himself owned in the North Strand area that had not been seriously damaged.

Darkness ignited the continuing controversy over lighting policy. Should Dublin douse all its lights tonight? Or fully illuminate the city? Which would provide greater safety if the planes returned? In the absence of a citywide, enforceable policy, it was again debated locally. Some people blacked out their homes, while others along the street lit every lamp, resulting in the same absurd chequerboard pattern as before. Even Frank Wearen, the lamplighter, couldn't avoid the controversy as he made his rounds on Saturday night. While some people implored him to "put 'em all *out* now, will ya?" others told him to "put 'em *on*, mister, *please*, so we won't be in the dark tonight."

By eleven o'clock the North Strand was more quiet than it had been all day. Gone were the demolitionists, pneumatic drills, megaphones, and ambulance bells. However, groups of rescuers continued to work through the night, knowing that there were people still buried, quite possibly alive, always keeping in mind the many cases in London, Manchester and Belfast where victims were pulled from the ruins days later, their lives saved. This thought motivated Alec King and other rescuers to continue working with great intensity.

At 11:15 p.m. it paid off. At one site, additional rescuers were quickly called over with their torches, and stretcher-bearers were shouted for. Police at their cordons turned to watch, seeing men frantically pulling away the last bricks and blockages. Someone had been found. *Two* people. Other rescuers halted their work and gathered around to see who it might be. Then they heard the name: "Fitzpatrick". It was Noel and Madge, together. They were lifted out, brushed off, then placed on stretchers where Red Cross nurses bent over them. Everyone remained still, wondering if they were breathing. Then they got their answer, as two sheets were carefully drawn over them. They were placed together in an ambulance and taken directly to the City Morgue. The Sunday morning newspapers would increase their death report by two.

As people climbed into their beds for the night they found their auditory senses heightened. Especially those around the North Strand, where things were still settling, cracking, falling. A single tumbling brick or slipping slate could cause a loud crash. Loose glass from windows kept smashing, jolting people over and over again. The harder some people sought sleep, the more this fear gripped them.

It wasn't a reactive fear, like that following the bomb explosion the night before, rather a more awful *anticipatory* fear, what the *Evening Mail* called "suffering the agonies of suspense."[2] It could be a gradually rising, torturing sort of terror. "You'd *keep thinking* about it," Bridie Byrne remembers, "that he was going to come back *again*—that was the fear. People *terrified!*" Around his part of the city, along North King Street and Queen Street, claims Noel Hughes, "*everyone* feared the Germans were going to bomb us again." Chrissie Byrne recalls: "We couldn't go to bed, couldn't sleep, worried that something was going to happen—so we said the Rosary."

Thousands of Dubliners lay awake in one form of misery or another—wondering, worrying, *waiting.*

———

Among the multitudes sorely in need of sleep were the Lynskey family of number 46 Old Bride Street in the Liberties. With four other families they lived in a 150-year-old decrepit tenement house that was brittle, structurally unsound and highly dangerous. It was one of the houses described as the "death traps" of Dublin's notorious tenement world.

The Lynskeys' tenement house had been verified as one of the worst. Loud claps of thunder or heavy lorries rumbling past could shake the building perceptibly, as occupants heard walls and ceilings crack. The Lynskeys and their four children felt insecure, and desperately wanted to get out. They were now especially anxious to abandon the tenement because the night before when the bomb exploded at the North Strand they felt their dwelling shudder and heard it crack as never before. It was unnerving to all the occupants.

For years they had been on Dublin Corporation's list to receive a new house out in one of the developing estates around the city. Finally, a few days before the Whit weekend, Bridget Lynskey, aged thirty, and her husband received word that they had been selected for one of the new houses in Kimmage. They were overjoyed. On the morning of Whit Friday a corporation official showed up and placed in her hand the key to the door of their new, clean, modern, *safe* Kimmage house.

Bridget Lynskey especially wanted her children, the youngest being six-month-old Noel, to have a healthy and secure environment in which to grow up, and all the advantages she and her husband never had. She was now informed that she and her family could move any time they wished—even today, Friday, when she received the key. But she wanted a little more time for preparation, packing, and the many farewells. "No," she said, they would remain in their tenement house over the Whit weekend to get their belongings in order and say goodbye to friends. She told the corporation official that they would move in first thing on Tuesday.

All Saturday afternoon had been spent organising their move, gathering their well-worn belongings, readying the old furniture to be carried down the shaky stairs and loaded into a corporation lorry. Neighbours who had heard their good news dropped in steadily during the day to offer congratulations and say their farewells. Bridget loved to show everyone her key, to have them hold it in their hands. Friends had never seen her spirits so high.

With all the excitement and anticipation it was difficult to get the four children settled in for their last Saturday night in Old Bride Street. With the warm night temperatures, the windows were wide open. Tomorrow they would go to Sunday Mass, then home to enjoy their last Sunday-morning breakfast in the Liberties.

Some time about midnight, Bridget and her husband made it into bed, weary but happy. Her last thoughts probably were, "Only three more nights in the old place."

———

"Hysterical!" So Sally Burke described some of her neighbours along Portland Row when they felt a cold fear upon hearing the first piercing cracks of thunder, followed by angry swooshing gusts of wind. It struck suddenly, without warning. Buildings vibrated, and windows rattled crazily, loosening more bricks, slates and glass which smashed to the ground, causing people once again, she recalls, to feel "really frightened." It was an unusually violent thunderstorm that hit just after midnight. The roaring thunder and turbulent winds jarred people awake and out of bed to see what was happening. Powerful wind surges around the North Strand caused everything that was loose to shake and rumble and to fall. Sheets of rain lashed against walls and windows. Rescuers and policemen were drenched before they could run for shelter.

Everyone was taken by surprise and instantly alarmed, causing many at first to believe that another bombing was under way. Some scrambled for cover once again beneath stairs and tables. Eileen Pugh was in Jervis Street hospital, having been treated for a leg wound that laid her skin back and caused severe bleeding. She wasn't in much pain and was about to fall into sleep when the storm smacked into her side of the hospital:

> I remember in hospital we were upstairs and all the windows had wire on them, in case of more bombs. Then the night got stormy and they started

to shake—and I thought it was the plane, I thought it was the start of it again! I thought, "My God, how will I get out of here if anything happened?" That night was *dreadful*—it was traumatic for *everyone*.[3]

The storm didn't last long. But it left Dubliners jittery and more frightened than before. People crawled back into bed, but frayed nerves were to keep many from getting any sleep.

And German bombers were about to be heard once again in the skies over Ireland's east coast.

Chapter 19 ❧

WHIT SUNDAY
AFTERSHOCK

I saw bits falling off the wall—then someone shouted,
"Come on, quick, the house is falling!"
(PATRICK HANVEY TO THE *Irish Times*, 2 June 1941)

When the dust subsided, all that remained of the two houses
was a pile of bricks and masonry.
(*Irish Independent*, 2 June 1941)

German officials in Berlin said they had no confirmation of
reports that Dublin had been bombed … the whole matter
is regarded as somewhat strange.
(*Irish Press*, 2 June 1941)

"Did'ja hear that? Did'ja hear that?" People strained to pick up the sounds. This was no storm clatter. There was no mistaking the throbbing "drum, drum, drum" of German bombers. It was 12:30 a.m. on Whit Sunday morning. The planes seemed to be flying their normal northerly route; but this time they were not directly over Dublin and their engine drones were distant and faint. Those Dubliners blessedly asleep may never have heard them, but those who did braced themselves for another possible attack.

Residents of Dún Laoghaire had no trouble identifying the drones, for some of the Luftwaffe pilots were flying right over them this time. Searchlights began scanning the sky, but the number of planes could not be determined. Despite the bombing of Dublin less than twenty-four hours earlier, Air Defence Command gave no orders to send up warning flares or to fire anti-aircraft shells. Residents did not panic, though many sought safety under their stairs or in basements. Others repeated the foolish response of Dubliners by rushing to their windows to gaze skywards. The planes finally faded away without mishap.

Shortly thereafter, other German aircraft were heard over the Arklow area, loud enough to cause some people to sit up in their beds. They had grown accustomed to the rhythmic throbs of engines overhead, never before considering them threatening. But with Dublin's tragedy so fresh in mind they were nervous. Suddenly, at 1:07 a.m., the night silence was broken by a single loud explosion. Twenty families whose windows were blown out lurched to their feet. Their houses were within a few hundred yards of the bomb, which detonated in a soft open field, scooping out a good-sized crater. After the one bomb had dropped, the planes flew away. There were no casualties or serious damage. Fortunately, the Arklow bomb left an "unexploded portion," which Colonel Liam Archer and his colleagues at the Department of Defence would find of great value in matching with the North Strand bomb to prove that both were of German origin.[1]

Though spared this time, Dubliners were alarmed to learn that another bomb had fallen the very next night.

Whit Sunday morning religious services were attended in record numbers. Ordinarily, women liked to show off a new spring hat or scarf at the Whit Sunday services. But this was not a day for fashion: it was a day of sorrow and reflection. "Prayers for the dead and injured were recited in all the Dublin churches," reported newspapers. Priests and pastors did their best to offer comforting words about the mysteries of life and coping with tragedy. They neither made accusations against the transgressors nor offered explanations for the act.

In New York on Sunday 1 June, St Patrick's Cathedral began filling up earlier than usual. Much of the congregation consisted of people of Irish heritage. All had heard and read about the shocking German bombing of Dublin. As they squeezed into pews they wondered if Cardinal Spellman might mention the incident in his sermon. Discreetly, but with unmistakable fervour, he declared:

> The governments of man have Stuka-dived into paganism, strafed the Ten Commandments, and bombed the Sermon on the Mount.[2]

To the crowd of Irish-Americans seated before him, there was no doubt that he had in mind Dublin's catastrophe.

In Vatican City the Pope began his radio broadcast by sending Whitsuntide greetings to Catholics throughout the world. As the *Irish Press* reported, "Pope Pius XII broadcast over the Vatican radio a plea to the world upholding human dignity and freedom … the message being one of love and comfort in the present difficult times."[3]

Somewhat ironically, over in London the Whit Sunday church services included thanks for having had the past three weeks free of bombing raids, a blessed respite from hell for Londoners. The British, understandably, felt some ambivalence about Dublin's misfortune. Surely they had sympathy for the victims of the bombing; but there were those, bitterly opposed to de Valera's policy of neutrality, who didn't mind seeing the Irish get a good lick from the Germans—just to see what it was like. Perhaps now they might see Herr Hitler in a different light.

On Sunday afternoon in New York there was the arrival for the first time in months of a mammoth British liner, the *Britannic*. It had cautiously navigated its way through treacherous waters, heavily patrolled by German submarines prowling the North Atlantic for trophy British targets. It carried nearly two hundred British government workers, ranging from typists to diplomatic couriers. As passengers disembarked they described their tense "zig-zag voyage all the way from England."[4] Once ashore, one of their first acts was to get hold of a copy of the *New York Times* to find out in more detail about the surprising German bombing of neutral Ireland.

Dublin's Sunday morning newspapers were filled with fresh news of the North Strand bombing. The death toll had climbed to twenty-five and was expected to rise. An estimated eighty-eight people had been seriously injured and countless more suffered lesser wounds. Not all the injured victims were expected to survive. In fact the *Irish Press* confirmed that already "four who were stated to be seriously injured on Saturday were listed as dead on Sunday morning."[5] The paper informed readers that among the bodies laid out at the City Morgue was still "one baby girl, unidentified."

Although hordes of people had descended on the North Strand over the previous thirty-six hours, the majority of Dubliners had not personally seen the destruction. The Sunday papers were filled with graphic accounts and photographs presenting a vivid image of the scene. Readers commented that it looked exactly like all the photographs they had seen of London, Manchester and Belfast. But the photograph on which they tended to dwell was not one of demolished houses or rescuers at work: it was of just one man—Éamon de Valera. It struck people as powerfully telling in its simplicity, that of the Taoiseach standing at the lip of the crater, looking down into the depression. He was described as "staring dumbfounded" into the hole.[6] It was an expression on de Valera's face with which Dubliners were not familiar.

Throughout the remainder of the day, and the next, and the next, there was no official statement from de Valera or any other member of the Government on the bombing incident.

The press, however, was not reluctant to speak out. Newspapers wrote with candour and sharp criticism, especially about the blatant failure of the Government's protection system for citizens—the "hat-box" shelters, padlocked doors, useless gas masks, and the absence of a coherent lighting or black-out policy. And, most egregiously, the silent air-raid sirens. Even after three bombs had already fallen! Ireland's vulnerability was exposed. The *Sunday Independent* wrote in a brief editorial:

> Dublin has suffered heavily by bombs from belligerent aircraft. The sympathy of the whole Irish nation goes out to those people who have suffered so terribly and especially those who have had their nearest and dearest friends killed.
>
> We are sure that Mr. de Valera ... will protest vigorously to the belligerents concerned. Eire has been strictly neutral since the outbreak of war, and she has the right to respect—and to demand—that her territory and the air above should not be violated by any of the nations of the war.[7]

By comparison with editorials that would follow in other newspapers in coming days, it was a mild statement.

As readers pored over their Sunday newspaper, they were disquieted by seeing the term "refugees" applied to Dubliners, accompanied by photographs of bedraggled men, women and children, looking tattered and lost, carrying parcels of salvaged possessions through the streets against the skeletal backdrop of a smashed landscape. They looked every bit as pathetic as the refugees from France or Poland. The sight of these homeless people in the heart of Dublin was emotionally moving. Patrick Belton TD was extremely displeased with the Government's ill-preparedness for dealing with the refugee crisis suddenly at hand. What sort of plan, he wanted to know, had been established for coping with the inevitable homelessness in the event of a real air attack? Apparently none, as far as he could see. They all had to be taken in by charitable organisations. He demanded "to know what department of government was responsible for housing homeless victims of a raid."[8]

The Sunday newspapers also carried a disturbing notice. It was a joint appeal for funds from the Irish Red Cross Society and St John Ambulance Brigade. Only one day after the bombing, both organisations were running short of money and resources. Furthermore, Dublin's blood supply was lower than it should be. In a letter to the *Sunday Independent* the directors of the two organisations told how they had "rendered first-aid to hundreds of casualties," as well as "providing food, shelter and clothing for hundreds of others." In closing, they made their plea:

> Our organisations are definitely short of funds and they cannot carry out their work with empty hands. We appeal to the generosity and humanity of your readers.[9]

Citizens would respond with great generosity. Yet it was worrisome that the two largest medical aid organisations had seen their resources so depleted within twenty-four hours by four bombs, only one of which was truly large. People could not help but wonder what might happen if there was a blitz similar to that in Belfast.

With more than eight hundred people suddenly rendered homeless—and hundreds more sure to follow—a serious housing crisis had been thrust upon an unprepared Government. The temporary shelters into which they were being placed were already nearing their capacity. The continuing evacuation of dangerous buildings meant that the homeless population was sure to increase substantially over the coming days, possibly doubling. The temporary shelters were primitive, with people sleeping on floors with mattresses, no privacy and limited toilet facilities. People were uncomfortable and with each passing day would grow more discontented and impatient to have their own home and dignity once more. For the Government it was an urgent crisis that gave new meaning to the term "emergency".

On Whit Sunday morning P. J. Hernon, Dublin city manager, faced an emergency meeting of the Housing and Engineering Committees of Dublin Corporation. He described the problem at hand very succinctly: hundreds of homeless, traumatised, frightened citizens were sleeping on floors in shelters, in convents, in a library basement, on a theatre stage and even in an art gallery. It was a desperate, degrading situation. Dublin Corporation had a long history of moving at a glacial pace in dealing with housing problems for working-class citizens. But now a glaring public spotlight was upon them. They had to act decisively and swiftly by putting a plan into action.

———

Residents of the Liberties knew at first hand about housing problems. The majority lived in decrepit, dangerous tenements 150 to 200 years old. Generation after generation, investigative committees had inspected them, verifying their appalling condition: corroding brickwork, dry rot, woodworm infestation, water leakage, structural instability, cracked walls and ceilings. Some were so rickety and brittle that simply hammering one nail into the wall to hang a picture could bring the entire wall down. Tenements were declared "death traps" and "coffin boxes". Yet in 1941 Dublin's infamous tenements— known as the worst slums in Europe—were still standing. Some, barely.

Among the worst dwellings were those along the Coombe, Pimlico, Patrick Street, Ash Street and Old Bride Street. Every time a heavily laden cart or lorry rumbled past, the buildings would tremble. At 2:05 a.m. on Saturday morning when the 500-pound bomb exploded over on the North Strand it caused tenement houses in the Liberties to quiver and crack perceptibly. Tenants were frightened. Everyone must have said a prayer in thanks that the bomb had not been any closer.

Sunday mornings in the Liberties were always the most serene. People slept late after Saturday night "goings-on", then attended Mass and went home for their traditional Sunday breakfast of rashers, an egg, maybe black and white pudding, a slab of bread and tea. Those with a gramophone liked to listen to Caruso or McCormack on quiet Sundays. Along the Coombe, John Gallagher remembers, a woman who lived at number 8 would sing aloud every Sunday morning with the most lovely voice. "No matter *how late* she was up drinking the previous night, she'd start singing, for maybe two hours, and *everyone* would listen to her. *Beautiful* voice." She could easily have been on the opera stage, neighbours swore.

At 46 Old Bride Street the Lynskey family especially relished this tranquil Sunday morning, for they knew it would be their last in the street. In a few days they would be moving out to their new house in Kimmage. Bridget arose at about eight o'clock, before her husband and four children. She would wake her family later and get everyone ready for Mass.

As she put the tea on, she heard other residents in the old tenement house stirring. It was a tall, four-storey building, in which she had many neighbours. On the top floor lived the O'Brien family and on the ground floor two elderly sisters, Margaret and Mary Lawlor. In between lived a number of others, including Mrs Doyle and her eleven-year-old son, Jimmy. Bridget was fond of each of them.

Next to the Lynskeys, at number 47, lived Ann Hanvey, a widow, and her six children. After her husband died she had vowed to keep their small bicycle shop in business, for she needed the modest income to raise her family. Her fifteen-year-old son, Patrick, was a great help in the shop, filling his father's role as best he could. By necessity, he was mature beyond his years, responsible and hard-working. His mother depended on him. The Lynskeys and the Hanveys were good friends.

Directly across the street from the Lynskeys lived Catherine Murphy. The view out her window perfectly framed numbers 46 and 47 on the opposite side. She spent a good part of each day peering out her window at all the activity along the street below, calling down to neighbours, sometimes engaging them in a good ten minutes of conversation. She liked the Lynskeys. They would wave out the window to one another, shout out a few words if there was not too much noise in the street. She knew that Bridget and her family were leaving for their new house in another forty-eight hours and had expressed to her how much she would miss them all.

By about nine o'clock the street had a scattering of people going to and from Mass, as children played. With the warm weather, Bridget had her windows open wide. Just below, she heard men shuffling towards the old bird market in Bride Street, dating from the time of the Huguenots at the end of the seventeenth century. It was one of the oldest traditions in the Liberties, as avid bird-fanciers gathered every Sunday morning to look over the crop of chirrupy, coloured little feathered creatures in handmade cages. Many tenement-dwellers had a bright singing bird to cheer up their setting. For a few pennies or shillings one could take home a linnet or goldfinch or other breed. Bridget always liked hearing the men talk about birds as they passed her window, later returning with their cages, delighted with their acquisition.

As ten o'clock approached, many people along the street were preparing to depart for Mass. Her children, already dressed and ready, were about to go down into the street to play for a few minutes. On Sunday mornings, parents always warned their little ones to be careful outside, because, with the lighter horse and bicycle traffic, large lorries had the habit of speeding along faster than usual.

At 10:02, as local people pinpointed it, a heavily laden lorry rumbled along Old Bride Street at a good clip, bouncing over the cobblestones, making a racket and causing tenement houses on both sides to vibrate. This was not unusual on Sunday mornings. Nor was the lorry heavier or speedier than many others that often rumbled past. But this was the first one since 2:05 on Saturday morning.

Young Patrick Hanvey was still in bed, just coming out of sleep, when he thought he heard a slight, strange sound. A sort of crumbling. Residents were used to hearing cracking when their building was jarred, but this was an unfamiliar sound to everyone in numbers 46 and 47. Everyone heard it, paused, and listened. In Patrick Hanvey's room it was followed by a curious flutter of tappings on the floor, like small pebbles dropping, then larger ones. On other floors the same thing was happening. He sat straight up. Then, as he later told the *Irish Times*, he heard a desperate shout, as everything around him began breaking apart:

> I saw bits falling off the wall—then someone shouted, "*Come on, quick*, the house is falling!" Part of the wall of number 46 collapsed, and then our house fell as I reached the door. Something hit me and I fell. After a minute or two I managed to crawl out.[10]

At the same moment, from across the street, Catherine Murphy was watching the horrible spectacle from her window, as if viewing it on a cinema screen:

I was getting ready to go to Mass when the window darkened and there was a roar that I thought was caused by a bomb. I saw the house tumbling into the street. I raised the alarm, and men ran over to free the people trapped. There was a terrible smell of gas.[11]

What she was witnessing was the slow collapse of the two weakened buildings, attached to one another, as they lazily sagged, then fell in upon themselves. The Lynskeys' tenement, number 46, began collapsing first, pulling with it number 47. Because the buildings disintegrated gradually, rather than instantly, as if by a bomb blast, there were precious seconds during which tenants were able to react and flee. "Widow Ann Hanvey and her six children saw the walls crumbling," reported the *Irish Independent,* "and were able to rush out into the street before the upper floors fell in."[12] Younger occupants, more fleet and agile, were able to respond and evacuate most quickly. Yet, the newspaper said, the elderly Lawlor sisters had "a wonderful escape, although the whole house had fallen on top of them."[13] The paper failed to explain exactly how this remarkable feat was accomplished. Eleven-year-old Jimmy Doyle darted out of number 46 within seconds. Once safely out, he recalled seeing his pal Tommy Lynskey back inside. As the *Irish Press* verified, without hesitation he acted:

Finding that he could get out, he went back in again to where he had seen 9-year-old Tommy Lynskey, at the bottom of the stairs. He found him and half carried him through the gap he had made in the debris.[14]

As soon as Tommy had been dragged free from the rubble he looked around for his mother, but she was nowhere in sight.

During the first few minutes, tenants were struggling to save themselves and others, as neighbours rushed to their aid. Before any police or rescue services could reach the scene, 31-year-old Patrick Murphy, who lived and worked as a cook in the Salvation Army hostel in Bride Street, was bolting towards the ruins. Without thought for his own safety, he plunged into the debris to find victims, aware of the smell of escaping gas and its danger. In modest manner, he later described his actions (verified by witnesses) to the *Irish Press:*

I brought out four children aged between five and twelve years. One woman I found inside was unconscious and I struggled to get her out. Then I found an old man pinned down under a beam and got him out. And I got two elderly women, they were unconscious.[15]

Could these have been the Lawlor sisters? It was later determined that Patrick Murphy's courageous actions, reported the newspaper, "saved those whom he rescued from much more serious injury, as all the time gas was escaping."

Following the rumble of the tenement collapse, wrote the *Irish Independent*, "the whole street was enveloped in dense clouds of dust."[16] Like Catherine Murphy, many people took the loud noise and dark sky to be another bomb explosion. Local residents darted away down the street, casting glances back over their shoulder, shouting, "The houses are falling!" The great billows of thick dust could be seen streets away. Nearby, at the Garda station in Kevin Street, Garda Patrick O'Connor heard the crash and rushed to the window, where "he saw a great cloud of dust rising … heard the screams of women and children."[17] Within seconds, he and his colleagues were running directly into the dense cloud, which impeded their breathing. On arrival at the scene he ran into James Brennan, a neighbour, who gave him directions to where he believed people had been trapped. Together they worked as a team, reported the *Irish Independent*, as "they began to pull away beams of wood, and they first found Mrs. Doyle. Some moaning amid the debris then led to the discovery of another woman buried beneath bricks and heavy beams."[18]

Meanwhile other policemen, firemen, ARP wardens and members of the LDF, Red Cross and St John Ambulance Brigade arrived on the scene from all directions. Father T. Walsh from the nearby Carmelite church in Whitefriars' Street raced over, followed by several doctors from the Adelaide Hospital. All were choking in the dust as they went about their work. Some of the firemen who arrived from Tara Street fire station had just returned from long hours spent at the North Strand bomb site. With little chance to recuperate, here they were again at another disaster.

After thirty minutes or so the street was jammed with rescuers and onlookers behind cordons. One by one, most occupants had been pulled free, though a number were injured. Rescue efforts seemed under control. Then, at 10:35, a deep, guttural "swoosh!" was heard as a third adjacent tenement house just got tired of holding itself up and sank to the ground, raising another dust cloud and sending rescuers scrambling. Fortunately, the occupants had been evacuated. But this collapse confirmed what the authorities feared most: the possibility of a "domino effect" occurring along the tenement rows. Fallen houses left a tooth-gap space that not only weakened adjacent buildings but reduced the structural strength and integrity of the entire terrace. If one went down, others might well follow. It could happen in minutes, hours, days or weeks later. And there was no certain way of knowing how unstable other structures might have become. The sequence of the Old Bride Street tragedy, described by the *Irish Independent*, illustrated this danger:

It was found that the four-storey tenement house No. 46 had collapsed pulling with it No. 47, the three-storey house adjoining. No. 46 had collapsed, floor on top of floor, burying people who lived there in debris. When the dust subsided, all that remained of the two houses was a pile of bricks and masonry from which protruded tables and chairs.[19]

An entire connected row of weak, destabilised houses could possibly collapse in neat, linear order once one or more had toppled. Bombings in British and other European cities showed how easily this could happen. Firemen, rescuers and housing authorities in Dublin were worried. Evacuations would have to be carried out for safety's sake.

By noon, things finally seemed under control. Trapped occupants had been freed, the gas main shut off, and neighbours evacuated. Fifteen injured people had been taken by ambulance to the Adelaide Hospital. All had been identified. The O'Brien family, who occupied the top floor of number 46, were among the most seriously injured. Survivors standing behind cordons looking over at the heap of rubble that only minutes before had been their home must have wondered how they ever got out alive.

Three people seemed not to have, for they were missing. They were 72-year-old Samuel O'Brien, 30-year-old Bridget Lynskey, and her six-month-old son, Noel. Mr Lynskey and their three other children had been found unharmed. He immediately informed the authorities that his wife and baby son were still in the ruins. According to the *Irish Independent*, "rescuers redoubled their efforts when it was found that Mrs. Lynskey and her infant child were still unaccounted for … as they tore away at the debris."[20] Doctors stood by, as well as a priest ready to administer the Last Rites if necessary.

After an hour and a half of intense search there was still no trace of mother and child, nor of Samuel O'Brien. A contingent of soldiers was called in to assist with the rigorous manual removal of bricks and timbers. It paid off at 12:30 p.m., when Samuel O'Brien was found alive, but near death. He was rushed off to hospital. His discovery gave hope that the remaining two would be found soon.

Just after one o'clock two forms, one of them tiny, were spotted beneath crushed mortar and thick dust. It was John Doherty, a soldier, who came upon them. He felt sickened when he realised the nature of his find. Later he told an *Irish Press* reporter, "She had the baby in her arms, and she seemed to have tried to cover it with bed clothes. They were dead when I found them."[21] They were placed together in an ambulance and taken away to the Adelaide Hospital, where the house surgeon, Dr Yvonne Mallet, pronounced mother and child "dead upon arrival," their deaths "due to shock and haemorrhage."[22] By this time Samuel O'Brien had also died at the hospital.

News of the deaths of Bridget Lynskey and her baby spread through the crowd. Within hours, word of the tragic discovery had swept across the Liberties. The next day the *Irish Independent* revealed a poignant footnote to their deaths:

> Mrs. Lynskey was found with the baby clasped in her arms ... a tragic feature of her death was that she had just got the key for her new house.[23]

The key was never found.

The collapse of the tenement houses had duplicated many of the visual and auditory features of a bomb blast: a roar, smashing of glass, crunching of bricks, billowing dust cloud, smell of escaping gas, screams for help, and sense of panic. As the *Irish Press* confirmed, it "presented a picture which recalled the scenes of horror and destruction witnessed after bombs had fallen on the city 30 hours earlier."[24] Understandably, many people at first thought it was indeed another bombing. That perception was soon dispelled. However, in people's minds there was implanted a strong *connection* between the North Strand bombing and the tenement collapses only hours later. In the immediate wake of the Old Bride Street tragedy, other tenement-dwellers came forward to tell how their buildings too had been shaken and destabilised by the bomb explosion, with its earthquake-like tremors. Nan Davis recalls what most people were saying around her part of the Liberties: "When that woman was killed down there, when the house collapsed, that was the *result* from the bomb. Oh, yes! It was the result of that bomb—because it *shook* that tenement." There was a strong consensus among Dubliners knowledgeable about the decrepit, dangerous tenements that the link between the thunderous bomb blast and the following building collapses was logical and verifiable, not mere coincidence. As one citizen, J. J. O'Sullivan, wrote to the *Evening Mail*:

> The danger confronting tenement dwellers arising out of the bomb attack is only too obvious to anyone familiar with these dreadful eyesores ... the worst slums in Europe.[25]

The only surprise, many people contended, was that *more* tenements had not crumbled as a result of being shaken and weakened by the explosion.

Ordinary citizens may have seen a clear connection between the two incidents, but the authorities were hesitant to concede this. For generations they had endured harsh criticism for not eradicating the tenement "death traps". Neglecting to provide decent, safe housing for the city's working people was immoral and scandalous. During his tenure at the *Irish Times*, R. M. Smyllie had seen many negligent officials come and go, and plenty of tenement investigation reports filed away. In this case, he wanted to get to the truth himself. On Sunday afternoon, before the dust had settled along Old Bride Street, he had his best reporters searching around for evidence and interviewing local tenement dwellers. His resulting "autopsy" of the tenement tragedy was shared with readers:

> The collapse of the buildings is believed to be due to a combination of factors—the old houses were shaken when the bombs fell in Dublin on Saturday morning, and then a heavy lorry passed the buildings a short time before they collapsed.[26]

During Sunday's meeting on the housing crisis, Hernon was updated on the unfolding tenement tragedy in Old Bride Street. It was bad news, for it meant that more homeless people and evacuees would need housing. His problems seemed to grow worse by the hour, and everyone was feeling the pressure. Indeed, by early Sunday afternoon, the *Irish Times* reported, "108 persons unexpectedly arrived [at the offices of the Red Cross] and somehow they managed to accommodate them."[27] The director of the Red Cross Society, Rory Henderson, must have been wondering when the flow of refugees to his door would cease. It would become worse in the days ahead.

By this time there were at least nine hundred homeless people scattered about in temporary shelters, a figure certain to exceed a thousand and possibly 1,500 or more. Most of them would need permanent housing. Hernon presented what he regarded as a feasible plan, the only one he could imagine that might work. Several new housing projects were already under construction in Cabra, Crumlin, Kimmage and Ballyfermot, intended for the neediest tenement-dwellers. The bombed-out victims could be considered needier, as they now had no roof over their heads. But most of the new houses were not due to be completed for many months, even years. This was far too long to expect homeless people to remain in primitive shelters, sleeping on the floor.

To succeed, Hernon explained, the housing development scheme would have to be greatly accelerated. Months would have to be compressed into weeks. Kimmage and Cabra offered the best prospects, as they were furthest advanced. Some houses in Kimmage were already completed; others were still only shells or skeletal frames. Contractors would have to agree to the terms and get their carpenters, bricklayers, plumbers and other tradesmen to work longer hours, probably in shifts around the clock. Only a completely co-operative effort could succeed. They would face an unprecedented deadline in completing construction. But if it was successful, hundreds of homeless bomb victims *could* be housed within a matter of weeks.

There were questions. What about the quality control of construction under such pressure? Hernon conceded that he too was concerned about this matter. They would first have to place their trust in the contractors to produce houses of decent quality. The goal was to see that the houses were *habitable*, not necessarily *comfortable*—the new owners could take care of that themselves in time. Everyone agreed that it was indeed good fortune that the housing projects were already under way. A reporter from the *Irish Times* covering the meeting was given the final decision: "It was decided to place at the disposal of the homeless about 100 houses in the Cabra section."[28]

While Hernon and the city councillors were conferring about the housing crisis, military investigators spent Sunday afternoon sifting through all five of the bomb sites, the four in Dublin and one in Arklow. Meanwhile Éamon de Valera was drafting an official protest to be delivered in Berlin. All knew that the bombs were of German origin, but hard evidence was necessary to back up claims and protests. Military experts microscopically examined pieces of the casing, tiny bomb fragments and residue of the explosive powder. Several larger pieces clearly showed the German lettering and Nazi eagle emblem. All evidence was properly assembled to be handed over to the authorities.

By Sunday afternoon there had been no communication between the Irish and German governments regarding the bombing incident. In fact there had been no official confirmation from the Government that a bombing had even occurred. The national and foreign press, however, had been documenting the tragedy in detail, with photographs of the destruction and first-hand accounts by survivors and witnesses. On Sunday afternoon, when officials at the German Foreign Ministry were queried by the foreign press, their response was curiously insouciant, as reported in the *Irish Press*:

> German officials in Berlin yesterday (Sunday) said they had no confirmation of reports that Dublin had been bombed. Both at the Wilhelmstrasse [Foreign Ministry] and in political circles in Berlin it was stated that the whole matter is regarded as somewhat strange. Spokesmen stated that they heard of the explosions only from foreign press reports.[29]

German military officers at lower levels and members of Berlin's "political circles" indeed seemed genuinely surprised at the news from the foreign press. Some even seemed amused. What would be the purpose of attacking neutral Dublin?

Higher powers in Berlin were silent. They were concentrating on rather larger military matters. It would be only weeks before they would embark on their fateful campaign to invade the Soviet Union.

———

The staff at Kirwan's undertakers were concentrating on their own challenge. "We had only five cars," Tom Kirwan remembers, "so we *had* to borrow over a dozen hearses." Dublin Corporation had just informed them that the two funerals for the bomb victims would be held on Wednesday and Thursday, the latter to be the public funeral, with many official figures present. Time was tight.

Mr Kirwan had been ringing up country undertakers to help him out, with some success. He felt confident that by Monday he would have the hearses he needed. As he well knew, it wasn't merely a matter of the *number* of hearses and drivers, they had to be *good* ones. For all Dublin would be viewing the public funeral procession. On arrival in his yard, even handsome hearses would be cleaned immaculately after their journey to Dublin, to be made spotless and gleaming. Hopefully, the weather would be sunny and dry on Thursday for one of the biggest public funerals to be held in the streets of Dublin.

Gravediggers and cemetery attendants had been given their orders by Sunday afternoon. At short notice, everything had to be made perfect. Jack Mitchell, later to become head gravedigger at Glasnevin Cemetery, knew many of the men on duty in 1941, old-fashioned gravediggers with nicknames like "the Lump" and "the Swanker". Strong men, hard-working, with only one day off a year, Christmas Day. They were out in the worst of elements in their moleskin trousers, be it drenching rain, sweltering heat, bitter cold, or ice and snow. People died every day of the year, and they had to be buried.

They had seen it all. But they were particularly touched by the tragedy that had befallen the most innocent people of the little North Strand village. The gravediggers were local people themselves. The bombs could have struck them and their families. They felt honoured to play a role in preparing their final resting place.

Ordinary Dubliners spent their Whit Sunday carrying out their holiday plans or simply relaxing and reflecting upon the past thirty-six hours. It had been a whirlwind of tragic events and emotions. As the shock of the experience subsided, people began to wonder why it had happened. Would it occur again? At first, simple explanations were comfortably embraced, especially the widespread belief that it must have been an unfortunate mistake or accident. In days and years ahead, more complex hypotheses would emerge.

Whit Sunday was drawing to a close. It had been the second consecutive day of unexpected disaster and death. The death toll was now nearing thirty, and the number of homeless people reaching almost a thousand. Dubliners went to bed wondering what the third day of the Whit holiday weekend might bring. In the week ahead, they would brace themselves for the inquest and for two intensely mournful funerals.

Chapter 20 ✌

WHIT MONDAY: AN
UNEASY RESPITE

The Irish people have been horrified by this terrible tragedy.
Even the outside world ... has been shocked by the news.
(*Irish Independent*, 2 June 1941)

The capital of Ireland is to-day a city of sorrow. The bombs
which caused this havoc have been proved to be of German
origin ... [this] calls for the most vehement condemnation.
(*Irish Press*, 2 June 1941)

W hit Monday was to be a day of respite between the previous two
days of tragedy and the forthcoming sorrowful funerals on
Wednesday and Thursday. By week's end, Dubliners would feel as
if they had been through an emotional wringer.

Monday morning's *Irish Times* had the headline "GERMAN BOMBS
WERE DROPPED ON DUBLIN," while the *Evening Mail* reported that
"speculation as to the origin of the death-dealing plane was stopped when the
Government announced that the bombs had been identified as German."[1] In
truth, there had been little speculation, as almost everyone knew perfectly well
that the bombers were German.

Positive confirmation came within less than forty-eight hours. The
evidence gathered by military investigators was abundant and conclusive. By
good fortune, at the Arklow crater a large unexploded portion of the bomb
was found. Microscopic examination of metallic fragments, fibrous
substances, explosive powder, nuts, bolts and paint chips all fitted the puzzle
perfectly. Furthermore, adds Captain A. A. Quigley, "the remnants of those
bombs were clearly stamped with German insignia and German
instructions."[2] One fragment found at the Summerhill site showed the
imprint of the German eagle. The military's final report, to be submitted to
the Secretary of the Department of External Affairs on 20 June, would even
contain revealing evidence about the German plane that dropped the bomb:

The fin rings are painted in blue enamel and appear to have been treated with a black sooty dope, evidently for camouflage purposes. This finish is similar to that of the under-surface of the wing and fuselage of the German Heinkel bomber ... the bombs were probably carried externally because of their size.[3]

Verification that the planes and bombs were German was beyond dispute. But some people had a further, disturbing question: were the *pilots* German as well?

Official declaration that the bombs were German allowed newspapers to print strong editorials assigning blame and demanding action from the Government. Despite censorship regulations, editors felt compelled to speak forcefully about such a despicable act. The editorial in the *Irish Independent* noted the international reaction:

The Irish people have been horrified by the terrible tragedy of Saturday morning. Even the outside world, hardened as it may have been by the daily toll of calamity on land and sea since the outbreak of this hideous war, has been shocked by the news that people could be killed by bombs in their homes in the capital of a neutral state.[4]

Every newspaper's editorial displayed outrage about what was seen as a barbaric act of murdering innocent citizens in their beds in a neutral country. All expressed in the strongest terms the hope—indeed, demand—that the Taoiseach would passionately protest, as the *Irish Press* wrote:

The capital of Ireland is to-day a city of sorrow. Thirty innocent men, women and children have been killed. At least ninety have been injured and many homes and business premises have been destroyed.

The heart-rending scenes in the devastated areas have brought into the minds of all who saw or read about them a feeling of the deepest resentment that so grievous a hurt should be inflicted on our capital and its unoffending people.

The bombs which caused this havoc proved to be of German origin ... this is a neutral state, it has maintained its neutrality with a correctitude which is evident to all belligerents. That it could, nevertheless, suffer the horrors of last Saturday morning calls for the most vehement condemnation.[5]

On Monday the Government announced that "the Irish Chargé d'Affaires has been instructed to lodge a vigorous protest to prevent further violation of our neutrality."[6] The Government's official message issued on the same day to the Irish people hardly rang with outrage and condemnation:

> In an official message, the Government expressed the sympathy of the whole nation with those bereaved or who have suffered injury or loss, and tributes to the "splendid services" of the many organisations engaged in rescue work.[7]

By contrast, messages and condolences expressing profound sympathy, and anger, were pouring into Ireland from abroad, from governments, organisations and individuals. Much heartfelt sentiment cascaded down from Northern Ireland, where people were immensely grateful for the asssistance of Dublin Fire Brigade during their recent blitz, and for taking in refugees. On Monday evening Denis Ireland, president of the Ulster Union Club, spoke at their general meeting in Belfast and expressed the feelings of many in the North:

> We send our deepest sympathy to the injured, the homeless, and the relatives of the citizens of Dublin who lost their lives in this latest attack upon a peaceful country. As a token of our feelings of our kinship as Irishmen, I propose that we in this club raise a subscription ... [for] a city that responded so nobly to the call of humanity in our time of need.[8]

The sense of kinship forged between the North and South during their shared wartime tragedies was felt strongly on both sides of the border. What was no longer felt by those in the North was safe sanctuary when visiting Dublin.

Apart from their powerful editorials, Monday's newspapers updated events and statistics: thirty now confirmed dead and at least ninety seriously injured. Thirty-one people were classified as missing. Several unidentified bodies still lay in mortuaries. There was no news about Mrs Fagan or Patrick McLoughlin and his two-year-old son, William, known to be still buried in the rubble. The newspapers also published a plea from the Red Cross Society for gifts of clothing, "for persons rendered homeless by the bombs ... Clothing of all kinds is required and the need for men's attire is most urgent."[9] The Lord Mayor of Dublin, Kathleen Clarke, said she would be happy to accept clothing parcels delivered to the Mansion House, as a convenience to donors. Contributors from all parts of the city soon began showing up, with not only clothing but food, pots and pans, and other items. Before long, the Mansion House would be swamped with donated goods.

Two Monday morning newspapers carried some "helpful" advice. The *Irish Times*, quoting an "authority on air-raids", offered Dubliners some advice in the event that more bombs should fall upon them. It was his professional opinion that "there would have been fewer casualties at the North Strand if people had remained in their beds ... the protection afforded by bed clothes would have saved some of them from injury."[10] The *Irish Press* published an advertisement with some uplifting words for people who were feeling "down" in life. It was for Carter's Little Liver Pills, which promised people a cheerier "world outlook":

> Wake up your liver bile—and you'll jump out of bed in the morning full of vim and vigour.[11]

As it explained to readers, "when you get constipated you feel sour, sunk, and the world looks punk." They guaranteed that their pills would "make you feel 'up' again." There was no denying that Dubliners could use a bit of a lift after what they had been through.

On Monday morning the city manager and Dublin Corporation flew into action, issuing three immediate orders: heavy traffic was to be diverted around dangerous tenement streets, a mass inspection of tenement buildings was to be undertaken, and evacuations were to be carried out wherever tenement dwellings were considered unsafe for occupation. Over the past twenty-four hours the homeless situation had worsened. At least eleven families had lost their homes in Sunday's collapses, and twenty-three more families were evacuated from adjacent unstable buildings. Then, on Monday morning, the authorities condemned two more four-storey tenements in Empress Place, off Portland Row, before they too might topple to the ground. This meant another seventy or so evacuees in need of shelter. All trekked over to the Red Cross offices in Mespil Road, where they were assigned to crowded temporary shelters.

Meanwhile, out in Cabra a battalion of building workers had worked through the night in response to Hernon's call to complete a hundred houses far ahead of schedule. An *Irish Times* reporter was sent out to investigate their progress:

> All last night (Sunday), workers were rushing to complete the lighting, sanitary, and other arrangements in these homes, which were not scheduled to have been completed for at least three weeks hence.[12]

Over the coming weeks, newspapers would report that they had never seen tradesmen work so feverishly or purposefully, without a hint of grumbling about the long hours and night shifts. It was hoped that most of the hundred houses could be made habitable within four to six weeks, rather than the planned four to six months. But there remained an underlying worry about the quality of work and the comfort of the houses once they were completed.

———

It was about ten o'clock on Monday morning, and Alec King was worn to the bone, with skin scraped off his hands, elbows and knees. He and his Rescue and Demolition crews had arrived at the North Strand at 2:20 a.m. on Saturday, only minutes after the bomb exploded. After nearly sixty consecutive hours of the most gruelling and gruesome work he had lost not only skin but some fingernails, his watch and his glasses. He had expended every ounce of energy in his body. When he finally returned home, emotionally as well as physically spent, he was alarmed to find what else had happened to him:

> I never had a break—*sixty* hours. *Mentally*, everything was drained out of me. I was tired, I was hungry, my bones were sore. When I did get home on Monday morning, longing for a lovely bath, I got a rude awakening. After a "welcome home" from my family, I went upstairs and ran myself a hot bath.
>
> As I took my socks and boiler suit off, I was down to my vest and underpants. My wellington boots were thrown out the window. Then I had a look at myself. I was covered in blood. My fingernails were gone, there was nothing but red, pussy sore things. And I was cut and bruised all over the place. But at the time, you were numbed to it. That was a minor thing—because you had people there who were far worse, with no arms and legs, maybe no head, like that woman. You didn't think about it, you just kept going.
>
> When I stripped down in the bathroom, took off my underpants, I discovered that I had a ring around my stomach, about two inches of raw flesh. I had been *eaten alive* by all kinds of bugs. They had come up from my feet, but they couldn't get any farther because of the elastic. So they decided to eat underneath it.
>
> The rim around my waist was on fire; the pain was awful. Panic at last set in. I got a big bottle of Jeyes Fluid and I lashed the whole lot into the bath, and I got in. And the *pain* around my stomach was something, from the raw flesh and the Jeyes Fluid.

As King was luxuriating in the steaming bath water, over in Stephen Street horses were neighing wildly and thrashing against the sides of their stalls as flames licked up around them. The large premises of Dublin Bakery Company had suddenly caught fire, and flames were feeding ravenously on huge stores of fats. It was spreading rapidly in a highly congested area. If not contained quickly, the entire street might catch fire. Bakery workers ran frantically to free the horses from the stables as the "frightened animals stamped and neighed in the swirling dust and smoke."[13] As the horses were being led away, people rushed past them towards the fire scene. Within minutes, flames and clouds of smoke were visible streets away. The alarm bell rang at Tara Street fire station, and within 59 seconds firemen were again on their engines and heading to Stephen Street at breakneck speed. People along their route heard the fire engine bells clanging, saw the black billowing smoke and naturally wondered—once again—if another bomb had fallen, or another tenement house had collapsed.

Dublin's firemen were being pushed to their limits. They still had men and engines over at the North Strand; only twenty-four hours earlier they had been at the Old Bride Street tenement disaster; and now they were called to fight a fire that was threatening to engulf the surrounding district. As the retired fireman Tom Geraghty expresses it, "as bodies were still being recovered from the North Strand bombing, the fire brigade was again dealing with a major fire … it was to test the fire brigade organization to the full."[14]

For hours, firemen pumped water on the flames from all angles. But the fire kept feeding itself from within, until it had consumed all its fuel. Meanwhile, firemen were trying their best to prevent flames from jumping across to other buildings. Finally, after five hours of battling, the fire was under control. As the firemen packed up their gear and mounted their engines to head back to Tara Street, a few men were ordered to remain on the site for a few more hours to keep watch for any eruptions from the smouldering ruins.

By contrast, Whit holidaymakers were having great fun. Transport terminals were as jammed as they had been the two previous days. "From 11.00 in the morning until late in the afternoon," reported the *Irish Press*, "a long queue of people stretched along Eden Quay, waiting for the G.N.R. buses to take them to the sea at Howth or Portmarnock. Bus and rail facilities were availed of to an extent scarcely ever equalled."[15] It was as if people were trying to salvage at least one tragedy-free day of the holiday. A railway official at Harcourt Street station estimated that more than eight thousand people went by train to Bray on Monday, the opening day of the summer season. Another large crowd would attend the Rathmines Festival that evening.

All day long, throngs flowed into the Phoenix Park. They were picnickers, zoo-goers, strollers and curiosity-seekers wanting to have a look at the large crater gouged out in the soft earth by the third bomb that had fallen by the

Dog Pond, demolishing Mr McNally's house and damaging the Cricket Club. At the zoo everyone wanted to visit Sara, the gentle and astonishingly resourceful elephant who carried out her much-publicised escape after being frightened by the bomb blast. While some other zoo animals still seemed fidgety, Sara appeared perfectly calm. If it were true that elephants possessed good memories, Sara seemed to be nicely repressing her recollections of that terrifying night.

Late on Monday morning, the City Coroner, Dr D. A. MacErlean, announced details of the inquest to be held in the City Morgue the next day. It was his firm belief that the autopsies conducted on all the victims should be made known to the relatives and the public, for the historical record. He knew that some of the findings would be painful but it was his duty to be precise. He further stated that attention would first be devoted to the seven members of the Browne family, as relatives had informed him that they wished to remove the remains immediately to Edenderry for burial the next day at Drumcooley Cemetery.

At 11:45, about the time Dr MacErlean was speaking to reporters, another body was found at the North Strand, to be added to the autopsy list. Mr Fagan's vigil of nearly two-and-a-half days had finally ended as his wife, Josephine, was pulled out of a deep pocket in the rubble. The entire time, he had waited stoically, saying little to rescuers. When her face was cleaned of filth he identified her, saying only what was necessary, after which he turned and walked slowly away.

By this time, Alec King had been in the bath for nearly an hour, adding hot water from time to time, dozily absorbing the pleasant sensation into every pore of his bug-bitten, weary body. Hunger was now paramount on his mind; then sleep. But first he had to rise, dry off and dress, which he dreaded:

> I started to push the scum down toward the end with my hands, and when I pulled the stopper out it took a long time to drain away. I had to get a bucket to clear out all the bugs.
>
> Then, after I washed away the blood with lukewarm water, I got the best disinfectant you could get: a bottle of whiskey! And I poured whiskey over my stomach. And by that time I was up around where the electric light was with the *pain* of it! *Really stung*—but it *worked!* Then I had a right good feed—and I went to bed.

After devouring the meal his wife had prepared, he went upstairs and fell into sleep within seconds. Eight to ten hours of solid sleep would make a new man of him.

By mid-day on Whit Monday, Dublin pub men were into their third day of holiday drinking. With all the nerve-racking events, most were drinking more heavily than usual. Many had spent little time with their families since 2:05 a.m. on Saturday. A number of pubs managed to stay open nearly around the clock, with the blind eye turned.

With their tongues well lubricated and Germany officially declared the culprit, pub pundits were now speculating freely about what Hitler was up to. As Mary Cooke exclaims, "there were a *million* stories! And I guarantee you, if you went into every pub you'd get a different story." In the elite city pubs, such as the Palace, the Pearl, and McDaid's, journalists, literati and politicians delved cerebrally into the political and diplomatic ramifications of the incident. In working-class locals, men were spouting off and speechifying with their own earthy insight. Every pub in the city was crackling with lively conversation about the bombing.

Four of the most popular public houses around the North Strand— Crowe's, Creighton's, Maguire's and Fagan's—had either been blown up or seriously damaged. Their thirsty regulars had to seek new watering-holes. Many gravitated towards Killane's pub on the corner of Gardiner Street and Parnell Street, always a hive of stimulating chat. It was Dublin's most famous boxers' pub, with the likes of the legendary "Spike" McCormack, Irish middleweight champion, as well as Peter Glenn, Mickey Gifford and Blackman Doyle, and a host of lesser-known fighters. Gardiner Street had in fact been christened the "street of champions". Normally, publicans imposed a prohibition on the two subjects of religion and politics, to avoid the outbreak of verbal brawls or even real fisticuffs. But in Killane's, if a man didn't like a particular politician or archbishop, he came right out with it. In this pub, fighters, dockers and coal men all had their say.

By Monday afternoon the talk in Killane's about the German bombing was reaching near fever pitch. While many Dubliners at this early stage either believed or hoped that the bombing had been an unfortunate mistake, many men in Killane's saw it differently. Quite a few had served in the British army and knew about war and the German military cruelties. Some lashed out at Hitler and the Luftwaffe pilots who had "blown up" their city. Every speaker had his own view on it. But no-one was putting any logical reason *behind* it— telling *why* it happened.

Finally, up stood "Big Bob" Darcy, a towering, tough man, fully six feet four inches and over eighteen stone.[16] Known for his thoughtful insight, he didn't dispense oratory on just any subject: it had to be of some importance. Otherwise, he let it pass to the pub's amateurs. For two-and-a-half days Bob had sat back in Killane's, holding his tongue while listening to the other men jabbering away about the bombing. That he was so conspicuously silent on such a colossal subject made his mates wonder what was on his mind. He had, indeed, been thinking deeply, concluding that it was more than merely an isolated accident. When he felt the moment to be right, and the scene to his liking, "Big Bob" rose to speak, and every man in Killane's turned on his stool or sat back in his chair to hear what he had to say. With the pub hushed, he stood to his full height:

> I'll tell yiz why the Germans bombed the North Strand. Ya have to remember a few weeks before the North Strand. The Germans sent their whole bloody air force to blow Belfast off the map. Gave them an awful hammering for two solid days.
>
> And do you remember what we did down here? We sent our fire-brigade units up to help with the fires. We were supposed to be a neutral country, but we openly went and gave the boys in Belfast a hand. Belfast is part of Britain as far as them Germans are concerned—Hitler was telling de Valera to stop helping the Brits.[17]

"Mr Killane behind the bar was up like a flash to Bob with a fresh pint," recalls his nephew Bill Cullen. "'There you are, Mr Darcy, that's on the house.'"[18] Then Bob proceeded to remind his listeners about the Wexford creamery bombing, which was "supposed to be an accident, too." What really happened, he explained, was that the Germans discovered abandoned British supplies on the beaches of Dunkirk after the British retreat. Among them were wooden crates with the name of Campile Creamery, County Wexford, boldly stencilled on them. This was taken as another sign of neutral Ireland aiding the enemy. Then he drew attention to the recent, and glaring, violation of Dublin taking in thousands of bombed-out Belfast refugees, all British subjects. These acts were all indisputable breaches of neutrality. As Darcy had it worked out, there was a price to be paid for such interference. He summed it up:

> The bloody Germans were paying us back, telling us to keep quiet and mind our own business ... a warning, to keep out of this war, or else.[19]

The common sense of his argument brought nods from every corner, followed by pats on his back. Within seconds Mr Killane was on the spot, handing him another free pint for his stellar performance.

———

Alec King was awake. When he looked over at the clock in his bedroom he was astonished to see that it was still afternoon. At best, he had been asleep for about four hours. His subconscious had stirred him, calling him back to the bomb scene. When he arose and began to dress, his entire body felt bruised or raw. His red and infected hands found it difficult to fasten buttons and tie shoelaces. With his boiler-suit and boots caked with dirt and blood, he had to dress in civilian clothes this time. He went downstairs to look for his glasses, then remembered he had lost them at the scene. His wife was surprised to see him up and dressed after such a short spell in bed. Was he all right? He assured her that he was well enough but felt a strong calling to return. As usual, he couldn't explain it. As usual, she didn't ask him to. He would be back home within a few hours, he told her.

Efforts were now under way to comb the ruins for personal possessions. Larger items, such as furniture and clothing, were being identified by their position and then taken by Dublin Corporation lorry to a collection centre, to be reclaimed later by their owners. Smaller objects had to be handled with care. Scattered about the site was every imaginable personal possession: glasses, false teeth, artificial limbs, photographs, family bibles, religious relics, toys, Rosary beads, birth and wedding certificates, combs and brushes, undergarments, medicine bottles, delph, eating utensils, and indescribable ornaments and mementoes—all the treasured minutiae of people's lives.

Discovered letters and diaries were like voices from the grave, unearthing the most poignant sentiments, many containing messages of love, endearment, cheeriness and good news. Some mentioned the anticipation of the coming Whit holiday, the last entry being on 30 May 1941.

The discovery of money was an important matter, carefully handled. Most city-dwellers lived on a week-to-week bare-bones budget. Coming up a few shillings short at week's end could bring the threat of a bare table, or even eviction. The timing of the bombing was unfortunate, coming as it did at the end of the week, when people had just collected their wages. Despite the ever-present financial pinch, mothers tried to put away a few extra shillings, growing into pounds over time, for special occasions, such as Christmas, first Holy Communion, christenings, weddings and wakes. In an age when many lower-income families did not rely on banks, their paltry savings were often hidden away beneath floorboards, behind chimney bricks, or stuffed into a brass bedpost, the base of a religious statue, in the mattress, or just into the pocket of trousers or a handbag. Then the bomb blew everything to high heaven.

The authorities gave strict orders regarding the discovery of money. Every shilling had to be handed over to ARP wardens and documented by its position. "From many of the houses," reported the *Evening Herald*, "purses and women's bags were brought out containing the house-keeping money for the week."[20] Those who had savings hidden in their homes were frantic to retrieve them. Forbidden entry by the police, some dared to try to sneak through the cordons, as did one of Dermot Ring's neighbours:

> There was one fella that went back through the police cordon and climbed up through the ruins, 'cause he was looking for a pair of trousers—'cause he had over a *hundred pounds* in it! And he *found* it! Hanging on the end of an old bed rail. Oh, he was happy!

Late on Monday afternoon, just before King returned to the scene, there was another tragic discovery. Mr and Mrs John Foran of 152 North Strand, who had been on the missing list, were found buried beneath chunky debris. Their bodies were brushed off and placed in an ambulance to be taken to the City Morgue. It was not possible to know whether they had died instantly or had suffered a prolonged death. Two more names would be struck from the missing list, two more added to the death toll. With each new discovery of bodies, hope was revived that Patrick McLoughlin and his infant son, William, could still be found.

When King returned he identified himself to the police at the cordons and was given permission to re-enter the ruins. He first went to meet his men and see how their rescue and demolition work was proceeding. To his surprise, "as I moved about the destruction, now that I was in clean and decent clothes, no-one recognised me." When he greeted them, all were astounded to see him back again so soon. Then he began shuffling around the rubble on his own. Without at first realising it, he found himself searching once again. By now his eyes were trained to detect the smallest tell-tale protruding object that warranted further exploration. Occasionally, he'd pause and bend down to turn over a brick or other object, or just poke it away with the toe of his shoe.

After about an hour of rambling and scanning the ground, his vision picked out a tiny object missed by everyone else over the past three days. It was only about half an inch in size, but it brought him to an instant halt:

> I saw *that much* [indicating] of a woman's shoe, just the little pointed toe. A lady's shoe sticking out of the ground—it was a black winkle-picker style. And I went to lift this up, and I couldn't get any movement out of it at all. So I started to excavate a bit—and I discovered there was a foot in it! And from the foot I discovered there was legs in it! And from the legs, I discovered there was a body on it!

Then three other workers came over and we started excavating. And after more work the three of us uncovered a young woman of about twenty. She had evidently been hit by either a block of timber or an iron girder, which had injured her very badly. Her nose and breasts were sheared off like you would see with an electric carving knife. It had just come down and severed her.

After the body was recovered it was immediately placed on a stretcher and covered, so that no-one else would see her in such condition, at least until she arrived at the morgue. Once again, covered in filth and blood, Alec King returned home for a late supper.

On Monday evening the holiday weekend was drawing to a close. It would stand as the most memorable Whitsuntide in Irish history. Holidaymakers were streaming back into the city, some not having heard about the tenement collapses along Old Bride Street on Sunday morning, or the huge fire at the Dublin Bakery Company. All were eager to catch up on the latest news.

About eight o'clock that evening, the Olympia Theatre presented its new review, "Let Laughter Loose". One critic lauded it as a "well balanced production with sketches, snappy songs and dancing, and colourful sets ... comedy was liberally dispensed."[21] Every seat in the theatre was filled, and all eyes were cast upon one young man: the replacement for Noel Fitzpatrick. Nothing could have been in greater contrast than the bright lights, gaiety and cheerful songs on the Olympia stage and the cold, silent, grey City Morgue in which Noel was laid dead upon a slab.

As the Olympia's first number was under way, another body was found. To everyone's surprise, it was discovered very near Newcomen Bridge, somehow passed by for days beneath a pile of thick debris and dust. Once retrieved, no-one around the North Strand could identify who it was. So, the body was sent to the City Morgue to join seven other unidentified remains by Monday night.

Just before 11:30 p.m. rescuers came across another find. Not a whole body this time. As the *Evening Herald* described it, "a head and some bones were removed from the charred remains of No. 157 North Strand."[22] The skeletal remains were carefully picked up, fragment by fragment. Then the ground was raked for smaller bones. Most had been cleaned bare by fire, but some had bits of flesh intact. To whom did the skull and bones belong? Speculation arose that it could be Patrick McLoughlin. Perhaps the coroner could work it out.

At midnight, the Whit weekend was over. Most Dubliners were in bed, finally sleeping soundly. Between one and two o'clock bombers swept through the sky. Searchlights snapped on as a barrage of anti-aircraft fire awakened thousands of people. Bombs fell and exploded. "Large fires were started," wrote the *Evening Mail*, "material damage was done by the raiders ... there were a number of casualties, some fatal."[23] Citizens were terror-stricken.

But this time it wasn't Dublin. It was Berlin. A small, daring force of British pilots penetrated German defences and struck at the heart of Hitler's regime, giving the Germans a strong dose of their own medicine. It was a modest military success but a huge psychological boost to British morale.

Dubliners, meanwhile, enjoyed a night of sleep without the slightest disturbance. Like the "good old days," people would be saying the next morning.

Chapter 21 ∾

THE CORONER'S VERDICT

The most solemn inquest scene that Dublin has seen in many years.

(*Irish Press*, 4 June 1941)

There are some remains so shattered and maimed that identification is impossible.

(*Irish Times*, 4 June 1941)

Tuesday morning's newspapers provided schedules and full details of that day's coroner's inquest as well as of the funerals to be held on Wednesday and Thursday. Throngs of mourners would attend all three—a massive turn-out of grieving Dubliners, beyond anything imagined.

The newspapers now all agreed that the death toll had climbed to thirty-four. This did not include the three victims of the Old Bride Street tenement collapse. The number of serious injuries was also steadily mounting as hospitals tried to cope, but their space and resources were severely strained. The list of missing was also nudging upwards.

As Dermot Ring finished his breakfast, having scanned the morning newspaper, he headed over to Coláiste Mhuire in Parnell Square to take his Leaving Certificate exam. As he ascended the stairs and entered the room he was surprised to hear "great cheers, like I was a conquering hero! They had assumed that I was in the middle of the dead!" He rather enjoyed the fuss over his survival. Many residents of the North Strand area would receive a similar reception when they showed up at their work-places in days after the bombing, their friends greatly relieved to see that they were not among the dead, injured or missing. When his exam was graded, Ring was "happy with the results; I got as many honours as I expected to get … it didn't affect my performance."

As he had been taking his examination, Dublin's hospital administrators were trying to devise a better system for handling the surge of patients. "Bomb casualties had taxed to the utmost the accommodations of the 30 participating hospitals," reported the *Irish Press*, "the Mater and Jervis Street

Surviving Charleville Cottages. Note the bricks on the ground at right, which were sent flying through the air by the blast. (*Courtesy of Dublin City Archives*)

ARP wardens combing the ruins. (*Courtesy of the* Irish Independent)

Maura O'Toole witnessed looting during the first hour following the bombing.

Damage along North Clarence Street, showing the Clover Dairy and Kelly's Dairy at right. (*Courtesy of Dublin City Archives*)

Numbers 30 to 35 North Strand Road, showing the post office at right and dangling sign from Roddy's shop, a local favourite. (*Courtesy of Dublin City Archives*)

An enamel plate that fell from one of the German planes into Denis Dunne's back garden and was discovered the following morning. (*Courtesy of the Allen Library*)

Bomb fragment with the imprint of the German eagle clearly visible. (*Courtesy of the Allen Library*)

Sally Burke, who was caught out on the open street with her father when the big bomb exploded.

North Clarence Street, with tenement children in the foreground. (*Courtesy of Dublin City Archives*)

Less damaged section of North Strand Road at numbers 12, 13 and 14, showing the hard, dense cobblestone surface and steel tram track on which the big bomb detonated, causing such ferocious destruction. (*Courtesy of Dublin City Archives*)

St John Ambulance Brigade's new mobile canteen, at which rescuers and local survivors could get much-appreciated food and drink. (*Courtesy of Military Archives*)

Dunne Street, showing how destabilised houses had to be reinforced for safety. (*Courtesy of Dublin City Archives*)

Many were the stories of brave and daring rescues in all the newspapers. Dubliners couldn't get enough of the coverage.

Numbers 47 and 48 North William Street. Note the damage at right rear. Some houses toppled, while others stood shakily. (*Courtesy of Dublin City Archives*)

Survivors examining their salvaged possessions, with a garda at left and LDF man at right. (*Courtesy of the* Irish Independent)

hospitals had all their beds filled."[1] It had been expected that more patients would have been released from hospital after forty-eight hours or so, but because of the seriousness of their injuries this had not happened. So, on Tuesday morning Dublin's Hospital Commission declared a "bed crisis" and hurriedly established a "bed bureau" at its central office in Upper Mount Street. It served as a medical "command centre" at which information from all the hospitals could be collected and quickly dispensed to those institutions desperately seeking additional bed space. As a consequence, instead of hospitals functioning independently they would now share information and co-ordinate their efforts. Information gathered was charted on a large blackboard in the commission's central office; this enabled members of the staff to "assess at a glance" what accommodation was available and where, and immediately "furnish it to an enquirer" by phone. One reporter from the *Irish Press* was so impressed that he wrote, "The Bureau has devised an ingenious system":

> Covering the entire wall is a huge blackboard with the names of the hospitals chalked on the left-hand side ... with hooks forming columns ... coloured cardboard tags are attached to the hooks indicating beds available for men, women and children.[2]

In his estimation, neither Eisenhower nor Montgomery could have had a better visual chart with which to plan their campaigns.

Later on Tuesday morning, the city manager, P. J. Hernon, set up a crisis bureau of his own. This was the Dublin Corporation Bureau, established in the Charleville Mall Library, to deal with applications for alternative accommodation for people whose houses had been "rendered uninhabitable". According to the *Irish Independent*, nearly three hundred damaged houses had already been declared unfit for habitation, "leaving many hundreds of people homeless."[3] It was hoped that many of the houses could be quickly repaired and reoccupied. But the phrasing of the declaration by the housing authorities was worrying to occupants:

> In the cases of dwelling-houses capable of being rendered fit for habitation, arrangements are being made by the Corporation to undertake structural first-aid through several firms of building contractors.[4]

The term "first aid" was a cause for real concern. They knew all too well that the corporation, even under the best circumstances, was known for often carrying out poor-quality work. They feared that this would be a hasty, shoddy "patch-up" job, a mere bandage on their damaged homes.

Nonetheless, most homeless families were so desperate to get back into their own homes that they were willing to accept even a barely habitable dwelling, at least for the time being.

To make matters worse, Dublin ran out of glass within the first three days. The city's entire supply had been used up by citizens and shopkeepers seeking to replace their broken windows. This left all the other people with "glass of secondary quality which would admit light through, but which it would be impossible to see [through] clearly."[5] This inferior, hazy glass did not allow for visual definition and created for many a feeling of claustrophobia. But it was better than a bare window frame. Then, when this translucent glass ran out, people had to hammer boards over their windows, making their home feel like a tomb.

Dublin Corporation assured residents that the so-called "blind" glass would be temporary, replaced with normal glass very soon. In 2004, two-thirds of a century later, it was still to be seen in some houses around the north inner city. Passers-by who sometimes enquired about the strange glass were told a good story.

There was also a problem with furniture and bedding. Most bombed-out victims had lost most, if not all, of their sparse furniture. Some of the families scheduled to move into the hundred houses being completed in Cabra had not a stick of furniture. Not a single chair. The Government had no plan to provide furniture, bedding, cooking utensils or the like for those who had lost everything. The *Irish Independent* wanted to bring to the attention of Dubliners the fact that the refugees and evacuees were often not only homeless but possession-less as well:

> The problem of furnishing the houses for people, nearly all of whom lost personal and household belongings, is a big one. Unless furniture and bedding are provided immediately, many people will be faced with the prospects of moving into empty houses.[6]

To assist victims in acquiring essential furnishings and getting their life back together, the *Irish Times* and other newspapers began a daily "subscription funds" effort, listing the names of contributors and their donations. It caught on immediately, as good citizens wanted to help out. The majority of contributions ranged from one to three pounds, but about a third were measured in shillings. Some individuals and companies gave a hundred pounds and more. Many preferred not to be identified by name—rather as "A Sympathiser from Ennis", who offered five shillings, or "Delighted to Help", who sent in twenty pounds. Eveline Smyth gave two pounds, while Sunbeam Wolsey Ltd, the hosiery manufacturers, donated a hundred pounds.

Donations of a single shilling were listed with all the others. Contributions flowed in from every county and from every district in Dublin, including the poorest of the tenement districts, all equally happy to do their part.

The newspapers had made no mention of looting, though surely some of their reporters had picked up stories about theft in the streets and shops during the first chaotic hour after the bombing. It was an editorial decision carefully weighed. A few culprits, however, had been caught in the act and brought to court. These cases were briefly mentioned in the press. Though the stolen items were of small value, several of the thefts were viewed as despicable because of their nature. One involved picking up a pair of used boots. But the *Evening Herald* jumped on the story, calling it a crime of "stealing a pair of boots of a man killed"—that man being Richard Fitzpatrick, the butcher.[7]

Michael Cleary, aged thirty, of St Joseph's Mansions, Killarney Street, was charged in Dublin District Court with the crime. He had been employed by Dublin Corporation as a temporary worker to help clean up the bomb site. Somehow, he got hold of an ARP badge and pinned it on his shirt, giving him licence to roam the ruins of homes and rummage about. He was caught in the act by two witnesses, Detective-Sergeant M. Byrne and an ARP warden. The detective testified that he "saw the defendant stooping down and picking up the boots which he rolled up in paper, which belonged to the late Mr. Richard Fitzpatrick."[8] He also took a packet of playing cards. Detective-Sergeant Byrne called over an ARP warden, J. J. MacDonagh, to examine the thief's credentials. He was immediately exposed as a fraud and sent off to jail. When he was later released he wisely kept out of sight, as he was viewed by local people as a most loathsome individual.

Shortly after 10:30 on Tuesday morning, fire engine bells were again heard and smoke plumes seen, as people in the streets looked around and wondered "what now?" It was another bakery fire, this time at Alexander's Bakery in Cuffe Lane, off Cuffe Street. Once again, firemen sped to the scene and laid out their hoses as gardaí pushed the crowd back. It turned out to be a fire of moderate size and intensity. Nonetheless, it took several hours to extinguish completely. Appreciative citizens held their fire brigade in high esteem for their untiring efforts over the previous four days.

At number 157 North Strand rescuers had now been excavating in the debris for three-and-a-half days. They had found the bodies of Josephine Fagan, Mary Boyle and Thomas Carroll, but still no trace of the two McLoughlins. Then, at 12:10, digging suddenly intensified as one rescuer shouted out for a stretcher. A body had been found. A priest was also called over, and nearby workers ceased their activities to watch. One man was seen to drop to his knees, bend over and gently lift a small limp body from the cavity. William McLoughlin had finally been found. The body of the two-year-old child was cleaned off, placed on the stretcher and taken by ambulance to the City Morgue, just in time to be delivered to the coroner, Dr MacErlean, and included in the inquest scheduled for later in the afternoon.

As word began spreading around the city that William McLoughlin had been found, two notifications had to be made. Kirwan's were informed that they would need one more small white coffin; and someone had to be despatched to the Mater Hospital to tell Mrs McLoughlin that her child had been found dead. It is not recorded to whom this wrenching task fell.

The infant, who had captured the hearts of all Dublin, had been buried beneath a mountain of bricks, mortar, slates and timber for more the eighty-two hours. In another forty-eight hours he would be buried once again, this time peacefully and eternally in Glasnevin Cemetery.

Kirwan's had been doing their best to prepare all the bodies for coffining. Given the number of bodies and their often appalling condition, the undertaker's men were challenged as never before. "We collected the bodies from the City Morgue or hospital morgues," explains Tom Kirwan. "And there was no embalming at that time, but there were other chemicals we used. And, of course, a wash and a shave was done by us." With some of the bodies mangled, charred and dismembered, reconstruction and cosmetic preparation were exceedingly difficult. Gaping wounds and other unsightly features had to be covered or disguised. Family members were allowed to view the remains if they so wished, but they were advised in advance of what they would be seeing. Most heart-rending, recalls Tom Kirwan, was placing the children in their small white coffins. "With a child … it's always very emotional … It took a tremendous toll on them."

———

The inquest was to begin in the afternoon at four o'clock. Public interest exceeded all expectations, and a large crowd began gathering outside the inquest chambers more than an hour in advance. After days of closely following in the newspapers the most personal details about the victims, Dubliners had become emotionally invested in their lives, and deaths. They had come to feel as if they knew the Brownes, the Fitzpatricks, the McLoughlins, and others. The particularly tragic circumstances of some deaths—Harry Browne with his hand clutching the doorknob, his wife with little Angela wrapped protectively in her arms, the infant William McLoughlin and Noel Fitzpatrick, as well as others—elicited profound compassion.

The inquest it was hoped would finally reveal answers about exactly how some of the victims had died. Had Richard Fitzpatrick really been decapitated, or had he suffocated in his ice chest? There was great public curiosity about the proceedings. Undeniably, there was an element of sheer excitement and drama. Many who gathered in the street outside the City Morgue simply wanted to be a part of it.

By three o'clock it was obvious that more police and cordons would be needed for crowd control. Flocks of people were already impeding traffic in surrounding streets. By 3:30 it was decided that additional help was needed, and "outside a detachment of the L.S.F. helped to control the large crowd."[9] Regular police handled the crowd directly outside the coroner's court to make certain they didn't interfere with the arrival of victims' relatives, friends and other witnesses. As the hour of the inquest approached, it had both the appearance and the feel of a crowd outside a court building awaiting the jury's verdict.

Inside the building the mood was just the opposite, as "the precincts of the morgue were filled with people long before the inquest began," reported the *Irish Press*.[10] Apart from officials, relatives and witnesses, were a few reporters and select visitors. These included several representatives of Edenderry Town Commissioners, who had come on behalf of the Browne family. With the warm weather and tightly packed people, the room became stuffy well before the proceedings began. All the bereaved family members were gathered in the same room, creating a collective sense of loss and sorrow. Handkerchiefs were clutched in hands and sniffling heard. The room would grow warmer, the air more stale, and emotions rise. Attendants were told to watch for signs of faintness.

It was almost 4:30 before the coroner, Dr MacErlean, entered the room and took his place. Accompanying him were his four assisting doctors: Dr Fergus O'Nolan, house surgeon, Mater Hospital; Dr J. J. Danaher, Jervis Street Hospital; Dr Kevin J. Cahill, Richmond Hospital; and Dr G. F. Duggan. All distinguished physicians, they had examined the bodies and would share their medical expertise. Dr MacErlean was highly experienced, known for his professional thoroughness and exactness. He was precise in his medical examinations as well as in the verbal clarity of his findings. He understood well his role in this unprecedented tragedy. It was his responsibility to make certain that the historical record was absolutely accurate. He knew that it would be very difficult for the bereaved to hear the graphic descriptions of the causes of some deaths, but it was absolutely necessary at the inquest that they should do so.

The coroner began by praising the ARP, the LDF and the various rescue services that had "worked night and day at their gruesome tasks … when bombs were falling, without regard to their own safety."[11] He particularly commended the work of the Irish Red Cross Society and the St John Ambulance Brigade for their swift response and superb medical treatment at the scene. Were it not for their skill and dedication, he said, the morgue would surely be filled with many more bodies.

Then began the formal inquest, as reporters readied their pens and pads. An *Irish Times* reporter jotted down his opening statement:

> When he opened the inquest, the Coroner addressed the jury, and said that during the course of considerable aerial activity over the city on the night of May 30–31 a number of bombs fell, causing considerable damage and resulting in the death and mutilation of a number of people. Whole families were wiped out.[12]

Everyone in the courtroom had in mind the thirty-four people now listed in the morning newspapers' death toll, particularly the Browne and Fitzpatrick families. Dr MacErlean continued:

> We have succeeded in identifying all the bodies, scattered as they were through the city hospitals and morgues. There are some remains, however, that are so mutilated and maimed that identification is impossible.[13]

Upon hearing these last words, a few in attendance audibly gasped. In print it seemed abstract, but hearing these words in the inquest room sickened one's stomach. Several women sobbed, and a few were taken out for fresh air.

In his statement, Dr MacErlean distinguished between "bodies" basically intact that were identifiable and other "remains" that were impossible to identify. Then there were the "partial remains". He and his assisting physicians had done their best to fit together pieces of human puzzles, to make an identifiable body; but in several instances it was not possible. Then he revealed a most unexpected conclusion.

> Further investigations, coupled with inquest proceedings, established the fact that 28 deaths occurred as the result of the bombing. It had previously been believed that 34 people were dead, but this error was due to the discovery of portions of bodies in different places. The total now given includes three unidentified remains.[14]

No-one was more surprised than reporters whose own papers had printed that very morning a firm death toll of thirty-four. Now the figure had been *reduced*. People in the inquest chamber appeared confused, trying to envisage how three unidentified remains could have been counted for so many bodies. For some, it was too grotesque to contemplate. The *Irish Press* tried to sum it up for readers, leaving it open to some interpretation. "Twenty-five identified dead, and some others so mutilated that their exact number cannot be stated."[15] Perhaps the "partial remains" did bring the total to thirty-four people, but there was not enough medical evidence to verify it. And Dr MacErlean was a man of exactness. But the figure would soon rise into the thirties again.

Identification of the bodies revealed the indiscriminate nature of the 500-pound bomb. Seven of the victims were children aged seven or under. Two were only two years old, and one only two months. Of the eighteen adults, ten were women, four of whom were in their thirties and one twenty-six. Six of the men were fifty or older.

Making it even worse were the identified causes of death—asphyxiation, burning, bleeding to death, severe head injury, being crushed, decapitation, heart failure due to shock, being blown apart. A few in the inquest room had never heard the word "asphyxiation". Those seated nearby explained that it meant being smothered after being buried alive. They listened, said nothing. Every victim had died a terrible death, some agonisingly prolonged.

Next came the mandatory calling out of the names of the deceased. At this point the room fell silent once more. For veteran morgue attendants, doctors and reporters, this moment inevitably brought to mind scenes of a quarter of a century earlier, a similar chilling calling out of names, many now historically renowned. The *Irish Press* placed it in historical perspective:

> The calling out of the list of the dead at the general inquest recalled to the officials of the mortuary the great Church Street tenement collapse of 26 years ago, the protracted enquiries that followed the Easter Rising, the succession of inquests in the Civil War.[16]

However, in the mass slaughter of innocents, this inquest was unprecedented.

Then began the formal identification process in which relatives and friends of the deceased stepped forward, one by one, to give personal testimony. It was an unpleasant but necessary formality. By request, the Browne family was dealt with first, as they were to be transported home to Edenderry at about five o'clock. The grim duty of identifying all seven family members—Harry, his mother, Mary Browne, his wife, Molly, and their four children, Maureen, Nan, Edward and two-year-old Angela, the "little angel" to the public—fell to John McGlinchey of Clontarf who was married to Harry's sister, Minnie. As he stepped into the witness box every person in the room pictured in their mind the pathetic story of the Brownes being "wiped out",

Harry dashing madly homewards, grasping the doorknob as the bomb exploded, Molly enveloping the baby in her arms, all seven perishing in a great flash. "It *couldn't* have been more heartbreaking," people said. After McGlinchey was seated, the causes of death were identified. Medical evidence confirmed that the six family members inside the house died from asphyxia and heart failure following "severe burns." Harry died from massive head injury. Yet he didn't release his grip on the knob; his fingers had to be prised off.

Upon the completion of all testimony pertaining to the Brownes, those in attendance on their behalf were dismissed from the proceedings so they could accompany the stricken family on their homeward journey to Edenderry. Their chairs were offered to others who had been standing in the stifling room.

Next came the Fitzpatrick family of 28 North Strand, the beloved butcher, his wife, daughter Madge and son Noel. Another son, Richard Fitzpatrick of Manor Street, had been chosen by surviving family members to identify his parents, sister and brother. Medical evidence then revealed that Mr and Mrs Fitzpatrick had died from "severe head injuries, and from shock." Madge had "suffered head and body injuries, death being due to shock." By contrast, "there were no extreme marks on Noel Fitzpatrick," his death being due to asphyxiation.[17] Unmarked in death, despite being found beneath layers of rubble, he appeared in his coffin as natural and handsome as on the Olympia stage.

What of all the gory rumours going around about the butcher's death? No evidence offered at the inquest directly supported any of those stories. Dr MacErlean and Dr Duggan, who had examined his body, recorded only that he had died from "severe head injuries." Could this have been a discreet phrase for decapitation, some people wondered? Despite the inquest records, folklore would persist that Mr Fitzpatrick, the butcher, "got his head cut off" when the bomb fell.

Then there were the "other" Fitzpatricks: Alice Fitzpatrick, aged thirty-eight, her son Desmond, aged five, and baby James, only two months old, of 156 North Strand. They were the "forgotten" Fitzpatricks. Inexplicably, the newspapers had given them little coverage. This is curious, as their story seemed equally tragic: a young mother and her two children killed. But the well-known local butcher, his family and theatrical son were the "big story" for newspapers. The other Fitzpatricks were just ordinary people. They were not identified in death by relatives; instead, Paddy Finlay, a fireman and family friend, agreed to carry out this task. He had seen violent death many times before and had just returned from the bombing of Belfast six weeks earlier, but it was emotionally hard for him to identify the two small children, of whom he was very fond. The mother and two children had died of asphyxia.

Following Paddy Finlay, wrote the *Irish Times*, "a procession of weary-eyed relatives passed through the witness box giving brief evidence of identification—one of his wife, another of his son, and others of near relatives."[18] One by one they stepped forward, a few appearing frail or shaky, needing assistance. Then, half way through the proceedings, disruptive noises were heard from the rear of the morgue. Everyone was drawn to them. An *Irish Press* reporter positioned in the yard covered what was happening:

> While evidence was being given, the rumble of a lorry towards the rear of the morgue attracted attention. Within, the coffining of the bodies of the seven members of the Browne family was being completed. The lorry came from the Mater Hospital with the bodies of some of the family. Those in the yard saw the sad reunion of death.[19]

The family, for some reason, had been separated in the two morgues. Now they were rejoined for their journey home. After the other six coffins had been placed in the lorry, that of Harry Browne, a member of the LDF, was ceremonially handled by a guard of honour of the LDF formed up under Captain W. Hamilton. They draped the Tricolour on his coffin and it was shouldered by the men to join the others. Then members of the guard of honour reversed arms and the cortege slowly began to pull out of the morgue yard toward the gates.

The crowd outside in the streets quickly guessed what was going on, and they began to push their way towards the rear to watch. The police and LSF politely but firmly kept them back as the lorry with the seven coffins rolled out onto the street. People who had been jostling for a good view fell motionless when they saw the lorry pulling out, as described by the *Irish Times*:

> Poignant scenes were witnessed around the City Morgue as the Brownes' bodies were removed. A great hush fell upon sad throngs lined along the streets and far up Amiens Street embankment, as seven coffins, loaded on a lorry, gave a grim picture of the tragedy of the Brown family, completely wiped out.[20]

People lining the route out of Dublin watched as the lorry rumbled past, remaining until it had faded from sight. Meanwhile, residents of Edenderry were planning to walk to the outskirts of the town to catch the first sight of the lorry bringing the Brownes home for the last time.

Inside the inquest room, witnesses continued with their testimony. Dr

MacErlean allowed them to give a brief personal statement about their lost loved ones. Dubliners now knew a great deal about the Brownes and the Fitzpatricks but virtually nothing about the others who had died. Relatives welcomed the opportunity to humanise their mother, father, son, or sister, to give them some meaningful identity before they were buried and forgotten by most. Those in the room visibly responded with interest as each victim was brought to life once more.

John Sweeney proudly told of his father, Charles, a native of Derry who, before he came to Dublin and worked in a petrol station, had been "a well-known railway official ... served as chief clerk at Pennyburn and was stationmaster at Ballylifflin and Carndonagh," a hard-working, well-respected man. In death, said his son, people should know that about his father.

Next came Patrick Murray, who took the witness box to inform everyone in the room that his father, John Murray, had been a widower and a carpenter by trade—a *good* carpenter. James Foran, a warder at Mountjoy Prison, came forward to identify his son John and daughter-in-law Mary Foran, buried together beneath a heap of bricks. His son, he revealed, was a jockey and horse-trainer, well known and liked. Joseph Montgomery then spoke about Patrick Callely, his brother-in-law, a chemist with one child, and how he loved his work helping people. Corporal John Daly served as witness for his sixty-year-old cousin, Elizabeth Daly, who was unmarried and a dressmaker. She had outfitted countless girls and young women over her life, asking little recompense but receiving much gratitude for her skill. There wasn't much more to tell. She had died from severe leg injuries. Mary Stoat then spoke on behalf of Mrs Holten, who, she said, did not work, but her husband, a former British soldier, had died a few years ago, leaving her with "some small means." Christopher Fagan lovingly told of his sister-in-law, Josephine Fagan, and her father, Thomas Carroll, who had enjoyed his life as a GNR employee. Mr Fagan, who had kept vigil at the entombment of his wife, Josephine, for several days, was apparently unable to attend the inquest.

And so it went, one witness following the next, most well composed, straightforward with their few words. Telling of the dead, how in life they had been a carpenter, dressmaker, chemist, jockey, railway employee. Beloved father, mother, son, wife. Innocents all.

Then came William McLoughlin, two years of age, who only five hours earlier had been buried beneath rubble. Coroner's doctors had immediately conducted his autopsy so that the child could be included in the inquest with all the others. His mother, still in hospital, was unable to attend the inquest, and Francis McLoughlin took the witness box to speak for his nephew. There wasn't much to tell of a life that spanned only two years. He was a cherished son, full of life and laughter.

None of the seven children killed, all under the age of seven, could be identified by career or accomplishments. They had been given no chance to grow up, marry, have a family, become a carpenter or dressmaker. Young lives snuffed out prematurely, and cruelly.

After all the witnesses had passed through the box, "they were followed by the doctors who were equally brief."[21] Dr MacErlean did not want a prolonged inquest, for everyone's sake. However, at the end of the testimonies he allowed for a brief statement by Seán MacBride, who represented the next of kin of the Browne family. According to the *Irish Times*, his voice was firm and words measured, carrying the "deep sense of horror and resentment which he had felt by the tragedy":

> It is not our function at this inquest to say who is responsible, but I think it only right to say that whatever the circumstances which led to this tragedy immediate steps will be taken to ensure that it will never happen again, and that just retribution and compensation will be made to those so grievously injured, and to the relatives.[22]

To the bereaved gathered in the inquest chamber, compensation was hardly on their mind. In the months and years to come, this would change.

When MacBride had concluded his statement, J. J. Walsh, representing Dublin Corporation, expressed the sympathy of the city manager, the corporation and the citizens of Dublin with the bereaved. Then Superintendent Peter Heffernan, on behalf of the Garda Síochána, rose to associate himself with those remarks. There was only one official act remaining:

> The formal verdicts were returned, stating that the persons died as the results of injuries received when their houses collapsed due to aerial bombing. The formal verdicts were signed by the foreman of the jury, and the inquest was over.[23]

The inquest had lasted fifty minutes.

———

As people were filing out of the building, at the back of the morgue the wreathed coffins were being placed in Kirwan's hearses to be taken to St Agatha's and St Laurence O'Toole's churches. It was now after 5:30 and, in addition to the crowds outside the inquest, people were lining the streets between the City Morgue and the two churches. Others were already queuing up outside the churches to pay their last respects. Kirwan's hearse-drivers, especially those from small towns, were astonished to see such huge crowds along their route. "We took the coffins to the church," says Tom Kirwan, "and there were *thousands* of people." Their orders were to drive slowly, so that onlookers had a chance to get a good view of the passing hearses.

Approaching 6 p.m., the hearses arrived at St Agatha's Church. At the doors waiting to receive the remains were Rev. John McGuirk, Rev. J. Masterson, and Rev. D. Daly. With the crowds from the City Morgue and the streets now descending on the churches, the police and LSF had to impose order. Maurice Walsh, on duty at the church, remembers the large crowds as calm and well mannered. Eyes were fixed upon each coffin as it was carried up the stairs, as described by the *Irish Press:*

> The streets were lined as the procession made its way to St. Agatha's church. The church itself is darkened—its windows were smashed by the bomb blast and are boarded up. On the steps of the church people murmured the names of the dead as they were borne in. L.S.F. men stood at the salute in the street.[24]

Sympathisers were especially moved by the sight of the coffins bearing the bodies of the four Fitzpatricks, as the *Irish Independent* noted that the church was "not 100 yards from their wrecked home" at 28 North Strand.[25] The priests directed the bearers to the front of the church where the coffins were aligned beside one another. Once they were properly arranged, people were allowed in to pay their last respects. All through the evening people streamed past the coffins, many unable to contain their emotions. Among them were many fans of Noel Fitzpatrick who knew him personally or had seen him on the stage. The Olympia Theatre, at which he was to have been appearing, was represented by Lorcan Bourke and J. Graham. Cast members came as well to say goodbye. Beside the Fitzpatricks were the coffins of Charles Sweeney and Marion Holten, all scheduled to be buried on Wednesday. Also to be buried the next day were Mrs Boyle, whose coffin had been taken to the Church of the Visitation in Fairview, and John Murray at St Laurence O'Toole's church.

Those who bade farewell at St Agatha's that night have their own memories. Bernadette Pierce attended with her granny: "I remember people saying, 'Oh, God bless them all.'" Some said prayers and others muttered personal goodbyes as they passed each coffin. Elizabeth Smullen remembers: "Madge Fitzpatrick was a good friend of mine, I used to go dancing with her ... I missed her." As a young girl, Colleen Heeney recalls being nervous, and somewhat scared, being so close to the coffins. Yet she was touched to see how many people lovingly placed their hands on them as they paused beside each one, in an almost caressing manner:

> We all went up to St Agatha's to see all the coffins. People were all going and praying over all the coffins. And I was a little bit frightened, because there was bodies *in* the coffins. And I'd see people going along and they'd put their hand on them.

> There were such large and sorrowful crowds gathered outside of St Agatha's Church that a passser-by, not knowing any better, might well have assumed that they were there to pay last respects to a beloved fallen head of state.

Chapter 22 ∿

A MUFFLED PEAL OF
BELLS

*Accompanied by sorrowing thousands, eight of the North
Strand bomb victims were laid to rest this morning.*
(*Evening Mail*, 4 June 1941)

*The town of Edenderry stood still. The final sad journey
took place ... [as] the funeral cortege turned into
Drumcooley, and up the hill to the graveyard. The Brownes
had, sadly, come home."*
(JOE O'REILLY, "From Dublin to Drumcooley")

L ocal Boy Scouts awoke with excitement on Wednesday morning. They
had been chosen to participate in the funeral procession from St
Agatha's Church out to Glasnevin Cemetery. Too young to grasp the full
meaning of the tragedy, they just wanted to look smart in their uniforms and
hope they could march in step before the crowd of thousands. A big day in
their lives.

It was a big day for all Dublin. For all Ireland. Fifteen of the bombing
victims were to be laid to rest. The seven members of the Browne family were
to be buried in Drumcooley Cemetery outside Edenderry. In Dublin the four
Fitzpatricks, Marion Holten and John Murray were to be interred in
Glasnevin Cemetery, while Charles Sweeney and Mary Boyle would be buried
at Dean's Grange. The staff at Kirwan's were up at dawn, attending to every
detail of hearse presentation, collection of the coffins at the churches, the
route, and cemetery ceremonies. Today would be their "dress rehearsal" for
the huge public funeral on Thursday. Also up early were members of the LDF
and LSF guards of honour that would march behind the hearses.

A Requiem Mass was to be held at St Agatha's for six of the victims. Similar
Masses were planned at St Laurence O'Toole's for John Murray and at the
Church of the Visitation for Mary Boyle. All were scheduled for ten o'clock so
that the funeral procession could be co-ordinated. By nine o'clock, relatives,

friends and perfect strangers began arriving, many milling outside, talking quietly before entering. The front pews were reserved for the victims' relatives and dignitaries. Outside, police cordons had been set up to keep the crowd back so they would not interfere with the hearses and marchers. Reporters and photographers also arrived early to position themselves by the front doors of the church to get the closest coverage, to better see the coffins being carried out, to study expressions on the faces of mourners as they departed. This was just good reportage.

By 9:45 the church was nearly full. With its boarded-up windows and thick layers of dust everywhere, the church had a dark and dismal look about it. Mary Dunne, one of those fortunate enough to have gained a seat, recounts: "I remember the funeral, the church with all its lovely stained glass blown out. And the Mass. I can still see the priests and the mourners all in black clothes … and the white bonnets of the nuns." Shortly before ten o'clock, black motor cars pulled up carrying members of the Government and the military. Heading them were Seán T. O'Kelly, the Tánaiste, and Seán Moylan TD, parliamentary secretary to the Minister for Defence. Mass was said by Canon McGuirk, Rev. C. Daly and, of course, Father Masterson, whose premonition on Whit Friday night had led him to this sorrowful moment. Scores of people showed up only to find they could not fit in, so they stood outside and tried to participate in their own way. Says Maurice Walsh, who was on crowd duty near the front steps, "The funeral mass, *oh, packed!* People *standing outside!*" He found there was no need to "control" the orderly crowd of solemn sympathisers.

The first pews were taken up by the chief mourners, particularly for the Fitzpatrick family. Their chief mourners were their surviving sons Richard, Gerald and Patrick, daughters Mona Fitzgerald and Mrs Dillon, and brothers Bernard and Patrick Fitzpatrick. People in the church glanced over when they recognised several theatrical figures from the Olympia Theatre taking their seats, especially Noel Purcell, the well-known variety star, and May Stanley and Bella Byrne, two of the Barry Olympia Girls.

During the Mass, Kirwan's hearses pulled up outside the church's front door to await the coffins, causing a stir in the crowd. Meanwhile, all the various members of the funeral procession were readying themselves to march behind the hearses once the procession began to pull away towards Glasnevin. Only fifty or so paces away, rescue and retrieval work continued at the North Strand bomb site.

Upon the completion of the Requiem Mass, the church doors were pushed open and the coffin-bearers strode forward to take their positions. This alerted the crowd to what was about to follow, as reporters and photographers prepared to cover the scenes. Slowly, one by one, the coffins were carried out and placed in the rear of the hearses, a spectacle captured by a reporter from the *Evening Mail*:

> Outside of St. Agatha's, crowds thronged the streets. A guard of honour of the L.S.F. men in uniform was drawn up opposite the two motor hearses which were to bring Richard Fitzpatrick and his wife, Ellen, and his children Noel and Margaret to the cemetery.
>
> In the background and standing like some horrible spectre were the gaunt stripped ruins of the victims' former happy homes. Behind their smashed walls occasionally a screaming railway engine. Crowds spoke in whispered tones of horror which had descended upon so many of their friends. Old men and young men bent their heads in silent prayer as the four coffins were brought out and reverently put into the two hearses.[1]

As the coffins were borne from the church, a guard of honour of the LSF was drawn up to give a last salute. Then Mr and Mrs Fitzpatrick were placed in the first hearse, Noel and his sister in the second. In the following hearses were put the coffins of Charles Sweeney and Marion Holten.

The Requiem Masses for John Murray at St Laurence O'Toole's Church and for Mary Boyle at the Church of the Visitation were ending close to the same time. They had been attended by far fewer people, but no less sorrowful. The funeral mass for Mrs Boyle drew particular sympathy because she was only twenty-six and left behind a thirteen month-old child. The *Evening Mail* called it the tragic "funeral of a young wife."[2] Officiating at the Mass was Rev. C. Finnegan, who spoke of the loss of a young mother and a child left behind forever without her love and comfort.

On the same morning, at the same hour, another requiem service was going on over at the Carmelite church in Whitefriars' Street. This one was for Bridget Lynskey, her two-year-old son, Noel, and Samuel O'Brien, who had perished in the Old Bride Street tenement collapse. Bridget Lynskey's story was an especially pitiful one, not only because she lost her son, cradled in her arms when found, but because she left behind three other young children, Thomas, Esther and Kathleen. And, of course, everyone knew how she had just received the key to their new house, and new life, the day before the bombing. Emotions rose even more when it was learnt that she and her baby son had been placed "in the same coffin for interment at Mount Jerome Cemetery."[3] When the coffin was removed from the church, blessed by Rev. W. J. Brennan, bitter tears were shed by onlookers. All along the hearse's route to the cemetery, wrote reporters, "thousands of people lined the streets" in shared sorrow.[4]

The simultaneous funerals for the victims of the North Strand and Old

Bride Street further confirmed in people's minds that they were linked, caused by the same bomb explosion. One was simply a delayed catastrophe. On Wednesday morning at Christ Church Cathedral the Dean, Rev. E. H. Lewis-Crosby, implicitly connected the two disasters when he spoke from the pulpit with passion about the loss of all their lives and of the evil behind the act. The *Evening Mail* shared his sermon with readers:

> A muffled peal of bells was rung at Christ Church Cathedral to express sympathy with the victims of Saturday morning's bomb incident and with the sufferers of Sunday morning's calamity.
>
> The Dean, preaching on the work of the Holy Spirit, said that the spirit of God was the world's hope … the cause of the world's troubles was man who, if left to himself, became desperately wicked. We know not, he said, at what moment we ourselves suddenly may have to face danger or death.[5]

The dull sound of the great muffled bells cast a funereal gloom over the heart of the city, a death knell that some said gave them "shivers".

At 11:20 a.m. at St Agatha's Church the funeral cortege was about ready to wend its way towards Glasnevin Cemetery. Directly behind the last hearse were the Boy Scouts with their black-creped flags, looking very serious now, followed by columns of LSF, LDF, ARP, Red Cross and St John Ambulance Brigade members. Just across the road on the North Strand, "workers who were still digging in the debris paused to pay tribute when the funerals began."[6] Men removed their hats and bent their heads. Some dropped to their knees in prayer. The butcher, his wife and two children were leaving their village for the last time. As the hearses slowly pulled away they parted a sea of mournful faces.

————

Normal life in Edenderry was suspended. Townsfolk, still shocked and in disbelief, were to bury their own that day. The evening before, a cluster of people had trekked to the outskirts of the town to spot the lorry and be the first to welcome the Brownes home. It had been especially difficult for Edenderry residents to accept the awful fate that had befallen the local family who had moved to Dublin only a few years before. To them, the war had seemed so remote as to be almost an abstraction. Theirs was not a world of air-raid shelters, gas masks, air-raid exercises and siren alerts. Apart from shortages and rationing, it hardly touched their lives. They had, of course, read about Hitler, Churchill, the fall of France and the London blitz. But the daily rhythms and routines of small-town life consumed their thoughts and energies. That the German air force would intrude upon their peaceful life by "wiping out", as the newspapers worded it, one of their own families was hard to imagine, or to accept.

Tuesday evening had brought that reality when the lorry that had collected the seven bodies appeared at the edge of the town. Within the town, people lined the streets as the driver followed the old custom of halting at certain points along the route to St Mary's Church, where the remains were to be kept overnight:

> The town of Edenderry stood still. The cortege with the seven coffins on the back of the lorry wound its way along St. Brigid's Road, up Fr. Kearns Street, then up past the Town Hall and down J.K.L. Street where there was another pause outside the house of the Browne family, up past the National and convent schools which Harry had attended, and finally up St. Mary's Street to St. Mary's Church where the remains were received by the parish priest, Fr. Tierney.[7]

As the coffins were lifted off the lorry, Harry's was easy to spot, as it was draped in the Tricolour. The children's coffins too could be identified by their small sizes and white colour, seven-year-old Maureen's being the largest, two-year-old Angela's the smallest. After the coffins were arranged at the front of the church, townspeople, from the elderly hobbling with canes to young friends of Maureen's and Nan's, began shuffling slowly past. At each coffin they envisaged the person inside when they had last seen them so full of life. Now the newspapers referred to them as "the remains". As violent death was virtually unknown to local people, it had been especially difficult for them to read in the newspapers how they died from asphyxiation, burning, being crushed. People in Edenderry normally just "passed away" when their time had come. But the Brownes had not lived full lives: their time had been stolen from them.

On Wednesday morning the Requiem Mass, to be celebrated by Father Tierney, was to begin at ten o'clock. Though almost everyone was up early, the town was shut down. Doors of businesses remained closed, and all normal activities were suspended. From all parts of County Offaly mourners were heading by horse vehicle, bicycle or foot towards Edenderry to attend the mass and the funeral. Condolences were pouring in from all over Ireland and from Britain and the United States. The Brownes' tragedy had been profoundly felt far beyond their Edenderry home.

By shortly after nine o'clock every pew was filled. The overflow crowd had the choice of waiting outside the church or getting an early start on their trip

out to Drumcooley Cemetery, where they might at least get a position close to
the graveside. Relatives and friends of the Browne and Corrigan families took
up considerable space in the little church. Also in attendance were some
official representatives, including Lieutenant C. A. Clarke, Curragh,
representing the Defence Forces, District Leader P. Egan of the North Offaly
LDF Command and T. O'Hanlon of the National Union of Vehicle Builders.
Also present were men with whom Harry had worked as a coachbuilder and
GNR decorator. A few Dublin reporters had also been sent to cover the event.
They generally found Edenderry people close-mouthed when asked personal
questions about the Brownes.

One of the bearers for Harry's flag-draped coffin was Ned Usher, a close
friend. He felt honoured in his role. The family's tragedy had affected him so
profoundly, and lastingly, that half a century later when asked by a writer to
reflect upon the day of the burial he found himself utterly unable to do so.[8]

Following Mass, the funeral procession crept at a snail's pace towards the
ancient cemetery, some mourners walking ahead, others trailing behind.
Those on bicycle passed them by. The Brownes' "final, sad journey," as it was
written, followed a meandering course from town to cemetery, wending its
way up St Mary's Road, turning left at Killane, over Colgan's Bridge, up Fann
Hill, and turning left into Drumcooley,[9] then slowly up the last hill to the
graveyard. The earliest recorded grave there was that of a sixteen-year-old girl,
Mary Galgan, who was interred in 1731. Two of Edenderry's best-known
patriots, Father Moses Kearns and Colonel Anthony Perry, were hanged in
1798 and buried there. It was fitting that Harry Browne, also regarded as a
hero for his dash home to save his family, would be buried there as well.

As those in the crowd gathered around the grave waiting for the burial
service to begin, they looked at the serenely beautiful view sweeping around
them:

On a small and often windswept hill on the south-western outskirts of the
town of Edenderry, lies Drumcooley graveyard. It is overlooked by an
ancient motte crowned by a circle of trees which stands as if on guard over
graves of people buried nearby. From the graveyard, one gets a panoramic
view of the surrounding area. To the south-east stands the neighbouring
Ballykillen Hill, itself adorned by a similar covering of trees. Turning back
towards the town, the Downshire Bridge over the Grand Canal comes into
view.[10]

Few cemeteries in Ireland are as idyllic, as tranquil, as Drumcooley. So restful
that one might look forward to taking up permanent residence there some
day.

Members of the Browne and Corrigan families stood together as Father Tierney gave the final blessings. Group leader J. O. O'Connell, standing before the LDF guard of honour, gave the order to fire volleys over the grave. Startled, a few birds enjoying the spring morning in nearby trees flapped away into the sky. Then the funeral was over. Many people, however, were reluctant to leave, talking quietly to one another, offering condolences to relatives. Over and over it was said that the Brownes had finally "come home."

As the last of the funeral crowd were ambling down the hill, gravediggers were already at work covering the large coffins and the small ones together beneath a single large stone slab:

Of the many gravestones that bedeck this ancient spot, none could bear witness to a sadder tale than that of the Browne family ... their names and memories handed to the wind and rain of Drumcooley forever.[11]

——

The staff of Glasnevin Cemetery were standing at the gates when the cortege from St Agatha's Church came into view. Outside the railings stood a large crowd watching the hearses pull in and draw up outside the small chapel. Mourners from the Fitzpatricks' family emerged from their vehicles and appeared to welcome the fresh air. The church had been stuffy, as had their cars. Hearses bearing the coffins of John Murray and Marion Holten arrived just behind them. Once inside the cemetery grounds, "the people at Glasnevin were directing the families," explains Tom Kirwan, "and the coffins went into the chapel for about five minutes and there were prayers."

Then the coffins of Mr and Mrs Fitzpatrick, Margaret and Noel were borne to the open grave, where family and close friends gathered. Canon P. McGuirk officiated at the graveside. His eulogy, which was not reported, was brief. Relatives and mourners closest to the grave seemed composed. Then, wrote the *Evening Herald*, "a nearby church had just tolled the Angelus, when the first shovel of earth was thrown upon the coffins,"[12] causing some emotions to waver. The old tradition of having mourners stand right beside the grave as earth was shovelled atop the coffins, says Glasnevin gravedigger Jack Mitchell, was primitive and traumatic, emotionally wrenching to watch, and worse to have to *listen* to:

But that was the tradition. You can picture four men lowering the coffin, a big heap of earth there, and people standing around as they filled it in. And you'd *hear* the "thud, thud, thud," a dull sound, till it actually became covered. Ah, it was an emotional thing

One thud at a time, the Fitzpatricks slowly disappeared beneath the earth. Then the mourners turned and began to walk away.

As the Fitzpatricks were being buried, elsewhere in the cemetery John Murray was "being parted with by many broken-hearted relatives,"[13] while Marion Holten was "being laid in her last resting place by a few distant relatives."[14] Family and friends lingered around the front gates of Glasnevin for at least an hour before departing for home—or to the pub to continue their "sympathising".

Newspaper reporters left the cemetery immediately after the funerals to get their stories to press. There was still time for the evening papers to include the entire day's funeral news. As they were doing so, in mid-afternoon a late news item came in from the North Strand. Another skull had been found. It was taken to the City Morgue and handed over to Dr MacErlean. To whom it belonged may never be known. But the death toll was raised by one more.

On Wednesday evening a large crowd queued up outside St Laurence O'Toole's Church to pay their last respects to the bombing victims who were to be buried the next day.

Elsewhere, another crowd was gathering, this one to attend a fund-raising event being put on by Bohemia Amusements for the victims who had lost so much. It was to be a dazzling show of music and dancing, featuring the Shadows, a very popular group, along with Peter Melia's Céilí Band. "A record attendance is expected," it was announced.

Once again, Kirwan's staff would be up late into the night. Thursday was to be the public funeral for twelve of the bomb victims, attended by the Taoiseach, Éamon de Valera, other members of the Government, the Dáil and Seanad, senior military officers, religious hierarchy and throngs of mourning Dubliners. Wednesday's funerals had gone well for Kirwan's, but the arrangements for the far larger funeral were considerably more challenging. The only thing for which they could not meticulously plan was the weather. If the day was dry they were confident the funeral would go well. Rain was an undertaker's enemy.

Chapter 23 ✎

AS THE HEARSES PASSED BY

Never had the capital felt or expressed such sorrow.
(*Evening Mail*, 5 June 1941)

Pathetic scenes were witnessed as the cortege passed through the streets crowded with sympathisers ... as the twelve hearses passed along women wept bitterly.
(*Evening Herald*, 5 June 1941)

Dawn broke grey and gloomy, threatening rain. The staff at Kirwan's looked out their windows and shook their heads. Full rain gear would have to be brought. Glasnevin gravediggers cursed the morning sky. Sodden, mucky ground made it extremely difficult to push and pull coffin-laden trolleys from the visiting chapel to the graves. Pooling surface water could flow into open graves, eroding the edges and collecting at the bottom. For gravediggers, balancing on the slippery side of a grave while trying to lower a heavy coffin into the deep pit was treacherous, then having to cover the coffins with shovels of thick, saturated soil. It looked like it was going to be an ugly day.

Reporters and photographers were out early in the morning, posted at strategic points. For the most important public funeral in nearly a quarter of a century, newspaper editors wanted every angle covered in detail: the Requiem Mass, removal of coffins to waiting hearses, attending officials, lengthy cortege, crowd scenes, burials at Glasnevin. Newsmen jostled for best positions and competed to stake out prime vantage spots. To gain panoramic shots, some photographers got permission from landlords and tenants to use their windows or rooftops. Of course, they had been counting on good weather and visibility.

The Requiem Mass for the twelve victims was scheduled for ten o'clock at St Laurence O'Toole's Church, named after the patron saint of the city. "Overnight the remains had rested in the high-steepled church," wrote the *Evening*

Mail, "down the centre aisle in front of the High Altar the 12 coffins stood."[1]
At the Mass to "celebrate the eternal repose of the victims' souls," the chief
mourners occupied the front pews. Most of the deceased had at least eight to
ten chief mourners, some as many as twenty-five. Standing out sadly was
sixty-year-old Elizabeth Daly, the dressmaker, who had but one mourner,
Corporal Daly, her nephew, who had identified her as well.

By 9:30 the church was packed to the doors, except for the seats reserved
for the officials, who began arriving in large cars shortly before ten o'clock.
Prominent were Seán T. O'Kelly, the Tánaiste, P. J. Ruttledge, Minister for
Local Government, Oscar Traynor, Minister for Defence, Seán Lemass,
Minister for Supplies, Seán MacEntee, Minister for Industry and Commerce,
Gerry Boland, Minister for Justice, and Lieutenant-General Daniel McKenna,
chief of staff. All arrived looking sombre, saying not a word as they entered
the church and took their seats.

The sight of de Valera lifting his lanky frame from the official car caused
quite a stir among the huge crowd gathered outside. As he ascended the steps
his posture looked slightly stooped. Some said he did not appear as tall as
usual. The burden he was carrying was conspicuous to all who saw him at
close range. A reporter in the church for the *Evening Mail* who was in a
position to discreetly study de Valera's visage wrote:

> An Taoiseach looked very pale as he bent his head in prayer for his people
> whom he had endeavoured to spare from the terrible sufferings that had
> crashed from the sky.[2]

As he sat in the church, all eyes upon him, he knew people were
wondering—*worrying*—about his neutrality policy, their security, the future.
And he must surely have felt their sympathy for him. Perhaps their discontent
as well. As he sat in the church surrounded by the victims' relatives, mourners
and national leaders, he had never looked quite so alone.

The majority of people in attendance who had arrived early found time for
reflection. Their most indelible memory more than half a century later is that
of the twelve coffins so perfectly aligned across the nave of the church. Seeing
the twelve coffins laid side by side conveyed the feeling of an indiscriminate
"mass killing" of innocents. In the coffins were the bodies of Alice Fitzpatrick,
her sons James and Desmond, Patrick Callely, John and Mary Foran, Thomas
Carroll, Josephine Fagan, Elizabeth Daly, William McLoughlin, and two
unidentified victims. It was particularly looking upon the small coffins that
moved many in the crowd to tears. "I remember mainly the white coffins, for
children," says Frederick McBain. In the very smallest slept the "waxen babies"
that Jack Conroy had seen carried from the ruins. It was most profoundly

moving for mothers, noticed a reporter from the *Evening Mail*:

> The sight of tiny coffins bearing simple wreaths wrought their hearts as
> keenly as if a loved one of their own family lay within.[3]

Since leaving the bomb scene late on Saturday morning, nurse Ann
Leonard had spent most of her time at home, recuperating physically and
emotionally. She spoke little to her mother about what she had witnessed. But
she wanted to attend the Requiem Mass for the twelve victims, to pay her last
respects. Unexpectedly, she found that it brought strong emotional release:

> You walked into that church and you saw these coffins, the next size and
> the next size. And when I saw these *little* coffins, I *stood back*. I thought it
> was a horrible thing to have to look at. *Horrible* ... young girls and boys.
> I'll never forget it, those coffins—the children would have been in their
> beds! People were heartbroken. Including *myself!* For all the people that
> were gone.
>
> Oh, and I'd think about their families that was left behind. *That* was
> sad. Like, "My God, *imagine*, they'll never be together again ... never seen
> again together." It struck me terrible.
>
> And I remember well that tears came down and I said, "May God
> *forgive* you, Hitler! Because *we* can't forgive you.

During Mass the clouds thickened and lowered as a steady drizzle made the
streets slick. Members of the many organisations marching in the procession
knew they were in for a good soaking. Included were the LDF, LSF, ARP, Red
Cross, St John Ambulance Brigade, Catholic Boy Scouts, Gardaí, and Dublin
Fire Brigade with a fully manned fire engine. Even the Dublin Harbour Police
and Pilots formed their own guard of honour. The formal order of the cortege
had been arranged in advance. Everyone knew their proper place. It was even
printed in the morning newspapers, so that the public could follow each
group as it passed by in the extremely long procession:

(1) Advance Party of Gardaí with Band
(2) Hearses
(3) Relatives of victims
(4) Government Party
(5) Corporation Party
(6) L.D.F. Contingent
(7) L.S.F. Contingent
(8) A.R.P. Wardens

(9)   Fire Service Party
(10) Rescue Services Party
(11) St. John Ambulance Brigade
(12) Red Cross Society
(13) Other Organisations
(14) Public

It was the inclusion of the last two that required some tactful last-minute handling by the organisers. Some little-known organisations showed up to participate, several in disarray. The authorities whipped them into presentable form and placed them in the ranks. Public participation was welcomed at the end of the procession, which would snake its way through the streets. It had, after all, been proclaimed a public funeral. This meant that any and all mourners could simply fall in and follow.

As the Mass was drawing to a close, at about 11:20, a chain of hearses, mourning carriages and official cars was aligned and waiting. The drizzle had now turned to rain, and a sea of umbrellas popped up. Apart from Kirwan's hearses and mourning vehicles there were those of other undertakers, of which a few were horse-drawn. Attendants stood beside the doors with large umbrellas to cover the officials and the coffin-bearers. Photographers were ready to take pictures as they emerged. A reporter for the *Evening Mail* covered the scene:

> After the Mass the coffins were brought out to the waiting hearses. Sobbing relatives helped by sympathetic friends, lovingly placed wreaths and were then assisted into the mourning carriages.[4]

As each hearse and mourning carriage was filled, it pulled forward so that the next could draw up beside the steps. Ahead of the hearses, at the front of the cortege, the advance party of Gardaí with the Garda Band stood in wait for their order to march.

About half way through the process of getting all the coffins and mourners into their vehicles, Mother Nature, as if on cue, unleashed a squall of rain, accompanied by sharp gusts of wind. As coffin-bearers sought to balance themselves, hats blew off and umbrellas were sucked into inverted pyramids. Photographers caught out in the open struggled to protect their cameras. With the wind whipping in every direction, many people in the massive crowd conceded defeat and folded up their umbrellas, men raising their collars for a bit of protection. De Valera and other officials held their hats as they rushed towards open car doors. Stalwart guards of honour stood their ground.

As the cortege finally prepared to depart from St Laurence O'Toole's Church, "the thoughts of the city turned towards the route to Glasnevin Cemetery."[5] At a crawl, the long line of dark vehicles began to move forward, one closely behind the other, giving the appearance of a ponderous train pulling slowly out of the station. Once en route, the procession stretched over a mile and a half in length.

As the procession "wended its sorrowful way" towards Glasnevin, wrote one reporter, the Garda Band at the head, their instruments muffled in black crepe, began playing Panne's "Regrets".[6] People lining the streets could hear their approach streets away. The route could not have been a more dramatic one. It lay across Seville Place and crossed the junction of Amiens Street and then directly past the North Strand, "within 20 yards of the victims' homes," noted the Evening Mail.[7] Then along the North Circular Road close to where the first two bombs had fallen.

Along the way, vehicles passed "hundreds of houses with smashed-in windows."[8] This route, directly past all the points of major destruction, gave mourners and Government officials a grim rendering of the whole tragedy. Through the fogged, rain-streaked windows of their cars, de Valera and his colleagues looked hard at what they were seeing. Many had not been back to the bomb scene since their brief Saturday-morning visit. As the Evening Herald described it, the cortege coiled its way along "through rain-swept streets, some of which bore scars inflicted by the bomb that had hurled them into the unknown."[9]

Huge throngs lined the entire route to Glasnevin Cemetery, and as the long procession passed by, "many thousands followed in its wake."[10] The multitudes were beyond counting, as newspapers didn't even hazard a guess. Photographs taken by rooftop photographers, who somehow managed to protect their lenses from the lashing rain, showed people lining every street, typically five to ten deep or more, peering out of windows and atop buildings everywhere. Streets are seen flooding with water, along the kerbs flowing like small streams. At points where drains were choked, ponds were forming, flowing over onto footpaths, soaking bystanders' shoes. Through all this the hearse tyres sloshed as miserable marchers dutifully held their ranks. The heavy, charcoal-grey clouds hung low over the city's shiny slate roofs.

And yet the dark, sodden, dismal aura was perfectly befitting for the tragic occasion. Sunshine would have seemed sacrilegious.

Just as the cortege reached the rear entrance of the Mater Hospital, "wherein were recovering from their wounds many relatives of the dead," the Garda Band struck the first mournful notes of the Dead March from Handel's Saul.[11] Everyone in the hospital picked it up immediately. Those who could do so rushed to the windows to look out. Even patients were helped from their beds to see. Some staff members grabbed umbrellas and trotted out to the gates to watch the funeral procession pass by, many returning to the building with tear-streaked faces.

Hearing the funereal notes of the Garda Band, seeing the hearses pass by nearly within reach, imagining the bodies within the coffins, brought people's raw emotions to the surface. For five days Dubliners had endured one wrenching experience after another: the shock and terror of the bomb explosion, news of death and destruction, nightfall fear of more bombs, tenement collapses, coroner's graphic report, burial of the Brownes and Fitzpatricks. And now, directly before them, the hearses carrying children, babies and "unidentified remains". Dubliners may never have wept so openly. Mary Dunne remembers standing among the crowd, waiting for the lengthy procession to pass. Then, on hearing the first strains of Handel's Dead March, seeing people simply break down with the grief of it all. "I can *still see* the cortege and all the hearses, and everyone was crying. Oh, I mean *everyone* was crying." She had never seen men crying before. She watched as they became choked up, then tearful. One scene, captured by the *Evening Mail,* was especially poignant, that of a single hearse carrying two coffins:

> Saddest feature of an immeasurably sad event was the motor hearse containing two coffins, each of which was simply inscribed "Unidentified. Died May 31, 1941."
>
> Behind this hearse travelled two empty motor cars. No loving relatives were there to weep over them; their mourners were the nation.[12]

It was the pathetic aloneness at death that so profoundly moved people. The sight of Dubliners grieving so openly prompted one newspaper to write, "Never had the capital felt or expressed such sorrow."[13]

Nearing Glasnevin, as the head of the procession emerged into the Finglas Road, the Garda Band split into two groups outside the cemetery gates, and between their ranks passed each hearse, "bearing to their final resting place the victims of an awful event that has stirred the nation to pity and resentment," wrote the *Evening Mail.*[14] After a brief visit in the small mortuary chapel, the LDF guard of honour formed by the door. The coffins were then placed on trolleys to be brought to the St Patrick's Plot for interment, with the exception of that of Patrick Callely, who was laid to rest in the family grave.

With the drenching rain, gravediggers had done their best to cover the graves with tarpaulins, to prevent erosion and keep water out, but with limited success. Footpaths to the grave sites were mucky, with pools of water scattered about. Gravediggers strenuously pushed and pulled the trolleys as wheels became mired in the mud. They knew that it was unpleasant for mourners to see the coffins rocked and jerked about in such a way. It was awkward, but unavoidable.

Families of the victims felt it appropriate that all would be buried together in the St Patrick's Plot. Only twenty-four hours earlier, William McLoughlin was still buried beneath bomb rubble. Now he was being buried again. It is not recorded whether his mother was able to attend the funeral. At the graveside, the remains of the two unidentified victims, whose hearse had been so conspicuously followed by empty mourning carriages, once again captured the sorrowful attention of all present. As it was sympathetically portrayed:

> The two unidentified remains were placed together in the one grave. They may have been relatives, friends or strangers in life, but death had united them.[15]

As the gravediggers shovelled sodden soil onto the lids of the coffins it made more of a splattering than a thudding sound. Then the funeral was over.

——

About the time that the funeral crowds were dispersing, search co-ordinators at the North Strand made a decision. As a last resort, they would try to find the body of Patrick McLoughlin by draining a portion of the Royal Canal by Newcomen Bridge. They knew it was a long shot, but they had dug deeply for five days in the area where his son had been recovered, without turning up a trace. Knowing how bodies had been hurled great distances by the blast, even onto rooftops, they thought it was possible that he had been thrown into the canal. It was the only part of the landscape not yet probed. Furthermore, they might find other missing persons.

Ironically, as Dublin was burying its civilian dead—bombed in their homes on a perfectly clear night—the German government was angrily protesting at alleged deliberate bombings of its citizens:

> The Germans accused the Royal Air Force of deliberately bombing the civilian population on their raid of Berlin on Monday night. Despite the clearness of the night, a hospital and several dwelling-houses were hit, said the German News Agency. The British no longer trouble to conceal the fact that their attacks are directed against the civilian population.[16]

The Germans were particularly incensed that the bombing had occurred on a *clear* night—when British pilots could have "no excuse" for "mistaking" their targets.

Chapter 24 ∿

| FRIDAY NEXT

The Irish Chargé d'Affaires has been instructed to lodge a vigorous protest in Berlin.
(ÉAMON DE VALERA, 2 June 1941)

It is naturally absurd to suggest that a German plane "intentionally" bombed Dublin.
(GERMAN REPLY, *Irish Press*, 6 June 1941)

Friday 6 June 1941

By Friday morning, Dubliners felt they had survived what some were calling "a week of hell". It was difficult to believe that Whit Friday, when everyone had been in such high spirits, was only seven days ago. So much had happened in one week, leaving Dubliners feeling not only emotionally drained but unsure of Ireland's neutrality policy and of their own safety in coming days. The complacency for which they had been so often scolded had vanished, replaced with a more realistic, disquieting outlook.

After two days of sorrowful funerals, on Friday morning Dubliners tried to regain some normality by going about their daily routine. Lord Holmpatrick presided over the monthly morning breakfast of the Royal Zoological Society of Ireland, reporting that the cost of bomb damage to the zoo amounted to £400 but telling his audience that things could have been far worse. A decision could well have been made to shoot some of the animals, as had been done in Belfast. When he spoke of Sara's astonishing, and now famous, exploits, breakfast guests chuckled at the images. One of the few bombing stories with a happy ending.

Typical of Fridays, by mid-morning the streets of Dublin were jammed with people. No better time for the Irish Red Cross to launch their fund drive to replenish drained coffers. An army of Red Cross volunteers were on every street corner, collecting donations. Everyone knew of their superb performance in treating the injured, saving lives, taking in droves of homeless people, providing food, shelter and clothing. Now it was the Red Cross who needed help. The city responded with unprecedented generosity, as acknowledged by the *Irish Press*:

> Thousands of collectors moved through the streets of Dublin as the mass drive for funds was begun by the Irish Red Cross Society. Coal porters, carters, messenger boys, shopkeepers and housewives all subscribed with the same cheeriness. It is a rare sight to see the public approaching flag sellers with the money ready in their hands, yet that was the case in Dublin. By evening it was easier to count the citizens who were *not* wearing flags than those who were.[1]

The spirit of giving swept the city. Citizens of widely different occupation and social and economic rank stood shoulder to shoulder, coins or notes in hand, from ha'pennies to tenners. The paper flag worn by the tenement-dweller was just as meaningful as that on the lapel of the banker's pin-stripe suit.

Considerably larger donations were being sent in as well, by shop-owners, factory bosses, financial institutions and wealthy individuals. A few notable ones were made public. The President of Ireland, Dr Douglas Hyde, sent in £200, with a note from his secretary stating that "the President has been deeply moved by the tragic loss of life and widespread suffering."[2] He was promptly outdone by Archbishop McQuaid with a cheque for £500. A good number of Dubliners were quick to think, and to comment, that his generosity was really a gift from that of thousands of ordinary people placing coins on the plate at Sunday Mass.

Not all business bosses were kind and generous. As it turned out, some were quite heartless in their treatment of employees who were also volunteer members of the various rescue services. They had hastened to the North Strand following the bomb explosion at 2:05 a.m. on Saturday and had worked relentlessly throughout the night. Many continued their rescue work during Saturday morning and afternoon. Completely fatigued, or still needed at the site, many were unable to show up for work on Saturday. Some managed to show up late in a bedraggled state, assuming their boss would allow them to return home to recuperate. Instead, quite a few turned out to be callously insensitive to employees who gave their time and even risked their lives to rescue bomb victims, not only chastising them for missing work but docking their weekly pay—in effect, penalising them for their patriotism.

When word got out around the city about such "slave masters", they were exposed and criticised in print, as outraged citizens sent letters to the editors on behalf of the mistreated employees. The following, published in the *Evening Mail*, was typical:

> Sir—Last Saturday morning we in Dublin were awakened to the

horrors of war, and how the A.R.P. and other services reacted to such sorrowful but practical war conditions. They deserve the praise of all. They worked hard through the night and some all the next day, hoping against hope that they would be the means of saving a valuable life.

But here comes the awful sting.

We call ourselves a Christian country, but where is the charity, I ask you, for men who after working all night, on reporting to their work in one of the firms in the city were refused permission to go home and rest. God only knows how much these men deserved that little consideration from their employers.

And who will pay for men's time if the Christian firms deduct working time lost when the pay envelope comes along? After all, we are just humans, and if through helping your neighbour we find our table empty what do you expect many of our A.R.P. and other workers will do? Will they continue in these services? If they don't, the supposed Christian charity firms will have a lot to answer for.

—"A.R.P. Admirer"[3]

The consensus in Dublin was that rescuers had indeed worked under "war conditions" and, if anything, should receive some sort of recognition or reward for their selfless service. One person wrote to the *Irish Independent* suggesting that they might at least be offered a helping hand if they were unemployed, which many were:

Unemployed members of the L.S.F., A.R.P. and other services who were on duty for long periods in the bombed areas of Dublin … only asked time off for the purposes of signing at the Labour Exchange. I am sure that the contractors and others responsible for clearing and reconstruction in those areas will not omit to give them first preference when labour is being engaged.

—Mr. E. Saul, South Frederick Lane[4]

Dubliners could only wonder why such a reasonable and meritorious idea had not been expounded by their Government.

One week after the bombing, some 542 families had been added to the waiting list for housing.[5] It had not been calculated how many individuals this included, but it was thousands. Refugee shelters were bulging at their seams. In the first few days in a shelter, refugees were just glad to be alive; but after a week of sleeping on the floor in primitive conditions, congested, uncomfortable, noisy, their impatience and frustration were showing. People wanted *out*.

A number of them decided to try to sneak back into their damaged homes, in violation of the direction of the housing authorities, who had pasted up notices declaring the buildings dangerous and officially condemned. Mothers desperate to get back inside were not deterred by damaged roofs, smashed windows and cracked, even crumbling, walls and ceilings. They failed to understand the serious structural destabilisation of the buildings. They didn't believe they were putting their families at risk by clandestinely reoccupying their own house as illicit squatters.

Clever mothers knew that their best chance of getting through the cordons was under the cover of darkness. Women didn't fear getting caught, knowing they'd probably get a sympathetic hearing. So, like a little mob of bandits, some silently led their families back home beneath the cloak of darkness. Entry was usually gained by prying open chipboard from rear doors or windows, then putting it back in place. Mary Dunne's mother surreptitiously led her children back into their old home in North William Street. "Mam said, 'I don't care how bad it is, *I'm going home!*' So we did. The house was all boarded up with chipboard. There was no gas or light, so we cooked on the fire and had candlelight." Children were instructed to remain perfectly quiet to avoid detection from the corporation watchman making his rounds.

Agnes Daly's home in North Clarence Street was well beyond repair and highly dangerous. The authorities had warned her mother that it could collapse at any moment, words she didn't bother to heed:

> Our house was *condemned*. The man said it was going to fall in like a pack of cards—but my mother didn't *care!* She said, "I don't care what the house is *like*, if I can go *home*." Which we *did*. So Kevin and Ginny and myself and my mother slept there for about four or five nights.

The silent squatters knew the watchman's rounds, dousing candles and not making a peep as he passed by. The cat-and-mouse game lasted several days, until smoke from her mother's black range was detected. "My mother was cooking on the fire, and the man outside, he *runs* in to the hall." She was given a half-hearted scolding and promptly put out, as well as being reported to the Housing Department. But as a result of her violation, the family was placed high on the list for new housing in Cabra. Her mother's scheming had paid off.

Real progress had been made out in Cabra in only one week, as contractors cracked their whip over work crews to make houses habitable as soon as possible. In the light of the rising number of homeless families, the original goal of 100 houses had now been increased to 150. As the housing authorities phrased it, these were to be "uncompleted houses" brought up to "occupation stage" for families desperate to get out of shelters. At first not much scrutiny was given to these terms used; but new occupants of the "uncompleted houses" would find they had great meaning.

By the end of the week, the Housing Department had produced 1,342 blankets and 437 mattresses for new Cabra residents. But virtually no furniture. It was announced that "the Corporation has the authority to pay, after investigating, up to £50 for the loss of furniture." The phrases "after investigation" and "up to" were again subject to broad interpretation and would become points of sharp contention later on. At the time, however, citizens who were homeless and possession-less had no choice but to trust the Government—and hope for the best.

At the city's newspaper offices, reporters and editors were returning to the usual daily grind. Standard stories, regular deadlines, all now frightfully dull compared with the high drama of the past week. For the most part, editors felt satisfied with the quality of their reportage. They had covered the major stories accurately and fairly. The evening papers may at times have tended towards some dramatically heightened coverage, but their facts were nonetheless correct. The *Irish Times* provided highly professional and expansive coverage of the biggest story in a generation, giving valuable experience to younger reporters like Tony Gray who had earned his spurs in real action. Even under the strict censorship, R. M. Smyllie had managed to publish harsh condemnation of the Germans for their dastardly act of bombing citizens of a neutral country. But he had not been able to answer the consuming question of *why?*

There was cause for speculation about Germany's motives. On Thursday afternoon, following the public funeral, the Dáil convened. It began with members standing in silence for a few moments "in token of respect and mourning" for the bomb victims. Then de Valera stated: "It has been for all our citizens an occasion of profound sorrow ... the great number of our citizens who have been so cruelly bereaved by the recent bombings."[6] He concluded by assuring members that a protest had been made to the German government. William Warnock, the Irish chargé d'affaires in Berlin, had personally delivered the protest to the German Foreign Office along with full details of the military investigation and evidence. The *Irish Press* published Germany's reply, which stated, in part:

It is naturally absurd to suggest that a German plane intentionally bombed Dublin. If the bombs were dropped from our planes, it is obvious that the German airman must have thought he was over another city.[7]

The statement further questioned whether it was even "possible for a German plane to have dropped the bombs; that is to say, whether there were German aircraft in the area at the time."[8] Nonetheless, the German spokesman promised that "a strict inquiry into the incident is now taking place."[9]

To all those Dubliners who had for hours watched the Luftwaffe bombers at close range, the German statement was preposterous. Germany's cavalier attitude towards the tragedy—essentially a flat denial—was disquieting.

Some anti-German sentiments began to be expressed—not widely, but in certain forums. German businessmen, who had always enjoyed excellent relations with Irish colleagues, were now not always made to feel so welcome. And, as Una Shaw recalls, even the familiar Swastika Laundry became an undeserving target. "I remember people started firing stones at the van because of the swastika on it. People were very angry, because they thought they were Germans—but they weren't, actually."

For six consecutive days the newspapers had been filled with coverage of the bombings, tenement collapses, the inquest and funerals. Finally, on Friday there was other national and foreign news of interest to readers. At home, in the Irish countryside, another type of tragedy was occurring. Worsening, in fact. The *Irish Independent* declared that the foot-and-mouth disease that had been ravaging one part of the country after another was now "reaching epidemic proportions."[10] This catastrophe affected country people far more personally than had the capital's bombings.

On the international scene, one article in particular probably struck Dubliners far more meaningfully than it would have only one week before. It was a revelation that the "u.s. Congress approved a bill providing for the production of 40,000 new warplanes."[11] The article further confirmed that Germany's current monthly production was about 4,000 planes, with a potential output of 8,000. Previously, Dubliners may have found these figures abstract. But now they knew what just *one* plane dropping a *single* bomb could do to human life and property. With their morning tea they might have tried to comprehend the production of more than 100,000 warplanes per year, each one capable of carrying a bellyload of death and destruction.

The world beyond Ireland's shores appeared to be descending into absolute madness. And Irish people were no longer smugly confident that they were safe from this lunacy.

———

On Friday morning the staff at Kirwan's undertakers awoke after their first decent night's sleep in nearly a week. Tom Kirwan remembers his father telling him, "We worked for four or five days and nights straight." The pressure over acquiring the hearses, handling so many damaged bodies, arranging details for two consecutive public funerals, then coping with the rainy conditions had taken a toll on everyone, especially his father. "My father was a practical man, and he couldn't afford to get involved emotionally when he was looking after things—but I'd say afterwards he probably collapsed to a very low state." The city authorities and the victims' families praised the excellent job done by the small undertaking firm. States Tom modestly, "We obviously did a good job."

Six days after the bombing, rescuers were recuperating physically and emotionally as they returned to their normal life. Some had wandered back to the scene, others deliberately stayed away. There were those who said they *never* again wanted to see the North Strand and Newcomen Bridge. They knew the image of 31 May would remain forever frozen in their memory. Ann Leonard and Noel Brady of the St John Ambulance Brigade purposely stayed away from the site for years. Jack Conroy, stationed just around the corner at Buckingham Street fire station, saw the North Strand nearly every day. In fact it helped him to cope with his traumatic experiences of having come across the headless man and seeing "waxen babies" carried from the ruins. Gardaí Finucane and Walsh returned from time to time, mostly to see how reconstruction was progressing. They always left feeling discouraged on seeing how sad and neglected the area appeared.

Dick Eyres and Alfie Byrne faithfully continued to visit survivors and to champion the cause of renewal. Eyres, whose home in Shamrock Terrace had been damaged, would end up out in Cabra. But he would always be known as "Warden Eyres". Alfie Byrne's folkloric stature was enhanced by his dedication to Northstranders during their worst hours.

In the days following his sixty consecutive hours of gruelling rescue work, Alec King found his emotions strangely in conflict. Though he was physically and emotionally drained, he confessed, "When it was all over then, I felt sort of sorry that I had to stop ... I was so *hyped* at the time." It had been, he reasoned, the combination of adrenalin charge, the exhilaration of finding and saving victims, and the camaraderie. An awful experience—yet intensely exciting. Psychological let-down was only natural.

Up to Thursday he had not seen the men in his first rescue squad, the ones with whom he had flailed through the stubborn LDF cordon at the periphery of the bomb scene. All were friends. On Friday it was decided that they would get together again, just to chat, see how one another's bruised and torn bodies were healing. On this occasion they preferred not to meet in a pub. Instead, they'd gather at their supplies depot and talk over tea.

One by one, the banged-up bunch of men trickled in and sat down. Hands still raw, fingernails missing, cuts, scrapes and bruises all over. They were more reserved than usual, spoke more softly. No male bravado or bragging about the dozen or more victims dug out, dead and alive. Small talk as they looked over one another's wounds. "How'ya doing with that hand, Paddy?" For men who knew each other so well, had shared so much, talk was strangely tentative at first. A curious melancholy hung over the group.

Gradually, feelings began to seep out. All confessed that they had barely talked of their experiences to wife and family. They had found themselves unusually reticent, introspective, even reclusive over the past few days. With some reluctance, each candidly revealed that, like King, they had unexpectedly felt a "disappointment" or "let-down" when it was all over. Among themselves, they could make such an admission. It was not an age in which men shared deep feelings and emotions. Their few words and facial expressions told it all. There were silent pauses as they reflectively sipped their tea, or gazed down.

Then, Alec King remembers, "as we had the tea … some of us cried."

Chapter 25 ᴄᴠ

JUNE: REFLECTIONS AND REACTIONS

No sirens were sounded during the raid.
                                        (*Sunday Independent*, 1 June 1941)

All we got was searchlights—some warning *ought to have been given!*
                                        (CITIZEN, *Evening Mail*, 9 June 1941)

It must never be kept from our people that this war may yet engulf our nation.
                                        (*Irish Press*, 19 June 1941)

In the aftermath of the bombing, Dubliners reflected on all that had happened, tried to make some sense of such a seemingly senseless act: an air raid upon civilians in their neutral country.

Throughout June people's voices would be heard, in the street, in pubs and in the press. Their complacency had been replaced with both fear and distrust. They didn't know whether the Luftwaffe would strike again, whether de Valera and his neutrality policy could protect them. This left people unsettled, nervous about life.

Dubliners were distressed not only by Germany's actions but by their own Government's *inactions*. Questions were raised and criticism fired at politicians for the dismal failure of the so-called "defence system" based on air-raid sirens, shelters and a muddled black-out policy. In newspapers such terms as "negligence", "incompetence" and "stupidity" appeared. Feelings of frustration and anger surfaced. Abominable mistakes had been made and people now demanded explanations—and changes—before more bombing attacks occurred.

Public ire was particularly aroused over the ARP service's blatant failure to sound a single air-raid siren in the city during the entire period of the four bomb explosions. The day after the air raid the *Sunday Independent* printed the military's explanation:

> No sirens were sounded during the raid. It is considered that this is in accordance with practice because a neutral country does not give a general alert when aircraft from which it expects no attack appear overhead.[1]

The Department of Defence later went a step further in providing a rationale:

> Air-raid sirens were not sounded, as their use was not justified by the fact of foreign air-craft flying overhead or isolated bombings when the country was not at war.[2]

Dubliners were flabbergasted. Aircraft overhead from which the military *expects* no attack? Dublin was *under* attack. *Isolated* bombings? Four bombs had dropped on the city in the space of half an hour. Bombers remained menacingly overhead even after the raid. And yet not one siren was activated in Dublin.

The silence of the sirens had sent exactly the wrong message to citizens: telling them they were safe. This is what Winnie Brennan and her neighbours along Mountjoy Place believed when, "as time passed, there were no sounds of sirens going off." Mary Dunne confirms that residents along North William Street were also given a false sense of security, as "no-one heard a siren go off," even after the first three bombs had exploded and the mystery plane was swooping ever lower. Without sirens screaming, people did not feel they were in imminent danger.

Afterwards, citizens openly expressed their frustration in newspapers, as did one writer to the *Evening Mail*:

> Sir—It was stated in the Press that we, being neutral, should not sound alarms, or "alerts" as they are called. *Some warning ought* to have been given! All we got last Friday night was that of searchlights! Are sirens only to be used in *case of war!*
> —"Citizen"[3]

If the Government couldn't sound sirens when German planes were actually bombing the city, it was suggested that at least the citizens be allowed to ring all the church bells as a warning that real danger was upon them.

The bombing also proved, once and for all, that most Dubliners had no faith in the "hat-box" air-raid shelters. Instead they had fled *en masse* to basements, beneath stairs, under tables. Those few who did seek protection too often found them locked. One disgruntled citizen wrote to the newspaper:

"In the city I found the gates, one after another, iron-barred and padlocked."
The keyholders were nowhere in sight. Elsewhere, as at Gloucester Diamond,
frightened women and children had been rounded up like cattle by local ARP
wardens and "shoved" into dungeon-like shelters, many against their will.
Packed inside, shoulder to shoulder, they felt trapped, claustrophobic, even ill.
More frightened than they had been of the bombs outside, causing many to
become panicky. It was an experience they never wanted again.

The controversy over city lighting and black-outs was now elevated to a
new level of impassioned debate. Everyone in Dublin, it seemed, was fuming
over the issue. As before, citizens were fairly divided between those who called
for a total black-out and opponents who favoured a fully illuminated city,
which could be easily identified as neutral by pilots overhead. As John Ryan
wrote in his memoir, *Remembering How We Stood*, "Dublin had no blackout,
only restrictions on display lighting, so she must have been easily identifiable
as a neutral city."[4] Yet bombs had fallen on the capital.

To clarify the issue for the public, the *Evening Mail* printed the official
policy regarding lighting:

> On enquiry at the Department of Defence, it is learned that there is no
> restriction on private lighting ... [only] the use of sky signs and
> illuminated advertisements, etc.[5]

No mandatory black-out for private citizens. They could make their own
decision and act accordingly—which is why the city ended up with an absurd
chequerboard pattern of lighting along streets. Some neighbours lit up, others
blacked out.

Before the bombing, the lighting debate had been civil in tone. Now
neighbours openly squabbled. Accusations became personal, sometimes
insulting, while the Government was scathingly criticised for not settling the
matter. Caustic letters to the newspapers stoked the fires of controversy, as
illustrated by the following, written by an indignant ARP warden:

> Sir—The standard of intelligence possessed by certain people ... makes it
> necessary to point out that lights should *not* be in use during the presence
> of aircraft. On Friday-Saturday night last, I became infuriated by the
> criminal idiocy of these people. I trust this letter will come to their notice,
> and that in the future they will refrain from an act, the gross stupidity of
> which should be evident to any rational mind.
> —"A.R.P"[6]

Such letters ignited a firestorm of rebuttals. Then counter-rebuttals. Bickering back and forth in the press had its entertainment value in newspapers, as editors well knew. Opponents of "A.R.P." fired in their letters to set him straight:

> Sir—Without wishing to insult "A.R.P.", may I say that I consider it *he* who is guilty of criminal idiocy in advocating "lights out" when air-craft are overhead. Will he tell us how he thinks airmen can discriminate between neutral and belligerent territory when we are blacked out and anti-aircraft guns go into action? I think our only hope is to have some distinctive form of lighting in operation from dusk to dawn.
> —"Fiat Lux"[7]

Letters of moderation helped to tone down the combative rhetoric, such as that from one calm-tempered citizen:

> Sir—In reference to "A.R.P 's letter ... as this country is neutral, one would think that the more lights visible to aircraft the better, as they could not then make a mistake, which would be possible if we had a blackout.
> I also think it is not very helpful to the public when people in a position such as "A.R.P." become "infuriated" at such a time. A.R.P. men need to be cool and collected as much depends on a steady brain.
> —"Citizen"[8]

Dubliners wanted solutions, not endless controversy. What was needed was a *mandatory* and *enforceable* lighting policy applied throughout the city. One citizen's voice of reason was heard in the *Evening Mail.* "Everyone *wants* to do the right thing—it only remains to be *told* what the right thing is."[9] The Government had failed to do so.

In the absence of action from the Government, some Dubliners offered their own novel solutions. A few were quite innovative. One person put forward an idea that drew widespread praise:

> Sir—I put forward the following suggestion, which, if found practicable, would deprive of excuses any belligerent planes bombing or penetrating neutral Eire; our searchlights are to put out triple-coloured rays representative of the national colours embodied in the national flag. This could be made possible by fitting the searchlights with tri-coloured discs. And representatives of the belligerent's governments could be informed of this innovation.
> —"Helpful"[10]

Readers lauded his suggestion, wondering why the Government or military had not come up with such a rational scheme. Another person, writing in praise of Helpful's idea, was prompted to add, "I hope that everyone who agrees that something of this kind should be done will make their voices heard through the medium of the press, without delay."[11] The bombing had indeed rid Dublin of its crippling complacency, as citizens were now forcefully expressing opinions and direct criticism regarding the city's failed air-raid defence system. Whether the Government was listening was not yet certain.

On the weekend following the bombing, 7 and 8 June, work continued at the scene. The authorities stated that the repair of "broken gas mains was going on speedily, as well as the clearing of debris and demolition of dangerous walls." Local people, however, felt that progress was too slow. On Saturday more people were evacuated from the bombed area, "their homes being deemed unsafe." Most were accommodated at the Red Cross offices in Mespil Road. The *Irish Independent* once again reported that "there is still no indication of the fate of Patrick McLoughlin who is missing since the bombing."[12] There was now little hope for his survival. Crowds of people again queued up for Saturday afternoon confession, to have their souls freshly cleansed, especially if they had become tarnished during the past week.

By noon on Saturday there was a steady stream of curious country people showing up at the North Strand. Some came from as far distant as Counties Kerry and Donegal. "Oh, *crowds* came up from the country," Una Shaw attests, "because they couldn't *believe* what had happened in the city, in the capital." They had to see for themselves. Country people routinely came to Dublin on Saturday for shopping excursions, and a chance to see the bomb scene was an added incentive on this weekend. They stepped off buses and trekked straight over. They had seen photographs in the newspapers and were expecting the same dramatic sights. However, the shark-tooth jaggedness of standing walls and chimney stacks had been largely levelled by demolition. It was now mostly mounds of rubble on a depressing greyish wasteland. Some country visitors expressed disappointment that it was not a more exciting experience. They were, however, awed by the bomb's explosive power and massive destruction.

A good many "gawkers", particularly men, decided that they might as well collect a genuine specimen from the famous site to take back and show to their fellow-townsmen, hoping that it might bestow a bit of celebrity upon them, at least in their local pub. So they reached down and picked up a fragment of broken brick or slate, tucked it in their pocket, then began concocting a good story to go with it. To people back home, seeing the "real evidence" was as good as producing a certified chunk of moon rock.

For many months thereafter, when sporting matches were held in nearby Croke Park on weekends, men would amble over to the bomb site to have a look around. Local people were not pleased that the scene of their tragedy had become a "tourist attraction."

In the days following the bombing there was much speculation about the intended target of the German pilot—if, indeed, it had been an intentional attack. Many Dubliners still believed that the bombings in early January had been aimed at Jewish communities and their synagogue.

Some people were now contending that the bombs had been meant to strike nearby Amiens Street railway station, through which the Belfast refugees had arrived, and Buckingham Street fire station, which had sent firemen north to fight the flames of the blitz. In an effort to better educate the public about modern bombing accuracy—or inaccuracy—the *Sunday Independent's* military correspondent on 8 June explained that while daylight bombing might be reasonably accurate under favourable conditions, "night bombing is not much more precise than a blind man's essay at stone-throwing."[13] The notion that a German pilot could, even on a clear night, pinpoint and strike a specific building was highly questionable.

That very night, the Luftwaffe battered Birmingham in an unexpected attack, raining bombs down on the city, their pilots having once again flown along the east coast of Ireland en route to their targets.

———

The drenching rain that had made Thursday's public funeral so miserable had continued for several days. As it soaked deeply into cracked walls and foundations it further destabilised some bomb-shaken tenements. Housing inspectors, out in full force, responded to the dangers:

> With the rains of the past few days, it was found that some of the houses which had not previously been condemned, and in which people were still living, were not safe. It was necessary to evacuate the occupants.[14]

Evacuation meant more homeless people herded towards Red Cross headquarters. And more headaches for Hernon and his staff. It also increased pressure on building contractors working feverishly to get the new Cabra houses into at least habitable condition for their new occupants.

Dublin Corporation also despatched other inspectors, mostly older men, hired to go around to the tenement houses and other buildings to assess personal property losses, for which the corporation was supposedly to pay compensation. Most tenement-dwellers had few belongings, only a few sticks of old furniture, some glasses, plates and odd mementoes. But when word was spread by "bush telegraph" along Gardiner Street, Dominick Street, Parnell Street, North King Street and the Coombe that an "oul inspector fella" was coming around offering something called "compensation" for broken items, the mammies, legendary for their shrewdness and resourcefulness, saw a golden opportunity, a rare chance to squeeze a few quid from the mighty Corpo. And taking "compensation" from the government by dubious means wasn't like stealing money. Not at all.

Tenement women who survived by their wits successfully used guile and cajoling in dealing with landlords, pawnbrokers, money-lenders and the like. It wouldn't take much to fool an oul fella called an inspector. A bit of conniving, fabricating—fibbing, if necessary—could put a few shillings in their purse. All they had to do was provide some visible evidence of loss, backed by a sorrowful story. Many of the women had indeed lost a few fragile glass or delph items in the explosion. All they had to do now was embellish the scene a bit. They scoured around for some additional "evidence" to document their losses. Mary Cooke tells of her granny's scheme along Lower Gardiner Street:

> Funny thing was, within days there was this man, an inspector, sent around knocking at doors to see what damage was done in the tenements. Now all there would have been was a few drinking glasses and a few ornaments.
>
> So an old gentleman, the inspector, would be knocking at the door asking, "Was there any damage?" So the women who had a few broken glasses or ornaments, they would add to it—breaking up milk bottles and making the broken glass look tragic! And they were claiming compensation on the bottles, as damage done from the bombing. That was very funny.
>
> I'll tell you, they were wonderful, those Dublin women. For latching onto something smart! Oh, those mammies, they were up to *every scheme* going for to *get money* out of this thing. *I know this*—because my grandmother done it!

The most creative women scrounged around for milk bottles, jam jars and such, even sending their children out to the dumps to bring back some more "evidence" to scatter around. Back then a few extra shillings helped to pay the rent and put food on the table. It would have made an amusing scene for the Abbey Theatre stage—the canny mammies putting on their charade to wangle a few quid from the "oul inspector fella."

Meanwhile Seán Moylan, parliamentary secretary to the Minister for Defence, was receiving disturbing reports that clearance and restoration work at the North Strand site was not going well. Alfie Byrne may well have been his primary source of information. On 12 June he decided to march out and make an on-site inspection. He hiked from one end of the wasteland to the other, assessed the work force and their progress, and spoke to local people to get their opinions. Their strong consensus was that the work effort was lax. Further, they felt quite abandoned by politicians, whose faces they never saw after the morning of the bombing. His personal observations supported everything they were telling him. People mentioned the newsreels they had seen, showing how quickly bombed-out parts of London and Belfast were cleared and rebuilt. Why not their community? And the inevitable question: What if this had been Blackrock or Ballsbridge blown into rubble? Would progress be moving so slowly?

Moylan saw their dispirited state, felt sympathy for the victims. Returning to his office, he fired off an uncommonly critical letter to Hernon the same afternoon:

I visited the North Strand on the 12th and to say that I was amazed and shocked at the lack of progress is to put it lightly. Public morale demands that this matter should be dealt with swiftly and efficiently.[15]

Most hopeful were those homeless families selected to move into the new houses in Cabra. They were counting the days, envisaging a modern house with kitchen, bath, electric lighting, indoor toilet. Safe from collapse. Not merely a new home but a better life.

Yet they were rather worried that it might seem far away from the old familiar world of city life, with its daily hubbub, crowded streets, and excitement. They'd soon find out.

On the evenings of 11 and 13 June the Gresham Hotel in O'Connell Street held grand benefit events to raise funds for bomb victims and the Red Cross. The hotel's management and staff were very sympathetic towards stricken Northstranders and energetic in their efforts to help, in part probably because they were only a few streets from the bomb site and most of their employees were local people. On Wednesday 11 June they presented an impressive programme featuring "leading Irish singers, musicians, actors, authors and playwrights." As a co-operative effort it represented the cream of Dublin's literary, theatrical and entertainment world. A smashing success, it brought in generous contributions from an appreciative audience. Two nights later the hotel put on a grand dance and musical gala, made especially attractive by the raffle for a radio set. This too was a great success, with "500 guests ... dancing until a late hour" to the music of the Gresham Band."[16]

On 14 June the Minister for Defence announced, "I would like to see another 100,000 men in the LDF," asserting that "every able-bodied man capable of giving service" should step forward and do his part.[17] Once again new recruits, from fresh-faced farm lads to hobbling ex-soldiers from the First World War, queued up to sign their name on the form. And, as with earlier recruitment drives, as months passed they were confronted with the lack of proper uniforms, weapons and training. Their patriotic zeal soon faded.

Throughout June, newspaper coverage of the bombing gradually declined. There was brief mention of the two cases of looting at the North Strand that had previously been brought to light. In the Dublin District Court Justice Hannan dismissed the charge against Michael Cleary, accused of stealing Richard Fitzpatrick's boots, because of insufficient evidence that he had intended to commit a crime. However, William Moran, who had been "charged with larceny and illegal possession of a purse containing £8 10s" belonging to Thomas Carroll, killed by the bomb, was given a "suspensory sentence of two months."[18] Northstranders regarded the two men as despicable for stealing from the dead.

The papers continued to report that there was no word on the missing Patrick McLoughlin—as if he had disappeared from the planet. The authorities abandoned their plan to drain the Royal Canal to search for his body, considering it too great an effort for so slight a chance of success. If his body was there, it was reasoned, it would surface sooner or later.

The newspapers ceased listing the names of those injured people released from the hospitals, though they did give notice of patients who had died. One such death notice in the *Irish Independent* on 15 June caught the eye of readers. Annie Malone, aged eighty-eight, died in the Mater Hospital from her bomb injuries. At her advanced age she had few close friends left. Her surviving daughter's name, however, was familiar to all: Molly Malone.

For two weeks following the bombing, Dublin's pub men talked of little else. Then, in mid-June, their attention became riveted on another violent conflict. Not a battle in the skies over London or on the dark waters of the North Atlantic: this one was being fought some five thousand miles away on a 22-foot-square patch of canvas beneath dangling lights, surrounded by a crowd of men at near fever pitch with anticipation. It was the world heavyweight boxing championship between the title-holder, Joe Louis, and the challenger, Billy Conn, being held in New York.

By fight day, the tension in some Dublin pubs was as electric as at the ringside, particularly in Killane's, the "pugilists' pub", where the likes of Spike McCormack and his crowd of fighters hung out. Several of them had even been to New York to fight in the Golden Gloves. The bout was even more dramatic than they had anticipated, according to the description in the *Irish Independent*:

> Louis came out of his corner with face set firmly for the twelfth round, but there was an uproar as Conn continued to hand out punishment. Conn, however, lacked a knock-out punch, although he staggered Louis with two terrific lefts. Conn's round.
>
> The fight took a dramatic turn in the 13th round. Conn had opened strongly, having the better of the exchanges, when Louis unleashed a left hook that landed on the jaw. Conn staggered, obviously hurt. Louis sensed a chance, and let fly a barrage of blows, under which Conn went down, and was unable to rise. The fight ended with only two more seconds of the round left.

For days thereafter, boxing fans in Dublin's pubs dissected the fight blow by blow. It was good therapy, drawing their minds away from the tragedy so close at hand. What if Conn had survived the round, cleared his head? Would there be a rematch? And so on. Life was finally returning to normal.

———

On 18 June, Germany finally expressed regret over the North Strand bombing, but without actually confessing guilt or offering a formal apology. The *Irish Press* published the convoluted message:

> The thorough investigations made by competent German authorities concerning the dropping of bombs on Dublin on 31 May have not established the responsibility of German aircraft. It has been ascertained that a German aircraft flew over the east coast of Ireland by mistake in the early morning of May 31. The aircraft changed its course as soon as it recognised that it was over Irish territory, and, in any case, it did not drop any bombs.
>
> Since, however, the Irish Government have stated that their investigations have shown the bombs dropped in Dublin to be of German origin, and as the very strong prevailing wind at high altitude on the night in question may have driven German aircraft over the east Irish coast without the knowledge of the pilots, the possibility of such planes having dropped the bombs cannot be excluded.
>
> In the circumstances, the German government unhesitatingly expresses their sincere regrets to the Irish Government. Furthermore, the German

Government, in view of the friendly relations existing between the two countries, are prepared to give compensation for the deplorable loss of life and injury to person and property.[19]

Though the statement was ambiguous and contradictory, it did contain two elements that doubtless pleased de Valera: the references to continuing "friendly relations", and the pledge to pay compensation.

In the same edition the newspaper printed an editorial warning people not to draw a false sense of security from the words. "It must never be concealed from our people that this war may yet engulf our nation."[20] Hitler was not to be trusted. Many passers-by now viewed the large red, white and black swastika flag hanging outside the German Embassy in Northumberland Road as menacing.

Throughout June, ARP wardens tested the air-raid sirens. They worked perfectly. Their scream was now a reminder of negligence as people muttered, "*Now* we can hear them, all right!" Some citizens, especially the elderly, took their piercing cry as a real warning of another attack, upsetting them once again. Children were now commonly frightened as well. Mary Dunne's home in North William Street was close to the Sisters of Charity convent, on which was mounted a large siren. Its high-pitched shriek reverberated through the bricked canyons of terraced houses. On one occasion, she recalls, shortly after the bombing, "I remember my sister getting hysterical; she was five." Fortunately, Father Masterson was "passing up the street and he took her up like this [in his arms] and blessed her ... he comforted her." If the Government meant the frequent siren testing to instil confidence and calm, it had just the opposite effect on many.

In the third week of June, Hernon finally announced the imposition of a black-out policy for the city. At dusk, citizens were required to cover their windows with dark curtains, blinds or dyed sheets. About half the citizenry still believed that a brightly illuminated city was safer; but at least a decision had been made. As Margaret Pringle sarcastically comments, "Oh, *after* the bombing, *then* we had the black-out! My grandmother'd have the blinds down and you'd think we were all dead! The *dark*—and we'd be afraid." Enforcement was haphazard, as some local ARP wardens and police were strict, others lenient. In her inner-city district, says Una Shaw, "the wardens would *roar*, '*Put out* that light!'" Over in the Liberties, Garda Senan Finucane took his job seriously as well. "If you saw light, even if it was an *inch*, you'd knock on the door and say, 'There's light there.'" People hated entombing themselves in darkness, which some found claustrophobic. They missed seeing the pleasing night-time glow from the street lamps sifting through their curtains at bedtime.

Everyone wanted to play their part in helping bomb victims. Organisations and ordinary people from every part of the country were sending in financial contributions, clothing, blankets, pots and pans, Rosaries. And the National Association of Registered Egg Dealers was not about to be left out. They had eggs to contribute. The head of the association contacted the Irish Red Cross to see if they would serve as a collection centre at their head office in Mespil Road. Delighted, the Red Cross said to just deliver them to their door. On 18 June the association put out word to its members: "Registered egg dealers are asked to contribute at least one dozen eggs to the relief of the victims of the recent Dublin bombings." *At least* one dozen eggs. What the head of the association had failed to mention to Red Cross officials was that there were 14,000 members.

The scheme began smoothly enough when the Ballaghaderreen Branch of the association proudly delivered the first consignment of 120 dozen eggs. Shortly thereafter, the dam burst. It seemed that every few minutes a staff member at the door would shout out, "More eggs!" To exacerbate matters, citizens with a few hens began bringing in their eggs. To put Red Cross staff in even more of a dither, country people from every county were sending up eggs through the post. This was an accepted practice at the time. It was customary for country families to send their Dublin relatives fresh eggs. They were delivered by postmen, like Jeremiah Crean and Joe O'Neill. Jeremiah Crean explains: "You did the tricycle delivery with the basket on front, about three-and-a-half feet long—the balance wasn't so good." Egg-toting postmen became frustrated trying to pedal over cobblestones and tram tracks, swerving through buses and horse vehicles and pedestrians with their fragile cargo. The "great egg drive", as the newspapers called it, became a great headache for postmen and beleaguered Red Cross officials.

Finally, word was jointly put out by the National Association of Registered Egg Dealers and the Red Cross society: "No more eggs, *please!*" This was followed by an announcement by the latter on 27 June that "surplus eggs would be converted into cash."

————

As heavy demolition was gradually completed, sections of the North Strand site were made safe and cordons removed. The wasteland became a playground for children. They went treasure-hunting amid the dirt and rubble. Boys searched for pirate booty—real coins. Girls were delighted to collect fragments of richly hued stained glass, broken cups, saucers and crystal for their games of shop and chainies. Mammies warned them about the dangers of getting cut, and of rats. "Don't touch body parts," they were told.

Some children creatively used the "spoils of war". Gathering up bricks and wood, they made dolls' houses and club houses where at night young lads began telling stories of headless ghosts. A single board resting on a few bricks became a shop counter. Bernadette Pierce and her pals made a small fire and roasted a fine meal for themselves:

> It was still all blown to bits, but when the bodies were all gone, as children we would go into the rubble and build pretend houses with bricks. There were loads of sticks, and we'd get potatoes and throw them into the fire and roast them on a coat-hanger.

Children made up little songs and ditties about the bombing. "We had our little jingles and we'd sing them," recalls Winnie Brennan. The one that most sticks in her mind was sung to the tune of "My Bonnie Lies Over the Ocean":

> I remember the night of the bombing,
> The night that I lay in my bed,
> That night that I thought I was lucky,
> But the Germans were over my head.

She made up that song, she explains, because her mother used to tell her how lucky Irish people were to have their neutrality protection. "My mother used to say, 'You'll have no better luck now, because there'll be no bombing of the Irish.' But then *after that* she said, 'Look what they *done* to us!'"

Another small sign that life was slowly returning to normal was the sight of pigeons in the sky above the North Strand. After the ruinous explosion, local pigeon-raisers struggled to rebuild lofts and to calm their surviving highly distressed birds. For a time they didn't dare race them, for fear that shock and disorientation could cause them to go astray and become lost. After three weeks a number of pigeon men decided to test their birds. They took several baskets of the homing pigeons to a distant point outside the city and had them released, praying they'd see them again. Their owners then waited nervously by their lofts, constantly scanning the sky. The *Evening Herald* reported the happy results, quoting one relieved pigeon-owner: "I watched their manoeuvring to find directions. Their 'home' was the North Strand, and after making a few circles they soon headed full wing in that direction."[21] Cheers went up from loft to loft.

On the morning of 22 June, at the request of the ARP wardens in Number 3 Area, a Mass was offered at St Laurence O'Toole's Church by Rev. M. Daly for the "repose of the souls who lost their lives in the recent Dublin bombing."

The wardens assembled at Parnell Square, accompanied by groups of Boy Scouts, and the march proceeded to the church. After Mass the wardens marched through the bombed area as a token of respect for the dead. Local people lined their path to watch the small procession. The site was still raw, as were the emotions of participants and observers.

That night "at 11.20 an aircraft flew inland and was fired on by the ground defences in the Dublin area."[22] Searchlights were again seen sweeping the darkness to and fro. The bright beams and exploding shells jolted many people into sitting position in their beds, as others, once again, rushed to their windows. Nerves were on edge.

The next morning, Dubliners picked up their copy of the *Irish Independent* and were struck by the bold headline:

GERMANS INVADE RUSSIA—FIGHTING ON 1,500 MILE FRONT

Germany was proclaiming it "the greatest march-in the world has ever seen, [as] Herr Hitler launched his vast forces against Soviet Russia."[23] Newspapers around the world carried the stunning news. German radio declared that the "greatest battle in history will be fought on the plains of White Russia [Belarus] and the Ukraine," noting that the terrain was ideal for German motorised troops and tanks. Germany was supremely confident of victory.

In Ireland, people sought to interpret its significance for their own country. It reinforced the belief that Germany was seeking world domination. But some Irish people took it as good news not only because they perceived that it might be a colossal blunder by Germany but also because it would probably make Irish skies safer. By opening a massive eastern front, they reasoned, the Luftwaffe would probably have to reduce its British bombing missions, which would mean fewer bombers passing over Ireland's east coast, and less chance of "mistakes".

De Valera, however, was concerned that it might regenerate a creeping complacency. On 28 June, five days after Germany's invasion of the Soviet Union, at a conference of Fianna Fáil delegates in Ennis the Taoiseach gave a sobering address, calling for a pragmatic blend of preparation and prayer. The *Sunday Independent* summarised his remarks:

Speaking of the dangers which faced the country, Mr. de Valera said he wanted to warn the people that every day that passed while this war lasted would see the country more and more in a position of peril … war meant confusion, misery, destruction and death, but all those could be greatly lessened by wise planning in steeling themselves to meet whatever ordeal might come.

> God had spared them so far, and it might be His Will that they would
> be spared to the end, but they had no right to presume that. And they
> should, besides praying, make ready by every means to defend themselves.
> There was hardly a single home that could feel safe should war come.[24]

He concluded by emphasising that the "peril of people in the city was far
greater than that of people living in the country." Disquieting words to
Dubliners.

Sure enough, the very next day the "Battle of Dublin" broke out:

> Men rushed to their positions, garrisoning bridges and buildings, laying
> theoretical tank-traps, mining roads, guarding banks of rivers and canals
> … all was fair—infiltration, fifth-columnism, and sabotage.[25]

It was, of course, another LDF exercise, officially dubbed the "Battle of Dublin"
by army headquarters to give it a dramatic flair. To make it more realistic, in
the morning hours unsuspecting pedestrians were brusquely halted on the
street, ordered to thrust their arms skyward and submit to search. "Dublin's
citizens peacefully accepted cross-examination," reported the *Irish Press*, "only
vaguely aware that the city was at total war."[26] It later made a great story for
the pub, how they were "held at gunpoint" by unflinching soldiers. To add a
further touch of authenticity, the LDF even despatched carrier pigeons
carrying coded messages from one military post to another.

It is not clear whether the dramatic staging of the "Battle of Dublin", one
month after the big bombing, was meant to boost the military's morale or the
public's. To many citizens, it was simply more "play soldiering."

Chapter 26 ✿

FAITH, MIRACLES, AND "LOST SOULS"

They thought the end of the world had come! Their religion all came back to them.

(GABRIEL MOLONY, 82)

Oh, really and truly, people turned to their religion.

(MARY COOKE, 74)

Many stories of miracles mitigated the horror of the catastrophe.

(*Irish Times*, 2 June 1941)

In the wake of the terrifying bombing, Dubliners turned to their religion for consolation. It had always got them through life's hardships and crises, especially in the poorer district of the city. They filled the churches, stood in confession queues, carried Rosary beads. Patrick O'Leary, a chemist in the 1940s, says: "Religion was their anchor ... a rock. Their faith was unshakable, the *one thing* they could count on."

Irish Catholics were renowned for their devotion. For most, the bombing brought a renewed or deepened faith. For others, it was more of a religious revival, and for some of those who had strayed a rediscovery of faith long lost. Despite the horror of the bombing that had slaughtered so many innocent victims, people talked of "God's will" and "his plan". As Father Brendan Lawless explains, back in the 1940s it was still "an old type of faith ... an *unquestioned* faith" that Dubliners embraced, a type of faith in which there was absolute acceptance of whatever the Church, and parish priests, professed. If priests from their pulpits told Dubliners that God had "his ways", "his reasons", it was not for them to question his wisdom.

Yet some did. There were those who were greatly shaken and disillusioned by such a merciless act as killing innocent people in their beds. How could such an injustice possibly be the "will of God"? Brian Barton, in his book *The*

Blitz: Belfast in the War Years, found the same true in the North, where for "some people ... it shook their religious faith."[1] Louis Robinson knew of people whose faith was rattled by the brutality of the bombing:

> The first thing everybody did was say, "Thank God!" They were alive. But then they'd say, "*Why that?*" I mean, *why* would God, even if he's working in strange ways ... *why* would God *allow that?*

Most whose faith had been shaken questioned it introspectively. However, as nurse Ann Leonard recalls, some expressed it openly:

> Some people even forgot God after that. You know, "There couldn't *be a God!* When carnage like that was *allowed!*" There was people who said that—and I heard it myself—"there's *no God!*"—to let that happen.
> Oh, I thought that was a horrible thing to say. We *had* to trust in God.

Priests, in sermons and in private, tried to convince people that there was "God's will" as well as people's free will, which was granted by God. Events on earth might appear unjust, but in Heaven there would be supreme, eternal justice.

Miracles were also a matter of faith. And there were plenty of miraculous claims circulating—most of a minor sort, but several taken quite seriously. Newspapers cultivated stories that they called "miraculous". The *Irish Times* reported that "many stories of miracles mitigated the horror of the catastrophe."[2]

It is common for survivors of any calamity, be it a shipwreck, a hurricane or a bombing, to attribute their survival to a higher entity, often using the term "miracle" to describe their escape from death. And at the North Strand there were many stories of "miraculous escapes", especially about those victims "buried alive" for a time in the ruins. The *Irish Times* documented a remarkable case in which "a twelve-months-old baby was taken uninjured from a completely demolished house where six dead had been removed."[3] Everyone was calling it a miracle.

What some attributed to God's intercession, others simply put down to fate or good luck. As Diarmuid Hiney contends, "that Lady Luck was working overtime at the time of the bombing could not be disputed."[4]

Dermot Ring knew of a few remarkable incidents, including one where "a staircase disappeared and the fella was just falling—and then getting up and running away." Some said it was miraculous, others that he was just a "lucky fella". Many were the stories of people pinned under heavy bricks and beams yet somehow freeing themselves. Frail grannies trapped beneath debris managed to claw and climb their way to freedom. To many it was a miracle; others marvelled at the wonders of the human survival instinct.

There were countless cases of religious objects "miraculously" spared when all around them was in ruin. Most were statues of the Blessed Virgin, but there were also pictures of Christ, crucifixes, bibles and other religious artefacts. It was indeed curious to see partially collapsed houses in which religious statues and pictures remained on the mantelpiece or the walls when almost everything else had been blown away.

A few miracles were seriously proclaimed, and widely accepted. One occurred in the house where Chrissie Byrne was living with her aunt and uncle at number 25 North William Street. Every other house along the street suffered severe bomb damage, with windows smashed out and roofs ripped apart; but number 25 was left untouched. It stood out, and everyone commented on it. When they were told the story of Chrissie's uncle it began to take on a miraculous aura:

> My Uncle Tom, he was a very good religious man. He went around the house *every* night with a crucifix and blessed the house with holy water. Blessed the house *every* night, before he went to bed.
>
> And we were the *only* house where there wasn't even a *pane* of glass broken. As sure as I'm sitting here! And we always believed that it was saved through that, the crucifix and blessing of the house with holy water.

Seeing it with their own eyes was proof enough for most of the neighbours: a small miracle had taken place along their street.

Kathleen Roche tells of a different sort of miraculous event that occurred in her sister Mag's house at number 3 Shamrock Place:

> *Everything* was demolished. Chimney stacks come down and windows came in, everything *demolished* inside—bar a statue of the Blessed Lady in a shade. To *think* that the Blessed Virgin statue was *still standing*, in its shade—not *touched!*

Word spread quickly through the neighbourhood about the "miracle of the statue" in number 3. When a priest mentioned it in church, news of the "miracle" became known to the entire congregation. Later, when the statue was given to, and reverently accepted by, nuns at the convent it conferred further sanctity upon the relic. It is still remembered today.

"Lost Souls"

Some people were in a daze … looking wild … others were rigid, could not move.

(*Irish Press*, 31 May 1941)

With the impact of that bomb there was a *lot* of damage to the mind.

(MARY COOKE)

There was people that went into the asylum in Grangegorman, 'cause their nerves were shattered.

(STEPHEN LOFTUS, 85)

"Lost souls" they were called. No miracle had saved them from harm. They physically survived the bombing but were mentally never the same again. Theirs was a particularly pitiable tragedy, for their mental wounds were neither well understood nor adequately treated. They were not reported in the papers, yet were known to all local people. Many people said that God—or fate—had been kinder to those who perished quickly than to those left alive to suffer a life of mental illness. As Una Shaw puts it, "some people just 'went off their rocker.'" Their story was never told.

Northstranders had been particularly unaccustomed to violence and upheaval, theirs being an uncommonly peaceful village life. A tram accident or a runaway horse injuring a pedestrian was regarded as a real calamity. By temperament and daily life, most were used to a tranquil, safe existence.

With the shock of the sudden, thunderous explosion, the trembling earth, disintegration of buildings and death all around them, many people suffered mental trauma. The majority of those stunned soon regained their senses. Some people, however, "went haywire", as Margaret Ladrigan puts it, left with lasting psychological and emotional damage. As Jenny O'Brien witnessed, "mentally, there was people that were *never really* over it." As Paddy Walsh explains, it was the "point where you go *beyond* panic—your *mind* goes, completely!" Victims were deprived of their normal reasoning powers, and personality. In the local vernacular there were many terms for it: "loony", "queer", "gone dim", "gone mental", "off centre", "over the edge". In working-class society the terms "insanity" and "mental illness" were assiduously avoided, for they carried a powerful and lasting social stigma. It was quite acceptable to be "loony" or "queer in the head"—but not insane.

It was natural for those near the bomb blast to suffer bad nerves, insomnia, nightmares, jitteriness. Women afterwards commonly said to one another, "Me nerves are all gone bad over it." But even some people in distant parts of the city, miles removed from the explosion, reported fear and mental trauma, as did Tom MacDonagh, who lived in the Clanbrassil Street area:

> For me the roar of German planes over our back yard was just the beginning of nightmare. The world was no longer an innocent garden of delight. I felt threatened by violence. Visions of planes terrorising civilians … German tanks coming. The war had got to me. I was to fear the opening strains of Beethoven's Fifth. They were evil people.
>
> Darkness had descended upon my universe. I was afraid to go to bed, scared to sleep.[5]

Tony Gray recalls how, as a young *Irish Times* reporter in 1941, "I found the whole experience shattering."[6] The "lost souls" were those who were lastingly "shattered" in their mind. The *Irish Press* revealed that experts in London who had studied the psychological and emotional effects of the blitz on citizens found that with exploding bombs "the noise they make and the fear it inspired is more serious than the loss of life caused by them."[7] The article explained that certain people were so traumatised that they were pushed beyond the limits of their endurance, causing a mental snap that resulted in a lasting debility.

Una Shaw saw the sad transformation of one of her neighbours in Rutland Street, from the most docile, cheerful mother to a completely changed woman:

> Some people went "off their rocker." I *know!* One neighbour of mine, up the street, from the *next day* she *completely* "went". Her *mind*. Oh, she *went off* her rocker! She was a mother and she ran in under the table and stayed there, and the crash of the bomb was a terrible thing to listen to—and she just went *totally* hysterical.
>
> And she was then *never* the same again. And she was a lovely, lovely jolly woman. Often she'd send me to get her milk, and when I'd get back she'd give me a few sweets or a few coppers. A lovely, *jolly* woman. But *never* the same again!
>
> After that, she went off in her mind, because she was talking about strange things. So we children got frightened of her and kept away. That's one I know of—but God *knows* how many more!

Nearby, a nun who was rendered demented by the bombing was cloistered within her convent in North William Street for the remainder of her life. Her story, says Chrissie Byrne, who knew her well, was known locally. "She went off in her head ... just 'went mental.'" Though people knew of her condition, it was seldom mentioned openly.

Most of those mentally impaired by the bombing were protected at home by family. Their most conspicuous symptoms were changes in personality and behaviour, such as reticence, inattentiveness, inability to respond normally, incoherent mutterings. Sometimes periodic trembling, sobbing, sudden shouting, even the failure to recognise familiar faces and voices. Some had a vacuous, distant gaze, as if they were trapped in a cavernous place within their own mind, far removed from present time and place. A few were said to have a "wild" look in their eyes, which frightened children. Most could no longer function normally in daily activities.

In those cases where a person was severely demented they had to be watched carefully at home or committed to an asylum. As this was never chronicled, it is not possible to document the number of cases. But some known instances are revealed through oral history. Stephen Loftus knew of several women around Buckingham Street, just around the corner from the blast, who went "berserk" and had to be placed in Grangegorman mental hospital:

> There was people that went into the asylum, in Grangegorman, 'cause their nerves were shattered. A *lot* of them were affected—and a lot of them never come out. Ah, there was quite a few, people just mentally not able for to handle it.
>
> One man, he was a fine big Kerry man, and he had a couple of children, and his wife, they done their best for her ... but she *never got over it!* And they took her to Grangegorman. It was the *terror*, really. Yes, some of them *never* come out of it.

It was not an age in Dublin when therapy, medication or clinical treatment were available to those suffering shell-shock or similar psychological illness. No-one had yet coined the term "post-traumatic stress disorder". But they knew the terms "mental asylum" and, less kindly, "madhouse". To be institutionalised carried a certain stigma, not only on the person but on their family as well. So, most families tried to cope with victims at home. As they were never treated, most never got better, unable to live a normal life again. Brian Barton, in his analysis of the long-term effects of the Belfast bombings, found much evidence of permanent mental and psychological damage among victims:

> [The bombings] had a lasting effect. There were those, especially among

the elderly, who never fully recovered from the trauma and anxiety; it shortened their lives.[8]

No studies were done in Ireland of the short-term or long-term mental afflictions of bomb victims. But Tony Gray, in 2004, put it in historical perspective: "The emotional state of Northstranders would have been the same sort of shock as victims of any modern terrorist atrocity."[9] The profound difference, of course, is that today such victims can seek professional treatment. No miracle drugs or mental health schemes were available to Northstranders. Looking back on it, says Kathleen Martin sympathetically, "people could have done with some therapy ... their *minds*."

Most victims mentally crippled by the 1941 bombing managed somehow to hobble through life. Decades later, after most Dubliners had forgotten—or never known—about the origin of their mental problems, some of them were sadly reduced to local "characters", sometimes cruelly jeered, even tormented, by youngsters who had not been around in 1941. To older people, they sympathetically remained "lost souls".

Chapter 27 ∾

CABRA—"THE WILD AND WOOLLY WEST"

Cabra at that time, to those who were living in the city centre, felt like it was miles and miles out in the country. They looked at it like they were going out into the bogs!

(UNA SHAW, 75)

Now Cabra, they used to call it the "wild and woolly west"!

(WINNIE BRENNAN, 73)

They were sent out to Cabra—and they always wanted to get back. They all wanted to come back.

(MARGARET PRINGLE, 88)

For hundreds of homeless people desperate to escape the uncomfortable housing shelters, Cabra was imagined as the "promised land". They were soon to become pioneer settlers on the "wild" western frontier of Dublin.

What the new settlers were destined to find were unfinished dwellings and primitive living conditions in an isolated environment. Their disappointment, struggle, even depression in coping with their difficult new life were not recorded in Government documents, nor reported in the newspapers. However, oral testimony of the Cabra settlers is profuse and passionate.

On 24 June 1941 the *Irish Press* published Dublin Corporation's proud announcement that "one hundred and fifty uncompleted houses out in Cabra … have been brought up to the 'occupation point'."[1] Readers were impressed. The notoriously sluggish Housing Department had apparently made good on its promise to make the houses habitable within weeks rather than months. Similar housing projects were being vigorously pushed forward in Crumlin, Ballyfermot, Kimmage and Donnycarney. The new residents selected for the Cabra houses were about to receive their keys, full of hope for a better life. They were, however, apprehensive about moving so "far away" from the city and nervously uncertain about exactly what was meant by the term "occupation point".

Preconceived ideas of a new life out in Cabra varied widely. Most had never been there before, and their images were formed from hearsay or their own fantasies. The city's poor tenement-dwellers, understandably, had fanciful notions about having their own house. "It was the dream of most tenement mothers," says Lily O'Connor, "to be given a small corporation house out of the city."[2] In their minds it was a leafy, salubrious setting away from the congestion, dirt and traffic of the city. Most Northstranders, however, never had any wish to leave their happy life in the picturesque, peaceful city village beside the canal. They had been perfectly content where they were. Only those living in impoverished enclaves nearby, such as Quinn's Cottages, wanted to escape to a corporation house in a new development. But after the bomb destroyed their village, the corporation authorities told Northstranders that Cabra was to be their future—like it or not.

And many didn't. They were dead set against moving "out to the bogs," as it was phrased. They were city people to the core. Parochialism created a fear of moving anywhere else, especially out to the "country". Says Kathleen Martin: "Oh, my mother and grandmother, they were both widows and they were absolutely *devastated* to have to move—the very *thought* of going out to Cabra!" Some actually rejected the offer of a new house. Mary Dunne's home in North William Street had been severely damaged and was condemned. After three miserable weeks of living in the Baggotrath shelter, the corporation offered her family the key to a house in Cabra:

> Father and Mother were offered a house in Cabra. But my mother said Cabra was the *country*—and we were *city* people, you know. So she said, "I'm *not* going out in the country *anywhere*." Mam said, "Now what would I be doing out in the country? Cabra, *indeed!*"

No amount of coaxing could get her to budge. She declared that they would stay in the shelter until her home was repaired or they found another place in the city.

In the emotions of the moment, some refugees made hasty decisions that they would later regret. Margaret Ladrigan's house in Synnott Street was blown apart, beyond repair. But her mother somehow convinced herself that it would be rebuilt. The corporation sympathetically offered her a new house only a few streets away in Clonliffe Avenue in Ballybough:

> My poor mother, we were offered a house in Ballybough—but she wouldn't take it. She thought it was *too far away!* She wanted her *own*

home back. Like, she thought, "How *dare* they expect me to leave Synnott Street!" It was her *life*, her home, where she started.

So she refused that house—and they were *lovely* houses. Oh, *was she* regretful! She said, "When I *think* that I refused that house! And she *cried*.

Only weeks later, she had no choice but to accept a home far out in Dingle Road in Cabra—to her, light-years further away than Ballybough. For years thereafter she suffered great regret, feeling depressed, periodically crying over her bad decision.

On 25 June the new settlers began their westward journey, filled with both trepidation and excitement but mostly nervous uncertainty about what lay ahead. They were transported in corporation lorries, bringing with them the few parcels of clothing and other small personal items they had salvaged from their bombed homes. As the lorries bounced along the road, the houses and the hubbub of city life dwindled, then faded away. The landscape became more open, barren. Some already felt tinges of homesickness. As children merrily sang songs along the way, mothers nervously rubbed their hands together.

The first visions made some settlers feel sick to their stomach. As they approached they could see the houses in the distance, standing out in the open, aligned like barracks, in the middle of a muddy brown *nowhere*. As they cast their eyes over the width of the landscape they saw nothing that was green or alive, prompting a few to comment that it looked like a different planet. Seeing the alien colony at a distance churned up apprehension.

Everyone recalls their first impressions. "Oh, it was absolutely *primitive*," says Martin. "We were drawn into the unknown—we didn't know *where* we were! There were no other houses around us." Nor were there any "civilised" features such as footpaths, railings, gates, post boxes, or exterior house adornments—just boxy houses set out on a brown, barren open space. Some mothers were in tears before they even set foot on the ground. It was visual shock never forgotten by those who experienced it, says Ladrigan:

> It was a nightmare! We had nothing out there—a *field* it was. Absolutely *nothing*. All *muck*! It was like an Arab land. We had no footpaths, no railings, a wood plank to come into the house.
>
> Really, we were out in the *wilds. Really and truly*, lost. Oh, God, really now, we were out in the wilds!

As the lorries halted and the passengers climbed down, officials pointed out to each family which house was theirs. They were given their key, mattresses and blankets. That was about it. People later described feelings of being "dumped off" and promptly abandoned.

On opening the door they were at least greeted with the pleasing smell of fresh paint. Then they were struck by the stark emptiness and the unbroken straight lines of walls, ceilings, floors, and door frames. Many had never walked into a new house of any type before. It looked featureless and sterile. "When you walked in it was boards: we had no lino, no carpet," Ladrigan recalls. "The house was cold." As parents moved from room to room, noticing the modern amenities of electricity, plumbing, kitchen, range, bathroom, bath and toilet, the children scampered about with the excitement of exploration.

After touring their new home for a few minutes, the new residents began looking more carefully. On closer inspection, some work appeared unfinished and unrefined. Carpentry, finishing work and painting were not up to standard. Doors and windows were often not properly framed and fit, out of alignment. Evidence of poor craftsmanship showed everywhere in the kitchens and bathrooms. "The houses just *weren't ready!*" says Martin. "They should have been another six months before we moved in—they *had to rush.*" There was particular dismay over the poor quality of fireplaces. A reliable hearth was the centre of a home, providing warmth, drawing people together. Problems arose right away, says Martin:

> People lit their fire and they got a crack down their fire breast, and that was there for years. It was the heat, see; the house wasn't properly *dried*—and when we lit the fires it cracked. It needed another month for to dry out.

Ladrigan and her neighbours found that "our fireplaces needed to be blackened" as well. Windows were small compared with the ones in the old Georgian and Victorian houses, and the low ceilings felt confining. The houses simply felt "boxy", not "homely".

As the first day drew to a close there were more distressing realities. Normally, new residents settle in to their new home by unpacking possessions and arranging furniture. After putting their mattresses and grey army blankets on the floor, the new Cabra residents looked around only to realise just how possessionless they were. For mothers it was especially disheartening. Some sobbed, seeing their home devoid of beds, chairs, curtains, floor coverings, or table on which to eat. "We had *nothing* for ages," says Martin; "no furniture as such, other than a few straight chairs, wooden chairs; and we'd no oilcloth or nothing on them." Though distressed by the barrenness, mothers tried to appear optimistic so as to uphold the spirits of the family. In the days ahead they scrounged around the Dublin markets to find wooden boxes to use as small chairs and tables, went to charitable organisations seeking any household items to bring back, accepted whatever scraps of furniture they might be offered. They couldn't let pride stand in they way. Though they had plenty of clothing collected through the Red Cross, they had no money with which to buy other necessities:

> We didn't have *any* finances for to try and buy stuff. When I look back on it I think, "My God, we were *very poor*." With the upheaval of the bomb, and then the losses. *How* my mother survived at all I do *not know*."

Cabra settlers had assumed that the corporation would help them to make empty dwellings livable by providing at least some money and essential furnishings. Their assumption was wrong, as the corporation saw its responsibility as putting a roof over the refugees' heads; they then had to fare for themselves. Essentially, people had to "camp out" in their empty dwellings.

An unexpected blow was the new rent they were suddenly hit with by the corporation, commonly twice or more what they had been paying. In the confusion and strain of the circumstances, the new rental terms had either not been properly explained to them or they had not understood them. Martin's mother was among those caught off guard. In their former home in Synnott Street, "we paid only three and six, but in Cabra the rent was *ten* and something! It was an awful lot of money. Ma didn't see how she could pay that amount of rent." Fortunately, her mother and granny were both widows who had been living together, so the corporation allowed them to jointly assume responsibility for the rent. Nonetheless, her mother could manage only by getting a job over in Inchicore, where she cycled each day, in all weathers. All Cabra residents felt the new rent pinch and worried about it constantly. Others in the house had to seek jobs to help out.

Some new inhabitants were left virtually helpless. Nan Davis tells of the hardship of two widow friends, Ginny and her sister Rosie. The bombing had rendered them essentially destitute:

> Ginny's husband died and she was left with three children. Then her house was bombed. *Lost everything!* And the Government never done *anything* about it. They got *nothing*. Never got compensation … not a bed, not a cup. Just let them go, and they had to find their own way. That was an awful thing.

Nor did they receive any sympathy from one corporation official to whom they turned. Davis well remembers the day that Ginny and Rosie timidly went to the corporation office to seek some small compensation—any bit of help—

Survivors looking over their salvaged possessions loaded on a cart. (*Courtesy of the* Irish Independent)

Dublin Corporation arranged for lorries to haul away the surviving furniture of residents. (*Courtesy of the* Irish Independent)

BOMBS GERMAN: PROTEST BEING MADE TO BERLIN

Thirty Dead, Ninety Hurt: High Tribute To Rescuers

THE POPE DEFENDS RIGHTS OF MAN

THE death-roll from the bombs dropped by aircraft in Dublin early on Saturday morning is now 30, with 90 injured. A bomb was dropped near Arklow early yesterday, it is officially announced. No lives were lost but there was some damage to property.

It took military investigators only forty-eight hours to confirm that the bombs were German—which Dubliners already well knew. Note the photograph of the Taoiseach, Éamon de Valera, standing at the edge of the large crater, described by one reporter as looking "dumbfounded" when he arrived at the site.

Mr and Mrs Connell, who went in desperate search of their son Charlie at the City Morgue—the worst experience of their life.

Charles Connell (*left*), who was a teenage messenger for the local butcher, Richard Fitzpatrick, at the time of the bombing. His parents were frantic when he was missing after the blast.

At the coroner's inquest, huge crowds gathered outside awaiting the formal verdicts. The verification of mutilations and "partial remains" both horrified and fascinated the public.

Kirwan's undertakers, relative newcomers in the profession, played a major role in the public funeral, doing a splendid job under the most difficult circumstances. (*Courtesy of the* Irish Independent)

Massive crowds gathered for the public funeral of the bomb victims. Never had Dublin appeared so sorrowful, wrote one newspaper. Bitter tears were openly wept by men and women. (*Courtesy of the* Irish Independent)

GERMANY 'PLANNED' KILLER BOMB RAID

A RENOWNED Irish aviation investigator claims he has uncovered evidence suggesting the 1941 German bombing of Dublin's North Strand was no accident.

■■■ PAUL GUNNING

North Strand target for revenge: expert

Researching archive material at an Munich base, Galway man Leo Sheridan discovered the ...aid — codenamed 'Operation Roman Helmet' — was aimed at intimidating the Free State Government after a number of neutrality breaches.

A total of 25 people were killed in the raid, with 45 seriously injured.

Hundreds of houses were destroyed or damaged.

Mr Sheridan, based in France, said the scale of the North Strand catastrophe could have been minimised had the Irish military — on receiving a tipoff from British code-breakers — called a full-scale air raid warning.

The attack by Adolf Hitler's Luftwaffe was mainly aimed at a number of Dublin fire stations whose staff had helped in quenching bomb blazes that had gutted Belfast.

The operation also targeted Aras an Uachtarain — with President Douglas Hyde their main target.

"With the English press detailing accounts of Eire's fire fighters racing over the border to fight bomb fires

in Belfast, German intelligence saw this as a sign of weakness," Mr Sheridan said.

"They wanted to teach the Irish a lesson."

Taoiseach Eamon De Valera had accepted the April 1941 calls for help in fighting the bomb blazes in Belfast.

Targets

Fire tenders were sent from Dublin, Drogheda and Dundalk.

De Valera had attempted to dismiss German complaints, saying his government claimed a sovereign right over the North.

A Dornier DO17 bomber with six bombs — three of them primed — targeted the North Stand fire station.

It then attempted to bomb the Dorset Street fire

station, but the the bomb landed in the River Liffey.

Its final target was Aras an Uachtarain.

"However, an artillery gunner, having heard the plane, released some rounds and tailed its wing, forcing it to turn," Mr Sheridan said.

"The plane then made a rendevous signal with a German submarine 10 miles south of Kish lighthouse that it had been interfered with from ground attack."

It was "unclear whether the bomb dropped at the Phoenix Park exploded or not."

The air crew responsible for dropping the bombs reportedly never made it back to base.

An Irish-born RAF pilot said he shot down the bomber

FIRES: De Valera   BOMBINGS: Hitler

A sensational headline in the *Star* in 1998 claiming that Hitler deliberately bombed Dublin in revenge for alleged breaches of Irish neutrality.

Some surviving bomb fragments found their way into a box on the desk of the librarian at Charleville Mall Library.

The North Strand in 2004, showing the Strand Theatre on the left.

The North Strand, with Newcomen Bridge in the distant background. The memorial garden dedicated to those killed by the bomb can be seen between two large trees on the right, behind an iron railing.

The monument erected in the memorial garden dedicated to the victims of the German bombing. The funds for this project had to be raised by local people when the Government failed to contribute.

to get them through life. The man flatly turned them away, dismissing their tragedy in a huffy tone, telling them "it was Providence. Providence that happened—couldn't be prevented."

Equally dispiriting was what lay outside their houses. Nothing. Not a shop, pub, market, park, or cinema. Nor a tree or garden. No colour, no social activity, traffic or street life. The setting was isolated and lifeless. There were no traditional social places at which to congregate and interact. "People were far away from their natural habitat," says Margaret Pringle, "it wasn't the *same* … there wasn't the community spirit." There was no community, as they had known it. All the familiar daily rituals and patterns of city life were missing. Gone were the hubbub, excitement, spontaneity of streets, shops, pubs and markets. The emptiness and boredom were depressing. Cabra was a social desert.

One bright spot on Cabra's brown horizon was the periodic appearance of Alfie Byrne on his bicycle. He had promised to visit the refugees once they had been transplanted. He kept his word. Margaret Ladrigan recalls what a happy event it was when he was spotted. "Alfie—he was the genuine thing, he'd visit us here in Cabra, on his bicycle. He'd come up because we were refugees from the North Strand." Whenever he would show up along Dingle Road or Swilly Road, with a sack of lollipops in hand, everyone flocked to greet him. He was a link with their past, bringing news and gossip from "back home". All agreed that Alfie was a great tonic for homesickness.

But his visits were not a cure. Direct contact was needed. Within a few weeks, isolation out in Cabra began to feel like a prison. People longed to escape—back to "civilisation", as Ladrigan puts it, back into exuberant and stimulating city life, to the social flurry and commotion of Talbot Street, O'Connell Street, Henry Street, Moore Street. So, every Friday and Saturday, Cabra residents queued up *en masse* to climb aboard buses headed "home" into town. Within minutes of entering the bustling world of street life, clanging tram bells, busy shops and lovely chatter and clamour all around them, their spirits soared. They visited old friends, shopkeepers, market dealers and, of course, St Agatha's and St Laurence O'Toole's churches. Men, naturally, made a beeline to their pubs, engaging in gregarious socialising with their old mates.

Weekly escapes back to the city were exhilarating, liberating. But it was only a temporary fix for homesickness. On the return trip back to Cabra the day-trippers were often solemn, knowing they were headed once again into the boredom and dullness of life on the western frontier.

Most new settlers had a first cheerless Christmas, wondering what the new year would bring. They greatly missed the joy of colourful past Christmases around the North Strand. Many, like Kathleen Martin, remember it as the saddest Christmas of their lives. Hers was particularly sorrowful. Her brother Seán, only sixteen, was an apprentice carpenter, hoping to bring in money to help his mother pay for rent and food. On 18 December he died of TB. "I always remember that Christmas, sitting at a horrible old fire with wet turf, hardly any fire. Sitting on ordinary chairs … being so miserable."

As the cold of winter set in, people put their army blankets to better use. By now they had received better blankets from the Red Cross and charitable organisations. A few people got the idea of taking their blankets to a tailor and having them made into coats, which were not stylish but very warm and durable. Within days it became the rage. Agnes Daly claims that tailors "made coats for *everybody*" in Cabra. When they went into the city their grey blanket-coats identified them as bomb refugees. Some wore their coats as a badge of pride in their survival, others felt a certain embarrassment. Many wore their distinctive grey coats for years, even decades.

By all accounts, the great majority of Cabra settlers were unhappy in the early years of their new life. "They were put out in Cabra, and it was *never the same*," says Maura O'Toole. Homesickness could become a serious malady, leading to depression. The most common saying was "They left their hearts back in the city." It was true, Pringle insists, "They *all* wanted to come back … they *always* wanted to get back." There were no counsellors to help them adjust to their new life. Instead, mothers congregated in their homes over tea to share feelings in what today would be called "support groups".

Some adapted better than others. For the elderly, set in their ways and the least mobile, it was especially difficult. "Some *never did* adjust," says Una Shaw. It was often said simply that they were "not themselves any more." They seemed to lose their spirit, their zest for life. Family members said that it "broke their heart," leaving a lasting sorrow. It happened to Ladrigan's mother:

> My mother, it *broke her heart*—it *really* did! She was a real Northstrander, her *whole life* was back there.
>
> A sadness … a *heartbreak*. And there was no counselling, nothing like that, in our time. She cried for a solid twelve months … the heartbreak. Oh, my mother cried … she never *stopped* crying, God love her.

There were those who did eventually make it back home to the city—one way or another. Usually they moved in with city relatives or got on the corporation's list for any type of dwelling. Some were even willing to give up their house in Cabra for a tenement room back in the city. Lily O'Connor's mother stuck it out for a while before giving up. "After two years of living in

Cabra we moved back to the city. 'I miss the friendliness of the city,' Mammy said."[3] As simple as that. Others waited until their damaged houses were repaired and were offered back to them; they grabbed it.

The majority, however, made it back home again one day by a different route: upon death. They had been given a solemn promise by their family that when they died they would be returned to St Agatha's or St Laurence O'Toole's church for their funeral and burial in Glasnevin, promises that were faithfully kept. In their advanced years the thought of "being brought home" again was a comfort to them. Una Shaw observes that it is still the tradition:

> When any of them died, they *always* came back to their church—and *still do!* Even today, people who have lived out there for sixty years and more, they *still* come back to get buried. That'll give you an idea of how their *heart* was there.

Most Cabra settlers stuck it out in the "wild west", more by necessity than choice, and gradually saw the quality of their life improve. Furniture was slowly acquired, home improvements made, path, railings and gardens added. Shops, pubs and cinemas eventually sprang up, and a nice church was built. With convenient local amenities and places in which to meet and socialise, people no longer felt as compelled to return to town, though many still continued to make regular trips back by bus to visit friends, do certain shopping, or visit their native church.

But as any Cabra pioneer will tell you, life was never again as good as it had been before 2:05 a.m. on 31 May 1941.

Chapter 28 ∾

THEORIES, MYSTERIES, AND MYTHS

It's always been a mystery to me—why?

(LOUIS ROBINSON, 81)

There was a lot of theories about it, about that pilot. One was that he got lost, that he was to blow up Belfast. Or the British were interfering with his system and it put him off track. And another said he was trying to blow up Amiens Street station. Every sort of theory.

(BERNADETTE PIERCE, 75)

Irish neutrality has thrown up many myths.

(ROBERT FISK, *Independent on Sunday*, 24 January 1999)

Really and truly, looking back, we didn't get any good explanation for what happened.

(MARY COOKE, 74)

Robert Fisk calls it "the great mystery of Irish neutrality in the Second World War."[1] Why did thirty or so German bombers invade Dublin air space at 12:02 on 31 May 1941, hover menacingly overhead for two hours and then drop four bombs on the neutral city, the last a devastating 500 pound landmine that wiped out the North Strand? There was no apparent reason for the heinous act, no comprehensible motive for the crime. It has remained an unsolved mystery for more than sixty-five years.

Over the past two-thirds of a century many fanciful and credible hypotheses have been expounded. From parlours and pubs to the Dáil chamber, the mystery has been debated and dissected. At first, many assumed that Eduard Hempel, the likable German Minister in Ireland, had some foreknowledge of the air raid, and that de Valera surely must have had some idea why the bombing was carried out. But all evidence is to the contrary. De Valera appeared "dumbfounded" on Whit Saturday morning as he stood looking blankly into the bomb crater. Hempel was described as being equally flummoxed, as he "seemed fully to share the pervading incomprehension as to how the attack could have occurred. When he was informed of it, he records feeling 'staggered'."[2] In fact, he "went straight to the Department of Foreign Affairs to ask its Secretary, Joseph Walshe, what had happened."[3] Apparently having no information from his own government, he "suspected the British had dropped the bombs to force Eire into the Second World War."[4]

Though newspapers covered the incident in great detail, they did not engage in speculating about motives behind it. This left it up to ordinary citizens to try to work it out for themselves. In the first days and weeks after the bombing, most explanations were uncomplicated, easy to grasp, based mostly on common sense and some wishful thinking. In subsequent months and years, as more information came to light, explanations became more complex. Of all the theories put forward over the years, five have stood the test of time. Each has its own merits and weaknesses:

1. Mistake or error
2. Pilot's anger over being fired upon
3. German retribution for breaches of neutrality
4. British plot to bring Ireland into the war
5. "Bending the beam"

(1) *Mistake or error*
This was the first and the most widespread assumption. The pilot had "made a mistake"—a human error. People *wanted* to accept this explanation. It was the most comforting; to think otherwise meant it had been intentional, meaning also that more bombings might occur. Bernadette Pierce recalls that in the days following the bombing her granny sat in their kitchen in Shamrock Terrace with a few women neighbours talking about the tragedy:

> In my house, and to the people around the neighbourhood, he *didn't mean* to do it! He didn't do it *intentionally*. And that was a source of consolation. People in them years, they were forgiving. They were kind of innocent, not bitter.
>
> My grandmother and her friends, I *always* remember them saying, "Well, you can *forgive* the man if he didn't know what he was doing … if he didn't *mean* to do it, and he was a young pilot." They felt, "Well, he had to live with it."

The most common explanation for the "mistake" was that it was due to navigational error, technical malfunction or geographical disorientation on the part of the German pilots. Perhaps tricky winds at higher altitudes had blown the planes off course. Perhaps they thought they were over a British city. Along Clonmore Terrace, Dermot Ring and his neighbours believed the pilots were "going astray … thought they were over Liverpool." At Summerhill, says Margaret Pringle, it "was a mistake, the pilot thought he was over the North." Chrissie Byrne and her crowd in North William Street were convinced that the pilot "thought they were over England—it was a *mistake.*"

Another slant on the "error" theory was that the pilot was jettisoning his bombs over what he thought was the Irish Sea. This was logical, as in fact it was a common practice of German pilots when they were running low on fuel or were being hotly pursued by RAF Spitfires. By unloading their heavy bomb cargo they saved fuel and gained speed and manoeuvrability. This practice had been witnessed many times by Air Defence Command observers over the past several months. In this instance, it was thought that something had apparently gone wrong. Again, most probably due to some type of navigational miscalculation. At least this was Alec King's early conclusion:

> My own reading of the matter was that he just jettisoned his bombs. That particular plane had been flying around Dublin for about an hour, and after a while the army anti-aircraft pinpointed him. He said, "Look, I've got to get back, the fuel is going down"—and he pulled the lever and that was it! Then he headed out to sea and on his route.

Gabriel Molony feels that he "jettisoned his bombs, and he didn't give a damn *where* he dropped them—just dropped it to get away." Most people who subscribed to this explanation, however, preferred to believe that the pilot thought he was over the Irish Sea.

One incontrovertible fact conflicts with the comfortable "mistake" idea: the planes were flying low over Dublin on a crystal-clear night. With no black-out, the city was brightly illuminated, and easily identifiable.

Before 31 May, other German bombings had also generally been accepted as unfortunate mistakes. These included the bombs in County Wexford in August 1940 that killed three women at the Campile Creamery, two bombs falling on Dún Laoghaire in December 1940, and then the bombings of 1–3 January that struck five counties, including those on Terenure and Donore Terrace in Dublin. All were taken as mishaps by many Irish people. Sceptics, however, argued that this was hardly likely. In January 1941 the *Irish Independent* had contended that "it is difficult to conceive that these happenings have been due to a series of mistakes."[5] Their strongest argument was that Dublin was so brightly illuminated that pilots *must have seen* that they were over neutral Ireland. As the *Irish Press* put it:

It is hardly conceivable that any experienced airman could mistake our soil for belligerent territory.

What can be the possible explanation?[6]

Shortly after the North Strand incident there was lively debate in the Dáil, during which all sorts of explanations were bandied about. The terms "accident" and "mistake" were heard over and over, finally prompting one member to assert bluntly his absolute incredulity at such a naïve notion:

Is it not true that a one-eyed imbecile could see the difference between our cities and the belligerent's cities if he wanted to see it; but we know that he damn well did not![7]

"Mistake, *indeed!*" scoffed other sceptics, agreeing that, despite any navigational malfunctions, simple visual observation on a radiant night over the lit-up city would have clearly identified their position.

Nonetheless, because it was such an easily understandable and comforting explanation, scores of Dubliners held fast to their belief that it had been "just a mistake."

(2) *Pilot's anger*

Equally logical to many was the idea that the pilot had dropped the bombs out of anger over being so heavily fired upon by Irish anti-aircraft gunners. German pilots making their customary flights over Dublin on their way towards British targets were accustomed to a few "polite" anti-aircraft bursts to remind them they were over neutral territory. This night the barrages were intense, with heavy shells used. As several German pilots were apparently clearing out over Collinstown they were met by a sharp volley of fire. The logs of Air Defence Command record that they had just reached Collinstown and "when engaged by the anti-aircraft battery there, [they] turned south again,"[8] heading back over the heart of Dublin. It was an obvious, sudden reaction, as one pilot sharply reversed his course.

What was the reason for such a reaction? Was the anti-aircraft fire too intense, too close? Had one of the planes been winged by a shell? Was the pilot acting out of anger? Dermot Ring says that around his part of the city, "the supposition was that the German planes were trying to get away ... and some people blame the anti-aircraft fire being too intense," prompting a strike back. Louis Robinson, who clearly observed the entire episode, agrees, "At the time we were saying that this popshooter must have aggravated the pilot." Captain A. A. Quigley, a member of the Air Corps at the time, similarly speculates, "Was it anger at the guns?"[9] Was it to teach the Irish gunners a lesson?

Questions arise. Normally, retaliation stemming from the emotion of anger is swift. Yet just the opposite had occurred. The "mystery" plane had circled above the city for half an hour before releasing the 500-pound bomb, during which time the pilot repeatedly swooped low and seemed to be scanning the landscape as if for a target. If he was acting out of anger, why would he have waited so long, taken such chances of being struck by anti-aircraft fire? Was he waiting for orders permitting such a bombing? But three bombs had already been dropped, half an hour before. Was higher authority required to drop the "big one"?

(3) *Retribution for breaches of neutrality*

The German Foreign Minister, Joachim von Ribbentrop, was specific and vehement regarding the Irish Government's policy of neutrality. He would honour it as long as the Irish *strictly* abided by the terms of complete non-involvement in the war. This meant absolutely no "taking sides" in the conflict, no interference or "meddling" of any sort. Von Ribbentrop was a man accustomed to having his orders followed to the letter.

Ireland failed to adhere to the rules of "staying out of it". Germany found out that Ireland was shipping cattle to Britain from the docks at Dundalk. Then, wooden crates of butter clearly carrying the stamp of Irish creameries were discovered by the Germans on the beaches of Dunkerque left by British troops. Providing food to the British, as they had long done, may have seemed natural enough to Irish people, but to the Germans it might be construed as assisting the enemy.

William Joyce, better known as "Lord Haw-Haw", was familiar to all Irish people. During the war they listened to his blustery broadcasts, though his rantings were mostly taken as entertainment. He used the radio waves as a channel through which German displeasure could be transmitted to Britain and Ireland. On occasion he would issue strong criticism, even warnings. Edward Flynn, later to become a colonel in the British army, recalls one particular broadcast he listened to when home from boarding-school in England in which Joyce issued an explicit warning:

> I remember hearing a broadcast by William Joyce in which he warned that Amiens Street railway station in Dublin might be bombed. I also remember Joyce complaining that the Irish were shipping cattle to Britain from the docks at Dundalk, and threatened it would be bombed if this continued.[10]

As Joyce was always full of bombast, de Valera and other Irish officials were not inclined to take his threats very seriously. It certainly did not deter them from continuing to ship provisions to Britain.

Then came the April blitzes of Belfast. Without hesitation, de Valera despatched fire engines, ambulances and medical supplies to the North. He did so on *three* separate occasions within a period of thirty days. Dublin also took in several thousand refugees from stricken Belfast, providing shelter, food, medical treatment and sanctuary. Some stayed for months. Rendering such help to British subjects was surely regarded as a breach of neutrality. De Valera had acted from his heart in what he regarded as a humanitarian act of assisting people in the North—which the Constitution of Ireland regards as part of Ireland—in time of terrible tragedy. Even Hempel later admitted that he fully understood the emotional and political reasons behind de Valera's act of humanity. As he told an Irish journalist, "it was a deed of sympathy for your people, your Irish people, and we fully understand what you felt. Your own people were in danger."[11] He too may have understood and felt genuine sympathy; but he didn't speak for Hitler.

Newspapers in Ireland, North and South, in Britain, Continental countries and the United States hailed the heroism of Irish firemen who dashed across the border to aid their fellow-humans. Press coverage was expansive and glowing, read by millions. Hitler and his command could not have been pleased, for it may have made Germany look soft on the rules of neutrality. Was it time to "teach the Irish a lesson" for meddling?

William Joyce apparently thought so, for shortly after Dublin's "interference" he made it the subject of several of his threatening broadcasts. Bernadette Pierce and her granny, along with thousands of other Irish people, listened to his angry words one evening as he clearly warned of retribution. "He'd be giving us *warnings*. He *said* that Dublin was going to be bombed ... because the Irish, though they were neutral, they *interfered!*" He specifically cited the sending of fire engines north and taking in Belfast refugees. There was no mistaking his words. He even predicted "that particularly Amiens Street station would be bombed." Irish listeners had heard him spouting angrily many times before; he didn't frighten them. His threats of German bombs falling on neutral Dublin were just more rabid rhetoric.

Following the bombing of the North Strand some six weeks later, many people immediately recalled his words of admonition and concluded that he had indeed prophesied a retaliatory strike. It hardly seemed like a coincidence. Proponents of this theory have held fast over the years. As Brian Barton contends in an article in *History Ireland*, "the 'accidental' bombing of Dublin's North Strand was probably in retaliation for fire-fighting assistance previously rendered in Belfast."[12] He concludes that it was "no accident ... but a deliberate attempt to intimidate the Southern Government."[13] It was more likely retribution for the *cumulative* breaches of neutrality carried out over nearly a year. If this retribution theory is correct, it is probable that the primary target was indeed Amiens Street Station, through which provisions had been sent north and refugees brought south into Dublin. The railway station is only a couple of streets from the North Strand. By night-flying standards, the pilot would have barely missed his target, the bomb skimming over the station and landing on the tram tracks in the centre of the North Strand. There has been further speculation that the first two smaller bombs may have been intended for the nearby Buckingham Street fire station, from which a number of firemen had come who assisted Belfast.

However, for years after the bombing the Germans continued to deny vehemently that it had been an intentional act. And no documentary evidence was found to prove that it was a planned attack.

(4) *British plot*

This was a particularly intriguing theory, a fanciful one on the surface. To proponents, however, it was backed by solid motives and feasibility. It has some of the elements of a good mystery: motives, scheming, subterfuge, trickery, credibility, and a cast that included Churchill and daring RAF pilots. It was taken seriously by a good many people, some "high-level officials". Eduard Hempel himself held to this explanation, at least at first.

It was no secret that Roosevelt and Churchill were displeased with de Valera for declaring his country neutral, safely "sitting on the fence," as the British put it, watching the conflict from afar. It was, after all, more than a battle for Britain's survival: it was a struggle for freedom throughout Europe, and beyond. That the Irish allegedly "played it safe" aroused the open ire of Churchill and Roosevelt.

Britain could well have used Irish land and naval bases, foodstuffs and manpower. It would have strengthened their position, as well as assuring it that Germany could not decide to grab the country for its own military and strategic purposes. Churchill particularly fumed over de Valera's refusal to allow the British to use the three "Treaty ports" of Cóbh, Castletown Bearhaven and Lough Swilly. British naval vessels needed those ports for refuelling, for taking on provisions and for protection from lurking German submarines. Their use, Churchill argued, could save the lives of British seamen. Nonetheless, de Valera steadfastly refused. To exacerbate matters, Churchill had the suspicion that "de Valera was secretly allowing German u-boats to refuel in the west of Ireland ports, and their crews to come ashore,"[14] a claim later to be proved false. Yet, Robert Fisk states, it caused Churchill to become "outraged" at de Valera's refusal to help the British at a time of such need.

From late 1940 there was speculation that Britain might try to lure—or provoke—the Irish into the conflict on its side. The motives were clear. There were various possible schemes through which this might be attempted. By the latter part of 1940 one particular rumour was circulating in Britain and Ireland, as well as in Germany and the United States, about a British plot of deception to draw Ireland into the war. In essence, Britain would drop a few bombs on Ireland, making it appear that the crime had been committed by Germany. The plan would be carried out by RAF pilots flying captured or reconstructed German planes, using German bombs. Britain presumably possessed the means by which to do this.

By the spring of 1941, as the war worsened, such rumours gained credibility. In fact the German government began openly suggesting that the British might be up to such a trick. Then, only three weeks before 31 May, a seemingly prescient statement was made in a German radio broadcast:

> A curious transmission over the German radio's English language service … commented on Britain's need for the Treaty Ports … concluding that "it is conceivable that, to gain their ends, the British intend to bomb Eire and then declare [that] this crime was committed by Germany.[15]

The timing and phrasing of this prediction—or warning—"seemed to carry some foreknowledge of the incident."[16] If not, it was surely a remarkable coincidence. Hempel, on the morning of 31 May, personally believed that the British had carried out the bombing in order to provoke the Irish into the war on their side. Others shared his conviction. Germany, too, intimated that the British might be culpable.

But most Irish people could not believe that Churchill would attempt such a deception, one that had been overtly speculated about—even predicted— months in advance. It was unimaginable that RAF pilots would be ordered to drop bombs in the heart of Dublin, a deed that would surely come to light after the war.

Furthermore, why would it take twenty to thirty "reconstructed" German bombers, which remained aloft over Dublin for hours, at the risk of being hit by anti-aircraft fire, to drop four bombs? To opponents, the "British plot" theory runs counter to logic. Yet it hung around in Dublin's pubs like stale smoke, brought up time and again by pub men anxious to stir up more debate.

(5) "Bending the beam"

The theory most commonly known as "bending the beam" has persisted for two-thirds of a century. The most complex, it gained credibility in the years following the bombing as more information was obtained about new German and British aerial navigation technology. Because it was based on solid scientific data, proponents embraced it with confidence.

In June 1940, Churchill was informed that Germany was developing a sophisticated navigation system called *Knickerbein* (crooked leg) to guide its bombers precisely to targets in darkness and bad visibility. This was alarming news, for it would give the Germans a significant advantage in the skies. The *Knickerbein* system relied upon transmitting radio navigation signals on intersecting lines. These directional beams came from three sites, in France, Norway and Spain. Calculating their position relative to these beams allowed pilots to unleash bombs accurately, regardless of darkness or inclement weather.

The British, determined to catch up with this technology, committed great resources and effort, making remarkable progress in a short time; and by the spring of 1941 they had not only matched but were improving on the German system. Talented British scientists also developed a counter-measure for disrupting the *Knickerbein* guidance system. This was done by "bending" the beam that directed German planes to their targets, so that the directional co-ordinates did not converge accurately. The consequences, Richard Hawkins confirms, could be grave:

> An aircraft so deprived was liable to make errors, possibly great errors, in trying to find its target.[17]

It could cause disorientation, confusion and frustration in Luftwaffe cockpits as crews struggled to regain their correct position. This meant they would have to slow their normal flight pattern or even "hang around" or wander over an area as they endeavoured to get their bearings by relying on conventional methods. When possible, they would try to visually identify landmarks, coastlines or the lights of a particular city—an imperfect process.

Early on, there was an important misconception, held by many, regarding Britain's successful "beam-bending" technology. This was the belief that, by distorting or curving the guidance signals and throwing German pilots off their designated course, they could also then be *redirected* towards a different target.

It is not known whether Irish military scientists in the spring of 1941 were well informed about British beam-bending technology. But it may well have been used in Northern Ireland early in May. On the night of 4/5 May during the Luftwaffe's last raid on Belfast, bomber crews were thrown into confusion, reporting "total interference with the radio navigation system."[18] The German pilots clearly attributed this to British interference with their *Knickerbein* directional system.

A more intriguing, and significant, incident occurred directly over Dublin on 28 May—only three days before the North Strand bombing. According to the Air and Marine Intelligence file for 28 May 1941, the Air Corps noted that about fifty planes flew across the south-east of Ireland just after midnight, heading northwards. The plotting map shows that the German bombers flew up the Wicklow coast, passed over Dalkey and proceeded towards Rush, County Dublin. Then something odd occurred. As some of the planes proceeded north, one turned around when it reached the border near Cootehill, County Cavan, while another was recorded by ground observers nearly eighty miles to the south at Mountmellick, County Laois. Then the "formations of aircraft ... suddenly divided up in confusion ... [and] disorientation of the pilots who flew in different directions," suggesting that the "land below them no longer matched their bomb-aimers maps."[19]

Shortly thereafter, flashes and explosions were spotted over the Irish Sea as German pilots jettisoned some of their bombs before finally fading away. This action, Robert Fisk concludes, suggests that it may have been "an air raid that was aborted at the last minute, perhaps when air crews realised they were over Ireland and not Britain."[20]

On 31 May, at 12:02 a.m., about thirty German bombers again appeared over Dublin, at first following their usual northerly route. Then, once again, they apparently became disoriented, falling into disarray and meandering over the skies above Dublin. Air Defence Command noted the striking similarity between the two incidents—but with tragically different results.

Following the bombing, few Dubliners knew anything about German and British scientific technology, and so this was not one of the early theories heard around the city. But senior Irish military officers and Government officials knew enough about it to suspect that it may have played a role in the bombing tragedy. This was confirmed in a letter of 29 July from F. H. Boland, Assistant Secretary of the Department of External Affairs, to the Department of Defence, in which he stated:

It is thought possible something had gone wrong with their direction finding radio system.[21]

It was later learnt that on the night of 30/31 May there was widespread German bombing of Cardiff, Newport, Bristol and Merseyside. Belfast may originally been a target as well.

This raised a grave question. Had the British not only bent the German guidance beams, steering them away—at least temporarily—from British targets but also redirected the bombers over Dublin? At least some suspected so. According to Colonel Doyle, "it has been claimed ... that the beam was deliberately bent to cover Dublin ... [that] some crews, given the wrong coordinates, mistook Dublin for Belfast."[22]

Throughout the war years, as more information leaked out about navigation technology, there was increased talk of the possibility of this having happened. At the time, this was thought to be scientifically feasible. However, as Duggan affirms, such technology had not yet, in fact, been developed. "The British had discovered a method of deflecting the beams guiding bombers ... this method, however, hardly had the precision to deflect the plane to a specific target."[23] The knowledge that the British did not possess this capability came out only near the end of the war in 1945.

The British may indeed have used their counter-technology to interfere with the German *Knickerbein* system on 31 May. This would probably have caused the apparent disorientation and confusion of pilots as described by observers. However, it would not have accounted for the bombing itself. As the night was clear and Dublin well illuminated, pilots should have been able to easily identify it as the neutral Irish capital—especially after hovering overhead for hours, even skimming low over rooftops. Yet they dropped four bombs over a thirty-minute span. How could this have been attributed to fouled *Knickerbein* navigation?

Nonetheless, after the war Churchill expressed his personal belief that the bombing of Dublin had simply been an "unforeseeable result of British interference with the radio beams used by the Luftwaffe bombers to find their targets in Britain."[24] Hempel eventually subscribed to this explanation too, though he continued to believe that the British had the scientific capability of directing the bombing of Dublin.

So, too, did many Irish people. By the end of the war the story about the British bending German beams and deliberately sending the pilots over Dublin was embedded in many people's minds. Like so much myth, it endured over the years, contrary to all fact. Many of the "old crowd" of survivors believe it to the present day.

———

For more than half a century after the war, no new information emerged. People had formed their opinions, selected their explanations, and held to them. The incident passed into distant history.

Then, just as the century was drawing to a close, two stories broke, ostensibly shedding new light on the mystery of the German bombing of Dublin. In 1997 and 1998, newspapers, radio and television gave coverage to new claims and "revelations" about the incident, stirring renewed public interest. Many Irish people had long forgotten about the tragedy, while the younger generation had barely heard of it. Like exhuming a cold-case file from an old police archive, the new claims raised hopes that the mystery might finally be solved. Plenty of people still wanted to know—*why?*

In 1997, Leo Sheridan, an Irishman living in France and identifying himself as an aviation investigator, claimed that he had discovered new information about the bombing. According to the *Irish Times*, "he claims he had uncovered evidence which strongly suggests that the May 1941 German bombing of the North Strand was not accidental."[25] He said he had been researching archival material in a Munich army base and "discovered that the raid, code-named 'Operation Roman Helmet', was aimed at intimidating the government after a number of neutrality breaches."[26]

He further contended that the bombing had been directed at Dublin Fire Brigade stations that had assisted Belfast, presumably those at Tara Street, Buckingham Street and Dorset Street. The intention was also, he said, to bomb Áras an Uachtaráin, President Douglas Hyde being the principal target, because he was a Protestant and perceived by German Intelligence to have "sympathies with Northern Ireland." He summed up his revelations by explaining that when British newspapers praised Southern firefighters for assisting Belfast, "German Intelligence saw this as a sign of weakness—they wanted to teach the Irish a lesson."[27]

He made two other statements, and these cast serious doubts on his credibility. Firstly, he claimed that one bomb, supposedly intended to strike Dorset Street fire station, had "landed in the Liffey." Secondly, he stated that it was "unclear whether the bomb dropped at the Phoenix Park exploded or not."[28] The first statement is completely contradicted by the empirical evidence; and his uncertainty about whether or not the Phoenix Park bomb exploded seems incomprehensible.

Sheridan couldn't provide any proof of his discovery in the Munich archives: no hard evidence or photocopies verifying the documents' existence. His story about "Operation Roman Helmet" had a dramatic flair, but his claims were unsubstantiated, and his statements about the bomb falling into the Liffey and uncertainty over the Phoenix Park explosion seriously undermined his credibility.

One year later, in 1998, "Heinrich" materialised from the mists of the past. From an undisclosed location in Canada an eighty-year-old man gave an interview to RTE, calling himself only "Heinrich", claiming that he was one of the German pilots on 31 May 1941. Their intended target, he claimed, was Belfast, but a mistake was made and Dublin bombed instead. This was due, he alleged, either to a problem with the plane's navigational guidance system or because the "weather was so bad" that night."[29] The RTE interviewer described him as extremely wary, unwilling to provide any evidence to document his story. Without even a last name, it was not possible to trace his identity in German military records and to verify his claim of having been a Luftwaffe pilot on that date.

His claim of bad weather on 31 May was, of course, completely incorrect. And his contention that the German target was Belfast raises the question why the planes, when they finally left Dublin, did not proceed north and strike that city. Instead, several cities in Britain were bombed that night.

And why did he wait fifty-seven years to come forward with his story? There was no Gestapo around to haul him in for his talking publicly. In essence, "Heinrich" was an unidentified voice on the radio, of no value as historical evidence.

If anything, the emergence of these two men further muddled the mystery, for they told completely opposite stories, one claiming that he had found a German archival document proving that the bombing was intentional and planned, the other claiming to have been a Luftwaffe pilot on the scene and stating that the incident was an unfortunate mistake.

Around the north inner city, old beliefs die hard. After some sixty-seven years, people have heard all the stories and claims. Those like Sally Burke, Colleen Heeney, Maura O'Toole and many other "old-timers" stick to their original belief: "it was all a mistake." That's all they feel they need to know.

Two-thirds of a century after the tragedy, Una Shaw sits in the kitchen of her home in Rutland Street, which was damaged by the bomb back in 1941, pensively sipping tea as she recalls how the whole event unfolded, from the first sounds of the German bombers, the searchlights, anti-aircraft fire, the menacing manoeuvres of the "mystery plane", then the screaming of the bomb and its thunderous explosion, all the way through to the funerals. All she fails to understand is "why?" "To this day, no-one has *ever* given it a logical reason."

Noelle Dowling, in *Mud Island*, a general history of the North Strand and Ballybough, concluded that "the whole question of why the bombings occurred is still debatable."[30] At the end of the century, in December 1999, Colonel E. D. Doyle wrote a most lucid article about the North Strand bombing in the *Irish Times* in an attempt to place the incident in historical perspective. His conclusion is probably the most valid:

Whatever the truth … it is unlikely ever to come to light.[31]

Chapter 29 ∾

| IN YEARS THEREAFTER

In the eyes of de Valera and perhaps the public at large, the bombing was a political and defence issue, as opposed to the destruction of a community.

(NOELLE DOWLING, Mud Island)

It was sad, because it left a vacancy that nothing *and* nobody *will ever fill … there's an emptiness … the people, the* whole lot, gone*! An emptiness that'll never be filled.*

(JENNY O'BRIEN, 75)

1942

When the 1942 Whit weekend rolled around, the *Irish Times* lamented about Dublin not that it was frightening, but that it was frightfully *boring*:

Anybody who spent Whit in Dublin would have found it difficult to detect any indications of excitement.[1]

It was memorable for being uneventful. Nobody was complaining. As usual, throngs departed for day trips to the seaside or the country, while others made longer excursions to resort areas. People who stayed at home were reflective about the events of one year ago. Dublin was quiet. It seemed fitting.

On the first anniversary of the bombing various commemorative events were held. Memorial Masses took place at St Agatha's and St Laurence O'Toole's churches. Both were filled to the doors. As memories cascaded through people's minds, some sobbing was heard. Following the Masses there was a large parade comprising members of all the rescue services that had participated. More than five thousand marchers wended their way past the North Strand, now barren wasteland. It was cleared but with no signs of renewal. The crisp white uniforms of the Red Cross nurses gliding past the backdrop of the bleak, tortured terrain only accentuated the deadness of the site.

The parade proceeded to the Central Model School in Marlborough Street, where the salute was taken by Seán Moylan, Parliamentary Secretary to the

Minister for Defence. The large crowd gathered around to hear his words:

> On exactly this day a year ago, a number of citizens were hurled into
> eternity, and a larger number received injuries, the marks of which they
> will carry all their lives.[2]

Before him stood victims hobbled, missing limbs and eyes. Moylan expressed
his sympathy to the bereaved relatives and to the injured. Trying to end on a
bright note, he said: "If there was a silver lining to the cloud which hung over
the North Strand it was displayed in the courage and efficiency" of the rescue
services.[3]

Over the Whit weekend there was a smaller but more lovely
commemoration that went unreported in the press. It might well have been
called the "children's procession and Mass", for it comprised girls and boys
from local parishes. Begun by parish priests, it included no uniformed
marchers, officials or speeches. Its poignancy was its simplicity. Columns of
young children, the girls in white dresses and veils, raised their voices in song.
It was to become an annual event. Every year, Mary Cooke looked forward to
participating:

> I remember it so well. *Every year* on the anniversary of that bombing we
> went as children. There would have been a couple of hundred children.
> They came from *far and wide* to the Mass on that day. It was held on the
> very site, on the ground where they had cleared away the rubble.
>
> All the children would dress up in white dresses, and some of us would
> have our Communion veils on, 'cause it was May, you see, and children
> would have just made their first Holy Communion. But if you hadn't got
> the gear you could still walk in the procession. All of us children would
> head for the North Strand in procession, singing hymns, and then the
> Mass was held there.

To those watching, the children, dressed in white, voices joined in song on the
very ground where the horror had occurred, was a moving sight.

————

Some ten weeks before, on St Patrick's Day, there had been another hopeful
sign, of a different sort. On a soccer field in Belfast a spirited friendly match
took place between a Northern team and a Southern one, followed by hearty
handshakes, slaps on the back, laughter and hours of camaraderie over pints

at the local pub. They were all firemen.

This unlikely event had blossomed from the ruins of the Belfast blitz in April 1941, when firefighters from the South and the North had bonded in a special way. To maintain their friendship, Belfast firemen invited their Dublin colleagues to come up for a soccer match. The Dublin men thought it a grand idea. There was only one problem, recalls Paddy Walsh, who was twenty-six at the time and in prime physical form: "They all played soccer up there—but we played *Gaelic* football." Nonetheless, they accepted the challenge. "Oh, we took it *very seriously*. We got a team together, and we *trained*. It was the first time I played soccer." Fortunately, a few of the lads had played the game before, and they taught others the essentials.

The invitation was for a three-day visit which required the team to get from the Dublin Fire Brigade Major J. J. Comerford's permission to be away that long, as the war was still on. They were quite unprepared for the lavish treatment they received, recalls Walsh:

Now *they* were all Protestants, and *we* were all Catholics. And we attended Mass up there on St Patrick's Day—and they arranged for the cardinal to give that Mass. And to *meet* us after the Mass and have a chat. And in the billets where we were staying they had a holy water font—they arranged *that*. It made me feel different ... about them. There was a *bond* between us.

On the field, however, there was fierce competition. Both sides were quite determined to win. "They beat us by one goal. I acquitted myself fairly well— we *all* did." As far as he can recall, apart from the soccer match it was all socialising between the two groups. "We had a great set-up there for three days. Oh, the pints ... we didn't *see* for three days!" The experience was so successful that it was mutually decided to make it an annual event, playing alternate years in Belfast and Dublin.

1943

One morning in 1943—he can't remember which month—Alec King reached into his post box and withdrew a handful of envelopes. One, he noticed, had a slight bulge in it. He sat down, put the others aside, and opened it first. Out of curiosity.

As he removed the contents he felt something metallic. It turned out to be a medal, along with a letter from the Department of Defence. Not personally written to him, but a standardised printed form. He read the words on the paper, "something about 'gratitude for service rendered on 31 May 1941.'"

He sat back in his chair and fingered the medal, turning it over several times, feeling its weight. Then he held it in his open hands—the same ones with which he had held the woman's severed head—and just stared at it for a while. How long, he doesn't recall. But long enough to take him back to 2:05 a.m. on that Whit Saturday morning. A stream of vivid recollections swept him through his sixty unbroken hours of rescue work amid the devastation, smoke, cries for help. He thought of how courageously the men in his rescue squad had carried out their duty, often at great personal risk. What a beating their bodies and emotions took! Then he placed the medal on top of the letter and sat silently for several more minutes. Neither had much meaning to him. In fact, they left him feeling empty. Some fifty-three years later he confided:

> That's the only thing I have to show for it, a bit of an old medal—they sent it out to me, the Department of Defence. Got that years later. No ceremony at all—just *sent out* to me.

Why, he wondered, could the Government not have gathered the eighty men under his command—as well as all the other dedicated rescuers—and personally handed their medals to them? With a handshake, and simple "Thanks", or "Job well done!" *That* would have given the medal some real meaning.

1945

On Tuesday 8 May 1945, the bold headline in the *Irish Independent* gave Dubliners an assurance that the coming Whit weekend would be a joyful one:

SURRENDER BY GERMANY

People were jubilant. When the news broke they burst forth from their homes, shops, offices, spilling out into the streets of the city to celebrate, shouting, singing, crying. The *Irish Times* wrote:

> Dubliners' reaction to the stoppage of hostilities found expression in the parading of the principal streets by thousands of people, who felt relief from the five years' strain too much to keep them in their normal occupations and recreations. Main thoroughfares were thronged.[4]

Once again, Garda Finucane was on crowd control duty, this time in the midst of unbridled happy emotions. But there was no need to "control" the crowd. People, he felt, were entitled to "let loose" in their own ways. He watched them cheering, whistling, hugging one another, prancing about like children. And he shared every emotion they were feeling:

It was a scene of joy everywhere; *everybody* was delighted. They prayed, especially women, saying "*Thank God* it's over! Now we'll be able to get a bit of coal, tea, candle, sugar." It was a weight taken off their shoulders.

Northsiders were particularly happy and relieved. Finally, no more fear of engine drones in the night, whistling bombs, almighty explosions. To them, peace was personal.

Scores of Dubliners headed for churches to give thanks for bringing them through the war safely. All Irish people, wrote the *Irish Times* in its editorial, should praise the Lord for their survival:

> Europe's war is over. In this tremendous moment the first impulse of all civilized people must be to render thanks to the Almighty. We, in this little island, owe a particular debt to Providence.[5]

The *Irish Independent* provided an extensive recounting of wartime events from 1939 to 1945, covering major campaigns and battles in several continents, in the air, on land, and at sea. The conflict had lasted for 2,094 days, or 526 days longer than the First World War of 1914–18. Of the more than two thousand days of warfare, Dubliners had known but one day of destruction and death. In its expansive coverage of the entire war the newspaper simply wrote of Ireland's tragedy, "May 31, 1941 was the date of the big bombing in Dublin."

Several weeks later another Whit holiday arrived. It was a delight, with plenty of sunshine and everyone in high spirits. Dubliners were drawn outdoors to enjoy all the usual holiday activities. Over the Whit weekend the *Irish Times* published a small item possibly missed by many busy, carefree Dubliners, but it must have given pause to those who saw it:

> Dr. Theodore Morrell, Hitler's personal physician since 1936, described Hitler as a "psychological phenomenon that happens once in 1,000 years."[6]

1954

On 10 December 1954, a headline in the *Irish Independent* was hauntingly reminiscent to Dubliners:

EVACUEES DESCRIBE NIGHT OF TERROR

"Terror-stricken residents called for help ... hundreds flee," wrote the paper. This time the disaster was caused by nature. It would become known as the "great Dublin flood" of 8–10 December 1954.

The parts of Dublin hardest hit by the natural calamity were the North Strand and Ballybough. For the second time in thirteen years, Northstranders found themselves struggling for survival. Exceptionally heavy rain for several consecutive days had swollen rivers and left the ground sodden. The North Strand area provided a natural catch-basin for the overflow of water, as described by the *Irish Independent*:

> A state of emergency was declared in the North Strand, Fairview and Ballybough areas … where firemen and soldiers used boats to rescue people from their flooded homes … houses were flooded to a depth of from eight to ten feet. Terror-stricken residents called for help as they saw the waters swirling through the ground floor of their houses.[7]

People tried to swim to safety, to grab hold of rescue boats, or to cling to higher floors and roofs. A 75-year-old woman living in St Brigid's Cottages had come through the German bombing in 1941 when she was sixty-two. But her hearing had since failed and she was now nearly deaf, and "she did not hear rescuers knocking at her door as the waters rose."[8] She didn't make it through her second tragedy.

In the wake of the great flood, Northstranders who had survived the German bombing found it hard to believe that they had been struck a second time. Once again, they stoically went about putting their lives back together. As before, sympathy and support from other Dubliners flowed in to help their recovery.

1958

Finally, in 1958, seventeen years after the bombing of Dublin, the Germans accepted responsibility—without admitting guilt—and paid the Irish Government £327,000, against a total claim of £481,878. Victims had been promised by the Government fair compensation for their loss of home and possessions. Many testify that, apart from the army blankets and mattresses, they received a measly £10 to £12, at most, as reimbursement for lost furniture and personal possessions. They resented it then and they still resented it more than sixty years later. It was seen as a broken promise, an injustice. They had suffered enough without being mistreated by their own government—that's the way they saw it.

1960

The 1960s were a decade of unprecedented economic growth, building development and rising prosperity among the middle and upper classes in Dublin. As the city's wealthier areas flourished, the working-class inner city essentially stagnated.

Affluent Dubliners in shiny new cars heading towards the airport or elsewhere often passed by a depressing patch of wasteland beside a charming stone bridge over the Royal Canal, now contaminated with filth and debris. Younger passengers sometimes asked, "What's that ugly littered ground over there?" To which those over the age of forty replied, "Oh, that's where the German bomb fell back in 1941." German bomb?

A full generation after the tragedy, a large swath of the North Strand still stood blatantly derelict, forgotten by the authorities. To local people the barren, scarred ground was a constant reminder of official neglect. "Years later, England, after the blitz, was all built up again," says Winnie Brennan, "and we couldn't *believe* it, 'cause the North Strand was *still* in rubble, still a bomb site." Members of the Traveller community would regularly park their caravans there as part of their nomadic life, with open fires and scrap heaps, sometimes leaving behind unsightly rubbish. In the light of the visible progress in more affluent areas, inner-city residents could not help but feel resentful that it had been left so despoiled, neglected. Of the Government, people said, "They just don't give a damn!" The site stood out, year after year, as a symbol of past tragedy and glaring negligence:

> Up to the end of the Sixties a vast vacant space on either side of the North Strand Road was a remaining reminder of the awful events that visited the area.[9]

After nearly thirty years, Dublin Corporation finally decided to build some flats on part of the site. Stark and sterile, they looked like high-rise barracks, architecturally incompatible with the older surrounding Georgian and Victorian buildings. They were occupied by people from beyond the area, who had no interest in the North Strand's rich historical past. Mary Dunne explains: "We welcomed them in, but they weren't *belonging* to the area, they weren't really part of the *old stock* … It wasn't the same." Soon afterwards, juvenile crime, such as theft and vandalism, arose. To native Northstranders it changed the character of the area. A sad irony resulted when some transplanted Cabra residents who had long hoped to "return home" finally had an opportunity to do so but declined, because they no longer felt they would fit in, or be safe, in the new North Strand life.

1971
The annual soccer match between Belfast and Dublin firemen had been held for nearly a third of a century. "We played right through the war, 1942, 43, 44, 45," Tom Geraghty writes, "and that lasted up to 1971. Then times changed."

The armed conflict in the North erupted in the late sixties. Prejudice deepened as violence broke out. Firemen were not immune to political and religious feelings. This was manifested on the soccer field during the 1970 match, when there were some tensions and angry exchanges. Original players, such as Paddy Walsh, Jack Conroy and Paddy Finlay, who had established the tradition in 1942, were now in their fifties. The younger firemen on the two teams were of a different generation. They cared little about the history of it. They were shaped by events of their day.

The 1971 match doomed the tradition. "That match turned into a free-for-all because of all the problems of the North and civil unrest," Tom Geraghty comments, "all that boiled over onto the football field. Unfortunately." It was the last of the annual contests. "Old-timers" from both sides who had been friends for three decades were saddened. A few of the men, including Paddy Walsh, kept up their relationship through letter-writing. At eighty-eight, with pride and nostalgia, he reveals, "I still have a programme of the 1944 match."

1991

The fiftieth anniversary of the bombing was approaching. Half a century had passed, and no memorial had been erected to mark the event and honour the victims. In 1989 local citizens had begun a grassroots effort to raise funds and seek resources for a memorial plaque and "Garden of Remembrance". They were proud citizens, and they would succeed where the Government had failed. They would look after their own.

With the help of Landlife, an environmental group specialising in landscaping derelict city sites, they began salvaging cobblestones, railings and granite from around the city to create a memorial garden. They succeeded in securing the site of number 164 North Strand, one of the houses destroyed by the bomb, only a few feet from the crater. The memorial garden was to be a place of rest and reflection for local people and visitors.

On 31 May 1991, the anniversary began with Mass at St Agatha's Church. The ornate stained-glass windows blown out by the blast had long ago been replaced by new ones, plain by comparison. The altar had been renovated, and there were other cosmetic changes. But the setting looked essentially the same as it had fifty years earlier. Slowly, the pews filled with mostly grey-haired men and women, survivors of "that night". Once seated, they glanced around, nodding and smiling to others in recognition. Then they fell into reflection, visualising the funeral Mass and the coffins those many years ago. Some perhaps found themselves thinking about young Noel Fitzpatrick, who would now be eighty-two, wondering if he would have achieved stardom on the Dublin stage.

The memorial ceremony was held in the Garden of Remembrance at 2:30

in the afternoon. As they filed through the small gate, participants praised the charm of the garden with its lovely landscaping and comfortable benches. Some people found themselves gazing across the railing out onto North Strand Road, trying to pinpoint the spot where the bomb had struck. Sleek new cars were whizzing past. How many motorists realised they were driving directly over the site of a terrible wartime tragedy? Would they care?

The small Garden of Remembrance quickly filled. Other people stood outside looking in. Michael Donnelly, Lord Mayor of Dublin, had the honour of unveiling the granite monument. It was an imposing seven-foot high tablet of granite from Walshe's quarry in Sandyford, carved by Broe and Sons, the well-known Dublin stone sculptors. People gathered around closely as the granite tablet was unveiled to applause and smiles. Its inscription was brief and simple:

IN MEMORY OF ALL WHO LOST THEIR LIVES IN THE BOMBING OF THE NORTH STRAND ON MAY 31, 1941.

Then Donnelly said a few words:

Today's unveiling and dedication will serve to show the resilient nature of the human spirit, and the granite memorial will provide enduring witness to the consequences of war, even for the innocent. The North Strand bombing has left a mark on the city which remains until the present day.[10]

His next statement caught everyone's attention:

Thirty-seven people were killed—twenty-eight immediately; nine died later.[11]

People had always wondered about the final death toll. Alec King, in attendance, remained convinced that it was higher: "I still think there were people buried there that were reported missing and never found. Down underneath it all." Garda Senan Finucane agrees. Over the years he made it his business to carefully follow the number of deaths. In 1992 he gave a firm figure: "From that one bomb there were forty-one killed." He had documented each one, he asserted. And his figure did not include the three people killed at the Old Bride Street tenement collapse. Alec King would eventually place his final total closer to 45. This is probably an accurate figure. It will never be known for certain.

After the dedication ceremony, most people approached the granite monument to have a close look for themselves. Many wanted to reach out and touch it. Here, at last, was a solid testament to the tragedy that had so profoundly touched their lives, yet had been so easily forgotten by others.

That evening a reunion was held in the red-brick Charleville Mall Library, directly beside the Royal Canal, just down from Newcomen Bridge and the Lynches' cottage. As the guests, most between their late sixties and eighties, and some in their nineties, slowly made their way inside, many instantly recalled how they had scrambled down the stairs in terror that night to the safety of the basement. As the room filled, people greeted old friends not seen in ages. Survivors had been scattered all over Cabra, Crumlin, Kimmage, and Ballyfermot. Some had not seen one another since the very night of the bombing. The air in the library was suffused with remembrances, good stories, pure nostalgia. As Una Shaw recalls, "there were plenty of smiles ... and plenty of tears."

And there was still frustration over the silence of the air-raid sirens that could have saved lives; disappointment, and lingering anger, over poor treatment by the Government in new housing and furniture; and much criticism of the Government for not properly rebuilding the North Strand village so that life could be renewed there for its inhabitants. Some in the room grew teary talking about the Browne family and the Fitzpatricks, about Patrick and "baby William" McLoughlin, and the white coffins on that black rainy Thursday.

But there were mostly smiles and laughter. They could still joke about the "hat-box" air-raid shelters, smelly gas masks, bone-dry water tanks, or the long, lively debate over a black-out policy. Some were amused when talking of the folklore that had arisen from the bombing, how local children grew up with scary tales of "headless men" and zombies appearing in the night, stories of people still buried and calling out for help, of unexploded bombs embedded beneath the ground. Someone brought up "Heaven, Hell, and Purgatory"—what ever happened to the battling Byrne sisters? Or the strolling woman with the lovely operatic voice? Agnes Daly chimed in, "I heard that after the bombing she went to America, and became famous." It may well have been so.

Dick Eyres—still "Warden" Eyres to everyone—received much attention. He was, of course, asked once again to tell the story of how he found the wedding cake in the midst of bomb blight. Then he shared another little story, laced with irony. When asked how he was spending his retirement out in Cabra, he told those gathered around him that his favourite pastime was going out to the Phoenix Park to fly model planes. Among his favourites were the Spitfires, Lancasters, Messerchmidts—and especially the German Dornier and Heinkel bombers.

Conversation occasionally turned serious, especially about the failure to restore the North Strand to its original architectural character. The consensus was that this surely would have been done in an affluent community. Everyone agreed that the Government had failed to comprehend the loss of a *community*, a traditional way of life. As Noelle Dowling contends, "in the eyes of de Valera" and apparently other Government authorities, and the general public, the bombing was basically "a defence and political issue" rather than the destruction of an irreplaceable community.[12]

To the victims and other local people, however, it was a profound human tragedy. As Jenny O'Brien expresses it, the loss of the little village "left a vacancy that *nothing* and *nobody* will ever fill ... *gone!*"

Towards the end of the evening another disquieting subject arose. Why had no book been written about the 1941 bombing? Rory Farrelly, who lives a few houses down from the library, said people were still seeking what he calls the "real story" of what happened back then. Fifty years later, people knocked on his door at number 10 Charleville Mall, asking him about "my granny, my da" and other relatives who were killed. As one of the originals along the street, word somehow got out that he was a fella who knew all about it. He could never turn anyone away—but he hardly had all the information they were seeking. A *book* was needed. Everyone nodded. The *entire* story needed to be documented. Only the survivors themselves could provide the wealth of oral history needed. Each year their numbers were dwindling. Time was not on their side.

The evening had begun as a social gathering of old friends; it ended with a feeling of extended family. As goodbyes were being exchanged, people promised to keep in touch, hopefully have another reunion in a few years— possibly a fifty-fifth or sixtieth anniversary—to which a good many joked that they doubted they would be around for the next one. As they walked out into the fresh spring evening they heard the canal water gently cascading over the lock. Looking to their right they saw Newcomen Bridge and the Lynches' stone cottage, now at least two hundred years old—two enduring links with the past, both looking as they had before the bombing.

As they drifted apart, fading from the lamplight into the shadows of the night, heading home, they felt a pleasant sense of final closure.

The next day those who had attended picked up newspapers hoping to read something about their fiftieth anniversary ceremonies. They were disappointed. The *Irish Times* made no mention of it. The *Evening Herald* printed a brief article headed "Look Back To a Night of Fear for City," characterised by shoddy research and flawed writing. It claimed that that Dick Eyres and his wife had "dodged the bombs at Shamrock Terrace" and that four bombs fell on Dublin, "three on the North Strand, one in Terenure."[13] In fact *one* bomb had fallen on the North Strand, two others at the North Circular

Road and Summerhill, and another in the Phoenix Park. The Terenure bomb had fallen in January, five months earlier.

The *Irish Press* published an article entitled "Night of Hell on the North Strand," based mostly on the remembrances of Alec King. It had not bothered to despatch a reporter to cover the anniversary events; but at least it gave Alec King an opportunity to express his displeasure with the Government for failing to erect a monument bearing the names of the bomb victims:

> Fifty years on, the people of the North Strand still seek a monument bearing all the names of those killed. I see no reason why our Government should not give a helping hand in this endeavour. They bore their tragedy those many years ago with great dignity; that dignity, as well as the memory of those who perished should be remembered appropriately.

Once again, these were words that fell on deaf ears.

1995

In 1995, on the fiftieth anniversary of the ending of the Second World War, an unexpected invitation arrived at the headquarters of Dublin Fire Brigade. It was not addressed to the chief fire officer (as the superintendent is now called) but to those survivors who had dashed north to assist blazing Belfast in April 1941. Only four of the men who had made the perilous journey that night were still alive.

The invitation was not to attend some commemorative function marking the end of the war but a personal one to attend a gathering at Hillsborough Castle in County Down and to meet Prince Charles. Three of the surviving men declined the invitation but the fourth, Tom Coleman, made the trip on behalf of all the other men to receive a formal "recognition for his colleagues' solidarity at such a critical time" in history.[15] What a shame, he must have thought, that all the lads could not have gone together to be so honoured.

2001

A new century had dawned. To most Dubliners, 1941 was now ancient history. There was no sixtieth anniversary of the event, as most survivors had realistically known. Nor had any book been written.

However, Alec King and his supporters had successfully raised the funds for a granite memorial, with all the names of the victims inscribed for posterity. It stood beneath a shaded tree in a peaceful corner of the Garden of Remembrance on North Strand Road.

To mark the anniversary, the municipal library in Pearse Street opened its archives on the subject, which had been inaccessible for nearly two-thirds of a century. Only a few years earlier the records in the Military Archives were declassified and made available to the public, some of which had been labelled "secret" for nearly six decades.

A little-known but fascinating historical object had found its unlikely way into the desk drawer of Pat O'Connor, librarian at Charleville Mall Library. It was the most authentic, tangible relic imaginable: a ten-inch-long metallic piece of the 500-pound bomb itself. Originally embedded in the crater, the fragment came to "live in a box in my desk," as Pat O'Connor likes to tell it. "It was rescued from an Office of Public Works clear-out by a historical-minded civil servant," she explains, "when he took a job abroad, he gave us the piece of the bomb, along with a letter detailing its provenance." Curious visitors are allowed to look at, even hold, the fragment, always expressing surprise at how cold and how heavy it is. Some have suggested that it should be placed in a museum. But local people feel it should remain exactly where it is, only about seventy yards from where it fell at 2:05 a.m. on 31 May 1941—on Whit Saturday. It, too, is a survivor.

The year 2001 saw an event an ocean away that vividly brought to the mind of survivors their own horrifying experience. They watched on television the terrorist attack of 11 September on the Twin Towers in New York. Seeing the devastation, the smoke, charred and fearful faces, rushing firefighters and ensuing panic brought back a flood of emotions. It positively gave Mary Cooke the chills. "I'm telling you, that 9/11 in America, it was on a scale like *that* for *us!* That people were murdered … and terrible devastation. *Really and truly*, it was, for us, equal to 9/11 in America." Others said the same.

May 2004

Another Whit weekend was approaching, the sixty-third anniversary of the German bombing of the North Strand. Every year at this time members of the Sancta Maria Ladies' Club in Cabra fell into natural reminiscence about what they all went through that night. The club was founded in the 1990s by women who shared their roots and childhood around the North Strand area. "We all lived in North Strand, North Williams Street, Clarence Street, Synnott Street when we were kids," says Mary Dunne, "all had the same spirit of being good friends … all those years ago." Now in their seventies and eighties, they remained closely bound by their shared experience two-thirds of a century earlier.

Over tea and cake they talk of what each went through—their fear, homelessness, personal losses. Who died. How village life just vanished in one mighty sunburst. In today's frenetic world their mental images of life around the North Strand back in 1941 are more idyllic than ever before. The sadness of it never goes away. Mary Dunne says softly, "It still lives on in our hearts."

So long as it is *remembered*, avows Jenny O'Brien, it is not truly gone:

There will always be the memory of what that place was *before* it was hit by the bomb.

* * * * *

NOTES

Prologue (p. 1–12)
1. "Bombing Incidents, 31-5-41" (Military Archives, Dublin).
2. "Twenty-Five Killed by Bombs," *Sunday Independent*, 1 June 1941, p. 1.
3. "Night of Horror," *Evening Herald*, 31 May 1941, p. 1.
4. "Provisional Estimate of Dublin Casualties," *Evening Mail*, 31 May 1941, p. 3.
5. "The Bombing of the North Strand, Dublin, 31 May 1941," Civil Defence School, 6 December 1951, p. 71 (Military Archives, Dublin).
6. Correspondence from Dublin City Manager, P. J. Hernon, to Mr J. Hurson, Secretary of Department of Local Government and Public Health, 8 September 1941 (Military Archives, Dublin).
7. "The Dublin Bombing," *Irish Press*, 2 June 1941, p. 2.
8. "Bombs on Dublin," *Irish Independent*, 2 June 1941, p. 2.
9. Fisk, *In Time of War*, p. 434.
10. "Time of the Greatest Danger to Our Nation," *Sunday Independent*, 26 January 1941, p. 1.
11. "Ireland—Suburb of a City on Fire," *Irish Press*, 7 February 1941, p. 3.
12. "Impressive Scenes at Public Funeral," *Evening Mail*, 5 June 1941, p. 3.
13. Dowling and O'Reilly, *Mud Island*, p. 162.
14. Dowling and O'Reilly, *Mud Island*, p. 162.
15. Geraghty and Whitehead, *The Dublin Fire Brigade*, p. 225.
16. Cullen, *It's a Long Way from Penny Apples*, p. 13.
17. Gray, *The Lost Years*, p. 130.
18. Robert Fisk, "Why the Nazis Bombed Dublin," *Irish Independent on Sunday*, 24 January 1999, p. 13.

Chapter 1 (p. 13–30)
1. O'Keeffe, *Down Cobbled Streets*, p. 186.
2. Share, *The Emergency*, p. 2.
3. Share, *The Emergency*, p. 58.
4. Gray, *The Lost Years*, p. 6.
5. "Minister Wants to Destroy 'The Illusion of Security'," *Irish Press*, 1 July 1940, p. 3.
6. Gray, *The Lost Years*, p. 182.
7. Dukes, "The Emergency Services," p. 66–71.
8. Share, *The Emergency*, p. 58.
9. Share, *The Emergency*, p. 58.
10. Share, *The Emergency*, p. 58.
11. Doyle, *Rory and Ita*, p. 115.
12. Ryan, *Remembering How We Stood*, p. 7.
13. Matthews, "Powder and Ball Company, L.D.F.," p. 71.
14. Matthews, "Powder and Ball Company, L.D.F.," p. 71.
15. Share, *The Emergency*, p. 67.
16. Share, *The Emergency*, p. 45.
17. Doyle, *Rory and Ita*, p. 117.

18. Doyle, *Rory and Ita*, p. 117.

19. Gray, *The Lost Years*, p. 45.

20. "Dublin's Air-Raid Shelters," *Irish Press*, 8 January 1941, p. 1.

21. Share, *The Emergency*, p. 36.

22. Bracken, *Light of Other Days*, p. 110.

23. "Our Dumb Friends," *Evening Herald*, 1 January 1941, p. 8.

24. "The Smithy's Anvils are Busy Again," *Irish Press*, 18 February 1941, p. 1.

25. Ryan, *Remembering How We Stood*, p. 12.

26. "Bombs on Eire," *Irish Independent*, 4 January 1941, p. 4.

27. "New Swiss Protest," *Irish Independent*, 24 December 1940, p. 5.

28. "It was a Happy Ending Despite the War," *Irish Independent*, 24 December 1940, p. 5.

29. "It was a Happy Ending Despite the War," *Irish Independent*, 24 December 1940, p. 5.

30. "It was a Happy Ending Despite the War," *Irish Independent*, 24 December 1940, p. 5.

31. "It was a Happy Ending Despite the War," *Irish Independent*, 24 December 1940, p. 5.

32. "It was a Happy Ending Despite the War," *Irish Independent*, 24 December 1940, p. 5.

33. "A Happy Christmas to All Readers," *Irish Independent*, 24 December 1940, p. 4.

34. "The New Year Made Its Entry," *Irish Independent*, 1 January 1941, p. 5.

35. "How 1941 Was Welcomed," *Evening Herald*, 1 January 1941, p. 3.

36. "How 1941 Was Welcomed," *Evening Herald*, 1 January 1941, p. 3.

37. "Almost An Air of Normalcy in the Streets," *Evening Herald*, 1 January 1941, p. 1.

38. "Almost An Air of Normalcy in the Streets," *Evening Herald*, 1 January 1941, p. 3.

39. "War Due to Spiritual Malady," *Irish Independent*, 1 January 1941, p. 7.

40. "The New Year is Passing," *Irish Independent*, 3 December 1940, p. 4.

41. "Almost Silent Welcome in Dublin," *Evening Herald*, 1 January 1941, p.3

42. "The New Year Made Its Entry," *Irish Independent*, 1 January 1941, p. 5.

Chapter 2 (p. 31–42)

1. "1941 Year of Destiny—World's Future to be Decided," *Irish Times*, 1 January 1941, p. 5.

2. "Muffs Are 'In' Again," *Irish Independent*, 2 January 1941, p. 8.

3. "Three Bombs Dropped in Drogheda," *Irish Times*, 2 January 1941, p. 5.

4. "Three Bombs Dropped in Drogheda," *Irish Times*, 2 January 1941, p. 5.

5. "Women Die in Wrecked House," *Irish Independent*, 3 January 1941, p. 5.

6. "Women Die in Wrecked House," *Irish Independent*, 3 January 1941, p. 5.

7. "How Death Came to Sleeping Family," *Irish Press*, 3 January 1941, p. 1.

8. "Lone House Struck," *Irish Independent*, 4 January 1941, p. 6.

9. "Thrilling Rescue Scenes in Dublin Suburbs," *Irish Press*, 3 January 1941, p. 7.

10. "Lone House Struck," *Irish Independent*, 4 January 1941, p. 6.

11. "Bombs Dropped in Irish Counties," *Evening Herald*, 2 January 1941, p. 1.

12. "Residents Tell of Bombings," *Irish Times*, 3 January 1941, p. 6.

13. "Bombs Fall on Five Irish Counties," *Irish Times*, 3 January 1941, p. 5.

14. "Residents Tell of Bombings," *Irish Times*, 3 January 1941, p. 6.

15. "Thrilling Rescue Scenes in Dublin Suburbs," *Irish Press*, 3 January 1941, p. 7.

16. "Thrilling Rescue Scenes in Dublin Suburbs," *Irish Press*, 3 January 1941, p. 7.

17. "An Irishman's Diary," *Irish Times*, 3 January 1941, p. 4.

18. "An Irishman's Diary," *Irish Times*, 3 January 1941, p. 4.

19. "Series of Bombs Dropped," *Irish Times*, 3 January 1941, p. 5.

20. "Tragic Inquest Story," *Irish Independent*, 3 January 1941, p. 6.

21. "Rescues by A.R.P. Men," *Irish Times*, 4 January 1941, p. 6.

22. "Rescues by A.R.P. Men," *Irish Times*, 4 January 1941, p. 6.

23. "Freakish Effects of Bomb Blast," *Irish Press*, 4 January 1941, p. 7.

24. "Freakish Effects of Bomb Blast," *Irish Press*, 4 January 1941, p. 7.

25. "Vivid Stories of Bombing," *Evening Herald*, 3 January 1941, p. 1.

26. "Dublin Families' Ordeal—Agonising Scenes Follow Bombing Havoc," *Evening Herald*, 3 January 1941, p. 1.

27. "Dublin Families' Ordeal—Agonising Scenes Follow Bombing Havoc," *Evening Herald*, 3 January 1941, p. 1.

28. "Dublin Families' Ordeal—Agonising Scenes Follow Bombing Havoc," *Evening Herald*, 3 January 1941, p. 1.

29. "Bombs Fall on Five Irish Counties," *Irish Times*, 3 January 1941, p. 5.

Chapter 3 (p. 43–54)

1. "Surprise in New York," *Irish Times*, 4 January 1941, p. 5.

2. "The Irish in U.S. Make Protest," *Irish Press*, 6 January 1941, p. 7.

3. "A Statement in Berlin," *Irish Independent*, 4 January 1941, p. 6.

4. "Bombs on Eire," *Irish Independent*, 4 January 1941, p. 4.

5. "The Bombings," *Irish Press*, 4 January 1941, p. 6.

6. "Dublin City Manager and A.R.P.," *Irish Press*, 6 January 1941, p. 7.

7. "Bomb Damage in Dublin," *Irish Times*, 4 January 1941, p. 4.

8. "Dublin May Have a Stricter Black-Out," *Sunday Independent*, 5 January 1941, p. 1.

9. "Air-Raid Precautions," *Irish Times*, 7 January 1941, p. 4.

10. "Air-Raid Precautions," *Irish Times*, 7 January 1941, p. 4.

11. "Air-Raid Precautions," *Irish Times*, 7 January 1941, p. 4.

12. "The Night Bomber," *Irish Independent*, 3 January 1941, p. 6.

13. "Well Done," *Irish Press*, 10 January 1941, p. 4.

14. "An Irishman's Diary," *Irish Times*, 5 June 1941, p. 5.

15. "Dublin to Have Big A.R.P. Test," *Irish Press*, 18 January 1941, p. 7.

16. "Dáil Tribute to Army Morale," *Irish Press*, 21 February 1941, p. 1.

17. "Time of the Greatest Danger to Our Nation," *Sunday Independent*, 26 January 1941, p. 1.

18. "Around the Theatres," *Irish Independent*, 4 January 1941, p. 6.

19. "North Had Its Snowstorm," *Sunday Independent*, 26 January 1941, p. 3.

20. "L.D.F. Manoeuvres in Dublin," *Irish Independent*, 3 February 1941, p. 5.

21. "City Manager on Dublin A.R.P. Plans," *Irish Press*, 4 February 1941, p. 5.

22. "City Manager on Dublin A.R.P. Plans," *Irish Press*, 4 February 1941, p. 5.

23. "City Manager on Dublin A.R.P. Plans," *Irish Press*, 4 February 1941, p. 5.

24. "A.R.P. For Animals," *Irish Times*, 14 March 1941, p. 4.

25. "Women's Protest," *Irish Independent*, 9 May 1941, p. 4.

26. "Women's Protest," *Irish Independent*, 9 May 1941, p. 4.

27. "Broadcasting in Ireland," *Sunday Independent*, 25 May 1941, p. 4.

28. "St. Patrick's Day Honoured Everywhere," *Irish Press*, 18 March 1941, p. 1.

29. "St. Patrick's Day Honoured Everywhere," *Irish Press*, 18 March 1941, p. 1.

Chapter 4 (p. 55–69)

1. "Dublin See 20,000 in Parade Spectacle," *Irish Independent*, 15 April 1941, p. 5.
2. Gray, *The Lost Years*, p. 118–19.
3. Gray, *The Lost Years*, p. 118.
4. Geraghty and Whitehead, *The Dublin Fire Brigade*, p. 225.
5. "Many Killed in Mass Air-Attack on Belfast," *Irish Independent*, 17 April 1941, p. 5.
6. Geraghty and Whitehead, *The Dublin Fire Brigade*, p. 226.
7. Geraghty and Whitehead, *The Dublin Fire Brigade*, p. 226.
8. Geraghty and Whitehead, *The Dublin Fire Brigade*, p. 229.
9. Geraghty and Whitehead, *The Dublin Fire Brigade*, p. 227.
10. Interview with Tom Geraghty, April 2004.
11. Duggan, *Herr Hempel at the German Legation in Dublin*, p. 134.
12. Fisk, *In Time of War*, p. 430.
13. Fisk, *In Time of War*, p. 430.
14. "A Terrible Beauty," *Irish Times*, 17 April 1941, p. 2.
15. "A Terrible Beauty," *Irish Times*, 17 April 1941, p. 2.
16. "Aid for the Homeless," *Irish Independent*, 18 April 1941, p. 4.
17. "Devastation and Mourning in Bombed City," *Irish Press*, 22 April 1941, p. 1.
18. "400 Bodies in Belfast Ruins," *Irish Press*, 19 April 1941, p. 1.
19. "400 Bodies in Belfast Ruins," *Irish Press*, 19 April 1941, p. 2.
20. "A Terrible Beauty," *Irish Times*, 17 April 1941, p. 2.
21. Geraghty and Whitehead, *The Dublin Fire Brigade*, p. 229.
22. "The Barbarous Bombs," *Irish Times*, 19 April 1941, p. 4.
23. "A Terrible Beauty," *Irish Times*, 17 April 1941, p. 2.
24. "The Barbarous Bombs," *Irish Times*, 19 April 1941, p. 4.
25. "Sympathy for Belfast," *Irish Independent*, 21 April 1941, p. 5.
26. "A Terrible Beauty," *Irish Times*, 17 April 1941, p. 2.
27. "An Irishman's Diary," *Irish Times*, 23 May 1941, p. 3.
28. "Our Readers' Views," *Irish Independent*, 3 May 1941, p. 6.
29. "Dublin's Bright Lights Gone," *Irish Independent*, 23 April 1941, p. 6.
30. "Hold What We Have," *Irish Independent*, 26 April 1941, p. 5.
31. "Hold What We Have," *Irish Independent*, 26 April 1941, p. 5.
32. "Hold What We Have," *Irish Independent*, 26 April 1941, p. 5.
33. "The Barbarous Bombs," *Irish Times*, 19 April 1941, p. 4.

Chapter 5 (p. 70–78)

1. Harold C. Brown, "Motoring—A New Army Machine," *Irish Times*, 24 May 1941, p. 9.
2. "Letters to the Editor," *Irish Times*, 4 June 1941, p. 6.
3. "Letters to the Editor," *Irish Times*, 4 June 1941, p. 6.
4. "An Irishman's Diary," *Irish Times*, 4 March 1941, p. 4.
5. Ryan, *Remembering How We Stood*, p. 15.
6. Share, *The Emergency*, p. 121.
7. "An Irishman's Diary," *Irish Times*, 23 May 1941, p. 3.
8. "Betting and Gambling," *Irish Times*, 28 May 1941, p. 2.
9. "Mobile Canteen for Dublin," *Irish Press*, 25 February 1941, p. 5.
10. Geraghty and Whitehead, *The Dublin Fire Brigade*, p. 230.

11. Geraghty and Whitehead, *The Dublin Fire Brigade*, p. 230.
12. Barton, *The Blitz*, p. 248.
13. "Irish Will Resist Any Attacker," *Irish Independent*, 5 May 1941, p. 6.
14. "Imaginary Air Raid on Dublin—A.R.P.'s Biggest Test," *Irish Times*, 26 May 1941, p. 5.
15. "H.M.S. Hood was Sunk in 'Million-to-One Chance'," *Irish Times*, 26 May 1941, p. 1.
16. "Bismarck Sunk After Chase of 2,000 Miles," *Irish Times*, 28 May 1941, p. 1.
17. "How Bismarck and Hood Sunk," *Irish Independent*, 31 May 1941, p. 5.
18. "Mr. Roosevelt on U.S. War Policy," *Irish Times*, 28 May 1941, p. 2.
19. Barton, *The Blitz*, p. 248.
20. "An Irishman's Diary," *Irish Times*, 29 April 1941, p. 4.
21. Fisk, *In Time of War*, p. 434.
22. Fisk, *In Time of War*, p. 434.

Chapter 6 (p. 79–86)
1. "Bombs German—Protest Being Made to Berlin," *Irish Press*, 2 June 1941, p. 1.
2. "Bombs German—Protest Being Made to Berlin," *Irish Press*, 2 June 1941, p. 1 p. 1.
3. O'Reilly, "From Dublin to Drumcooley," p. 19–21.

Chapter 7 (p. 87–96)
1. "Whit Railway Facilities," *Irish Independent*, 31 May 1941, p. 3.
2. "Entertainment at Bray," *Evening Mail*, 31 May 1941, p. 6.
3. "Comedy and Drama," *Irish Times*, 26 May 1941, p. 6.
4. "Olympia," *Irish Times*, 27 May 1941, p. 4.
5. "An Irishman's Diary," *Irish Times*, 30 May 1941, p. 5.
6. Gray, *The Lost Years*, p. 15.
7. "Roosevelt Sends Secret Plans to Churchill," *Irish Times*, 2 June 1941, p. 2.
8. "Crete Battle," *Irish Independent*, 31 May 1941, p. 5.
9. Hiney, "Personal Memories," p. 10.

Chapter 8 (p. 97–102)
1. "Bombing Incidents, 31-5-41" (Military Archives, Dublin).
2. O'Farrell, "The North Strand Bombing," p. 283–4.
3. Quigley, "The Day They Bombed Dublin."
4. "The Dublin Bombing," *Evening Mail*, 7 June 1941, p. 2.
5. "Bombing Incidents, 31-5-41" (Military Archives, Dublin).
6. "Bombs German—Protest Being Made to Berlin," *Irish Press*, 2 June 1941, p. 1.
7. "Twenty-Five Killed by Bombs," *Sunday Independent*, 1 June 1941, p. 1.
8. Barton, *The Blitz*, p. 247.
9. "Bodies Taken From House," *Evening Herald*, 31 May 1941, p. 3.
10. "Tour of the Bomb-Stricken Areas," *Irish Times*, 2 June 1941, p. 5.
11. O'Farrell, "The North Strand Bombing," p. 284.

Chapter 9 (p. 103–13)
1. "Gallant Rescue Scenes in Dublin," *Evening Mail*, 31 May 1941, p. 6.
2. "Bodies Taken From House," *Evening Herald*, 31 May 1941, p. 3.
3. "Bombs German—Protest Being Made to Berlin," *Irish Press*, 2 June 1941, p. 1.

4. "Bodies Taken From House," *Evening Herald*, 31 May 1941, p. 3.

5. "Tour of the Bomb-Stricken Areas," *Irish Times*, 2 June 1941, p. 5.

6. "Gallant Rescue Scenes in Dublin," *Evening Mail*, 31 May 1941, p. 6.

7. "Gallant Rescue Scenes in Dublin," *Evening Mail*, 31 May 1941, p. 6.

8. "Gallant Rescue Scenes in Dublin," *Evening Mail*, 31 May 1941, p. 6.

9. "Gallant Rescue Scenes in Dublin," *Evening Mail*, 31 May 1941, p. 6.

10. "Graphic Story of N.C.R. Bombing," *Irish Independent*, 31 May 1941, p. 1.

11. "Graphic Story of N.C.R. Bombing," *Irish Independent*, 31 May 1941, p. 1.

12. "Summerhill Scenes," *Irish Independent*, 31 May 1941, p. 1.

13. "North Strand Bombings," p. 46.

14. "North Strand Bombings," p. 46.

15. "Summerhill Scenes," *Irish Independent*, 31 May 1941, p. 1.

16. "Tour of the Bomb-Stricken Areas," *Irish Times*, 2 June 1941, p. 5.

17. "Tour of the Bomb-Stricken Areas," *Irish Times*, 2 June 1941, p. 5.

18. "Tour of the Bomb-Stricken Areas," *Irish Times*, 2 June 1941, p. 5.

19. "Tour of the Bomb-Stricken Areas," *Irish Times*, 2 June 1941, p. 5.

20. "Tour of the Bomb-Stricken Areas," *Irish Times*, 2 June 1941, p. 5.

21. "Two Family Tragedies," *Irish Independent*, 1 June 1941, p. 1.

22. "Two Family Tragedies," *Irish Independent*, 1 June 1941, p. 1.

23. "Elephant Toppled by Bomb Blast," *Irish Times*, 2 June 1941, p. 5.

24. "This Elephant Laughs at Locks!" *Irish Independent*, 2 June 1941, p. 3.

25. "This Elephant Laughs at Locks!" *Irish Independent*, 2 June 1941, p. 3.

26. "This Elephant Laughs at Locks!" *Irish Independent*, 2 June 1941, p. 3.

27. "This Elephant Laughs at Locks!" *Irish Independent*, 2 June 1941, p. 3.

28. "Elephant Toppled by Bomb Blast," *Irish Times*, 2 June 1941, p. 5.

29. Gray, *The Lost Years*, p. 125.

Chapter 10 (p. 114–18)

1. "Bombing Incidents, 31-5-41" (Military Archives, Dublin).

2. "Bombing Incidents, 31-5-41" (Military Archives, Dublin).

3. "Provisional Estimate of Dublin Casualties," *Evening Mail*, 31 May 1941, p. 3.

4. Quigley, "The Day They Bombed Dublin."

5. "North Strand Bombing," p. 46.

6. "Bombs on Dublin This Morning," *Irish Independent*, 31 May 1941, p. 5.

7. Fagan and Hiney, *Larriers*, p. 31.

8. "Search of Ruins at North Strand," *Evening Mail*, 2 June 1941, p. 3.

Chapter 11 (p. 119–28)

1. Gray, *The Lost Years*, p. 125.

2. Personal correspondence with Tony Gray, 1 April 2004.

3. Gray, *The Lost Years*, p. 125.

4. "Bodies Taken from House," *Evening Herald*, 31 May 1941, p. 3.

5. "Bombs in Dublin This Morning—Many Killed," *Irish Times*, 31 May 1941, p. 1.

6. "Bombs on Dublin This Morning," *Irish Independent*, 31 May 1941, p. 5.

7. O'Farrell, "The North Strand Bombing," p. 283–4.

8. Fagan and Savage, *All Around the Diamond*, p. 37.

9.   Fagan and Hiney, *Larriers*, p. 31.
10. "Bombs in Dublin This Morning—Many Killed," *Irish Times*, 31 May 1941, p. 1.
11. "Bombs in Dublin This Morning—Many Killed," *Irish Times*, 31 May 1941, p. 1.
12. "Bodies Taken from House," *Evening Herald*, 31 May 1941, p. 3.
13. "Bombs in Dublin This Morning—Many Killed," *Irish Times*, 31 May 1941, p. 1.
14. "Bodies Taken from House," *Evening Herald*, 31 May 1941, p. 3.
15. "Bodies Taken from House," *Evening Herald*, 31 May 1941, p. 3.
16. Quigley, "The Day They Bombed Dublin," p. 2.
17. "Detective Escapes," *Evening Herald*, 31 May 1941, p. 3.
18. "Bombs in Dublin This Morning—Many Killed," *Irish Times*, 31 May 1941, p. 5.
19. Barton, *The Blitz*, p. 106.
20. Barton, *The Blitz*, p. 106.
21. Barton, *The Blitz*, p. 106.
22. Barton, *The Blitz*, p. 106.
23. O'Farrell, "The North Strand Bombing," p. 284.
24. Barton, *The Blitz*, p. 117.
25. "North Strand Bombings," p. 47.
26. Department of Defence, "The Story of the Bombing of the North Strand," p. 71.
27. Fisk, *In Time of War*, p. 434.

Chapter 12 (p. 129–45)
1.   "Tour of the Bomb-Stricken Areas," *Irish Times*, 2 June 1941, p. 5.
2.   "An Irishman's Diary," *Irish Times*, 11 June 1941, p. 4.
3.   "Tour of the Bomb-Stricken Areas," *Irish Times*, 2 June 1941, p. 5.
4.   "Twenty-Five Killed by Bombs," *Sunday Independent*, 1 June 1941, p. 1.
5.   Department of Defence, "The Story of the Bombing of the North Strand," p. 71.
6.   "Bombs in Dublin This Morning—Many Killed," *Irish Times*, 31 May 1941, p. 1.
7.   "Bombs in Dublin This Morning—Many Killed," *Irish Times*, 31 May 1941, p. 1.
8.   O'Farrell, "The North Strand Bombing," p. 283.
9.   "Bombs on Dublin This Morning," *Irish Independent*, 31 May 1941, p. 5.
10. "Bodies Taken from House," *Evening Herald*, 31 May 1941, p. 3.
11. "Tour of the Bomb-Stricken Areas," *Irish Times*, 2 June 1941, p. 5.
12. "Tour of the Bomb-Stricken Areas," *Irish Times*, 2 June 1941, p. 5.
13. "Bombs German—Protest Being Made to Berlin," *Irish Press*, 2 June 1941, p. 1.
14. "Bombs German—Protest Being Made to Berlin," *Irish Press*, 2 June 1941, p. 1.
15. "Tour of the Bomb-Stricken Areas," *Irish Times*, 2 June 1941, p. 5.
16. "Tour of the Bomb-Stricken Areas," *Irish Times*, 2 June 1941, p. 5.
17. "Bombs in Dublin This Morning—Many Killed," *Irish Times*, 31 May 1941, p. 1.
18. Fagan and Savage, *All Around the Diamond*, p. 31.
19. Fagan and Savage, *All Around the Diamond*, p. 37.

Chapter 13 (p. 146–54)
1.   "Huge Crater—Houses Crash," *Irish Press*, 31 May 1941, p. 1.
2.   Geraghty and Whitehead, *The Dublin Fire Brigade*, p. 233.
3.   "North Strand Bombings," p. 47.
4.   "North Strand Bombings," p. 46.

5. "North Strand Bombings," p. 47.
6. Personal correspondence with Tony Gray, 1 April 2004.
7. Personal correspondence with Tony Gray, 1 April 2004.
8. Personal correspondence with Tony Gray, 30 April 2004.
9. "Scenes of Havoc," *Irish Independent*, 31 May 1941, p. 5.
10. "Bombs in Dublin This Morning—Many Killed," *Irish Times*, 31 May 1941, p. 1.
11. "Provisional Estimate of Dublin Casualties," *Evening Mail*, 31 May 1941, p. 3.
12. "Bombs in Dublin This Morning—Many Killed," *Irish Times*, 31 May 1941, p. 1.
13. "Mr. Cosgrave's Sympathy," *Evening Herald*, 31 May 1941, p. 2.

Chapter 14 (p. 155–79)

1. "Bombs in Dublin This Morning—Many Killed," *Irish Times*, 31 May 1941, p. 1.
2. "Twenty-Five Killed by Bombs," *Sunday Independent*, 1 June 1941, p. 1.
3. "Bombs in Dublin This Morning—Many Killed," *Irish Times*, 31 May 1941, p. 1.
4. Fagan and Savage, *All Around the Diamond*, p. 37.
5. "Huge Crater—Houses Crash," *Irish Press*, 31 May 1941, p. 1.
6. "Rehousing for Bombed Area," *Irish Press*, 4 June 1941, p. 3.
7. "Bombs in Dublin This Morning—Many Killed," *Irish Times*, 31 May 1941, p. 1.
8. "North Strand Bombings," p. 46.
9. Dowling and O'Reilly, *Mud Island*, p. 97.
10. Neary, *North of the Liffey*, p. 31.
11. "Search of Ruins at North Strand," *Evening Mail*, 2 June 1941, p. 3.
12. "Gallant Rescue Scenes in Dublin," *Evening Mail*, 31 May 1941, p. 6.
13. "Rescuers Form Human Chain," *Irish Press*, 31 May 1941, p. 1.
14. "Huge Crater—Houses Crash," *Irish Press*, 31 May 1941, p. 1.
15. "Provisional Estimate of Dublin Casualties," *Evening Mail*, 31 May 1941, p. 3.
16. "Dublin Bombing Victims," *Irish Times*, 4 June 1941, p. 5.
17. Fagan and Hiney, *Larriers*, p. 127.
18. "Bombs on Dublin—Many Dead," *Irish Press*, 31 May 1941, p. 1.
19. Gray, *The Lost Years*, p. 127.
20. Gray, *The Lost Years*, p. 127.
21. Gray, *The Lost Years*, p. 127–8.
22. "Bombs on Dublin This Morning," *Irish Independent*, 31 May 1941, p. 5.
23. "Bombs in Dublin This Morning—Many Killed," *Irish Times*, 31 May 1941, p. 1.
24. "Bombs German—Protest Being Made to Berlin," *Irish Press*, 2 June 1941, p. 1.
25. "Provisional Estimate of Dublin Casualties," *Evening Mail*, 31 May 1941, p. 3.
26. "North Strand Bombings," p. 42.
27. "Provisional Estimate of Dublin Casualties," *Evening Mail*, 31 May 1941, p. 3.
28. "Bombs in Dublin This Morning—Many Killed," *Irish Times*, 31 May 1941, p. 1.

Chapter 15 (p. 180–87)

1. Newman Devin, *Speaking Volumes*, p. 187–8.
2. "The Dublin Bombing," *Evening Mail*, 7 June 1941, p. 2.
3. "Bombs in Dublin This Morning—Many Killed," *Irish Times*, 31 May 1941, p. 1.
4. "Twenty-Five Killed by Bombs," *Sunday Independent*, 1 June 1941, p. 1.
5. Gray, *The Lost Years*, p. 128.

6.   "Mounting Death Toll of Bomb Victims," *Evening Herald*, 2 June 1941, p. 1
7.   "North Strand Bombings," p. 43.
8.   "Bodies Taken From House," *Evening Herald*, 31 May 1941, p. 3.
9.   Department of Defence, "The Story of the Bombing of the North Strand," p. 12.
10. Department of Defence, "The Story of the Bombing of the North Strand," p. 10.
11. "Tour of the Bomb-Stricken Areas," *Irish Times*, 2 June 1941, p. 5.

Chapter 16 (p. 188–207)

1.   Personal correspondence with Cathal O'Shannon, 23 February 2004.
2.   Personal correspondence with Tony Gray, 1 April 2004.
3.   Personal correspondence with Tony Gray, 1 April 2004.
4.   "Bombs on Dublin This Morning," *Irish Independent*, 31 May 1941, p. 5.
5.   "Provisional Estimate of Dublin Casualties," *Evening Mail*, 31 May 1941, p. 3.
6.   "Bombs on Dublin This Morning—Many Killed," *Irish Times*, 31 May 1941, p. 1.
7.   Gray, *The Lost Years*, p. 129.
8.   "Bombs on Dublin This Morning—Many Killed," *Irish Times*, 31 May 1941, p. 1.
9.   "Provisional Estimate of Dublin Casualties," *Evening Mail*, 31 May 1941, p. 3.
10. "German Bombs Were Dropped on Dublin," *Irish Times*, 2 June 1941, p. 1.
11. "Bombs German—Protest Being Made to Berlin," *Irish Press*, 2 June 1941, p. 1.
12. "Mr. Cosgrave's Sympathy," *Evening Herald*, 31 May 1941, p. 2.
13. Neary, *North of the Liffey*, p. 32.
14. Personal correspondence with Tony Gray, 1 April 2004.
15. "Whit Holiday in Dublin," *Evening Mail*, 2 June 1941, p. 3.
16. "Provisional Estimate of Dublin Casualties," *Evening Mail*, 31 May 1941, p. 3.
17. "Search of Ruins at North Strand," *Evening Mail*, 2 June 1941, p. 3.
18. "Protest to Berlin by Irish Government," *Irish Independent*, 2 June 1941, p. 2.
19. "Huge Crater—Houses Crash," *Irish Press*, 31 May 1941, p. 1.
20. "Night of Horror," *Evening Herald*, 31 May 1941, p. 1.
21. "North Strand Bombings," p. 46.
22. "Provisional Estimate of Dublin Casualties," *Evening Mail*, 31 May 1941, p. 3.
23. "Provisional Estimate of Dublin Casualties," *Evening Mail*, 31 May 1941, p. 3.
24. "Birds Singing in Debris," *Evening Herald*, 31 May 1941, p. 3.
25. O'Reilly, "From Dublin to Drumcooley," p. 19.
26. O'Reilly, "From Dublin to Drumcooley," p. 19.
27. O'Reilly, "From Dublin to Drumcooley," p. 19.
28. "How Bismarck and Hood Sunk," *Irish Independent*, 31 May 1941, p. 5.
29. "Raiders over Six Counties," *Irish Press*, 31 May 1941, p. 1.

Chapter 17 (p. 208–20)

1.   "Mounting Death Toll of Bomb Victims," *Evening Herald*, 2 June 1941, p. 1.
2.   "Gallant Rescue Scenes in Dublin," *Evening Mail*, 31 May 1941, p. 6.
3.   "North Strand Bombings," p. 46.
4.   Fagan and Hiney, *Larriers*, p. 31.
5.   "Park Favourites to Fore," *Irish Times*, 2 June 1941, p. 3.
6.   "Tour of the Bomb-Stricken Areas," *Irish Times*, 2 June 1941, p. 5.
7.   "Gallant Rescue Scenes in Dublin," *Evening Mail*, 31 May 1941, p. 6.

8. "Search of Ruins at North Strand," *Evening Mail*, 2 June 1941, p. 3.
9. "Death Roll is Now 34," *Irish Independent*, 3 June 1941, p. 3.
10. *Irish Press*, 2 June 1941, p. 4.
11. "Provisional Estimate of Dublin Casualties," *Evening Mail*, 31 May 1941, p. 3.
12. "Night of Horror," *Evening Herald*, 31 May 1941, p. 1.
13. "Gallant Rescue Scenes in Dublin," *Evening Mail*, 31 May 1941, p. 6.
14. "British Steamers Sunk," *Evening Mail*, 31 May 1941, p. 6.

Chapter 18 (p. 221–7)
1. "Housing the Homeless," *Irish Times*, 3 June 1941, p. 5.
2. *Evening Mail*, 9 June 1941, p. 4.
3. "North Strand Bombings," p. 42.

Chapter 19 (p. 228–42)
1. Letter from Col. L. Archer, Intelligence Branch, to Secretary of Department of External Affairs, 18 June 1941 (Military Archives, Dublin, G.2./x0755).
2. "Stuka-Dive Into Paganism," *Evening Mail*, 5 June 1941, p. 3.
3. "Bombs German—Protest Being Made to Berlin," *Irish Press*, 2 June 1941, p. 1.
4. "Big British Liner Reaches New York," *Irish Independent*, 2 June 1941, p. 1.
5. "Bombs German—Protest Being Made to Berlin," *Irish Press*, 2 June 1941, p. 1.
6. Fisk, *In Time of War*, p. 434.
7. "The Bombs of Dublin," *Sunday Independent*, 1 June 1941, p. 4.
8. "Housing the Homeless," *Irish Times*, 4 June 1941, p. 5.
9. "Joint Appeal for Funds," *Sunday Independent*, 1 June 1941, p. 1.
10. "Dublin Houses Collapse," *Irish Times*, 2 June 1941, p. 1.
11. "Three Die, 11 Hurt as Dublin House Caves In," *Irish Press*, 2 June 1941, p. 3.
12. "Dublin Tenements Collapse," *Irish Independent*, 2 June 1941, p. 3.
13. "Dublin Tenements Collapse," *Irish Independent*, 2 June 1941, p. 3.
14. "Three Die, 11 Hurt as Dublin House Caves In," *Irish Press*, 2 June 1941, p. 3.
15. "Three Die, 11 Hurt as Dublin House Caves In," *Irish Press*, 2 June 1941, p. 3.
16. "Dublin Tenements Collapse," *Irish Independent*, 2 June 1941, p. 3.
17. "Dublin Tenements Collapse," *Irish Independent*, 2 June 1941, p. 3.
18. "Dublin Tenements Collapse," *Irish Independent*, 2 June 1941, p. 3.
19. "Dublin Tenements Collapse," *Irish Independent*, 2 June 1941, p. 3.
20. "Dublin Tenements Collapse," *Irish Independent*, 2 June 1941, p. 3.
21. "Three Die, 11 Hurt as Dublin House Caves In," *Irish Press*, 2 June 1941, p. 3.
22. "Inquest on Bomb Victims," *Irish Independent*, 4 June 1941, p. 3.
23. "Dublin Tenements Collapse," *Irish Independent*, 2 June 1941, p. 3.
24. "Three Die, 11 Hurt as Dublin House Caves In," *Irish Press*, 2 June 1941, p. 3.
25. "Letters to the Editor," *Evening Mail*, 12 June 1941, p. 2.
26. "Dublin Houses Collapse," *Irish Times*, 2 June 1941, p. 1.
27. "German Bombs Were Dropped on Dublin," *Irish Times*, 2 June 1941, p. 1.
28. "German Bombs Were Dropped on Dublin," *Irish Times*, 2 June 1941, p. 1.
29. "German Comment," *Irish Press*, 2 June 1941, p. 3.

Chapter 20 (p. 243–55)

1. "Search of Ruins at North Strand," *Evening Mail*, 2 June 1941, p. 3.
2. Quigley, "The Day They Bombed Dublin."
3. "Dublin Bombing—31 May, 1941," document sent by G.2 [Intelligence] Branch to Secretary, Department of External Affairs, 20 June 1941 (Military Archives, Dublin).
4. "Bombs on Dublin," *Irish Independent*, 2 June 1941, p. 2.
5. "The Dublin Bombing," *Irish Press*, 2 June 1941, p. 2.
6. "Search of Ruins at North Strand," *Evening Mail*, 2 June 1941, p. 3.
7. "Bombs German—Protest Being Made to Berlin," *Irish Press*, 2 June 1941, p. 1.
8. "North to Help Bomb Victims," *Irish Times*, 3 June 1941, p. 5.
9. "Death Roll is Now 34," *Irish Independent*, 3 June 1941, p. 3.
10. "Turn Off The Gas," *Irish Times*, 2 June 1941, p. 5.
11. *Irish Press*, 2 June 1941, p. 5.
12. "German Bombs Were Dropped on Dublin," *Irish Times*, 2 June 1941, p. 1.
13. Geraghty and Whitehead, *The Dublin Fire Brigade*, p. 235.
14. Geraghty and Whitehead, *The Dublin Fire Brigade*, p. 235.
15. "Thousands Made Long Journeys," *Irish Press*, 3 June 1941, p. 1.
16. Cullen, *It's a Long Way from Penny Apples*, p. 18.
17. Cullen, *It's a Long Way from Penny Apples*, p. 61.
18. Cullen, *It's a Long Way from Penny Apples*, p. 61.
19. Cullen, *It's a Long Way from Penny Apples*, p. 62.
20. "Mounting Death Toll of Bomb Victims," *Evening Herald*, 2 June 1941, p. 1.
21. *Irish Times*, 3 June 1941, p. 2.
22. "Baby Boy's Body Found at North Strand," *Evening Mail*, 3 June 1941, p. 4.
23. "R.A.F. Start Large Fires in Berlin," *Evening Mail*, 3 June 1941, p. 4.

Chapter 21 (p. 256–69)

1. "Bed Bureau at Work," *Irish Press*, 4 June 1941, p. 3.
2. "Bed Bureau at Work," *Irish Press*, 4 June 1941, p. 3.
3. "Dáil Tribute to Dublin's Dead," *Irish Independent*, 6 June 1941, p. 3.
4. "Rehousing for Bomb Areas," *Irish Press*, 4 June 1941, p. 3.
5. "Aftermath of Bombing," *Irish Independent*, 4 June 1941, p. 4.
6. "Death Roll is Now 34," *Irish Independent*, 3 June 1941, p. 3.
7. "Alleged Theft of Boots, Property of Bomb Victim," *Evening Herald*, 4 June 1941, p. 4.
8. "Bomb Victim's Boots," *Irish Independent*, 4 June 1941, p. 4.
9. "Dublin Bombing Victims," *Irish Times*, 4 June 1941, p. 5.
10. "Bomb Inquest Stories," *Irish Press*, 4 June 1941, p. 1.
11. "Dublin Bombing Victims," *Irish Times*, 4 June 1941, p. 5.
12. "Dublin Bombing Victims," *Irish Times*, 4 June 1941, p. 5.
13. "Dublin Bombing Victims," *Irish Times*, 4 June 1941, p. 5.
14. "Inquest on Bomb Victims," *Irish Independent*, 4 June 1941, p. 3.
15. "Bomb Inquest Stories," *Irish Press*, 4 June 1941, p. 1.
16. "Bomb Inquest Stories," *Irish Press*, 4 June 1941, p. 1.
17. "Rescue Squads Praised by Coroner," *Irish Press*, 4 June 1941, p. 1.
18. "Dublin Bombing Victims," *Irish Times*, 4 June 1941, p. 5.
19. "Bomb Inquest Stories," *Irish Press*, 4 June 1941, p. 1.

20. "Public Funeral To-Morrow," *Irish Times*, 4 June 1941, p. 5.
21. "Dublin Bombing Victims," *Irish Times*, 4 June 1941, p. 5.
22. "Dublin Bombing Victims," *Irish Times*, 4 June 1941, p. 5.
23. "Dublin Bombing Victims," *Irish Times*, 4 June 1941, p. 5.
24. "Bomb Inquest Stories," *Irish Press*, 4 June 1941, p. 1.
25. "Removal of Remains," *Irish Independent*, 4 June 1941, p. 4.

Chapter 22 (p. 270–77)

1. "Dublin Bomb Victims Laid to Rest," *Evening Mail*, 4 June 1941, p. 6.
2. "Dublin Bomb Victims Laid to Rest," *Evening Mail*, 4 June 1941, p. 6.
3. "Dublin Bomb Victims Laid to Rest," *Evening Mail*, 4 June 1941, p. 6.
4. "Public Funeral of Bomb Victims," *Irish Times*, 5 June 1941, p. 5.
5. "Cathedral Bells Rung in Sympathy," *Evening Mail*, 4 June 1941, p. 2.
6. "State and Civic Chiefs Will Attend Funeral of Bomb Victims," *Irish Press*, 5 June 1941, p. 3.
7. O'Reilly, "From Dublin to Drumcooley," p. 21.
8. O'Reilly, "From Dublin to Drumcooley," p. 21.
9. O'Reilly, "From Dublin to Drumcooley," p. 21.
10. O'Reilly, "From Dublin to Drumcooley," p. 19.
11. O'Reilly, "From Dublin to Drumcooley," p. 19.
12. "Dublin Bomb Victims Laid to Rest," *Evening Mail*, 4 June 1941, p. 6.
13. "Dublin Bomb Victims Laid to Rest," *Evening Mail*, 4 June 1941, p. 6.
14. "Dublin Bomb Victims Laid to Rest," *Evening Mail*, 4 June 1941, p. 6.

Chapter 23 (p. 278–85)

1. "Impressive Scenes at Public Funeral," *Evening Mail*, 5 June 1941, p. 3.
2. "Impressive Scenes at Public Funeral," *Evening Mail*, 5 June 1941, p. 3.
3. "Impressive Scenes at Public Funeral," *Evening Mail*, 5 June 1941, p. 3.
4. "Impressive Scenes at Public Funeral," *Evening Mail*, 5 June 1941, p. 3.
5. "Mourning City As Twelve Killed by Bombs are Buried," *Irish Press*, 6 June 1941, p. 3.
6. "Impressive Scenes at Public Funeral," *Evening Mail*, 5 June 1941, p. 3.
7. "Impressive Scenes at Public Funeral," *Evening Mail*, 5 June 1941, p. 3.
8. "Funeral of Bomb Victims," *Irish Independent*, 6 June 1941, p. 4.
9. "Impressive Scenes at Public Funeral," *Evening Mail*, 5 June 1941, p. 3.
10. "Funeral of Bomb Victims," *Irish Independent*, 6 June 1941, p. 4.
11. "Public Funeral for Twelve Victims," *Evening Herald*, 5 June 1941, p. 3.
12. "Impressive Scenes at Public Funeral," *Evening Mail*, 5 June 1941, p. 3.
13. "Impressive Scenes at Public Funeral," *Evening Mail*, 5 June 1941, p. 3.
14. "Impressive Scenes at Public Funeral," *Evening Mail*, 5 June 1941, p. 3.
15. "Impressive Scenes at Public Funeral," *Evening Mail*, 5 June 1941, p. 3.
16. "German Comment on Berlin Raid," *Irish Times*, 6 June 1941, p. 5.

Chapter 24 (p. 286–93)

1. "Dublin Red Cross Drive Successful," *Irish Press*, 7 June 1941, p. 3.
2. "President's Gift for Bomb Victims," *Irish Press*, 7 June 1941, p. 1.
3. "Letters to the Editor," *Evening Mail*, 4 June 1941, p. 2.
4. "Our Readers' Views," *Irish Independent*, 12 June 1941, p. 2.

5.   "Re-Housing Dublin's Bomb Sufferers," *Irish Press*, 24 June 1941, p. 1.
6.   "Dáil Tribute to Dublin's Dead," *Irish Independent*, 6 June 1941, p. 3.
7.   "Protest Note Received in Berlin," *Irish Press*, 6 June 1941, p. 1.
8.   "Protest Note Received in Berlin," *Irish Press*, 6 June 1941, p. 1.
9.   "Dáil Tribute to Dublin's Dead," *Irish Independent*, 6 June 1941, p. 3.
10. "Cattle Disease," *Irish Independent*, 6 June 1941, p. 3.
11. "Huge War Bill for U.S.A.," *Irish Independent*, 6 June 1941, p. 3.

Chapter 25 (p. 294–308)

1.   "Shelters Open, But No Sirens," *Sunday Independent*, 1 June 1941, p. 3.
2.   Department of Defence, "The Story of the Bombing of the North Strand," p. 12.
3.   "Letters to the Editor," *Evening Mail*, 9 June 1941, p. 4.
4.   Ryan, *Remembering How We Stood*, p. 14.
5.   "Letters to the Editor," *Evening Mail*, 4 June 1941, p. 2.
6.   "Letters to the Editor," *Evening Mail*, 4 June 1941, p. 2.
7.   "Letters to the Editor," *Evening Mail*, 9 June 1941, p. 4.
8.   "Letters to the Editor," *Evening Mail*, 7 June 1941, p. 2.
9.   "Letters to the Editor," *Evening Mail*, 7 June 1941, p. 2.
10. "Letters to the Editor," *Evening Mail*, 4 June 1941, p. 2.
11. "Letters to the Editor," *Evening Mail*, 4 June 1941, p. 2.
12. "More Evacuations in Bombed Areas," *Irish Independent*, 9 June 1941, p. 3.
13. "Effort to Combat the Night Bombers," *Sunday Independent*, 8 June 1941, p. 1.
14. "Bombing Aftermath—More People Homeless," *Sunday Independent*, 8 June 1941, p. 1.
15. Letter from Mr Seán Moylan, Department of Defence, to Mr P. J. Hernon, Dublin City Manager, 13 June 1941 (Military Archives).
16. "Dance in Aid of Irish Red Cross Society," *Irish Times*, 4 June 1941, p. 4.
17. "L.D.F. Needs 100,000 More," *Irish Press*, 14 June 1941, p. 1.
18. "Dublin District Court—North Strand Bombing Sequel," *Irish Times*, 17 June 1941, p. 2.
19. "Germany Expresses Regret," *Irish Press*, 19 June 1941, p. 1.
20. "Join Now," *Irish Press*, 19 June 1941, p. 2.
21. *Evening Herald*, 23 June 1941, p. 4.
22. *Irish Press*, 24 June 1941, p. 1.
23. "Germans Invade Russia—Fighting on 1,500 Mile Front," *Irish Independent*, 23 June 1941, p. 1.
24. "Eire Pledged to Defend," *Sunday Independent*, 29 June 1941, p. 1.
25. "L.D.F. in 'Battle of Dublin'," *Irish Press*, 30 June 1941, p. 1.
26. "L.D.F. in 'Battle of Dublin'," *Irish Press*, 30 June 1941, p. 1.

Chapter 26 (p. 309–15)

1.   Barton, *The Blitz*, p. 255.
2.   "Tour of the Bomb-Stricken Areas," *Irish Times*, 2 June 1941, p. 5.
3.   "Bombs in Dublin—Many Killed," *Irish Times*, 31 May 1941, p. 1.
4.   Hiney, "Personal Memories," p. 10.
5.   MacDonagh, *My Green Age*, p. 130.
6.   Gray, *The Lost Years*, p. 130.
7.   "Endurance," *Irish Press*, 4 July 1940, p. 6.

8. Barton, *The Blitz*, p. 255.

9. Personal correspondence with Tony Gray, 30 April 2004.

Chapter 27 (p. 316–23)

1. "Re-Housing Dublin's Bomb Sufferers," *Irish Press*, 24 June 1941, p. 1.

2. O'Connor, *Can Lily O'Shea Come Out to Play?* p. 137.

3. O'Connor, *Can Lily O'Shea Come Out to Play?* p. 162.

Chapter 28 (p. 324–36)

1. Robert Fisk, "Why the Nazis Bombed Dublin," *Independent on Sunday*, 24 January 1999, p. 13.

2. Fisk, *In Time of War*, p. 435.

3. Robert Fisk, "Was the Bombing of Dublin Really a Luftwaffe Mistake?" *Irish Times*, 23 December 1999, p. 6.

4. Robert Fisk, "Was the Bombing of Dublin Really a Luftwaffe Mistake?" *Irish Times*, 23 December 1999, p. 6.

5. "Bombs on Eire," *Irish Independent*, 4 January 1941, p. 4.

6. "The Bombings," *Irish Press*, 4 January 1941, p. 6.

7. Barton, *The Blitz*, p. 429.

8. "Bombing Incidents, 31-5-41" (Military Archives, Dublin).

9. Quigley, "The Day They Bombed Dublin."

10. Robert Fisk, "Why the Nazis Bombed Dublin," *Independent on Sunday*, 24 January 1999, p. 13.

11. Fisk, *In Time of War*, p. 430.

12. Brian Barton, "The Belfast Blitz, April–May 1941," *History Ireland*, vol. 5, no. 3 (1997), p. 55.

13. Brian Barton, "The Belfast Blitz, April–May 1941," *History Ireland*, vol. 5, no. 3 (1997), p. 55.

14. Robert Fisk, "Why the Nazis Bombed Dublin," *Independent on Sunday*, 24 January 1999, p. 13.

15. Fisk, *In Time of War*, p. 435.

16. Fisk, *In Time of War*, p. 435.

17. Richard Hawkins, "Bending the Beam: Myth and Reality in the Bombing of Coventry, Belfast and Dublin," *Irish Sword*, vol. 19, nos. 75 and 76 (1993–4), p. 143.

18. Barton, *The Blitz*, p. 429.

19. Robert Fisk, "Was the Bombing of Dublin Really a Luftwaffe Mistake?" *Irish Times*, 23 December 1999, p. 6.

20. Fisk, *In Time of War*, p. 435.

21. Letter from F. H. Boland, Assistant Secretary, Department of External Affairs, to G.2 [Intelligence] Branch, Department of Defence, 29 July 1941 (Military Archives, Dublin, G.2./x/0755).

22. Col. E. D. Doyle, "British Bent German Guidance Beams, said Belfast Newspaper," *Irish Times*, 23 December 1999, p. 5.

23. Duggan, *Herr Hempel at the German Legation in Dublin*, p. 135.

24. Fisk, *In Time of War*, p. 436.

25. "Nazi Bombing of Dublin was 'Not Accidental'," *Irish Times*, 19 June 1997, p. 5.

26. "Nazi Bombing of Dublin was 'Not Accidental'," *Irish Times*, 19 June 1997, p. 5.

27. "Nazi Bombing of Dublin was 'Not Accidental'," *Irish Times*, 19 June 1997, p. 5.

28. Paul Gunning, "Germany 'Planned' Killer Bomb Raid," *Star*, 19 June 1997, p. 1.
29. Frank Kilfeather, "German Flier Asks Forgiveness for Bombing," *Irish Times*, 23 December 1999, p. 5.
30. Dowling and O'Reilly, *Mud Island*, p. 165.
31. Col. E. D. Doyle, "British Bent German Guidance Beams, Said Belfast Newspaper," *Irish Times*, 23 December 1999, p. 5.

Chapter 29 (p. 337–50)
1. "Whitsuntide in Dublin," *Irish Times*, 26 May 1942, p. 1.
2. "Dublin Bombing Recalled," *Irish Times*, 1 June 1942, p. 3.
3. "A.R.P. Parade in Dublin," *Irish Independent*, 1 June 1942, p. 2.
4. "Peace To-Day in Europe," *Irish Times*, 8 May 1945, p. 1.
5. "Laus Deo," *Irish Times*, 8 May 1945, p. 3.
6. "Dubliners Enjoy Whit Monday," *Irish Times*, 22 May 1945, p. 1.
7. "Hundreds Flee From Floods," *Irish Independent*, 10 December 1954, p. 11
8. "Dublin Woman Drowned," *Irish Independent*, 11 December 1954, p. 9.
9. Hiney, "Personal Memories," p. 18.
10. "Monument Dedication & Unveiling, 31 May 1991," brochure in Charleville Mall Library, Dublin.
11. "Monument Dedication & Unveiling, 31 May 1991," brochure in Charleville Mall Library, Dublin.
12. Dowling and O'Reilly, *Mud Island*, p. 5.
13. "Look Back to a Night of Fear for City," *Evening Herald*, 30 May 1991, p. 15.
14. "Night of Hell on the North Strand," *Irish Press*, 31 May 1991, p. 20.
15. Geraghty and Whitehead, *The Dublin Fire Brigade*, p. 232.

BIBLIOGRAPHY

"Aid for the Homeless", *Irish Independent*, 18 April 1941, p. 4.

"Air-Raid Precautions", *Irish Times*, 7 January 1941, p. 4.

"Alleged Theft of Boots, Property of Bomb Victim", *Evening Herald*, 4 June 1941, p. 4.

"Almost An Air of Normalcy in the Streets", *Evening Herald*, 1 January 1941, p. 1.

"Almost Silent Welcome in Dublin", *Evening Herald*, 1 January 1941, p. 3.

"Around the Theatres", *Irish Independent*, 4 January 1941, p. 6.

"A.R.P. For Animals", *Irish Times*, 14 March 1941, p. 4.

"A.R.P. Parade in Dublin", *Irish Independent*, 1 June 1942, p. 2.

"Baby Boy's Body Found at North Strand", *Dublin Evening Mail*, 3 June 1941, p. 4.

"The Barbarous Bombs", *Irish Times*, 19 April 1941, p. 4.

Barton, Brian, "The Belfast Blitz, April–May, 1941", in *History Ireland*, VOL. 5, No. 3, p. 55.

Barton, Brian, *The Blitz: Belfast in the War Years* (Belfast: The Blackstaff Press, 1989).

"Bed Bureau at Work", *Irish Press*, 4 June 1941, p. 3.

"Betting and Gambling", *Irish Times*, 28 May 1941, p. 2.

"Big British Liner Reaches New York", *Irish Independent*, 2 June 1941, p. 1.

"Birds Are Singing in Debris", *Evening Herald*, 31 May 1941, p. 3.

"Bismarck Sunk After Chase of 2,000 Miles", *Irish Times*, 28 May 1941, p. 1.

"Bodies Taken from House", *Evening Herald*, 31 May 1941, p. 3.

"400 Bodies in Belfast Ruins", *Irish Press*, 19 April 1941, p. 1.

"Bomb Damage in Dublin", *Irish Times*, 4 January 1941, p. 4.

"Bombing Aftermath: More People Homeless", *Sunday Independent*, 8 June 1941, p. 1.

"Bombing Incidents, 31-5-41" (Dublin: document marked "Secret" in files of Irish Military Archives at Cathal Brugha, 1941, no reference number cited).

"Bomb Inquest Stories", *Irish Press*, 4 June 1941, p. 1.

"The Bombing of the North Strand, Dublin, 31 May 1941" (Dublin: document published by the Department of Defence Civil Defence School, 6 December 1951. On file at Irish Military Archives).

"The Bombings", *Irish Press*, 4 January 1941, p. 6.

"Bombs Dropped in Irish Counties", *Evening Herald*, 3 January 1941, p. 1.

"Bombs Fall on Five Irish Counties", *Irish Times*, 3 January 1941, p. 5.

"Bombs German: Protest Being Made to Berlin", *Irish Press*, 2 June 1941, p. 1.

"Bombs in Dublin This Morning: Many Killed", *Irish Times*, 31 May 1941, p. 1.

"Bombs on Dublin", *Irish Independent*, 2 June 1941, p. 2.

"Bombs on Dublin This Morning", *Irish Independent*, 31 May 1941, p. 5.

"Bombs on Eire", *Irish Independent*, 4 January 1941, p. 4.

"Bomb Victim's Boots", *Irish Independent*, 4 June 1941, p. 4.

Bracken, Pauline, *Light of Other Days* (Cork: Mercier Press, 1992).

"8,000 British Prisoners", *Dublin Evening Mail*, 4 June 1941, p. 6.

"British Steamers Sunk", *Dublin Evening Mail*, 31 May 1941, p. 3.

"Broadcasting in Ireland", *Sunday Independent*, 25 May 1941, p. 4.

Brown, Harold C., "Motoring—A New Army Machine", *Irish Times*, 24 May 1941, p. 9.

"Cathedral Bells Rung in Sympathy", *Dublin Evening Mail*, 4 June 1941, p. 2.

"Cattle Disease", *Irish Independent*, 6 June 1941, p. 3.

"City Manager on Dublin A.R.P. Plans", *Irish Press*, 4 February 1941, p. 5.

"Comedy and Drama", *Irish Times*, 26 May 1941, p. 6.

"Crete Battle", *Irish Independent*, 31 May 1941, p. 5.

Cullen, Bill, *It's A Long Way From Penny Apples* (Cork: Mercier Press, 2001).

Curran, C.P., "James Joyce as Man and Artist", *Irish Times*, 14 January 1941, p. 6.

Dáil Tribute to Army Morale", *Irish Press*, 21 February 1941, p. 1.

"Dáil Tribute to Dublin's Dead", *Irish Independent*, 6 June 1941, p. 3.

"Dance in Aid of Irish Red Cross Society", *Irish Times*, 4 June 1941, p. 4.

"Death of James Joyce", *Irish Independent*, 13 January 1941, p. 6.

"Death Roll is Now 34", *Irish Independent*, 3 June 1941, p. 3.

"Detective Escapes", *Evening Herald*, 31 May 1941, p. 3.

"Devastation and Mourning in Bombed City", *Irish Press*, 22 April 1941, p. 1.

Devin, Edith Newman, *Speaking Volumes—A Dublin Childhood* (Belfast: Blackstaff Press, 2000).

Dowling, Noelle and O'Reilly, Aran, *Mud Island: A History of Ballybough* (Dublin: The Allen Library, FAS Project, 2001).

Doyle, Col. E.D., "British Bent German Guidance Beams, Said Belfast Newspaper", *Irish Times*, 23 December 1999, p. 5.

Doyle, Roddy, *Rory and Ita* (New York: Viking Press, 2002).

"Dublin Bombing—31 May, 1941" (Dublin: Document sent by G.2. Branch, Department of Defence, 20 June 1941, to Secretary, Department of External Affairs. On file in Irish Military Archives).

"Dublin Bombing Recalled", *Irish Times*, 1 June 1942, p. 3.

"The Dublin Bombing", *Dublin Evening Mail*, 7 June 1941, p. 2.

"The Dublin Bombings", *Irish Press*, 2 June 1941, p. 2.

"Dublin Bomb Victims", *Irish Times*, 4 June 1941, p. 5.

"Dublin Bomb Victims Laid to Rest", *Dublin Evening Mail*, 4 June 1941, p. 6.

"Dublin City Manager and the A.R.P.", *Irish Times*, 6 January 1941, p. 7.

"Dublin District Court—North Strand Bombing Sequel", *Irish Times*, 17 June 1941, p. 2.

"Dubliners Enjoy Whit Monday", *Irish Times*, 22 May 1945, p. 1.

"Dublin Families Ordeal—Agonizing Scenes Following Bombing Havoc", *Evening Herald*, 3 January 1941, p. 1.

"Dublin Houses Collapse", *Irish Times*, 2 June 1941, p. 1.

"Dublin May Have Stricter Black-Out", *Sunday Independent*, 5 January 1941, p. 1.

"Dublin Red Cross Drive Successful", *Irish Press*, 7 June 1941, p. 3.

"Dublin Air-Raid Shelters", *Irish Press*, 8 January 1941, p. 1.

"Dublin's Bright Lights Gone", *Irish Independent*, 23 April 1941, p. 6.

"Dublin See 20,000 in Parade Spectacle", *Irish Independent*, 15 April 1941, p. 5.

"Dublin Tenements Collapse", *Irish Independent*, 2 June 1941, p. 3.

"Dublin to Have Big A.R.P. Test", *Irish Press*, 18 January 1941, p. 7.

"Dublin Woman Drowned", *Irish Independent*, 11 December 1954, p. 11.

Duggan, John P., *Herr Hempel at the German Legation in Dublin, 1937–1945* (Dublin: Irish Academic Press, 2003).

Dukes, Jim, "The Emergency Services," *The Irish Sword*, VOL. XIX, Nos. 75–6, 1993–4, p. 66–71.

"Effort to Combat the Night Bombers," *Sunday Independent*, 8 June 1941, p. 1.

"Eire Pledged to Defend", *Sunday Independent*, 29 June 1941, p. 1.

"Elephant Toppled by Bomb Blast", *Irish Times*, 2 June 1941, p. 5.

"Endurance", *Irish Press*, 4 July 1940, p. 6.

"Entertainment at Bray", *Dublin Evening Mail*, 31 May 1941, p. 6.

Fagan, Terry and Hiney, Diarmuid G., *Larriers* (Dublin: published by North Inner-City Folklore Project, no date cited).

Fagan, Terry and Savage, Ben, *All Around the Diamond* (Dublin: North Inner-City Folklore Project, 1991).

Fisk, Robert, *In Time of War* (London: Deutsch Publishers, 1983).

Fisk, Robert, "Was the Bombing of Dublin Really a Luftwaffe Mistake?", *Irish Times*, 23 December 1999, p. 6.

Fisk, Robert, "Why the Nazis Bombed Dublin", *Irish Independent on Sunday*, 24 January 1999, p. 13.

"Freakish Effects of Bomb Blast", *Irish Press*, 4 January 1941, p. 7.

"Funeral of Bomb Victims", *Irish Independent*, 6 June 1941, p. 4.

"Gallant Rescue Scenes in Dublin", *Dublin Evening Mail*, 31 May 1941, p. 6.

Geraghty, Thomas and Whitehead, Trevor, *The Dublin Fire Brigade* (Dublin: Dublin City Council, 2004).

German Bombs Were Dropped on Dublin", *Irish Times*, 2 June 1941, p. 1.

"German Comment", *Irish Press*, 2 June 1941, p. 3.

"German Comment on Berlin Raid", *Irish Times*, 6 June 1941, p. 5.

"Germany Expresses Regret", *Irish Press*, 19 June 1941, p. 1.

"Germans Invade Russia—Fighting on 1,500 Mile Front", *Irish Independent*, 23 June 1941, p. 1.

"Graphic Story of N.C.R. Bombing", *Irish Independent*, 31 May 1941, p. 1.

Gray, Tony, *The Lost Years* (London: Warner Books, 1998).

Gunning, Paul, "Germany 'Planned' Killer Bomb Raid", *The Star*, 19 June 1997, p. 1.

"A Happy Christmas to All Readers", *Irish Independent*, 24 December 1940, p. 4.

Hawkins, Richard, "Bending the Beam: Myth and Reality in the Bombing of Coventry, Belfast and Dublin", *The Military Society of Ireland*, VOL. XIX, Nos. 75 and 76, 1993–94.

Hiney, Diarmuid G., "Personal Memories", unpublished document on file at Charleville Mall Library, no date cited.

"H.M.S. Hood was Sunk in 'Million-to-One Chance'", *Irish Times*, 26 May 1941, p. 1.

"Hold What We Have", *Irish Independent*, 26 April 1941, p. 5.

"Housing the Homeless", *Irish Times*, 3 June 1941, p. 5.

"How Bismarck and Hood Sunk", *Irish Independent*, 31 May 1941, p. 5.

"How Death Came to Sleeping Family", *Irish Press*, 3 January 1941, p. 1.

"How 1941 Was Welcomed", *Evening Herald*, 1 January 1941, p. 3.

"Huge Crater: Houses Crash", *Irish Press*, 31 May 1941, p. 1.

"Huge War Bill for U.S.A.", *Irish Independent*, 6 June 1941, p. 3.

"Hundreds Flee from Floods", *Irish Independent*, 10 December 1954, p. 11.

"Imaginary Air Raid on Dublin—A.R.P's Biggest Test", *Irish Times*, 26 May 1941, p. 5.

"Impressive Scenes at Public Funeral", *Dublin Evening Mail*, 5 June 1941, p. 3.

"Inquest on Bomb Victims", *Irish Independent*, 4 June 1941, p. 3.

"Ireland—Suburb of a City on Fire", *Irish Press*, 7 February 1941, p. 3.

"The Irish in U.S. Make Protest", *Irish Press*, 6 January 1941, p. 7.

"An Irishman's Diary", 3 January 1941, p. 4.

"An Irishman's Diary", 4 March 1941, p. 4.

"An Irishman's Diary", 29 April 1941, p. 4.

"An Irishman's Diary", 23 May 1941, p. 3.

"An Irishman's Diary", 20 May 1941, p. 5.

"An Irishman's Diary", 5 June 1941, p. 5.

"An Irishman's Diary", 11 June 1941, p. 4.

"Irish will Resist Any Attacker", *Irish Independent*, 5 May 1941, p. 6.

"It was a Happy Ending Despite the War", *Irish Independent*, 24 December 1940, p. 5.

"Join Now", *Irish Press*, 19 June 1941, p. 2.

"Joint Appeal for Funds", *Sunday Independent*, 1 June 1941, p. 1.

Kearns, Kevin C., *Dublin Tenement Life: An Oral History* (Dublin: Gill & Macmillan, 1994).

Kearns, Kevin C., *Dublin's Lost Heroines* (Dublin: Gill & Macmillan, 2004).

Kilfeather, Frank, "German Flier Asks Forgiveness for Bombing", *Irish Times*, 23 December 1999, p. 5.

"Laus Deo", *Irish Times*, 8 May 1945, p. 3.

"L.D.F. in 'Battle of Dublin'", *Irish Press*, 30 June 1941, p. 1.

"L.D.F. Manoeuveres in Dublin", *Irish Independent*, 5 February 1941, p. 5.

"L.D.F. Needs 100,000 More", *Irish Press*, 14 June 1941, p. 1.

Letter from Colonel L. Archer, G.2. Branch of Department of Defence to Secretary, Department of Internal Affairs, 18 June 1941. On file at Irish Military Archive, reference No. G.2./X0755.

"Letters to the Editor", *Dublin Evening Mail*, 4 June 1941, p. 2.

"Letters to the Editor", *Dublin Evening Mail*, 7 June 1941, p. 2.

"Letters to the Editor", *Dublin Evening Mail*, 9 June 1941, p. 4.

"Letters to the Editor", *Dublin Evening Mail*, 12 June 1941, p. 2.

"Letters to the Editor", *Irish Times*, 7 March 1941, p. 3.

"Letters to the Editor", *Irish Times*, 4 June 1941, p. 6.

"Lone House Struck", *Irish Independent*, 4 January 1941, p. 6.

"Look Back to a Night of Fear for City", *Evening Herald*, 30 May 1941, p. 20

"Many Killed in Mass Air-Attack on Belfast", *Irish Independent*, 17 April 1941, p. 5.

Matthews, Frank, "Powder and Ball Company, L.D.F.", *The Irish Sword*, VOL. XIX, Nos. 75–6, 1993–4, p. 71.

MacDonagh, Tom, *My Green Age* (Dublin: Poolbeg Press, 1986).

"Minister Wants to Destroy 'The Illusion of Security'", *Irish Press*, 1 July 1940, p. 6.

"Mobile Canteen for Dublin", *Irish Press*, 25 February 1941, p. 5.

"Monument Dedication & Unveiling", 31 May 1991. Brochure on file at Charleville Mall Library.

"More Evacuations in Bombed Areas", *Irish Independent*, 9 June 1941, p. 3.

"Mr. Cosgrave's Sympathy", *Evening Herald*, 31 May 1941, p. 2.

"Mr. Roosevelt on U.S. War Policy", *Irish Times*, 28 May 1941, p. 2.

"Mounting Death Toll for Bomb Victims", *Evening Herald*, 2 June 1941, p. 1.

"Mourning City as Twelve Killed by Bombs are Buried", *Irish Times*, 6 June 1941, p. 3.

"Nazi Bombing of Dublin was 'Not Accidental'", *Irish Times*, 19 June 1997, p. 5.

Neary, Bernard, *North of the Liffey* (Dublin: Lenhar Publications, 1984).

"New Swiss Protest", *Irish Independent*, 24 December 1940, p. 5.

"The New Year Made Its Entry", *Irish Independent*, 1 January 1941, p. 5.

"The New Year is Passing", *Irish Independent*, 3 December 1940, p. 4.

"The Night Bomber", *Irish Independent*, 3 January 1941, p. 6.

"Night of Hell on the North Strand", *Irish Press*, 31 May 1991, p. 20.

"Night of Horror", *Evening Herald*, 31 May 1941, p. 1.

"North Had Its Snowstorm", *Irish Independent*, 3 February 1941, p. 5.

"North Strand Bombings", *Living in the City* (Dublin: North Inner-City Folklore Project, 1992).

"North to Help Bomb Victim", *Irish Times*, 3 June 1941, p. 5.

O'Connor, Lily, *Can Lily O'Shea Come Out to Play* (Dingle: Brandon Publishers, 2000).

O'Farrell, Lt-Col Padraic, "The North Strand Bombing", *An Cosantoir*, September 1981, p. 283–4.

O'Keefe, Phil, *Down Cobbled Streets* (Dingle: Brandon Publishers, 1978).

"Olympia", *Irish Times*, 27 May 1941, p. 4.

O'Reilly, Joe, "From Dublin to Drumcooley" (Dublin: article on file at Charleville Mall Library, no
    publication source cited, 1993).

"Our Dumb Friends", *Evening Herald*, 1 January 1941, p. 8.

"Our Readers' Views", *Irish Independent*, 3 May 1941, p. 6.

"Our Readers' Views", *Irish Independent*, 12 June 1941, p. 2.

"Park Favourites to the Fore", *Irish Times*, 4 June 1941, p. 3.

"Peace To-Day in Europe", *Irish Times*, 8 May 1945, p. 1.

Personal correspondence from Dublin City Manager, P.J. Hernon to Mr. J. Hurson, Secretary of
    Local Government and Public Health, 8 September 1941, on file at Irish Military Archive.

Personal correspondence from F.H. Boland, Assistant Secretary, Department of External Affairs,
    to G.2. Branch, Department of Defence, Parkgate, Dublin, 29 July 1941. Reference number
    G.2./x/0755 in files of Irish Military Archives.

Personal correspondence with Cathal O'Shannon, 23 February 2004.

Personal correspondence with Tony Gray, 1 April 2004.

Personal correspondence with Tony Gray, 30 April 2004.

Personal correspondence, 13 June 1941, letter from Seán Moylan, Department of Defence, to Mr
    P.J. Hernon, Dublin City Manager. On file at Irish Military Archives.

Personal interview with Tom Geraghty, April 2004.

"President's Gift for Bomb Victims", *Irish Press*, 7 June 1941, p. 1.

"Protest Note Received in Berlin", *Irish Press*, 6 June 1941, p. 1.

"Protest to Berlin by Irish Government", *Irish Independent*, 2 June 1941, p. 2.

"Provisional Estimate of Dublin Casualties", *Dublin Evening Mail*, 31 May 1941, p. 3.

"Public Funeral for Twelve Victims", *Evening Herald*, 5 June 1941, p. 3.

"Public Funeral for Bomb Victims", *Irish Times*, 5 June 1941, p. 5.

"Public Funeral To-Morrow", *Irish Times*, 4 June 1941, p. 5.

Quigley, Captain A. A., "The Day They Bombed Dublin" (Dublin: document on file at Irish
    Military Archives, no date or reference number cited).

"R.A.F. Start Large Fires in Berlin", *Dublin Evening Mail*, 3 June 1941, p. 4.

"Raiders Over Six Counties", *Irish Press*, 31 May 1941, p. 1.

"Re-Housing Dublin's Bomb Sufferers", *Irish Press*, 24 June 1941, p. 1.

"Rehousing the Bombed Area", *Irish Press*, 4 June 1941, p. 3.

"Removal of Remains", *Irish Independent*, 4 June 1941, p. 4.

"Rescuers Form Human Chain", *Irish Press*, 31 May 1941, p. 1.

"Rescue Squads Praised by Coroner", *Irish Press*, 4 June 1941, p. 1.

"Rescues by A.R.P. Men", *Irish Times*, 4 January 1941, p. 6.

"Residents Tell of Bombings", *Irish Times*, 3 January 1941, p. 6.

"Roosevelt Sends Secret Plans to Churchill", *Irish Times*, 2 June 1941, p. 2.

Ryan, John, *Remembering How We Stood* (Dublin: Gill & Macmillan, 1975).

"Search of Ruins at North Strand", *Dublin Evening Mail*, 2 June 1941, p. 3.

"Series of Bombs Dropped", *Irish Times*, 3 January 1941, p. 5.

Share, Bernard, *The Emergency: Neutral Ireland 1939–45* (Dublin: Gill & Macmillan, 1978).

"Shelters Open, But No Sirens", *Sunday Independent*, 1 June 1941, p. 3.

"The Smithy's Anvils are Busy Again", *Irish Press*, 18 February 1941, p. 1.

"State and Civic Chiefs Will Attend Funeral of Bomb Victims", *Irish Press*, 5 June 1941, p. 3.

"A Statement in Berlin", *Irish Independent*, 4 January, p. 6.

"The Story of the Bombing of the North Strand" (Dublin: published by the Department of Defence, 8 December 1951, on file at Irish Military Archives).

"St. Patrick's Day Honoured Everywhere", *Irish Press*, 18 March 1941, p. 1.

"Stuka Dive Into Paganism", *Dublin Evening Mail*, 5 June 1941, p. 3.

"Summerhill Scenes", *Irish Independent*, 31 May 1941, p. 1.

"Surprise in New York", *Irish Times*, 4 January 1941, p. 6.

"Sympathy for Belfast", *Irish Independent*, 21 April 1941, p. 5.

"A Terrible Beauty", *Irish Times*, 17 April 1941, p. 2.

"This Elephant Laughs at Locks!", *Irish Independent*, 2 June 1941, p. 3.

"This Monkey's a Real Firebrand", *Irish Press*, 3 February 1941, p. 5.

"Thousands Made Long Journeys", *Irish Press*, 3 June 1941, p. 1.

"Three Bombs Dropped in Drogheda", *Irish Times*, 2 January 1941, p. 5.

"Three Die, 11 Hurt as Dublin House Caves In", *Irish Press*, 2 June 1941, p. 3.

"Thrilling Rescue Scenes in Dublin Suburbs", *Irish Press*, 3 January 1941, p. 1.

"Time of Greatest Danger to Our Nation", *Sunday Independent*, 26 January 1941, p. 1.

"Tour of Bomb Stricken Areas", *Irish Times*, 2 June 1941, p. 5.

"Tragic Inquest Story", *Irish Independent*, 3 January 1941, p. 6.

"Turn Off the Gas", *Irish Times*, 2 June 1941, p. 1.

"Twenty-Five Killed by Bombs", *Sunday Independent*, 1 June 1941, p. 1.

"Two Family Tragedies", *Irish Independent*, 1 June 1941, p. 1.

"Vivid Stories of Bombing", *Evening Herald*, 3 January 1941, p. 1.

"War Due to Spiritual Malady", *Irish Independent*, 1 January 1941, p. 7.

"Well Done", *Irish Press*, 10 January 1941, p. 4.

"Whit Holiday in Dublin", *Dublin Evening Mail*, 2 June 1941, p. 1.

"Whit Railway Facilities", *Irish Independent*, 31 May 1941, p. 3.

"Whitsuntide in Dublin", *Irish Times*, 26 May 1942, p. 1.

"Women Die in Wrecked House", *Irish Independent*, 3 January 1941, p. 5.

"Women's Protest", *Irish Independent*, 9 May 1941, p. 4.

"1941 Year of Destiny—World's Future to be Decided", *Irish Times*, 1 January 1941, p. 5.

INDEX